LibraryPlus

Weston College LibraryPlus
Knightstone Road
Weston super Mare, BS23 2AL

Tel: 01934 411493   Email: library@weston.ac.uk
TXT 2 RENEW : 07860023339

Careers Library

Short loan of one week

CATT
EDUCATIONAL
LIMITED

Published in 2017 by John Catt Educational Ltd,
12 Deben Mill Business Centre, Old Maltings Approach,
Melton, Woodbridge, Suffolk IP12 1BL

Tel: +44 (0) 1394 389850   Fax: +44 (0) 1394 386893
Email: info@gap-year.com   Website: www.gap-year.com

First published by Peridot Press in 1992; Twenty-sixth edition 2018
© 2017 John Catt Educational Ltd

British Library Cataloguing in Publication Data.

ISBN: 978 1911 382 43 0

Designed and typeset by Theoria Design

Contacts

Editor
Meena Ameen
Email: editor@gap-year.com

Advertising
Tel: +44 (0) 1394 389853
Email: info@gap-year.com

Distribution/Booksales
Tel: +44 (0) 1394 389863
Email: booksales@johncatt.com

visit: www.gap-year.com

contents

contents ... continued

Your gap-year abroad

contents ... continued

Your gap-year in the UK

contents ... continued

Many thanks to all those who have given their time, advice and expertise to help us keep this book as up-to-date as possible, with particular thanks to Stefan Wathan at Year Out Group, Teeny Scott Barber at Art History Abroad, the team at DU Insure and James Tait at Workaseason. Thank you also to those who have shared their gap-year adventures with us.

Cover image, courtesy of itsskin/iStock by Getty Images

Preface

How gap-years have changed...

Preface: How gap-years have changed

Stefan Wathan, chief executive of the Year Out Group, offers an outline of what a 'gap-year' means in 2018

In 2016-17 the member organizations of Year Out Group arranged structured gap-year placements for people aged 17-70+ in over 90 countries across the globe. 70% of the participants were aged between 17 and 25 predominantly taking time between school and university or leaving university and taking up full-time work; 20% were between 26 and 40, mostly taking a sabbatical or career break or even looking for a change of career, while the remaining 10% are catching up on travel opportunities they may have missed out on and offering valuable skills in the process or even deciding that they too have a new potential career ahead of them.

How have gap-years changed?

Taking a gap later in life

The trend of also taking a 'gap' later in life seems to be continuing but a gap-year is more popular across the globe with 60% of participants coming from outside the UK in 2016 compared to 34% in 2006. The drive behind this may be that more people are looking for opportunities to gain experience outside of their own country. In the USA, demand is growing and their universities are becoming more proactive in their support of well-structured and purposeful 'gap' experiences. A growing number of middle class students in China and India may also be a factor.

Competition for gap-year places

Our members feel there is more and more competition in the gap-year experience market which also means there are more start up organisations and those adding some sort of gap experience to what might otherwise be considered a holiday. This means there is also more negative publicity out there so it's important that travellers do their research to find the best of what is on offer, rather than the cheapest, most convenient or the best looking website.

The average length of structured activity during a gap is 10 weeks. It can be as little two weeks or as many as 52 weeks. Participants are leaving it to later to book, which makes it harder for providers to plan effectively and to guarantee a place. It's not clear if this trend will continue but probably has something to do with ease of searching and booking via mobile devices. Year Out Group places an emphasis on telling participants to do some planning and to remember that there are selection processes for many programmes even if it is telephone interview. With oversees participants now dominating the market there is danger UK young people will miss out if they are not thinking ahead.

Last minute bookings

Those leaving it late are often disappointed when their preferred gap-year provider is unable to meet their demands. This is particularly the case with voluntary work placements where it is important that time is devoted to ensuring that the potential volunteer is right for their preferred project and vice versa. There is also the lead-time required to obtain visas and give important vaccinations time to take effect. Canada for example has a limit of the number of work visas it issues so late booking is not recommended. In exceptional circumstances, it may be possible to depart within in a week but four weeks is more realistic and eight weeks, or longer better still. The same criteria apply to an expedition but if there is a vacancy on a course and you meet the minimum requirements then you could be away in days. As gap-years become more popular in other countries such as USA, China and Japan and amongst older people, young Brits may find that others have beaten then to the post if they leave things to late, so best to plan ahead.

Why take a gap-year?

Understanding your reasons for taking a year out or even just a short trip, is important. It helps avoid disappointment or even curtailing an experience if you have thought through where, when and for how long you want to travel, work, train, volunteer or explore, so that you find the best match, something that's really motivating.

Those taking a gap-year between leaving school/college and going to university arrive refreshed and focused. After all, you may not have an opportunity like this for many years. Evidence shows students are more likely to complete their chosen course if they have taken a gap-year so long as, that is, they have planned for it. For those less certain about their degree subject, a gap-year may mean they decide university isn't for them or they may change their choice of degree. Some may take time to get back into academic mode but this is more than compensated for in their social maturity. Their completion of a demanding challenge that they have initiated, planned and implemented successfully boosts their self-confidence significantly. They are also more globally-aware, enabling them to provide a more broadly based contribution in tutorials. In short, they are better placed to make the most of their time at university and to succeed. They will also have acquired skills and experiences that will enhance their employability.

It is the enhancement to their employability that graduates most seek to gain from their gap-year through developing an understanding of, and communicating with, people from other cultures. More people with gap experiences means you may have to try that bit harder to impress so the important thing is to do something you really think you will enjoy and learn from. It is not just about ticking a box on the CV list.

For more information on Year Out Group, visit: www.yearoutgroup.org

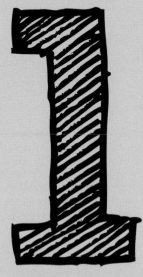

Tips for travellers

Sponsored by

düINSURE.com

The best, cheap backpacking onsurance providers

With medical travel emergencies potentially costing tens of thousands of pounds, it's important to ensure you have a gap year travel insurance partner to protect you during your travels abroad. Whether you're exploring America, visiting South East Asia or winging your way to Australia & New Zealand, we'll be there to ensure you are fully protected during your time abroad.

So why choose DownUnder?

DUInsure have been providing travel insurance since 1992 and are able to offer a great value product by not subsiding higher risk, older travellers who are over the age of 55. We believe our product is one of the best value for money policies around, giving you a tailored product that is perfect for your backpacking adventure. Our travel insurance policies are specifically designed with your needs in mind and cover a large number of adventure activities and extreme sports as standard — meaning you are protected in the event of injury without having to worry about sky high medical bills. We cover a wide range of adventure sports and activities as standard, including bungee jumping, BMX riding, canoeing, paragliding, rock climbing, scuba diving and over 50 further sports and activities in addition to these.

We do not require that you have a return flight booked for our single trip policy, rather you must be intending to return to the UK prior to the expiry of your policy. If your plans change, we can extend cover whilst abroad, up to a maximum combined total of 18 months.

When it comes to ensuring your health is protected abroad, our 24-hour medical emergency service is available for use at any time — you can call for immediate help in the event of illness or injury abroad. Our staff are able to provide support for a wide range of issues, for example liaising with doctors or arranging repatriation to the UK. We are able to provide help if you are struggling to discuss your treatment with your medical care provider, for example if you are in a country where English isn't a first language.

Our policies are also extremely flexible, allowing for that last minute change of plan that can often occur during trips abroad as you or a member of your group decides they wish to visit an area where you are not currently insured, or partake in a more extreme adventure activity. You can contact us at any point during your travels to extend your policy or expand your cover. Our policies also allow you to spend a percentage of your time travelling to other worldwide destinations outside of those originally covered on your policy, meaning you can be covered during last minute excursions to other regions that aren't covered on your original policy.

We also provide some of the most affordable policies on the market that allow you to work whilst you travel — an essential for many longer term travellers. We cover a variety of work including office and clerical work, retail and light manual work such as fruit picking, as standard, on our backpacking and gap-year policies.

You are able to purchase additional cover for valuables whilst abroad, in return for additional premium. You can cover electrical, computer or photographic items up to £1,000 any one item, £2,000 in total any one person, depending on which of our insurance policies you choose. Ensure your peace of mind, whilst travelling with your valuables.

We're also one of the few travel insurance providers who offer one way travel insurance cover — ideal for travellers who are either looking to emigrate or do not intend to return to the UK as they are returning home.

So, book that trip of a lifetime you've always wanted to experience or that gap-year holiday you've been dying to take and travel around the world safe in the knowledge you're covered by one of the best value travel insurance products available.

DownUnder Insurance — stay protected, pay less.

düINSURE.com

Tips for travellers

For starters, what do we mean by gap-year?

Well, according to the Oxford Dictionary, a gap-year is defined as:

'a period, typically an academic year, taken by a student as a break between school and university or college education.'

Typically, yes, but we'd contend that a gap-year can be and is much more than that nowadays. It's certainly not limited to school leavers. Nowadays people travel to volunteer, work and study. You might be taking a year out from work, spending a redundancy pay-out or enjoying your retirement.

Don't think your break would have to be for a year either — it could be as long and short as you like, or can afford!

But the one thing all such trips have in common is the fact that they're all about taking time out of the normal routine to do **something different, challenging, fulfilling, memorable** — so that is our definition of a 'gap-year'.

Who goes on a gap?

As we've just explained, anyone *can*. But who does?

It's difficult to give exact numbers because of the wildly different ways you can spend your gap, but we're likely to be talking hundreds of thousands — that includes young people (teenagers and those in their early 20s), career breakers and retired people.

The Year Out Group, which represents 24 of the leading gap-year providers in the UK, arranged structured gap-year placements for people aged 17-70+ in over 90 countries across the globe in 2016-17.

They say 70% of the participants were aged between 17 and 25, predominantly taking time between school and university or leaving university and taking up full-time work; 20% were between 26 and 40 mostly taking a sabbatical or career break or even looking for a change of career, while the remaining 10% were catching up on travel opportunities they may have missed out on and offering valuable skills in the process or even deciding that they too have a new potential career ahead of them.

"When African Conservation Experience started in 1999, it worked almost 100% with 'traditional' gap-year students — aged 17 or 18, and students during their university career" say our friends at African Conservation Experience. "Now about 25% of our travellers are professionals aged 25+, including quite a few retirees!"

So the answer is people of all ages and walks of life go on a gap.

John Hall Venice

Why should you take a gap?

There are as many reasons to take a gap as there are different opportunities on offer. Time out before further study? A break from the daily work routine? A memorable experience? To give something back? To learn something new? A way to gain work experience that will boost your career prospects? All are valid reasons.

The benefits of taking a gap-year are considerable. Younger gappers who have taken a structured trip are likely to arrive at university refreshed and focused. Research shows they are more likely to finish their chosen course.

If you feel like you're fed up with the daily grind of a 9-to-5 job, a career break can help you get out of your rut. Working full-time for even just ten years means roughly around 20,000 hours of sitting in an office staring at your computer screen. A career break will help you gain a new perspective on life and work and will be an experience you remember for the rest of your life.

Increasingly, young people planning a gap-year do so with improving their CV in mind and making sure they are more attractive to employers when they return. A well-planned gap-year that includes a work placement and learning new skills is likely to be of a huge benefit when you're back and looking for a job, particularly in tough economic times when work may be hard to come by.

Our friends at Pod Volunteer tell us: "Universities and employers like to see that you are going above and beyond the necessary and using your gap year to its full potential — by combining travelling and volunteering you are showing that you are motivated. It also offers the opportunity to develop decision making, language, problem solving, communication and organisational skills. It also shows that you can be confident and independent, build relationships successfully, embrace responsibility and work as part of a team."

Stefan Wathan from the Year Out Group highlights the key skills that employers are looking for and can be acquired through a structured gap-year: "More people with gap experiences means you may have to try that bit harder to impress, so the important thing is to do something you really think you will enjoy and learn from. It is not just about ticking a box on the CV list." Employers are looking for:

· Communication skills The ability to express oneself clearly verbally and in writing so that one can argue a position, persuade and inspire. The ability to relate to customers is also important.

· Courage to challenge and take risks The ability to manage a project, to identify and manage risk and to experience and learn from failure.

· Planning and organisation The ability to have an idea, to develop a plan and to implement that plan successfully.

· Initiative and adaptability The ability to think on one's feet, to act on one's own accord and to adjust a plan as and when circumstances change.

· Teamwork The ability to play a full part in a team. This links to adaptability as teams will often change as a project progresses.

· Internationalism Knowledge of languages and being at ease in diverse cultures is becoming increasingly important.

· Business acumen Understanding figures, an ability to negotiate and having some knowledge of maths and science in order to appreciate and make best use of emerging technology.

visit: www.duinsure.com

· The self-confidence that comes from a successful gap-year that enables you to start a job and draw on all your skills so that you become an effective member of staff as soon as possible.

Have tuition fees and the economy had an impact?

It's true that the uncertain economic times and the tuition fees from £9,250 a year, along with the scrapping of maintenance grants, have made people think much harder about what they do and how they spend their money.

As we've already mentioned, with the traditional route of going straight to university after finishing A Levels not proving as dependable as in previous years and a sluggish jobs market, more youngsters are considering vocational training or work experience on a gap-year abroad, allowing them to gain the hands-on experience that employers are looking for.

What's more, experts say the number of young professionals booking extended trips and work sabbaticals is still rising — up 30% in the past five years.

So, if anything, industry leaders are expecting to see more people taking a gap, despite the economy.

Planning your gap — the first steps

What do you want to do?

The beauty of the modern gap-year is the amount of choice and variety on offer: each is as unique as the individual participant, and each is an opportunity to create a tailored programme to meet their own personal ambitions.

You know your own personality, your interests, your strengths and weaknesses. Are you someone who likes to get stuck into something for a while — or do you want to be on the move a lot? If you're not confident about coping alone with unfamiliar situations you might want a more structured, group setting. On the other hand if you know you need time away from the crowds, you're bound to want to build in some independent travel.

FCO Advice Regarding Brexit

The EU Referendum held on 23 June 2016 delivered a clear vote for the United Kingdom to leave the EU. In a statement following the result, the Prime Minister reassured British people living in the EU, and European citizens in the UK, that there would be no immediate change to their circumstances, and that there would be no initial change to the way people can travel.

At the time of printing, the UK continues talks on leaving the EU but remains a member with all of the rights and obligations that membership entails. We would encourage all British nationals planning on travelling to Europe to do their research beforehand, and stay up-to-date by following the latest travel advice and information at **www.gov.uk/travelaware**

Voluntary work attracts the most placements and the greatest variety of projects, with placements available in nearly every country where gap-year providers operate.

Teaching is the most popular activity and is the ideal way to experience a country's culture and customs. When volunteering as an individual it generally follows that the longer the placement, the greater the benefit to both the volunteer and the host organisation.

Or perhaps you want to explore things you've always wanted to pursue but never had time? It could be anything from a spiritual retreat to meditation and yoga, art, photography, a new language or particular places and cultures.

Maybe you're particularly concerned about the state of the world and would like to do your bit environmentally or contribute to helping disadvantaged people? The possibilities are endless and many gappers end up constructing a programme that combines several elements.

Those with a full year at their disposal will perhaps have time for more than one activity, and might want to combine a structured element to their gap with some travel. The increase in cheap flights and wider access to previously unreachable destinations has made this even more possible.

Choosing the activity, destination and organisation most suited to the individual can be a difficult and time-consuming task. However, proper planning and research is crucial and will help ensure you get the most out of your time; a gap or career break can easily be wasted without planning ahead.

It is also important that you are aware of your responsibilities. Dropping out of a placement or programme before it has finished can be disruptive not only to you but also to others directly and indirectly involved.

A gap-year can also be used for spiritual reasons or for personal development and there are companies that specialise in emotionally and spiritually-enriching trips. But don't worry if all this sounds a bit heavy: the planning and preparation stage can be almost as much fun as the trip itself. And of course, this is where *the gap-year guidebook* comes into its own...

Where do you want to go?

The Year Out Group talk us through the latest most popular destinations for gappers:

"South Africa is consistently popular stemming from the diverse nature of the country and the availability of a wide range of suitable and worthwhile projects. These projects range from conservation work in the numerous private and national game parks, a wide variety of teaching placements, many opportunities to coach sports and volunteer placements in the care field including orphanages, health centres and HIV/Aids awareness programmes. Projects can last from a few weeks to a whole year. South Africa is also seen as a comparatively safe destination with plentiful flights and the cost of living is good value. Because of the scale of opportunities its important to chose wisely by asking questions of the provider about the benefits any projects are bringing to conservation and communities alike.

"Tanzania is home to some of the most famous of East Africa's attractions — from Africa's highest mountain, the snow-capped Mount Kilimanjaro to the incredible Serengeti National Park and the Ngorogoro Crater, which hold some of the largest concentrations of wildlife on the continent. Low living costs and safety make it an attractive option and there is real need away from the tourist areas for support in education. However a high visa cost does detract which may act against it if other countries like Kenya become safer in future.

"Both countries saw a drop in bookings during the Ebola crisis, despite the fact they are located far away from the outbreak. It shows that some travellers can be ignorant of geography and also of the importance of the programmes they volunteer on and their commitment to it. It highlights the importance of researching gap year options and knowing why you want to commit to any particular programme.

"Madagascar is the world's fourth biggest island and home to 5% of the known animal and plant species. Singing Lemurs, giant Baobab trees and some of the world's best street food make it an inviting place in which to trek and volunteer.

"Thailand continues to be popular. It is a favourite tourist destination so there are plenty of flights and there are hundreds of volunteering opportunities especially in teaching, community and conservation projects.

"Cambodia possesses a wide variety of activities available including teaching, care work and conservation projects. It is comparatively safe, the people are very warm and welcoming and once again the cost of living is low.

"Canada where there are now several more organizations offering winter sports activities ranging from ski and snowboard instructor courses that invariably lead to offers of paid work as an instructor on completion of the course, something which may lead to full-time career or a way of earning money during university holidays. For those that wish to venture further into the mountains there is now the possibility to train as a mountain leader. The companies are also making good use of the facilities in the summer months: as mountain biking increases in popularity so does the demand for instructors and the Canadian countryside provides the ideal terrain to gain the necessary skills and experience.

"Australia & New Zealand remain popular despite higher cost of living. Both countries are ideal staging posts to stop off for a few weeks or months, get a job and then

John Hall Venice

What's in fashion?

Year Out Group CEO Stefan Wathan provides a rundown of the most popular activities that gappers are currently taking part in

Voluntary Work attracts the most placements and the greatest variety of projects. Voluntary work placements are available in nearly every country where Year Out Group members operate.

Short and long-term placements are both very rewarding. Short-term bookings perhaps just for a week or two will get participants up to speed quickly so that the projects maximise the benefit of the volunteer's time, which also makes a valuable contribution locally. Projects that run for 3 to 12 months allow more time for volunteers to get into the routine and culture of community life and deeper relationships tend to be formed as a result, which is more rewarding for both parties.

Courses. Year Out Group members offer courses in art history, drama, diving, game ranger, languages, mountaineering, mountain leadership, sailing, windsurfing, skiing, and snowboarding amongst others. Expert instructors or guides lead these courses and most lead to internationally recognised qualifications. Some will use these to gain more expertise in their favourite past-time but for many it supplements study or offers another route to work either as a career or during holiday times.

Expeditions offer personal development opportunities through a variety of phases such as a community project, a conservation project and an adventure phase. Some expeditions involve small parties while others are designed for larger, often international groups. Some organisations offer guided travel opportunities, which might see participants travelling and trekking through regions and spending time along the way completing projects in the communities they pass through. All expeditions are led by experienced and carefully chosen leaders. Expeditions have become increasingly popular with graduates in recent years with many reporting success in the job market on their return.

Structured work placements & internship. A year in industry offers excellent opportunities for those planning to read engineering or related subjects at university to gain valuable work experience in engineering companies in the UK. Subsequently those on placements, who are often placed on the payroll of the host company and paid a fair salary (and no fee), are frequently supported throughout their degrees by their host companies and on graduation offered full time employment.

More and more members are starting to provide internships of some nature and across quite a wide variety of skills areas, including journalism, medicine, micro-finance and entrepreneurship. Unpaid internships may require a higher level of skill than volunteering placements but the distinction may be more about the intended outcome for the person taking part and it might involve working for a charity, government service or private company. For example a veterinary internship will help prepare you for a job in that profession but you might be expected to be studying it at university. By contrast, volunteering on a wildlife reserve may offer a broader experience, requiring less knowledge of the subject and suitable for those who are not looking at the placement as a career stepping stone.

move north to Indochina. The higher living costs are somewhat offset by higher earnings but many people will work in return for accommodation and food, on farms for instance and they can also get assistance through operators to find work whilst they are there. Needless to say, the natural environment of these countries is a draw and if you are looking to train in something technical like sailing then they are hard to beat.

"Costa Rica & Ecuador where Costa Rica's popularity again stems from the wide variety of activities available, comparative ease of access and its geographic position that enables gap-year travellers to go on to South America or the States. Costa Rica has a vibrant culture, has a good infrastructure (helped by the fact that it has no army and therefore spends more on public services) and fantastic wildlife accessible through their National Parks. Ecuador is a nature lovers dream and also a place of epic adventures that can take place in the Andes, jungle, the Galapagos and Pacific Coast.

"Nepal & India are both gaining in popularity as discerning British and international students and graduates seek to learn more about the culture and customs of an important and rapidly developing country like India, which offers a wide range of voluntary work placements and an increasing number of internship opportunities. Nepal remains both mystic and friendly and is much loved despite the earthquakes of this year, which means it'll need the support of tourists and volunteers to recover. Check with operators about their plans and how they make a difference to the country.

That gives you an idea of where others have gone. So where do you fancy?

If you want to visit several places you can let a cheap round-the-world ticket decide the framework for you. Otherwise you need to get your route clear in your mind.

Do you feel attracted to a particular area or to a particular climate? Unexplored territory or the popular backpacker places you've heard about? If you're unsure, try connecting with people who've been through the many gap-year internet messageboards.

Heading for unknown territory off the backpacker routes in search of something more unusual will usually mean higher costs, perhaps a longer wait for visas and less efficient transport systems — therefore more preparation and travelling time. A bit of netsurfing, a check with any contacts who know a country and a chat with a travel agent will help you get a better idea of what this might mean.

Then there's the risk factor. Obviously family and friends will want you to avoid danger zones. The political situation in some places around the world is serious, unstable and can't be ignored.

You want your gap travels to be stimulating, fun, to let you experience different cultures and meet new people, but do you really want to end up in the middle of a war zone with your life in danger? Foreign news correspondents and war reporters with large back-up organisations prepare properly, with proper insurance and safety and survival courses — and it makes sense for gappers too!

A good starting point is the Foreign & Commonwealth Office website (**www.gov.uk/travelaware**) where you can find country profiles and assess the dangers and possible drawbacks to places you're thinking of. The FCO updates its danger list regularly as new areas of unrest emerge, but it's not, and never can be, a failsafe.

How long have you got?

Now you have at least a rough idea of where you want to go and what you want to do. The next step is to consider how long you might need to get it all in. How much time you can spare depends on *when* you're taking your gap.

That's going to be dictated by when you have to be back for starting university or college or, for career breakers, how much time your employer's prepared to let you have, or even whether you're willing to risk quitting your job for more gap time.

We are hearing plenty of evidence that shorter placements of a few weeks rather than a few months are in increasing demand. Here, you need to consider what you want to get out of your gap, and whether you are getting value for money. University entrance tutors and employers will want to see how your gap made a real difference — they will be looking for commitment, determination to see a project through, planning ability, the ability to think on one's feet, to assess and manage risks, and to raise money and manage finances. If you've taken on a short placement just to 'tick the gap-year box', you may find you haven't really gained these skills at all.

And, while it may be tempting to look for last-minute bargains, there are plenty of reasons to get organised in good time.

Our friends at Kaya Responsible Travel, which offer a wide range of volunteering projects say: "It is important to remember that the longer you stay the more you will learn and the better relationships you can develop, which means the more you can do (the more you will be trusted to do) and the more you can help your project achieve. 6-8 weeks is the average time our participants sign up for, but the most consistent feedback we receive, across all projects, is that people wish they would have stayed longer.

"We recommend people plan 3-6 months ahead for their projects. Flights are a lot cheaper to buy this far in advance, and it gives you enough time to get your vaccinations and prepare for your trip. Having said that, we can arrange placements at very short notice — even a few weeks in advance, thought we do warn last-minute sign-ups to be prepared to be flexible if you are being accommodated for at the last minute. The summer is a particularly popular time, with people travelling in the holidays and many of the most popular projects for summer can get fully booked by late February, so if you have you eye on a particular placement, be sure to get in early to secure your space."

How much do you want to spend?

Estimates vary widely, but costs for a 'budget' gap-year in south-east Asia can be as little as £4,000, whereas a more luxury gap-year staying in hotels in Europe can cost £10,000 or more.

Much depends on where you're going and what you plan to do, and these days, if you care about the planet, climate change and ethical travel, you need also to include the costs of carbon offsetting. It's important to do as much research as possible, and a good place to start is **Chapter 2 — Finance**.

Our friends from DUInsure advise to "speak to people of the same age who have recently travelled to those countries you are going to visit. They will have a good idea about costs and help you work out a daily living allowance."

Consider the following ideas:

- Project opportunity — there is a cost to this as it isn't easy/possible to arrive in a country and wander into a school and offer your services for a few weeks!

- Project management — who is in charge, making it happen and looking after you whilst you are working there? Where do they live — with you or 100 miles away?

- Project materials — who is supplying them and paying for them?

- Accommodation, food and airport pickup? Home stay or company accommodation — close to the project sites?

- Are you on your own or with a team of people?

- 24/7 back up and communication with home should anything go wrong. How does this work and what are the company procedures?

- Call up the companies — which one do you like?

Do you want to go alone, or with friends and family?

It's totally understandable that you may want to share your experiences with friends or close family, and you may feel safer and more confident with company — and no doubt it will help the peace of mind of the family you leave behind. While safety should always be your first priority, don't be afraid of heading out on your own.

If you do travel with a friend or family, you have to be 100% certain you can spend 24 hours a day with them. We often hear of people going their separate ways during their trip because they are not accustomed to spending large amounts of time, including whole weeks and maybe months, together at a time with little to no break.

Before you go, get to know where you're going

The more you know about your destination, the easier your trip will be: India, for example, is unbearably hot and humid in pre-monsoon April to June, Australia has seasons when bush fires are rampant and then there are the cyclone seasons in South Asia and rainy seasons in South America — and the consequent risk of flooding.

It's also worth finding out when special events are on. It could be very inconvenient to arrive in India during Diwali, when everyone's on holiday and all the trains are full! Similarly Japan — gorgeous in cherry blossom season although it is recommended to avoid travelling in Golden Week.

Before visiting any country that has recently been politically volatile or could turn into a war zone, check with the FCO (www.gov.uk/travelaware) for information. Note: If you're from a country that qualifies for a Visa Waiver for the USA (and that includes UK citizens) you must now register online your intent to visit the USA and you *must* receive travel authorisation. Authorisation still doesn't guarantee you'll be granted entry and you may still be asked to go to the US embassy for an interview, but you have to go through the process before you can do anything else. You'll find the details here: **travel.state.gov/content/visas/en.html**

If you're intending to visit for longer, or are planning to work, you will need the correct visa (see **Chapter 5 — Working abroad**).

Sort the paperwork

If you need to get yourself a passport for the first time, application forms are available from Post Offices or you can apply online. But remember: passport interviews are a new part of the process and are required by all applicants, aged 16 or over, who are applying for a passport for the first time.

You can apply for and renew passports online (**www.gov.uk/browse/abroad/ passports**), but remember also that first time applicants can't use the fast track service.

There are interview offices around the country and you have to go to the correct one for where you live — see the map on the IPS (Identity and Passport Office) website: **maps.direct.gov.uk/LDGRedirect/MapAction.do?ref=passportinterviewoffices**

The standard adult ten-year passport currently costs £72.50 and you'll need your birth certificate and passport photos. It should take no more than a month from the time you apply to the time you receive your passport, but the queue lengthens coming up to peak summer holiday season.

You can use the Passport Office 'Check and Send' service at selected Post Offices throughout the UK or send it direct. The 'Check and Send' service gets your application checked for completeness (including documentation and fee) and is sent special delivery. It currently costs £82.25, which includes the passport application.

If your passport application is urgent and you're not applying for the first time, you can use the guaranteed same-day (Premium) service or the guaranteed one-week (Fast Track) service. Both services are only available by appointment at one of the seven IPS offices around the UK (phone the IPS Advice Line on 0300 222 0000), and both are more expensive (£128 for Premium, £103 for Fast Track). The services are only available for renewals and amendments and, although you'll get a fixed appointment, you will almost certainly wait in a queue after this for your passport.

To apply online visit: **www.gov.uk/government/organisations/hm-passport-office**

The FCO provided us with a checklist to help sort your travel documents:

- Check your passport is valid for the country you are travelling to — some countries require six months left to run after your return date to the UK so check this as soon as you can to allow plenty of time.

- Keep your passport in a safe place while you're away, ideally in the hotel safe. Pack a photocopy of the main personal details and photograph page for ID purposes, so it's easier to replace if it goes missing.

- If your passport does get lost, stolen or damaged while you are away, you'll need an Emergency Travel Document (ETD) issued by the Foreign and Commonwealth Office. It's important to remember that an ETD does not guarantee you entry to every country and will cost you time and money.

Make sure you've got the correct visa for the country you are visiting and allow plenty of time to research and prepare. Visit the Foreign and Commonwealth Office's travel advice page at **www.gov.uk/travelaware** to read up on country specific travel advice, information and entry requirements.

Leave someone in charge at home

Make sure you have someone reliable and trustworthy in charge of sorting things out for you — especially the official stuff that won't wait. Get someone you really trust to open your post and arrange to talk to them at regular intervals in case something turns up that you need to deal with.

However, there are some things you just have to do yourself, so make sure you've done everything important before you go. This particularly applies to any regular payments you make — check all your standing orders/direct debits and make sure to cancel any you don't need; and that there's money in your account for any you do need.

It's also worth contacting your bank about giving permissions to someone else that you trust whilst you're away. Should you encounter any issues with credit card bills, or withdrawing cash *etc*, it's always handy to have someone back home to help you out — even if to save on the long distance phone calls to the bank!

If you have a flat or house you're planning to sub-let, either use an accommodation agency or make sure someone you trust will keep an eye on things — it may be necessary to give them some written form of authority to deal with emergencies. There's more on all this in **Chapter 3 — Career breaks and older travellers**.

What to take

Start thinking early about what to take with you and write a list — adding to it every time you think of something. Here's a general checklist to get you started:

- Passport and tickets
- Padlock and chain
- Belt bag

· Daypack (can be used for valuables in transit/hand luggage on plane)

· First aid kit: including any personal meds: split between day pack and rucksack

· Notebook and pen

· Camera (with spare battery, memory cards and a lead)

· USB stick (to periodically back up any photos you take)

· Mobile phone and charger

· Headphones with built-in microphone (mic for when you are making a video call)

· Money: cards/travellers' cheques/cash

· Torch

· Sheet sleeping bag

· Universal adapter

· Pack of playing cards

· Spare specs/contact lenses

· Guidebook/phrasebooks — if doing several countries trade in/swap with other travellers en route

· Spare copies of ID cards if needed

· Photocopies of documents/emergency numbers/serial numbers of travellers' cheques (Also, use online storage such as Dropbox to keep a digital copy as back-up)

· Clothes and toiletries *etc*

Some of these checklist items will be more relevant to backpackers and people on treks, than to people on a work placement or staying in a family home. The list can be modified for your own particular plans.

Essential items

Packing for your gap-year can be tricky, and many travellers struggle to narrow their backpack contents down to the essentials. A general rule of thumb is to lay out everything you'd like to pack in a perfect world, then half this. Of course there are a few essential items you shouldn't leave without:

1. Travel towel If there's one travel essential every traveller should have in their backpack it's a travel towel. Compared to a standard towel from home, travel towels pack down to a fraction of the size and weigh a lot less. They are also quick drying and some come with anti-bacterial protection to reduce odours and stop mould developing in hot, sticky and damp conditions. The most common type of travel towel is made from a smooth microfibre material, but you can also get microfibre towels made from a soft-touch microfibre that feel more like towels you'd use at home.

2. Universal plug adapter. If you're going on a gap-year, chances are you're going to be visiting more than one country, which means you'll need different plug adapters for each destination. Packing multiple adapters can take up extra packing space you could put to better use, so getting an all in one adapter that covers multiple countries is a wise move. A universal adapter will also be much easier to find in your backpack.

3. Money belt. When travelling to countries with a high crime rate where security of your belongings can be an issue, a money belt is a must have. You'll find pick-pockets can be a problem in many destinations, especially in Latin America, Asia & Africa, as well as certain countries throughout Europe. Money belts come in many forms, including neck wallets and under clothes body wallets.

4. Combination cable lock. Another travel security essential, cable locks are a versatile accessory for travelling, enabling you to lock your luggage zips, as well as lock your backpack and other belongings to fixed or hard to move objects such as hostel bunk beds and railings. Due to their flexible coated steel shackle, they will fit through pretty much any backpack zip and can also be used to lock your hostel locker.

5. Sleeping bag liner. If the thought of sleeping on hostel bedding makes you cringe, you may want to invest in your own sleeping bag liner. Sleeping bag liners are available in a range of materials, including cotton, silk and fleece. If you want the lightest and most compact liner possible, silk is the best option, but cotton liners also pack down relatively small and are a cheaper option compared to silk.

6. First aid kit. Whether you create your own or opt for a travel specific first aid kit, a first aid kit for travelling is essential. The type of first aid kit you require will all depend on your destination and the activities you plan on taking part in. If you're travelling off the beaten track, where medical facilities are minimal or questionable, you should pack a first aid kit with sterile needles and syringes. These can be used by a medical professional should you require emergency medical treatment during your trip.

7. Packing cubes. This one may not seem like an essential, but if you've ever had to dig through a sea of tangled up clothes to find something inside you're backpack you'd definitely see the benefit of packing cubes. Packing cubes are a great way of organising your clothes inside your backpack and also help to keep them as compact as possible to maximise the amount of packing space available. Try

my
gap-year
Carys

I knew that during my gap year I wanted to volunteer for an environmental charity that relates to my interests. I wanted to have some time to go on adventures and see the world before jumping straight into a degree. By doing so, I would learn new skills, make lots of friends, and gain valuable life experiences. I was also unsure of what I wanted to study and where, and I didn't want to rush into such an important decision.

I chose Raleigh Expedition as it has such a wide variety of opportunities within one programme. Nowhere else provided that mixture of environmental, community and trek adventure projects. I wanted an adventure on my gap year, but I also knew that I wanted to make a difference and do more than just travel. I expected to develop a lot of skills on Raleigh, particularly leadership, and I expected the experience to be challenging and rewarding.

My team did a natural resource management project to help build a new bridge in the Danum Valley Conservation Area. This was to increase access for scientists to access the environment, plants and animals, contributing to the conservation of many rare species. It will also be beneficial for the breeding of monkeys as it will enable them to cross the river and get to the primary day forest area.

We collected materials from the river to mix cement, then used this for the pillars of the bridge and to fill holes. I am most proud of the construction work; it was really tough, but we completed the largest amount of work on what as probably the hottest day. I was surprised at how much we got done as it was all new to us — the materials and the skills needed. We really pulled together as a team, switching around roles to ensure people weren't getting too tired. It was good fun!

Overall, I think my Raleigh experience made me a much more confident person and definitely inspired my decision on what course was right for me. After my Expedition, I chose to study Geography at the University of Bristol, because the community projects opened my eyes to sustainable development and made me want to learn more about how we can achieve global equality. The environmental project made me also want to study the natural world and the huge threats that face it. Geography has the scope to be able to study both of these topics as well as many other global issues.

To find out more about Raleigh International, see their advert on pages 154

using a cube for t-shirts, a cube for shorts/trousers and a cube for underwear!

8. Water filtering bottle. When travelling to countries where the water isn't safe to drink or you're unsure of drinking water quality, a water purification bottle is a good way to ensure you can keep hydrated without taking any risks! The Water-to-Go bottle uses an inbuilt filter to eliminate 99.9% of bacteria, viruses and even heavy metals such as lead from (non-salt) water to make it safe to drink. Water purification bottles offer an easier way to treat water compared to traditional chlorine tablets and drops, as you simply fill up the bottle and allow the filter to remove contaminants as you drink.

9. Mosquito repellent. Insects tend to be an issue no matter where you travel, so ensuring you have a good quality mosquito repellent with you is essential. 50% Deet is classed as jungle strength and is strong enough for use in tropical conditions and areas with a risk of Malaria and other tropical diseases. In addition to mosquito repellent, you can also get mosquito repellent bands, which can be worn around your wrists and ankles to help deter insects. Be sure to pack some bite relief as well, just in case you manage to get bitten or stung during your trip.

10. Travel clothes line. You may well turn your nose up at this and think it's a bit of a gimmick, but a travel washing line is an extremely useful item for gap-year travel. The best way to save space in your backpack is to pack light and wash your clothes as often as possible during your trip, which means you'll need somewhere to hang everything up to dry. Draping your underwear over your hostel bunk may seem like a good idea at the time, but chances are the person in the bunk below doesn't want a curtain of your clothes hanging in their face! A travel washing line is a great way to avoid bugging your dorm room buddies and you don't even need pegs, as you simply tuck your clothes in between the twisted elastic."

Less is best

As airlines struggle with rising fuel costs, and diminishing passenger numbers, they are becoming increasingly inventive in dreaming up extra charges. Excess and overweight check-in baggage is one particularly fruitful area — and it's confusing as the rules vary from airline to airline. This makes it even more crucial to think very carefully about what you need to take — and what you could do without.

Basically, some charge per piece and others by weight, but that's not all. Some carriers limit you to one check-in piece, others, like BA, allow two. It can also depend on your route and your destination. Weight limits vary from as little as 20kg per bag to 40kg. Charges can even be different on outward and return journeys, with some carriers charging as much as £30 per kilogram over the permitted weight, or £90 per extra bag. It won't take much to wipe out all the money you've saved by searching for the cheapest available flights!

Inevitably if you fly business or first class the allowances are more generous but the above assumes that most people on a gap will be flying economy.

Packing tips

- Pack in reverse order — first in, last out.
- Heavy items go at the bottom.
- Pack in categories in plastic bags — easier to find stuff.
- Use vacuum pack bags for bulky items.
- Store toilet rolls and dirty undies in side pockets — easy for thieves to open and they won't want them!
- Take a small, separate backpack for day hikes *etc*. You can buy small, thin folding ones.
- Keep spares (undies, toothbrush, important numbers and documents) in hand luggage.
- Take a sleeping bag liner — useful in hostels.
- Take a sarong (versatile: can be a bed sheet, towel, purse, bag...)
- Travel towels are lightweight and dry fast.
- Remove packaging from everything but keep printed instructions for medications.
- Shaving oil takes less space than cream.
- Put liquids in squashy bottles (and don't carry liquids in hand luggage).
- Fill shoes, cups *etc* with socks and undies to save space.
- Tie up loose backpack straps before it goes into transit.

Now sit down and rationalise — cross off everything you don't really need. Pack enough clothes to see you through — about five changes of clothing should last you for months if you choose carefully. Don't take anything that doesn't go with everything else and stick to materials that are comfortable, hard-wearing, easy to wash and dry and don't crease too much. Make sure you have clothes that are suitable for the climates you are visiting and don't forget that the temperatures in some dry climates can drop considerably at night! You can find very lightweight waterproofs and thermals that can be rolled up easily.

Relax, you can't prepare for every eventuality if you're living out of a rucksack. The best way to know what you need is to ask someone who's already been on a gap what they took, what were the most useful things, what they didn't need and what they wished they had taken.

Maps, directions and vital information

You won't need anything too elaborate: the maps in guidebooks are usually pretty good. A good pocket diary can be very useful — one that gives international dialling codes, time differences, local currency details, bank opening hours, public holidays and other information.

Take a list with you of essential information like directions to voluntary work postings, key addresses, medical information, credit card numbers (try to disguise these in case everything gets stolen), passport details (and a photocopy of the main and visa pages), emergency contact numbers in case of loss of travellers' cheques and insurance and flight details — and leave a copy with someone at home.

Another way of keeping safe copies of your vital documents (even if everything you have is lost or stolen) is to scan them before you leave and email them as

attachments to your email address. However, it is well known that you shouldn't send sensitive information via email and it's not clear whether that advice also applies to attachments, given that they're all stored on a remote server, so you might prefer one of the many online secure data storage options. Or you could even put it all on a memory stick, which has the advantage of being small and easy to conceal and carry.

Those of you with a smartphone or an MP3 player on to which you can download apps will be able to input a mass of information and effectively 'carry' maps, timetables, hostel finders, information lists, and photographs of your valuable documents with you in one small, slim device. An app well worth looking in to is 'CityMaps2Go' as it offers an 'offline' map service. It downloads the map to your phone, so you don't have to worry about having a data connection to keep the map up to date, according to your latest position.

The FCO offers travel advice through social media updates and email alerts. You can subscribe to the alerts at **www.gov.uk/travelaware** selecting the country you are travelling to. Updates will also be issued via the FCO Twitter account **@fcotravel** and on their Facebook page: **www.facebook.com/fcotravel**.

Where to buy your kit

Some overseas voluntary organisations arrange for their students to have discounts at specific shops, like the YHA. The best advice on equipment usually comes from specialist shops, although they may not be the cheapest: these include YHA shops, Blacks, Millets and Camping and Outdoors Centres.

There are some gappers, of course, who might be more restricted by their budget and looking to go on a shorter trip, therefore cost is likely to be more of an issue. It's understandable that you wouldn't always want to buy the most expensive, high quality backpack for a trip of this type. A cheaper backpack or sleeping bag might mean it will only last for a couple of trips, but some gappers are fine with this as long as their gear lasts the duration of their trip. If you're travelling for a year or more, spending a little more on your backpack and travel gear is often worth the extra expense — the last thing you want is your backpack or sleeping bag falling apart half way through a year-long trip. It might cost more to replace it halfway through a trip than to buy one that is better quality and more expensive the first time around.

Ultimately, keeping in mind the duration of your trip, your budget, how frequently you may use your sleeping bag and carry your backpack around and the weather conditions you might meet — this is a decision you need to make!

Rucksacks

Prices for a well-stitched, 65-litre rucksack can vary greatly. Remember, the most expensive is not necessarily the best, get what is most suitable for your trip.

A side-opening backpack is easier than a top-opening one. You can get all sorts of attachments but if you don't need it why pay for it? A good outdoor store should be able to advise you on exactly what you need for your particular trip. Most of these stores have websites with helpful hints and lists of 'essential' items.

You should be able to leave your rucksack in most hostels or guest houses, if you are staying for more than a day, or in a locker at the train station. Always take a camera, passport, important papers and money with you everywhere, zipped up, preferably out of view. You could look to use a money belt to make sure they are hidden away.

visit: www.duinsure.com

Footwear

It's worth investing in something comfortable if you're heading off on a long trip. In hot countries, a good pair of sandals is the preferred footwear for many and it's worth paying for a decent pair, as they will last longer and be comfortable. If you're going somewhere cheap you could just pick up a pair out there but you're likely to be doing a lot more walking than usual, so comfort and durability are important.

Some people like chunky walking boots, others just their trainers, but it's best to get something that won't fall apart when you're halfway up a mountain. Take more than one pair of comfortable shoes in case they don't last, but don't take too many — they'll be an unnecessary burden and take up precious space in your rucksack.

Sleeping bags

Go to a specialist shop where you can get good advice. Prices vary widely and you can sometimes find a four-season bag cheaper than a one-season bag — it's mostly down to quality. You need to consider:

· Can you carry it comfortably and still have the energy to do all you want to do?

· Hot countries — do you need one? You may just want to take a sheet sleeping bag (basically just a sewn-up sheet).

· Colder countries: what will you be doing? Take into account weight and size and the conditions you'll be travelling in — you might want to go for one of those compression sacs that you can use to squash sleeping bags into. For cold countries, you need heat-retaining materials. You can usually — but not always — rent down-filled bags for treks in, say, Nepal.

35

First aid kit

Useful basics:

- Re-hydration sachets (to use after diarrhoea)
- Waterproof plasters
- TCP/Tea tree oil
- Corn and blister plasters for sore feet
- Cotton buds
- A small pair of straight nail scissors (not to be carried in your hand luggage on the plane)
- Safety pins (not to be carried in your hand luggage on the plane)
- Insect repellent
- Antiseptic cream
- Anti-diarrhoea pills (only short-term; they stop the diarrhoea temporarily but don't cure you)
- Water sterilisation tablets
- Antihistamine cream
- Your own preferred form of painkiller

You can get a medical pack from most chemists, travel shops or online from MASTA (**www.masta-travel-health.com**).

You can also look to buy specialised medical kits for travellers: the contents vary from sting relief, tick removers, blister kits, sun block and rehydration sachets to complete sterile medical packs with needles and syringe kits (in case you think the needle someone might have to inject you with may not be sterile).

You can also buy various types of mosquito net, water purification tablets and filters, money pouches, world receiver radios, travel irons and kettles. Not to mention a personal attack alarm.

Cameras

Picture quality on many mobile phones is now so good that you may not feel the need to take a camera as well, especially if you're going to be uploading your pictures on to one of the many photo sharing websites now available. However, very few people rely on *just* their phone when they are travelling. Firstly, taking photos will drain the phone battery quicker, and if you need your phone for staying in touch, or making a call in an emergency, a dead phone is obviously of no use. You also don't want to put all your eggs in to one basket with your devices. If you use your phone for absolutely everything, and it gets lost or stolen, you lose everything.

If you do want the back-up of a camera, check with your local photographic dealer about what will best suit your requirements. Make sure you get a camera case to protect from knocks, dust and moisture and don't buy the cheapest you can find. Cheap equipment can let you down and you need something that doesn't have software compatibility/connection problems.

Here are a few other tips:

- Digital cameras use lots of power (especially if using flash). Take plenty of batteries with you or take rechargeable batteries and a charger (you'll save money in the long run but check that they're usable in your particular camera).

- Don't risk losing all your photos. Back them up as you travel. Maybe visit an internet cafe occasionally and upload your best photos to a site such as Instagram, Flickr or Photobucket. You can upload them onto your Facebook profile, or even send them to your home email account.

- Don't walk around with your camera round your neck; keep it out of sight whenever possible to reduce the risk of crime.

- Remember certain countries charge extra for using a camcorder at heritage sites, safari parks and monuments, but often they don't charge for still cameras.

Looking after yourself...

Health

Note: although we make every effort to be as up-to-date and accurate as possible, the following advice is intended to serve as a guideline only. It is designed to be helpful rather than definitive, and you should always check with your GP, preferably at most eight weeks before going away.

It's not only which countries you'll be going to, but for how long and what degree of roughing it: six months in a basic backpacker hostel puts people at higher risk than two weeks in a five-star hotel.

Before you go you should tell your doctor:

- Your proposed travel route.
- The type of activities you will be doing.

Ask for advice, not only about injections and pills needed, but symptoms to look out for and what to do if you suspect you've caught something.

Some immunisations are free under the NHS but you may have to pay for the more exotic/rare ones. Some, like the Hepatitis A vaccine, can cost around £50, but this is not an area to be mean with your money — it really is worth being cautious with your health.

Also, many people recommend that you know your blood type before you leave the country, to save time and ensure safety. Your GP might have it on record — if not, a small charge may be made for a blood test.

If you're going abroad to do voluntary work, don't assume the organisation will give you medical advice first or even when you get there, though they often do. Find out for yourself, and check if there is a medically-qualified person in or near the institution you are going to be posted with.

People who've been to the relevant country/area are a great source of information. Some travellers prefer to go to a dedicated travel clinic to get pre-travel health advice. This may be especially worthwhile if your GP/practice nurse does not see many travellers.

Here are some options:

www.welltravelledclinics.co.uk is a UK travel clinic company, and part of the

the gap-year guidebook 2018

Liverpool School of Tropical Medicine, **www.e-med.co.uk** has a useful free travel service, which you can email for advice on immunisations, anti-malaria medication and what to watch out for.

www.fitfortravel.scot.nhs.uk

www.travelhealth.co.uk

Department of Health website:

www.nhs.uk/LiveWell/TravelHealth/Pages/Travelhealthhome.aspx

For safety advice try the Foreign and Commonwealth Office:

www.gov.uk/travelaware

Another good idea is to register with an organisation such as MedicAlert, a non-profit-making charity providing a life-saving identification system for individuals with hidden medical conditions and allergies. This service is particularly helpful for those who wish to travel. The MedicAlert emblem contains the international sign of medicine, and is recognised around the world. MedicAlert also has a 24-hour emergency number that can be accessed by medical personnel anywhere in the world and has a translation service in more than 100 languages. As a MedicAlert member, you wear a bracelet or necklet (known as an emblem) engraved with a personal identification number, main medical conditions and an emergency telephone number.

In an emergency, medical personnel have immediate access to vital information on the back of the MedicAlert disc. By phoning the emergency number, they can also gain further medical and personal information such as your name and address, doctor's details, current drug therapy and next of kin details. Membership to the service, including a tailor-made emblem, is £30 a year.

Accidents/injuries

Accidents and injuries are the greatest cause of death in young travellers abroad. Alcohol/drug use will increase the risk of these occurring. Travellers to areas with poor medical facilities should take a sterile medical equipment pack with them. Make sure that you have good travel insurance that will bring you home if necessary.

AIDS

The HIV virus that causes AIDS can be contracted from: injections with infected needles; transfusions of infected blood; sexual intercourse with an infected person; or possibly cuts (if you have a shave at the barbers, insist on a fresh blade, but it's probably best to avoid the experience altogether). It is not caught through everyday contact, insect bites, dirty food or crockery, kissing, coughing or sneezing. Protect yourself: always use condoms during sex, make sure needles are new and if you need a blood transfusion make sure blood has been screened, and don't get a tattoo or piercing until you're back home and can check out the tattoo shop properly.

Asthma and allergies

Whether you are an asthmatic or have an allergy to chemicals in the air, food, stings, or antibiotics, ask your GP for advice before you go. You will be able to take some treatments with you.

if you suffer from severe shock reactions to insect bites/nuts or any other allergy, make sure you have enough of your anaphylactic shock packs (most likely an EpiPen) with you — you may not be able to get them in some parts of the world. It is always best, if you are travelling with a friend or family, that someone else, apart from you, knows how to use an anaphylactic shock kit too in case a situation arises where you are unable to. Make sure to check the expiry dates on the anaphylactic shock kit.

Chronic conditions

Asthmatics, diabetics, epileptics or those with other conditions should always wear a medical ID necklace or bracelet or carry an identity card stating the details of their condition. Tragedies do occur due to ignorance, and if you are found unconscious a tag or card can be a lifesaver. See **www.medicalert.org.uk** for information on obtaining these items.

You should also keep with you a written record of your medical condition and the proper names (not just trade names) of any medication you are taking. If you are going on an organised trip or volunteering abroad, find out who the responsible person for medical matters is and make sure you fully brief them about your condition.

Contraceptives

If you are on the pill it is advisable to take as many with you as possible. Remember that contraceptives go against religious beliefs in some countries, so they may not be readily available. Antibiotics, some malaria treatments, vomiting and diarrhoea can inhibit the absorption of the pill, so use alternative means of contraception until seven days after the illness.

Condoms: unprotected sex can be fatal, so everyone should take them, even if they are not likely to be used. Keep them away from sand, water and sun. If buying abroad, make sure they are a known brand and have not been kept in damp, hot or icy conditions. Always check the expiration date.

Dentist

Pretty obvious but often forgotten: get anything you need done to your teeth before you go. Especially worth checking up on are wisdom teeth and fillings — you don't want to spend three months with toothache when you should be concentrating on exploring, travelling, having fun and discovering new things in another country.

Diabetics

Wear an obvious medical ID necklace or bracelet, or carry an ID card stating your condition (preferably with a translation into the local language).

Take enough insulin for your stay, although it is unlikely that a GP will give you the amount of medication needed for a full year of travelling — three to six months is usually their limit, in which case, be prepared to buy insulin abroad and at full price.

Ring the BDA Careline to make sure the brand of insulin you use is available in the particular country you are planning to visit. Your medication must be kept in the passenger area of a plane, not the aircraft hold where it will freeze.

Diabetes UK,
www.diabetes.org.uk
Careline: +44 (0) 845 120 2960, weekdays 9am-5pm.
Email: careline@diabetes.org.uk

Diabetes UK produces a general travel information booklet as well as specific travel packs for about 70 countries.

Diarrhoea

By far the most common health problem to affect travellers abroad is travellers' diarrhoea. This is difficult to avoid but it is sensible to do the best you can to prevent problems. High-risk food/drinks include untreated tap water, shellfish, unpasteurised dairy products, salads, peeled/prepared uncooked fruit, raw/undercooked meat and fish. Take a kit to deal with the symptoms (your doctor or nurse should be able to advise on this). Remember to take plenty of 'safe' drinks if you are ill and re-hydration salts to replace lost vitamins and minerals.

If vomiting and/or diarrhoea continue for more than four to five days or you run a fever, have convulsions or breathing difficulties (or any unusual symptoms), get someone to call a doctor straight away. Seek advice on the best doctor to call; the British embassy or a five-star hotel in the area may be able to offer some advice here.

To help lower the risk of diarrhoea when you're away, prepare your body before you go. For a couple months before you leave, include yogurt in your diet. It's filled with 'good' bacteria and probiotics, both of which can help regulate your digestive system whilst you're away.

Eyes

Contact lens wearers should stock up on cleaning fluid before going, especially if venturing off the beaten track; but if you're going away for a long period it might be worth switching to disposable types so there's less to carry — ask your optician for advice.

Dust and wind can be a real problem, so refreshing eye drops to soothe itchy eyes and wash out grit can be really useful. If you wear contact lenses, your optician should be able to offer you a range of comfort drops which will be compatible with your lenses.

Also most supermarket pharmacies, plus travel and camping shops, sell plastic bottles of mildly medicated hand cleanser that dries instantly. They're small and light to carry and you only use a small amount each time so it's worth packing a couple. They're really useful for cleaning hands before putting in contact lenses if the local water supply is suspect. It's also worth making sure you have glasses as a back-up, as it's not always possible to replace lost or torn contacts.

If you wear glasses consider taking a spare pair — they don't have to be expensive and you can choose frames that are flexible and durable. Keep them in a hard glasses case in a waterproof (and sandproof) pouch.

Malaria

This disease is caught from the bite of an anopheles mosquito and mosquitoes are vicious and vindictive. Highest risk areas are tropical regions like sub-Saharan Africa, the Solomon Islands and Vanuatu (Pacific), the Amazon basin in South America and parts of Asia. There's no jab, but your GP will give you a course of pills to take.

The most dangerous form of malaria is falciparum, which is particularly common in sub-Saharan Africa (places like Ghana, Gambia, DR Congo).

41

the gap-year guidebook 2018

It can cause liver, kidney, stomach and neurological problems and if left untreated, can be fatal.

One bite from a mosquito is enough. The parasite gets to your liver within 30 minutes and will reproduce there rapidly, infecting the blood stream. Once the parasites are in your blood stream you start to notice symptoms. Some versions can remain dormant in the liver, leading to repeat episodes of the illness.

The best protection is to try (as much as possible) to avoid being bitten. Here are tips for how:

- Use insect repellent, preferably containing either at least 30% DEET (diethyltoluamide), or extract of lemon eucalyptus oil.

- Keep your arms and legs covered between dusk and dawn and use a 'knockdown' spray to kill any mosquitoes immediately.

- Mosquito nets are useful, but they can be hard to put up correctly. It is often worth carrying a little extra string and small bits of wire so that the net can be hung up in rooms that don't have hanging hooks. Ideally the net should be impregnated with an insecticide, you can buy nets that are already treated from specialist shops and travel clinics.

- For some places, dual-voltage mosquito killer plugs are a good idea. *Holiday Which?* tested hand-held electric buzzers that claim to frighten off mosquitoes and found that they did not work on the anopheles mosquito.

- Another good idea is to spray clothes with permethrin — which usually lasts up to two weeks, although Healthguard has a product, called AM-1, which works for three months or 30 washes. Visit **www.healthguardtm.com** to find out more or call them on +44 (0)20 8275 1100.

The pills can be expensive, and some people, particularly on long trips, stop taking their pills, especially if they're not getting bitten much. Don't. Malaria can be fatal.

No one drug acts on all stages of the disease, and different species of parasites show different responses. Your GP, practice nurse or local travel clinic should know which one of the varied anti-malarials is best for you, depending on your medical history (*eg* for epileptics or asthmatics, for whom some types of anti-malarials cannot be prescribed) and the countries you are visiting. Visit your GP or travel clinic at least eight weeks before you go to discuss the options.

It's also worth doing a little research of your own before going to your GP or practice nurse. A useful website is **www.iamat.org/risks/malaria**

All the anti-malarial tablets have various pros and cons, and some of them have significant side effects. If you're going to an area where you have to use the weekly mefloquine tablets, MASTA recommends that you start taking the course two-and-a-half to three weeks before departure. Most people who experience unpleasant side effects with this drug, will notice them by the third dose. If you do have problems, this trial will allow you time to swap to an alternative regime before you go.

If you are in a malaria-risk area, or have recently been in one, and start suffering from 'flu-like' symptoms, *eg* fever, muscle pain, nausea, headache, fatigue, chills, and/or sweats, you should consider the diagnosis of malaria and seek medical attention immediately.

A traveller with these symptoms within several months after returning from an endemic area should also seek medical care and tell their doctor their travel history.

The correct treatment involves the proper identification of the type of malaria parasite, where the traveller has been and their medical history.

Sunburn

Wherever your gap-year takes you, the advice from Cancer Research UK's SunSmart campaign is to enjoy your time in the sun safely. This means not getting caught out by sunburn which, as well as being unsightly, is a clear sign that skin cells have been damaged. Over time, this damage can build up and may ultimately lead to skin cancer.

So while everyone needs some sun in their lives, too much can be harmful. The facts are worrying — skin cancer is one of the most common cancers in the UK and the number of people who develop it is increasing faster than any other type of common cancer. Every year over 11,000 people are diagnosed with malignant melanoma — the most lethal type of skin cancer — and almost 2000 die from the disease. It is diagnosed in a disproportionately high number of younger people, being the second most common cancer in young adults (aged 15-34) in the UK.

And as well as causing skin cancer, too much UV can cause premature ageing, making skin look old and leathery before its time. But the good news is that most cases of skin cancer can be prevented. When you're out in the sun, the most important thing is to make sure you don't burn. Get to know your skin type and how it reacts in the sun. As a general rule, the lighter your skin, the more careful you should be.

When your risk of burning is high, often during the hottest part of the day, spend time in the shade, cover up with a T-shirt or a towel and regularly apply plenty of sunscreen (at least factor 15 — but the higher the better) to protect your skin.

Whatever your skin type the message is simple — don't let sunburn catch you out. Anyone can develop skin cancer but some people have a higher risk and need to take more care, including those with fair skin, lots of moles or freckles, a history of sunburn or a family or personal history of skin cancer.

SunSmart is the UK's skin cancer awareness campaign, funded by the UK health departments. To identify your skin type, find out more about skin cancer, how to enjoy the sun safely, and the dangers of using sunbeds visit **www.sunsmart.org.uk**.

Tick borne encephalitis (TBE)

Ticks are second only to mosquitoes for carrying diseases to humans and immunisation is recommended for people who intend to walk, camp or work in heavily forested regions of affected countries between April and October when the ticks are most active. Your doctor or practice nurse can advise if you should have this immunisation for your travel destination.

Tick Alert say that TBE is "a viral disease contracted via the bite of an infected tick that is endemic in 27 countries in Europe. It leads to an annual average of 10,000 cases needing hospital treatment. Two in every 100 TBE sufferers will die from the disease." TBE incubation is six to 14 days and at first can cause increased temperature, headaches, fever, cough and sniffles, symptoms similar to a cold or flu. The second, more dangerous phase of TBE can lead to neck stiffness, severe headaches, delirium and paralysis.

There is no specific treatment for TBE. However, this is how you can protect yourself:

· Use an insect repellent that is effective against ticks.

· Avoid wearing shorts in rural and wooded areas, tuck trousers into socks, or cover all exposed skin with protective clothing (though not always practical in summer).

· Inspect your skin for ticks and remove any found as soon as possible. If using a special tool, follow instructions for use. If you are using fine-tipped tweezers, grasp the tick firmly and as close to the skin as possible. In a steady motion, pull the tick's body away directly outwards without jerking or twisting. Make sure you get the tick's head out as sometimes the head can remain embedded.

· Also, avoid unpasteurised milk which may also be infected with the TBE virus in endemic regions.

Vaccinations

Ones to consider:

· Hepatitis (A&B).

· Japanese Encephalitis.

· Meningitis.

· Polio.

· Rabies.

· Tetanus.

· Tuberculosis.

· Typhoid.

· Yellow Fever.

The NHS provide information on the vaccinations and diseases that you need to be aware of in the country you are visiting: **www.fitfortravel.nhs.uk**. Ask your GP for advice on vaccinations/precautions six to eight weeks before you go (some may be available on the NHS). Keep a record card on you of what you've had done. Certain countries won't admit you unless you have a valid yellow fever certificate.

Seeking medical advice abroad

You can expect to be a bit ill when you travel just due to the different food and unsettled lifestyle that your body is not accustomed to (painkillers and loo paper will probably be the best things you've packed).

While you're away:

· Keep a record of any treatment, such as courses of antibiotics, that you have when overseas and tell your doctor when you get back;

· Be wary of needles and insist on unused ones; it's best if you can see the packet opened in front of you, or you could take a 'sterile kit' (containing needles) with you; and

· If you don't speak the language, have the basic words for medical emergencies written down so you can explain what is wrong.

Is a gap-year safe?

Accidents can happen anywhere and so can earthquakes, floods, cyclones and other random events.

But there are some risks you can avoid by being alert, informed and prepared. You should take personal safety seriously and not put yourself in danger by agreeing to anything about which you have misgivings, just because you don't want to risk someone thinking that you're stupid or scared.

The Foreign & Commonwealth Office estimates that of the approximately 250,000 young people who take a gap each year, around 75,000 are prone to a reckless spirit that it calls the 'Invincibles'.

The FCO handles 'assistance cases' globally. While support includes visiting those who have been admitted to hospital or arrested, to rescuing British citizens from forced marriages abroad, the FCO launched Know Before You Go because it had found that the most common problems it was being called in on were the most preventable ones, such as inadequate or no insurance.

The FCO has a Twitter service, offering easy way to stay up to date with the latest advice about travel, and to get help before and during a trip abroad. Questions to @ FCOtravel are answered 9am to 6pm BST, Monday to Friday.

This service is provided by the FCO's dedicated travel advice and consular teams, who aim to respond within 30 minutes. Outside of 9am to 6pm questions are only answered in the event of a crisis situation. Others are picked up at the start of the next working day. Many questions about travel can be replied to on Twitter, but any inquiries that involve personal information are taken offline.

This service adds to the ways that British people travelling or living overseas can already get in touch with the FCO: by emailing the travel advice team — **traveladvicepublicenquiries@fco.gov.uk** — or contacting local consular staff: **www. gov.uk/government/world/organisations**.

The FCO has an online travel guide that you can find at:

www.gov.uk/guidance/gap-year-foreign-travel-advice

While the FCO deals with all travellers, not only those on a gap, we agree with the message about being as prepared as possible before you go and that's what this guidebook is for.

We also recommend that you consider taking a gappers' safety course before you go, to teach you how to recognise danger (from people as well as natural disasters), and how to look after yourself in a bad situation — it could be the thing that saves your life.

What the experts say

Planning a gap-year can be a very exciting time. In order to get the most out of and enjoy it to the fullest you need to plan and prepare for every eventuality. Staying safe is the key to having a good time.

These days research comes in many different forms, books, websites, fairs and courses. Safety courses have increased in popularity in the last few years particularly with celebrities such as Ewan McGregor and Charley Boorman taking part and training before their high-profile motorcycle trips.

There are a number of different courses run by various companies across the country ranging from two hours to two days, the one thing they all have in common is that they are run by instructors with first-hand experience, a priceless tool.

Why attend a course? Why not? Attending a specialist gap-safety course can be a vital tool in the planning and preparation of your trip, increasing self-awareness and enabling you to recognise danger and get yourself out of tricky situations.

Most of the courses follow a similar format, covering:

Before you go — research, cultural differences, preparation, insurance, documents and money.

What to take — the clothing you will need, first aid kits, gadgets, electrical items, security of your belongings and tips on economical packing.

Over there — accommodation, food and water, transport, local authorities and awareness of a new environment and laws.

Medical Issues — emergency first aid, staying healthy, self-defence, climate, bites, bugs and vaccinations.

Many of the courses will also run a 'for girls, by girls' session.

Make sure you know enough about what you want to do and where you want to go, talk to other travellers (there are many messageboards online). If you're travelling with an organisation, check them out; ask to speak to others that have done the same trip.

Ensure you have adequate travel insurance to cover everything you want to do including working both paid and voluntary plus any activities you have in mind to do.

Make sure you have copies of all of your documents, try an online document safe. Ensure you have telephone numbers of people to contact in an emergency; emergency medical assistance company, someone at home and if possible someone in the same country.

Travelling to unknown countries can be a great culture shock so a little preparation beforehand will ensure that you make the most of all of your opportunities without missing out. The point is that as long as you have done all you could to be well prepared with travelling essentials and knowledge, then you should go for it!

Personal safety and security checklist

We've canvassed lots of opinion about this, and we've had lots of suggestions. We think the following are among the most important:

- Don't drink too much or stay out too late, it is not like being at home and you will make yourself unnecessarily vulnerable.
- Hanging the 'Do Not Disturb' sign on your hotel door when you go out should help deter thieves.
- Always carry a business card from your accommodation. If you get lost, or want to get a taxi back, you won't have to remember the address.
- If you're worried about your belongings (whether in a hostel dorm or overnight travel), keep them in your sleeping bag with you for extra security.
- Having waterproofed documents (either laminating or in a secure plastic wallet), there is always a chance you will get caught in the rain or need to cross a river if trekking, this way your valuables and documents will stay dry.
- Walk with confidence and never use your guidebook, or get out your map. Find a café, sit and relax and read in peace, don't make yourself a target.
- Keep a small amount of change for food and drinks in a separate wallet so you don't have to keep going through your notes and avoid counting money in the street.

· If you have a 'weak' stomach avoid street stalls, eat in busy restaurants (where the locals are) and try and eat vegetarian if possible, although saying this salads can be some of the worst.

· If travelling alone, you are most vulnerable when you are sick and sometimes you feel like you have to travel that day, but our best advice would be to not to, If you feel ill, such as being intoxicated, don't travel and if you do make sure you are with another person you know well.

· Don't be afraid of approaching other backpackers — this is easier in non-western countries when you can generally tell who is a traveller and who isn't. Not only might you make new friends but also it's great to share experiences and good times as sometimes travelling can be very lonely.

· Talk to locals: the best way to get insight before you travel is to talk to trusted people who live there. Networks are springing up all over the place offering unique local insights based from food lovers, or culture vultures, try Tripbod: **www.tripbod.com**.

· Whatever happens, however bad — remember people are generally good and you will find people (other backpackers, locals, hostel owners *etc*) who will go out of their way to help you and make sure that you are safe and okay.

· If you are in trouble, whatever the local police tell you, contact the local British embassy or consulate — most of them are incredibly helpful and they will have dealt with situations like yours before and will know what you should do, make sure that you have several copies of their contact details to hand.

Remember, anyone can get lost. When you are on the road don't panic. Always agree meeting places before you go somewhere and play safe by having a back-up plan. Then if you don't turn up reasonably on time someone will be alerted to raise the alarm.

Before you do anything or go anywhere think about the consequences — this isn't about not having a good time, or being boring — it's about getting through your gap without taking foolish risks.

In many places, though, you'll find people are very hospitable and curious about you and you might find their unabashed and quite frank questions intrusive. While you have to be sensible about how much information you give, equally try not to be too suspicious about their motives.

What feels like an invasion of your personal space, or probing questioning, doesn't automatically mean anything sinister — remember the British in particular can be quite reserved so you'll notice the contrast. It's a question of balance and courtesy.

Caroline's Rainbow Foundation is a charity set up to promote safety awareness for young travellers. They gave us some additional pointers, all worth emphasising:

· Leave copies of all your travel documents, visas, insurance policies and bank card details with someone back home. If you lose them or they are stolen it is easier to report if you have all the details to hand. If you can store them on the computer and email the images to yourself, you will always have the documents where ever there is internet. Lock your passport and travel tickets in a safe if possible.

· If you plan to work abroad find out if you need a work visa and get it before you leave. Some countries will not let you work while on holiday. Try not to be tempted by the offer of cash in hand; if caught you could easily be deported or even imprisoned.

· If you take regular medication ensure you have enough for your trip. Also keep a note of what it is in case you lose it. You may be able get hold of it in another country

but this is not guaranteed. It may also be called a different name so try to have a note of the generic name of the drug rather than a brand name. Pharmacists can usually help with this. If taking a large amount of the prescription medication with you take a doctor's letter explaining what it is and why you need it. Easier than being mistaken for smuggling drugs.

· Try to learn a few simple phrases in the local language, if you find that hard or you do not understand the dialects at least you should learn to recognise them when written down. Knowing what the sign is for a bus stop, cafe, phone, police or hostel could be very helpful, particularly when arriving somewhere at night.

· Try to book your first night's accommodation in a new location, especially if you plan to arrive after dark. Make sure you know where the place is, how far it is from your arrival point and the best way to get there. Standing around with a map and large rucksack is a giveaway that you are new in town and could attract unwanted attention.

· Try not to carry lots of money around with you. Lock it away in a safe if you can, Most hostels have a safe at reception. Remember you can be watched using a cash point or inside a bank.

· Remember items such as condoms are often inferior in quality, especially in places such as Africa and South America; if you think you might need them it's probably best to take your own that you know are safe.

· Be aware of the food and dietary habits in the country/countries you plan to visit. While sundried grasshoppers may not be your normal diet, you might want to be prepared to try new foods. Hygiene abroad, particularly in developing countries, may not be the same as at home so be careful not to offend when offered food even if you think it

49

looks raw or disgusting. If you do get a 'gippy tummy' make sure you drink plenty of clean, ideally bottled, water to ensure you don't get dehydrated.

· Local transport is usually very different abroad, especially in developing countries. You may have no choice but to travel on a bus with worn tyres, too many passengers, or no seat belts to avoid being left in a deserted location, but it is worth finding out if there are any other options. Try to sit near to the main door or by an emergency exit if possible. It may seem fun to hang off the bus or sit on the roof like the locals but realistically this could be very dangerous.

· While travelling from place to place try to lock your luggage if you can not see it and do not leave any valuables in it. Take all valuables with you regardless of the mode of transport that you are taking.

· Be careful where and how you take photographs. It's often not a good idea to take photos of anything official, or anything which could be connected to the military, such as airports or border checkpoints. This could attract unwanted attention or hostile behaviour from the local people or officials.

· In hotel or hostel rooms, check that your windows and doors lock properly and keep them locked at night. Request a room that is not on the ground floor. Check the fire evacuation procedure from your bedroom in case of emergencies.

· Make sure that someone always knows where you are and when you can be expected to return. This is especially important in rural places where mobile phones may not work.

· Never leave your drink unattended — it could be spiked.

· If you are travelling in a hire car, keep the doors locked at all times, especially when

FCO Safety Advice

Drinking overseas

If you're drinking alcohol while you're away know your limits, don't leave your drink unattended and be aware that alcohol measures abroad may differ to those in the UK. It's important to stay hydrated, particularly if drinking in the sun and to be aware of your surroundings.

If you are planning on driving whilst overseas make sure you are aware of the local legislation. Many countries have a zero tolerance policy on drink driving, with penalties of suspension and in some cases imprisonment.

Drugs and detention

Even in countries where drugs seem easily available the punishments of the local authorities may be harsh and can result in significant fines, long term imprisonment and in some cases the death penalty.

Never carry luggage through customs for other people, even your friends. If you are found with drugs on you or in bags that are in your possession, you are liable to punishment whether you were aware of them or not.

If you do become unwell or are injured following the use of any illegal drugs, you are also likely to face a hefty medical bill as many travel insurance policies will be declared void as a result.

you are stuck in traffic. Make a note of contact numbers for the rental company in case of breakdown or theft. Be careful when parking your car as you may not be able to read or understand the parking rules. You do not want to return and find your car has been towed away.

- Nothing is worth more than your life. Money, cameras etc can be replaced, especially if you have insurance. If challenged do not put up a fight, letting go could save your life.

Caroline's Rainbow Foundation have a Safer Travel app which is definitely worth a look: **www.carolinesrainbowfoundation.org/safer-travel-app**

Safety

Your first impression of some countries will be a swarm of people descending on you, pestering you to take a taxi or buy something — at night, when you're tired from a long plane trip, it can be quite scary. If you're not being met by anyone, check whether there's a pre-pay kiosk in the airport and pay for a ticket to your ultimate destination. That way the taxi driver can't take you on a detour since they won't get their money until you're safely delivered and your 'chit' has been signed.

Some people advise that, if you arrive alone in the middle of the night (which is often the case on long-haul budget flights), it might be safer to wait until daylight before heading onwards. That's not a pleasant prospect in most airports, but it may occasionally be the sensible option.

In many countries of the developing world, where there are no social security or welfare systems, life can be extremely tough and leave people close to despair. That's likely to be even more the case, in the face of growing food shortages and escalating fuel and food costs as a result of the ongoing global recession. What may seem like a cheap trinket to you may be enough to buy them a square meal for which they are desperate enough to steal from you violently, so it is sensible not to wear too much jewellery.

These tips can help you to stay safe whilst on your gap-year:

1. Use your common sense, if something looks dangerous or unsafe, ask for assistance

2. Follow the advice of the Foreign Office for the countries you travel to.

3. If travelling with an organisation, the organisation should have completed risk assessments and inform you of the risks. There should also be support on the ground, should you need assistance.

Respect and behaviour

If you don't want to find yourself in real trouble, do some research. Each culture or religion has its own codes of behaviour and taboos and, while no one would expect you to live by all their rules, as an ethical and responsible traveller, showing respect for the basic principles is a must as a guest in their country, not to mention being a sensible precaution if you want to stay safe.

Bear in mind that, in most places, even the so-called First World, rural communities are usually far more traditional and straight-laced than city ones and casual western dress codes and habits can offend.

51

Also remember that a country's native people are not just part of the landscape, they are individuals who deserve respect and courtesy, so if you want to take a photo of them — ask first, or at least be discreet!

Dress codes

These are the sorts of things you should bear in mind: in most Asian and African countries don't wear a bikini top and shorts in city streets if you don't want to attract the wrong kind of intrusive attention. In any case an all-over light cotton covering will better protect you from sunburn and insect bites.

Men and women should dress modestly, particularly, but not only, in Muslim countries. Women especially should wear long sleeves and cover their legs. Uncovered flesh, especially female, is seen as a 'temptation' and you'll be more comfortable, not to mention finding people more friendly and welcoming if they can see you're sensitive to local customs.

You should also remember that, in Buddhist countries, the head is sacred and so it is unconventional to touch it.

Before entering temples and mosques throughout India and South Asia, you must remove your shoes. There are usually places at the entrances, where you can leave them with attendants to look after them.

Women are also expected to cover their hair — and in Jain temples wearing or carrying anything made of leather is forbidden. Even in parts of Europe you would be expected to cover your head and be dressed respectfully if you go into a church.

Culture and beliefs

Open gestures of affection, kissing or even holding hands between married couples can be shocking to some cultures.

visit: www.duinsure.com

However, you will often see men or boys strolling around hand in hand or with arms around each other's shoulders in India — don't misinterpret: they are very likely to be friends!

Remember also, that if you are speaking English with a local inhabitant, they may not understand or use a word with the same meaning as you do. Particularly in the area of emotional relationships and dating, remembering this and understanding the local religion, customs and morality can save a lot of misunderstanding, misery and heartache.

Sitting cross-legged, with the soles of your feet pointing towards your companions, is another example of a gesture regarded as bad manners or even insulting in some places and actually if you think about it, it's pretty logical if you're in a place where people walk around less than clean streets either barefoot or in sandals.

Since daily life and faiths are often closely interlinked, it helps to know a little about the major philosophies of life in the countries you visit.

These are the main belief systems you will encounter on your travels (we use the term belief systems because, arguably, some of these are closer to being philosophies of life than to religions or faiths in the sense most people would understand them):

· Bahá'i

· Shinto

· Taoism

FCO Travel Tips

It's important to research and familiarise yourself with the local laws and customs of the countries you intend to travel to as part of your preparation. A bit of local knowledge can go a long way to enhance your travel experience and earn you respect in the country you're visiting.

The FCO have put together some suggestions to help get you started:

· Get a good guidebook and make sure you know about local laws and customs, especially those relating to alcohol and drugs. It can also be useful to find a map of the area and a layout of the town or city you are visiting

· Learn some key phrases and words of the local language, these could be particularly helpful in the case of an emergency but can also improve your experience within the community

· Try to blend in to the local community: be conscious of any religious dress codes and dress accordingly. It's important to be respectful when you are visiting someone else's country

· Photographs: certain sites within a country can be sensitive, e.g. military bases, government buildings etc. Be mindful of what you are photographing. It's worth asking before you snap so as not to run into trouble or cause offence

· Book your first night's accommodation in advance. You're at your most vulnerable when you first arrive in a foreign country and are likely to be tired and uncertain of your surroundings

- Confucianism
- Shamanism
- Humanism
- Zoroastrianism
- Islam
- Judaism
- Hinduism
- Buddhism
- Jainism
- Sikhism
- Spiritualism
- Candomblé
- Santeria

For more information, or if you are interested in finding out about other religions, try: **www.bbc.co.uk/religion/religions**

Communication: Keeping in touch

Spare a thought for those you're leaving behind — friends as well as family. Not only will they be worried about your safety, but they may actually be interested in your travels too.

It's not just about keeping them happy: make sure you tell them where you are and where you are going — that way if something does happen to you, at least they know where to start looking. Backpackers do go missing, climbers have accidents, trekkers get lost; at least if someone is concerned that you have not got in touch when expected, they can then alert the police and relevant people. If you've promised to check in regularly with close family *make sure you do*, especially when you move on to another country. Of course, if you don't stick to what you agreed, don't be surprised if the international police come looking for you.

While you probably can't wait to get away, you may be surprised how homesickness can creep up on you when you're thousands of miles away. Getting letters or emails can be a great pick-me-up if you're feeling homesick, weary or lonely, so, in order to ensure a steady supply of mail, distribute your address(es) widely to friends and family before you go. If you're not able to leave behind an exact address then you can have letters sent to the local Poste Restante, often at a main post office, and collect them from there. Also, parcels do usually get through, but don't send anything valuable.

Keeping a diary/sketchbook to record places, projects, people, how you're feeling and the effect things are having on you, can help when you get an attack of the homesick blues or just feel a bit down.

Mobile phone basics

Make sure you've set up your account to allow you to make and receive calls and text messages in all the countries you'll be travelling to (and emails if you've got a smartphone). Try to limit use of your mobile to emergencies — they usually cost a

fortune to run abroad as you pay for all the incoming calls at international rates too.

It's worth insuring the handset, as mobile theft is common and if it's the latest model, try not to flash it around.

If you are staying in one country for several weeks, consider getting either a cheap local mobile phone or a local SIM card for your UK mobile. Don't forget to alert friends back home to the new number. Local texts and calls tend to be very cheap and incoming calls from abroad are free, which avoids the massive charges when using your UK mobile.

Snail mail

Aerogrammes are a cheap way of writing from most countries. Registering letters usually costs only a few pence (or equivalent) from Third World countries, and is definitely worthwhile. Postcards are quick, cheap and easy — though not very private.

www.pc2paper.co.uk: This website allows you to send letters worldwide from the internet and store addresses in your account. You type your message and they then convert it into an actual letter and post it for you. The costs vary depending on weight and size.

Email

If you can get to an internet café or access a wifi network on your smartphone or tablet in an airport, hotel, university, office or home when you're abroad, you can

my
gap-year
Riaan

After volunteering in 2015 with my parents, I decided to return to the Kevin Richardson's wildlife conservation project in 2017.

Kevin, his wife Mandy and their dedicated team are managing this project in Dinokeng Game Reserve, about 150km outside of Pretoria, South Africa. The project is based on taking care of wild animals like lions, hyenas and leopards who all are born and raised in captivity. They are no longer able to survive in the wild. To experience the unique bond between Kevin and the lions is amazing and heart-warming. Kevin is very open about his role in this and that is so useful for volunteers.

What makes being here so special? You become a part of a dedicated team with one main target: "Taking care of the animals and enriching their lives". While working with, and for, these animals you learn a lot of their behaviour. It gives me a lot of self-confidence. The main part of the work I did was preparing food, cleaning enclosures, fence patrol and assisting Kevin with film and photoshoots. Sometimes the work was tough, but I loved it. I also had a lot of fun during the project with the other volunteers.

One of the special activities is walking with the lions. Kevin goes out for walks with a few lions and we follow them by car. The lions are 100% relaxed and it is lovely to see them in their natural environment.

It is absolutely no holiday camp but a project that gives you the opportunity to come close to these animals and learn so much about their habits and problems.

I'm so proud and honoured to be a part of this story. This experience will guide me in my further life. And I thank Kevin, Mandy and their team for this experience.

I challenge you to join the project and make a difference in Wildlife Conservation. A short impression of the volunteer work: (https://youtu.be/dO6F-xTFbGw).

To find out more about Kevin Richardson Wildlife Sanctuary, see their advert on page 162

simply log in to your mailbox (remember you'll need your user ID and password if these are part of the package).

Newsletter

A great way to keep in touch with people at home is by sending out a newsletter email via a free service such as MailChimp (**www.mailchimp.com**). The service makes designing an email that is rich in images, captions, links and text easy, plus you can send the email to your whole mailing list at the touch of a button! It's a great way to keep your network back at home updated.

Internet cafés

Remember that internet cafés are much more than just a place to upload your latest batch of photos, check in with the folks at home and pick up the footie results along with your email.

In many places they're a lifeline for local people — to small farmers or traders, to families separated by war, poverty or natural disaster or a way of bringing education to children in isolated villages across the developing world — and, like any other kind of café, a place of crucial social interaction.

Equally if you are travelling independently and following your whims where better than to check with other backpackers for decent places to stay or get an idea of local customs and prices for food, transport, entertainment, whatever?

So even if you're travelling with the latest in e-technology it's worth taking your tablet or laptop to an internet café for a wi-fi hook-up. You'll get as much info from the people as you can from the machine!

Perhaps we should also include one note of caution — look for cafés with open spaces not curtained booths. Very often, particularly in very traditional societies where there is only minimal contact permitted between unmarried boys and girls, internet cafes with computers in closed booths are often male-only territory — and a place to check out the latest in 'adult' entertainment... not a good place to go if you're a gapper just wanting to check your email and say hi to mum!

Online journals

Another easy way to keep everyone up-to-date is to set up a travel blog — as many people now do. On Facebook, your photos and comments will be available only to your 'friends' (unless you relax the privacy settings for a particular post) but there is the added advantage of being able to send messages and pictures to specific people without having to remember their email address, providing, of course, they too have a Facebook account.

Other sites you might like to check out are:

www.travelblog.org
www.offexploring.com
www.fuzzytravel.com
www.travoholic.com
www.wordpress.com

And finally... back to earth

We've talked to enough people who have already taken a gap to know that returning home can be a shock to the system.

Returning to ordinary life takes time. It doesn't matter when you took your gap, you're likely to still go through the same sequence of feelings over the three months it generally takes to re-adjust.

How you respond, though, will depend on what you are returning to — if you went between school and university you might find yourself switching courses or storing up something else to explore later. Or you might be quite content to take up your course with renewed enthusiasm after a travelling break from study.

It's different again for people mid-career or over-50 mature travellers, but the pattern of adjustment is pretty much the same.

This feeling can be described as 'reverse culture shock':

A common response, experienced by people returning home from another culture, is reverse culture shock. It can often be worse than culture shock as it's often unexpected. Returning home should be the easiest part of the trip, and sometimes it is, however, your trip may have changed you, your values and expectations. Sometimes it may be difficult to acknowledge that you have changed and home is still the same. Your family and friends may have unrealistic expectations of you. This may be hard on you but it will also be hard on them.

You may feel a major loss upon returning home, almost as if you have been bereaved. There may also be a communication barrier between yourself and your family and friends back home. You may not be able to express the magnitude of what you have been through abroad.

Your view of your home country may have changed in the light of your overseas experience, and you might find yourself rejecting some of your old values and ways of living. This may cause conflict between you and your friends and family who may be affected by your lifestyle change.

You may try to re-adapt to your old lifestyle and re-connect with your old friends but find it hard to do so. Situations and relationships back home are bound to have changed in your absence; especially if you have been away for a long time. You may feel that you no longer belong and that joining in is hard.

If you have returned home without an immediate plan for the future you may feel as though there is a lack of purpose to your life, which sorely contrasts to when you were abroad and perhaps carrying out an important role."

All of the above can leave you feeling isolated, anxious, or depressed. It is important to remember that you are not alone in these thoughts, and that things can be done to help.

Here are some tips to help you adjust:

- Prepare: prepare yourself before you go by learning more about reverse culture shock.
- Keep in touch: keep in touch with your friends and family while you are away.
- Give yourself closure: say a proper goodbye to your friends and colleagues.
- Take a break: when you get home, take at least a few days off.
- Write: writing can be a cathartic experience and can help order your thoughts. If you have experienced some life-changing or difficult events, write about them.

· Avoid indulgences and rash behaviour: avoid self-indulgence in alcohol, drugs, and food — these comforts make you feel good in the short-term but are guaranteed not to help your recovery process. Also try to avoid making rash decisions; you may feel bored and want to accept the first offer that comes your way, but it is best to be patient and let your emotional state settle.

Usually you will settle down quickly, depending on certain factors such as the effectiveness of your coping strategies and the extent of your overseas experiences. The experiences from your international assignment are likely to become incorporated into your values and the way you live. You may find yourself drawing on them to inform your decisions and thoughts, and when advising others.

If, after a few months, you have not settled after your return we recommend you talk to a trustworthy friend or a psychological health professional. The length of time you've been away makes no difference to the feelings you go through on your return and even after six months you may still need time to adjust.

We've talked to people who've taken a two-week leave of absence from work through their company's charitable foundation and to people who've spent a year or more away. They all report coming back and finding themselves looking at everything through fresh eyes and questioning the importance of various aspects of homelife that they have previously taken for granted.

On average, it seems to take about three months between stepping off that last plane after a gap and getting back into life's routines. To start with, a commonly-reported phenomenon is the odd sensation of the body decelerating while the brain's still on the move. So, after the first three weeks of initial euphoria and sharing, be prepared to come down to earth with a bump. Having said all that, try and remember that you have done something really amazing. Yes, you'll be back home and missing your life on the road, but think how lucky you were to have had the chance to do something that most people only dream of.

my
gap-year
Sophie

I knew when I applied to study veterinary medicine at university that getting in was going to be difficult, so it came as no surprise when on results day I narrowly missed the grades for my offer to study at Liverpool. I quickly decided to take a gap-year and reapply, but wanted to make the most of my year out and do something I may never get the chance to do again.

I started looking online for gap-year trips where I could work alongside vets in other countries. Deciding on Africa was easy — its wildlife and beautiful landscapes are second to none. I soon found the African Conservation Experience website and looked at all of the different projects they offered. I filled out their online application and was contacted the next day with the offer of a place on my first choice of project; the wildlife veterinary experience.

When we landed in South Africa we were met at the airport by members of the ACE team who took us to our different projects. I arrived at my project and was met by a member of the host family I would be living with for the next month. The whole family were lovely, so welcoming and accommodating — they even spent their weekends driving us around, taking us to different sites and on day trips. They went to great lengths to ensure we got the most out of our trip, whether it was driving us for two hours to see elephants or getting up at 4am with us to meet the vet for early rhino dehorning.

Working with Dr Rogers was an incredible honour, I got to see and do such a massive range of things I never dreamed I would. I was not sat 100 yards away in a truck watching from a 'safe' distance, I was stood right there with the vet monitoring the breathing of the sedated rhinos and leopards, and even got the chance to administer drugs to the animals. I learnt so much, Dr Rogers is an incredible teacher and always explained what he was doing and why, and never got annoyed at having to repeat the long names of the drugs I couldn't remember (just make sure you pronounce the 't' in warthog, that does annoy him!). He always encouraged us to get involved, take lots of pictures and even let me take a ride in the helicopter, he is a genuinely nice guy and it was a pleasure working with him.

Every second of the trip, without exception, was perfect. I would give anything to go back and do the month again and wouldn't change a thing — except maybe never coming home.

For more information about African Conservation Experience, see their advert on page 168

What do you do now?

This one depends on what you had planned before you left and whether the option is still there — and if you still want to do it — once you are back.

Some people advise that, if you can manage it, putting aside some money for about three months of living expenses for your return, as part of pre-gap preparations, takes the pressure off if you're going to be job hunting. But, if taking time out isn't an option, don't panic.

If you already have work to go back to you may have to combine the post trip elation with a fairly quick return to the 'rat race'. And you'll need to think about how you interact with your colleagues. How much do you say about your trip? A spokeswoman for one major UK employer, which supports its staff in taking time out, and also has a foundation on whose projects they can do voluntary work, had this advice:

When you are returning to work it is important to have a plan. Returning to work after 18 weeks or more can prove difficult on both a psychological and logistical level. Keep your line manager up-to-date with the timings of your return to work. This will ensure that they can factor you into their resource planning and also help you integrate back into the working environment.

Do not rule out a degree of retraining when you return to work. Refreshing your skills will benefit most people in the work place, and, if you have been away from work for a long period of time, you should use the opportunity to familiarise yourself with new systems, procedures and practices.

When you return to work take into consideration reverse culture shock. Whilst you might be keen to talk about your travels for many months to come, your colleagues may not be so keen to listen.

You'll find more useful advice on this in **Chapter 3 — Career Breaks and Older Gappers**.

Deciding what next

While getting back to 'normal' life, you've no doubt been trying to process everything you've learned from your gap experience.

How do you feel? What's changed? What's been confirmed? Where to now? Is there something new you want to do next as a result? How to go about it? You'll almost certainly still be in touch with friends you made on your travels, maybe even had a couple of after-gap reminiscence meetings. Others may still be travelling and keeping you restless!

You may also still be in touch with the projects you worked on. It's a fairly common feeling to want to keep a link to something that's been a life changing, learning experience. Is this you?

The best piece of advice on dealing with the consequences of any life-changing experience is to be patient and give it time. Nothing but time can make things settle into some kind of perspective and help you work out whether you are in the grip of a sudden enthusiasm or something deeper and more long-lasting.

Change of direction?

In time you'll know whether your urge to travel has also become an urge to keep the links with the communities you visited now you're back.

What level of involvement do you want? Is it going to be something local like fundraising — doing local talks, letters to newspapers — or are you seriously looking to change your career?

If you have come back with the seed of an idea for a career change as a result of a volunteer placement, for example, there's nothing to stop you slowly exploring the options and possibilities.

Have a look at your CV. Try to talk to people working in the field you're considering moving into. Armed with some basic information, you could also consider talking through issues such as what transferable skills you have to add to your volunteer experience, what training you might need and how affordable it is, with a careers counsellor or recruitment specialist — preferably with an organisation that specialises in aid/charity or NGO positions.

Try these links:

www.totaljobs.com/IndustrySearch/NotForProfitCharities.aspx
www.cafonline.org
www.charitypeople.co.uk
www.peopleandplanet.org

To keep you going you should also never underestimate the power of synchronicity. You may find unexpected connections and information come your way while you're getting on with other things. If it's meant to be, you'll find ways to make it happen.

Please see the directory pages starting on page 253 for information on companies and organisations offering services and products to help you on your gap-year.

Finance

 **Finance**

How much money will you need?

It all depends on what you're doing, where you're going and for how long. Long haul flights are much more expensive than regional ones, for example, and insurance and visas vary country-by-country. As we've already mentioned in **Chapter 1**, costs for a 'budget' gap-year in south-east Asia can be as little as £4,000, whereas a more luxury gap-year staying in hotels in Europe can cost £10,000 or more, plus flights on top.

Heilwig Jones, from Kaya Responsible Travel, gave us this advice: "With regards to costs, these vary greatly. It is important to understand what you are getting for your fees. Lower-budget volunteer projects generally don't focus on individually matching people to the right project, or looking at how a person's skills are best used, because this is time-consuming. At the higher end of the price range, some organisations may include additional excursions and activities. So it is important to understand what you are looking at in making your choice. Some countries have a higher cost of living than others, some projects have higher costs of operation (for example marine conservation with diving, or wildlife research needing safari-vehicles). Invariably, while you have these costs upfront when you volunteer, you need to spend a lot less money in-country because your time is filled with the activity of your volunteer project. And longer-term placements can work out very economically."

What do you need to pay for?

A gap needn't break the bank, but it helps if you start by making yourself a list of all the things you might need to pay for, and then research how much it all comes to.

Look at your chosen locations and do a bit of research as to how much the essentials costs — accommodation, food and travel — vary between towns and countries.

This will give you your absolute base budget per day, on top of which you can add costs for activities — seeing sights, adrenalin activities (if that's your thing) and, of course, going out!

Here's a checklist of some essentials to help you get started:

Before you go:

· Passport

· Visas and work permits (check the FCO website for the relevant embassy — **www.gov.uk/travelaware**)

· Insurance

· Flights

· Fees for placements/organised treks *etc*

· Special equipment if needed

visit: www.gap-year.com

· Vaccinations — they're not all free — and a travellers' medical pack

· Don't forget regular payments, such as a pay-monthly mobile phone.

When you've gone:

· Accommodation (If travelling independently)

· Transport (if travelling independently)

· Food

· Entertainment

· Shopping — gifts and souvenirs

· Emergency fund

Avoiding money disasters

The list covers the absolute basics, but if you're not careful there are plenty of extra costs that could eat into your budget — ones you wouldn't necessarily think of at first. The FCO have produced some handy tips on where to start and how to manage the costs of your trip:

· Work out your budget before you go. Do some research on what activities you would like to take part in while you're away and what the expected costs of these will be. Think about how much you'll need to spend on a daily basis — such as food, accommodation and any additional activities — and then work that out for the number of days you'll be away

· Check the limits or cash available on any credit or debit cards you plan to take with you, as well as the validity and expiry dates so you don't get caught out overseas

· Make sure you have made arrangements for any credit card bills to be paid while you are away to avoid your card being stopped. It might be useful giving someone at home the power of attorney to look after your financial affairs in the UK while you are travelling

the gap-year guidebook 2018

- Notify your bank before you travel and inform them of the dates and countries you will be travelling through. Check your card/s can be used abroad and if any charges apply. Be sure to keep your cards safe, especially if you intend to use them throughout your trip
- Make a note of your credit / debit card details and the 24-hour emergency numbers and keep them separately
- Take at least two cards, making one your emergency reserve, and make sure you know the PIN numbers for both debit and credit cards. Keep the emergency card somewhere safe
- Make sure you have at least two forms of payment — take a mixture of cash (Sterling, Euros or US dollars), prepaid cards and credit cards. Don't keep them together in one place in case you lose them or they are stolen. It's often better to over budget in case of emergencies
- Purchase a return ticket, or make sure you have enough money to buy one. It's worth noting that many countries will refuse you entry unless you have a return ticket
- Always have some change in the local currency for when you arrive in case you need to make a telephone call. It is also advisable to have some local currency in small bank notes to catch a taxi or get something to eat or drink on arrival
- Look out for local ATM machines. Todays global network means you can withdraw cash from machines in most places abroad. Be sure to check before use as costs may apply
- Use a wallet for loose change and your day-to-day spending when carrying money around with you. Wear a secure money belt under clothing for your valuable documents and money

Raising the money

There's no doubt it's harder to raise money for gap travel in tougher economic times, when the competition for even low-skilled or part-time work is likely to be intense.

But, aside from the lucky few who can call upon major financial help from their families or wherever else, most people will have to go out and earn the money, so it may be a case of taking whatever is out there. It will be worth it to pay for your 'once in a lifetime' trip.

Do remember that how you raise the money could have lasting benefits. "Raising the money for a gap-year is seen as an important part of a gap-year both by the company you travel with and by employers," Stefan Wathan, of Year Out Group, told us, "Done well, it demonstrates commitment, initiative, an ability to plan, to appreciate money and to negotiate as well as communication skills."

If you already have a job look at how much of your salary you can realistically put aside each month for your travelling fund. It may mean six months or so of not having quite so many cocktails each week, or not being able to buy the latest iPhone, but it will be worth it! You can set up a separate account for your travelling fund and arrange a standing order to move money each month, which is really simple to do through internet banking.

There are other ways to raise some money however, such as a car boot sales or a sponsored run, bike ride or swim *etc* (donating half to charity, half to travel funds).

And the internet is a great source of money-raising ideas, from selling on eBay and Gumtree to new initiatives such as crowd-funding. Have a look at this website: **www.fundmytravel.com**. With a little imagination you could really lighten the financial load.

Sponsorship may be an option and local businesses may be interested if they think they can get some mileage out of it. You may able to get local media interested if you are doing something exceptional on your travels, and then you can give your business sponsors the free advertising they deserve.

Community groups, charities and religious organisations may well be interested in what you are doing and they may be willing to help in some way — particularly if you promise to give them a talk about your travels when you get back.

You could also apply for a grant. Have a look at the Directory of Grant Making Trusts. It is published each year and covers 2,500 grant-making trusts, collectively giving around £3 billion.

If you are planning to do a training course during your gap-year, you may be eligible for funding via a Career Development Loan. A CDL is a deferred repayment bank loan to help you pay for vocational learning or education. The Department for Education pays the interest on your loan while you are learning and for up to one month afterwards.

You can get more info from the National CDL enquiry line: 0800 100 900; or by visiting the government website: **www.gov.uk/career-development-loans/overview**

Top Tips to Raise Money
by Student Money Saver

Working to save up in advance of a gap-year is the most obvious way of financing a trip. However, don't worry if you feel like you can't successfully balance studies with paid work, there are lots of ways you can raise a little bit of extra money.

For starters, consider selling some old stuff. Start on eBay, but sites like Depop are ideal if you have clothes you no longer wear. You can also cash in on old CDs, DVDs or tech like smartphones - there are various sites on the internet providing this service.

Some young people are lucky enough to make some extra money through blogs and videos and YouTube has made household names of the likes of Zoella. But be aware that becoming rich from the internet is rarer than you might think, and making money online, even a small amount, is something that can really take time to work. So be patient and see this as a supplementary income source, at least to begin with.

As well as experimenting with making money online before you set off, setting up a blog could also be an option to explore during your gap-year as you share your experiences of travelling with the world.

Other ideas include becoming a TV or film extra, selling artwork on Etsy or freelance writing on **www.peopleperhour.com**.

visit: www.gap-year.com

Money savers

The International Student Identity Card (ISIC) gives you more than 40,000 travel, online and lifestyle discounts. It costs £12, is accepted in the UK and worldwide. There's also a 24/7 worldwide free call helpline for medical and legal assistance.

Many leading airlines also offer exclusive student/youth fares to ISIC (and IYTC) holders. Your travel agent can help you find the right one and advise if any age restrictions apply.

You can order your ISIC online at: **www.isic.org**

The card sees you right through the academic year: it's valid from each September, for up to 16 months, in other words until December the following year. You need to qualify for the year in which you'll hold the card:

· If you're a full-time student (15 hours weekly for 12+ weeks) at a secondary school, sixth form or further education college, language school, The Open University (60 points or more) or any UK university.

· If you've got a deferred/confirmed UCAS placement (then you can grab an ISIC for your year away).

If you're neither of the above, but under 26, you can get an International Youth Travel Card (IYTC) with a similar range of benefits. You can get the cards online at: **www.isic.org** or by phoning 0871 230 8546.

For budget flights and student discounts, you can check out the internet and we've included some hints in **Chapter 4 — Travelling and accomodation**.

If you're travelling independently, cut the cost of accommodation by: staying in the guest houses attached to temples and monasteries; camping or staying in a caravan park; as a guest in someone's home; sharing a room; or using budget hotels or hostels, but be careful to check for cleanliness and proper exits in case of an emergency. If you're a mature traveller, perhaps you could investigate a house swap for part of your time away, but see also **Chapter 3 — Career breaks and older travellers** for other ideas.

Buy second-hand: rather than spend a fortune on a backpack, do you know someone who's just returned from a trip and might be willing to lend or sell you any equipment they no longer need? Check the classified ads in your local paper, buy on eBay (or similar) or try some gap-year message boards.

Make sure that whatever you buy is in clean, sound condition, that the zips work, there are fittings for padlocks, and it's right for your body weight and height. If it's sound but a bit travel-worn, so much the better — you'll look like a seasoned traveller rather than a novice!

Money security

We've covered some of this earlier in this chapter, but it's worth explaining a bit further. It's best to take a mix of cash, travellers' cheques, credit/debit card and travel money cards, and here's how best to take care of them:

Cash: carry small change in pockets, not big notes. Distribute it between a belt bag, day pack and your travel bag so you have an emergency stash.

Travellers' cheques: record serial numbers and the emergency phone number for the issuer in case of theft. You sign each one when you get them from the bank but then there's a space for a second signature. Don't sign this second box until you're cashing it — if you do and your cheques get stolen, they can be cashed and you invalidate the insurance cover. Only cash a couple of travellers' cheques at any one time — get a mix of larger and small change denominations. Often street traders and snack stalls, or taxis and rickshaws, won't have change for a large note and it makes you vulnerable — you seem rich.

Hotel currency exchanges are more expensive, local banks can take a long time and require ID. If you can find a Thomas Cook centre they're the most efficient and speedy we've found. Street rates can be cheaper but be very careful. A lot of street money changers are trading illegally — don't hand over the cheque until you have your money and have counted it.

Credit card: essential back-up. The problem with a credit card is losing it or having it stolen — keep a note of the numbers, how to report the loss of the card and the number you have to ring to do so.

Both Visa and Mastercard are useful, in an emergency, for getting local currency cash advances from a cash dispenser at banks abroad. Remember, if you're using your credit card to get money over the counter then you're likely to need some form of ID (eg passport).

If you are paying for goods or restaurant meals by using your card, you should insist on signing bills/receipts in your presence and not allow the card to be taken out of your sight. This way you'll have no unpleasant surprises or mysterious purchases when you see your card statement.

Travel Money Cards: pre-pay travel cards are now a well-established alternative to travellers' cheques and can be used at an ATM using a PIN number. The idea is that you load them with funds before you leave, but beware — like credit and debit cards, most charge for every reload and for cash withdrawals. To find out more check out these two examples:

www.iceplc.com
www.travelex.com

DUInsure also advise the following when it comes to money security: "Never flash your cash in public. Never carry much cash when going out. Keep your money in an inside pocket, some in your wallet and some just in your pocket. DO NOT trust strangers to bring back change. Never change a lot of money with a street currency exchange seller. Avoid urban places where there are no crowds or poorly lit."

Wiring money

If you find yourself stranded with no cash, travellers' cheques or credit cards, then having money wired to you could be the only option. Two major companies offer this service:

MoneyGram — **www.moneygram.com**

Western Union — **www.westernunion.com**

Both have vast numbers of branches worldwide — MoneyGram has 180,000 in 190 countries and territories and Western Union has 379,000 agent locations in 200 countries and territories.

The service allows a friend or relative to transfer money to you almost instantaneously. Once you have persuaded your guardian angel to send you the money, all they have to do is go to the nearest MoneyGram or Western Union office, fill in a form and hand over the money (in cash).

It is then transferred to the company's branch nearest to you, where you in turn fill in a form and pick it up. Both you and the person sending the money will need ID, and you may be asked security questions so you need to know what the person sending the money has given as the security question *and* its answer. Make sure they tell you the spelling they've used and that you use the same.

There are now also smartphone applications for people to send money to each other. Barclays' Pingit allows its users to receive and send money, without charge, to anyone with a UK current account and a mobile phone number.

visit: www.gap-year.com

The service links users' current accounts to their mobile number. They can then 'Ping' money to another mobile phone number (the person receiving the money has to register with the service to access it). The service is protected by a passcode.

Older travellers with more assets will have specific financial concerns and perhaps more sources of funds than younger gappers, and we've included some detail in **Chapter 3 - Career breaks and older travellers**.

Sticking to a budget

How do you manage the budget when you're away? This totally depends on your style. You could be the person who loves an old fashioned spreadsheet, or someone who prefers to wing it and check your account weekly to see the damage and adjust your spending for the following week accordingly.

There are also apps that can help you with your budget, for example Expense IQ, where you input your budget, and spending each day (there's an alarm you can set up to remind you to do this). It's easy to use and very helpful if you tend to overspend! Other similar apps include Money Manager Expense and Budget. We also strongly recommend any currency converter app on your smartphone or tablet to help mange your budget.

Top tips to Make Your Money go Further
by Student Money Saver

Gap-years are usually planned on a strict budget, so finding bargains and avoiding being ripped off is a must while travelling.

Shopping in a local market rather than a big superstore can result in surprising savings, provided that you do it right. The number one rule to bartering in a market is to always fane disinterest — get practicing that poker face! If you are shopping with a friend, then agree on some codes, so that you aren't giving it away when you are really interested in something.

When it comes to taxis, it is best to agree fares before starting a journey, wherever possible. Remember that Uber exists in 76 countries around the world and can be a cheaper alternative.

When looking for accommodation, use online aggregate sites such as **www. booking.com**, **www.hostelworld.com** and **www.lastminute.com** and always remember to sort your search results on by price. To ensure that you don't end up booking a complete dive, filter by accommodation with an average review of around 7/10 and above.

If you are planning to travel home to visit family and friends during your gap-year, make sure you use flight comparison websites to get the best deals on your airfare. You can save hundreds by keeping a close eye on when flights are at their cheapest price and then booking them fast. The most comprehensive price comparison is www.skyscanner.net, and keep an eye out for student specific flight deals with Student Money Saver.

As a general rule you'll find your money will stretch quite a long way in most of the less developed parts of the world, and once you're in-country you can find out fairly easily from other travellers/locals the average costs of buses, trains, meals and so on.

Having said that, the global recession and rises in oil and food prices have had an impact on most countries' economies. They've particularly hit costs in the less developed world and the signs are that it may take time for things to settle down.

As you're planning some months ahead of your trip it may be sensible to add a little extra for potential inflation when you're working out your minimum and maximum spend per day. The trick then is to stick to it. Here are some tips:

Shopping: you're bound to find a zillion things that will make good souvenirs/gifts — best advice, though, is to wait. You'll see lots more wherever you are and the prices for the same goods in popular tourist and backpacker destinations will be much higher — and possibly of lower quality — than they will be in smaller towns and villages.

Do your buying just before you move on to the next destination, or return home, so you won't have spent too much money at the start of your trip, won't have to carry it all around with you and also by then you'll have an idea of what's worth buying and for how much. Another advantage of buying locally is that more of what you pay is likely to benefit the local community, and craftspeople, rather than the middle links in the chain.

If you buy souvenirs/gifts mid-trip, you could consider posting them home to save carrying them around with you but don't risk sending anything too valuable, and

visit: www.gap-year.com

make sure you know what's permitted to send (and what's not) since you'll almost certainly have to fill in a customs declaration slip, which will be stuck to the outside of the parcel.

Bargaining: make sure it's the custom before you do, and try to find out roughly what it should cost before you start. Also try to look at yourself through local eyes — if you're wearing expensive jewellery and clothes and carrying a camera or the latest mobile phone you'll find it much harder to get a real bargain.

Whatever you do, smile and be courteous. The trader has to make a living, usually in pretty harsh economic conditions, and you're a guest in their country. Not only that, but if you're a responsible traveller then ethically you should be offering a fair price, not going all-out to grab a bargain you can boast about later.

Don't give the impression you really, really want whatever it is. Don't pick it up — leave that to the market trader, then let them try to sell it to you. They will tell you how much they want and it's likely to be inflated, so offer a price the equivalent amount below the figure it should be and that you're willing to pay.

If they start the process by asking you how much you're willing to offer then mention that you've asked around local people so you know roughly what it should cost, before you name a price a little below what you're prepared to pay. From this point on it's a bit like a game of chess and it can be very entertaining — so don't be surprised if you collect an audience!

You might be told a heart-rending story about family circumstances or the trader's own costs, but you can counter that by saying that however much you like the item, you're sorry but it's outside your budget. Gradually you'll exchange figures until you reach an agreement. One technique is to pretend you're not that bothered and start to walk away, but be prepared for the trader to take you at your word.

Not getting ripped off by cab drivers: find out beforehand roughly what the local rate is for the distance you want to go. Then it's much the same principle as bargaining in a market. It's generally cheaper not to let hotels find you a cab — they often get a rake-off from the fare for allowing cabbies to park on their grounds, so it will cost you more.

Agree a price before you get into the vehicle and if you're hiring a car and driver for a day (which can often work out cheaper especially if you're sharing with friends) usually you'll be expected to pay for a meal for the driver so make sure you agree that the price of a stop for food is included in the deal.

In India there's a system of pre-pay kiosks, particularly at airport exits, where you can buy a chit — a paper that states a fair, and usually accurate, price for the journey. The driver can't cash it until you're safely at your destination, can't charge you more than is on the chit, and it has to be signed — usually by your hotel/accommodation before it can be cashed. So you can be sure you'll not be taking any long detours to bump up the cost. It's worth asking whether there are similar systems wherever you are.

Tipping: it's a bit of a minefield and you need to find out what the fair rate is. A tip should be a thank you for good service, so, for example, if you're in a restaurant and there's already a percentage on your bill for service you shouldn't pay more, unless of course you feel your waiter deserves it! Remember if you over-tip you raise expectations higher than other travellers — and locals — who may not be able or willing to pay.

Finding and affording a guide: find out if there's a local scheme for licensing/ approving guides and what the 'official permit' looks like. Nearly always there will be any number of 'guides' at the entrances to any interesting place you might want to visit. Some will be official — others will be trying their luck. You'll usually find out when you pay the entrance fee.

Insurance

It's important to take out comprehensive travel insurance, however long you are travelling for, and to check that it covers you for everything that you want to do while you are away. Should something go wrong while you are overseas, costs can quickly escalate with average prices ranging from £15,000 to over £100,000 (in Europe and America respectively) for treatment and re-scheduled flights back home.

Getting the proper insurance is important for when taking a gap-year. You can take out a good year or nine-month policy that will be specifically tailored to backpacker's needs.

As a backpacker your luggage is probably only going to consist of a rucksack with a few clothes in it, so most policies don't insure your luggage for a huge amount. However, the medical cover that you receive is the most important part as you may be travelling in developing countries where the medical services are not up to western standards.

It is worth noting that even in developed countries, health services work differently and you may have to pay more for certain things. Medical treatment is very expensive wherever you are, and if something really drastic happened to you whilst you were abroad, the costs could be astronomical. Most gap-year insurance packages cover repatriation costs, meaning that they would pay for you to be flown home if you were seriously ill. Some will cover the cost of having a family member flown out to you in an emergency.

It is therefore vitally important that when you take out a policy for your gap-year that you are covered for most eventualities so that you have peace of mind to really enjoy your year out. Scan all your documents and email them to yourself if everything gets lost, as long as you can find internet access you will have access to everything you need.

When taking out insurance we recommend that you ask the following questions about the insurance to ensure that you get the right one:

· How long am I going to be insured for?

· What parts of the world will the insurance policy cover me in?

· What happens if I lose or have my passport stolen or my wallet is stolen?

· What cover do I get if I decide to do an extreme sport and adventure activity?

· What happens if I need to go hospital?

· What happens if I miss my flight?

· What happens if I have to do exam retakes?

· Will I get flown home if I need to?

Some banks provide cover for holidays paid for using their credit cards, but their policies may not include all the essentials you'll need for a gap-year.

visit: www.gap-year.com

John Hall, Venice

Banks also offer blanket travel insurance (medical, personal accident, third party liability, theft, loss, cancellation, delay and more). You may be able to get reductions if you have an account with the relevant bank or buy foreign currency through it.

Who to choose?

You don't have to buy a travel insurance policy as part of a travel package through a travel company and there is intense competition between insurance companies to attract your attention.

FCO gives us this advice on choosing the right insurance company: "Make sure that you purchase travel insurance appropriate for your trip. Read up on the policy conditions and check that it covers you for all of the activities you intend to take part in whilst you are away. It's also important to be aware of any potential exclusions to claims before you travel."

Our friends at DUInsure add: "Always ensure that any backpacker policy covers emergency medical expenses and repatriation as a result of an unforeseen accident or illness. A £2 million limit should cover everything. Make sure that any pre-existing medicals are covered. Hazardous activities need to be covered, as well as expensive gadgets or smartphones."

Medical insurance

If you're going to Europe you can get a European Health Insurance Card (EHIC), which allows for free or reduced cost medical treatment within Europe, should you need it. You can apply online: **www.ehic.org.uk** or there's an automated application service on **0300 330 1350.**

If you need further help you can call Overseas Healthcare Team on 0191 218 1999.

my gap-year
Iggy

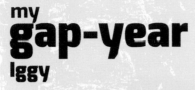

I left on my gap year in January 2017. I travelled to South Africa and Namibia for two weeks where the cage diving and safari experiences were incredible. Then I went off to South America for three months, during which I visited countries such as Brazil, Uruguay, Argentina, Bolivia, Peru and Ecuador. A few of the highlights were Machu Picchu, the Salt Flats, Buenos Aires, Rio and the Galapagos Islands where I did some volunteering on San Cristobal. The islands themselves were amazing.

After that I did the east coast of Australia, which was full of life everywhere I went; the Nomads 4X4 Fraser island trip was really good fun, driving round the island for three days seeing the various lakes on the huge sand island, beach parties and meeting some great people in the process. The last leg of my trip was spent in New Zealand. I spent a month in the South Island, which is very scenic everywhere you go, as well as a great little town called Queenstown where there's all sorts of activities like bungee jumps, skydiving, a variety of walks and plenty of bar crawls.

Afterwards, I travelled up to the North Island, where I followed the British and Irish Lions for their three tests vs the All Blacks. I was fortunate enough to acquire a couple of tickets; for me, it was the highlight of my six-month trip. The Lions and All Blacks fans were incredible, creating an unbelievable atmosphere. When it finally came to the end of mid-July, I was surprised at how much I was going to miss living out of a bag and seeing such amazing things in so many different countries, all with different cultures. Luckily, I only had to claim for a damaged iPad on my trip, but DownUnder Insurance were with me all the way!

For more information on DUInsure, see their advert on page 24

Your card is valid for three to five years and should be delivered to you in seven days. The EHIC card only covers treatment under the state scheme in all EU countries, plus Denmark, Iceland, Liechtenstein, Norway and Switzerland. You can also pick up application forms at your post office.

However, the EHIC is not a replacement for a travel insurance policy. It only covers necessary care and won't cover things such as repatriation to the UK in the event of a medical emergency

Countries with no health care agreements with the UK include Canada, the USA, India, most of the Far East, the whole of Africa and Latin America. Wherever it happens, a serious illness, broken limb, or even an injury you might cause someone else, can be very expensive.

Medical insurance is usually part of an all-in travel policy. Costs vary widely by company, destination, activity and level of cover. Make sure you have generous cover for injury or disablement, know what you're covered for and when you've got the policy read the small print carefully. For example, does it cover transport home if you need an emergency operation that cannot be carried out safely abroad?

Some policies won't cover high-risk activities like skiing, snowboarding, bungee jumping *etc* so you'll need to get extra, specific, cover and an insurance broker can help with this. Companies may also make a distinction between doing a hazardous sport once and spending your whole time doing them. Some insurance policies also have age limits.

If you have a medical condition that is likely to recur, you may have to declare this when you buy the insurance, otherwise the policy won't be valid. Also, check whether the policy covers you for the medical costs if the condition does recur, as some will not cover such pre-existing conditions.

Already covered?

If you're going abroad on a voluntary work assignment you may find that the organisation arranging it wants you to take a specified insurance policy as part of the total cost. You may also find you have a clash of policies before you even start looking for the right policy.

For example, if your family has already booked you a one-year multi-travel insurance policy to cover travel with the family at other times of the year, you may find you are already covered for loss of life, limb, permanent disablement, some medical expenses, theft and so on.

These multi-trip policies can be basic as well as quite cheap, but it's essential to check the small print of what the policy covers as it's possible that there may be a clause compelling the insured to return to the UK after a short period of time. DUInsure advises to: "Make sure that all proposed activities are covered, any pre-existing medical conditions have been declared and accepted and that the policy will cover any valuable electronic items such as smart phones, lap-tops or digital cameras."

Just like many of the 'free' insurance policies that come with bank accounts, many of these policies only cover for trips of up to 60 days at a time, at which point travellers had to return to the UK. In other words, great for a holiday or two or for a business traveller but no use at all if you plan to be out of the country for the whole year.

In this case you can start by finding out (through the broker or agent who sold you the policy) if any additional cover can be tacked on to your existing policy, though

the gap-year guidebook 2018

this can be expensive and most off-the-shelf policies won't do it. A specific gap-year or backpacking policy may be more appropriate and actually work out cheaper than trying to add stuff on.

Try to find a policy that doesn't already duplicate what is covered by an existing policy (they don't pay out twice), but some duplication is unavoidable and it's obviously better to be covered twice than not at all.

Making a claim

Read through the small print carefully before you travel and make sure you understand exactly what to do if you need to make a claim — most policies will insist that you report a crime to the police where this is possible (often within a certain time period), and that you send in the police report with your insurance claim. What you don't want to happen is to have a claim dismissed because you don't have the right paperwork to back it up.

Insurers won't pay you money unless you have complied with all their rules and many travel policies impose conditions that are virtually impossible to meet. For example, some policies demand that you report not only theft of items but also loss of items. Fine, but the police are likely to be pretty reluctant to write a crime report because you think you may have accidentally left your camera in the loo!

If you do have anything stolen and you have to get the local police to give you a report, it's a good idea to dress reasonably smartly when you visit them, be prepared to wait and try to be pleasant and polite no matter what!

The Foreign Office website **www.gov.uk/travelaware** has a good page about insurance and is worth checking out for advice and links. In addition to a list of what your travel insurance should cover, which is similar to the one at the start of this chapter, it suggests the following extras, which are not always included:

· Legal expenses cover can be useful as it will help you to pursue compensation or damages following personal injury while you're abroad — very important in countries without a legal aid system.

· Financial protection if your airline goes bankrupt before or during your trip — given the state of the airline industry this may be worth serious consideration for at least the next couple of years.

Our friends at DU Insure added that it is worth noting the excess on your policy — something that is often overlooked.

"Almost all policies have an excess attached to different sections of cover. That amount is deducted from the claim, normally for each person covered and for each relevant section of the policy. If you make a number of claims whilst you are travelling this can add up so think about taking out an excess waiver so that you have to contribute nothing. It may cost a little more but could save you a small fortune."

You'll also need to let your insurers know about any existing medical conditions before you head off: "If you don't declare a pre-existing condition, the entire policy will probably be invalidated. **If you are in any doubt, talk to the insurer before you buy**. Note also that, if you have an existing injury that is exacerbated by a second accident while you are travelling, cover for this may also be excluded."

What to do if you get an emergency call to come home

We all hope there'll be no family crises while we're away on our gap but it does occasionally happen that someone close is taken seriously ill, or even dies, and then all you can think about is getting home as quickly as possible.

We've talked to a couple of insurers about this and they reinforce our advice to *always* read the policy carefully before you set off on your travels.

Generally speaking, your gap-year travel policy ceases once you return home, but some insurers offer extra cover for one extra trip home (or more, up to four, but the price rises with each one) without your policy lapsing. In a backpacker/adventure policy of three to 18 months, one home return is in the region of £5 and four would be around £24 extra on your policy.

Most insurers are used to dealing with sudden early returns and have a 24-hour emergency assistance company to help you through the whole process.

You need to let them know anyway so you can set the ball rolling for claiming for the cost and they can deal with getting you from your gap location to the airport, or, if you have one, you can use the help of your placement provider's in-country reps, or even a combination of the two, so you don't have to deal with transport hassles when all you can think about is getting home quickly.

However, there are often restrictions. First off, your family emergency has to affect an immediate relative — so husband, wife, mum, dad, grandparents, sisters and brothers, children, grandchildren — but *not* aunts, uncles and other extended family. It has to be serious injury, illness or death of a relative — family feuds and divorces do not count!

If you have home return extra on your policy you're covered for one extra flight home; you're *not* covered for an additional flight back to resume your gap. But, if you have a return ticket, as most gappers do, the best way to go is to use your existing return, if the airline will reschedule, claim for it, then book another return flight. It's often cheaper to book a return flight than an extra one-way only.

If your ticket cannot be changed and you need to purchase a new ticket for your return journey, this can be arranged via a flight-ticketing agent or direct with the appropriate airline (subject to availability of flights and seats).

Websites such as Expedia and ebookers offer a wide selection of flights including single leg and one way tickets, which you can buy online and be allocated e-tickets, or collect them from the airline sales desk at the airport.

During peak travel or holiday times you might find the quickest way to get home may be to go to the airport and wait to pick up a 'no show' seat on standby.

Finally, make sure you read the small print. This may seem like a laborious task but it can pay as there are a few things you should always bear in mind before you hand over your cash:

· If you have an on-going illness like asthma and diabetes, make sure your policy covers them, as many don't.

· Ongoing medication and vaccinations are usually not covered.

· Dental treatment costs are usually for emergency treatment only.

· If an insurance company says they'll fly you home in a medical emergency, bear in mind that it won't be up to you — the doctors and the insurance companies will decide how serious it is.

· If you can wait until you get home to be treated, it's unlikely your cover will cover any costs of treatment you think you might need.

· If you're going to do sports, make sure they're covered — don't just assume. Many companies make you pay extra for adventure sports and activity insurance.

· If you're 'off your head' when you hurt yourself then there's a good chance you'll foot the bill.

· If your airline goes bust you're unlikely to be covered — unless you've got Airline Failure Insurance.

· If you forget to report a theft to the police, you probably won't be covered for the loss.

And don't forget to take the contact phone number of your insurance company with you in case of emergency. Carry it around with you in your money belt, in your rucksack and in your wallet. Also copy the policy number and any other reference you will need if you have to contact them. Photocopy the insurance documents and take them with you on your travels, or like mentioned earlier scan them and email them to yourself too.

Please see the directory pages starting on page 263 for information on companies and organisations offering financial and insurance services for gappers.

Career breaks and older gappers

Career breaks and older gappers

What exactly do we mean?

You will read the terms 'career break' and 'sabbatical' a lot in this chapter. They will essentially refer to the same thing: stopping work for a period of time to do something new or different. You would generally consider a 'sabbatical' to be a period of time away from your job, with the agreement to return at the end of it. A career break, however, might mean cutting loose altogether — quitting your job and seeing what happens; maybe with the intention of starting a whole new career when you're back, or just a leap into the unknown. Either way, it's what we'd consider a gap, so this chapter looks at how to do it and what you'll need to think about.

An emerging trend

They may still be in the minority in the gap-year market, but the number of career breakers is definitely on the rise. Taking a month, six months or a year out of your workplace is an excellent way to add new skills to your CV, re-assess your career (or maybe your life!), or just to recharge your batteries and get away from the routine.

There may be something you've always wanted to do or somewhere you've wanted to go — and maybe now you're in a better position to afford it? Or maybe you want to give something back after years in the 'rat race'?

You might have heard of the terms 'extravagapper','flashpacker' or 'grey gapper' to describe the more mature member of the gap community.

Extravagappers are thought of as newly-redundant city professionals with generous redundancy packages, who are taking the opportunity of a career break rather than plunge back into a possibly demoralising, recession-hit job market.

Flashpackers are those backpacking with 'flash or style', who typically spend freely, or even excessively, for activities at their chosen destination.

'Grey gappers' is a term used to describe people who are 50 and over, who have decided to take a gap-year.

These are caricatures, of course. People who take career breaks come from all sorts of backgrounds, and with varying degrees of affluence.

Some people opt for a luxury gap-year. Forget cheap hostels and grubby clothes, luxury gap-years are perfect for those who want to travel but would rather have a home from home. For more information see **Chapter 4 — Travelling and Accommodation.**

Taking a career break for one month to a year is the fastest growing sector of gap-year activity and there's some anecdotal evidence that the global recession is increasing the numbers. Around 90,000 people take a short sabbatical each year in the UK — in other words a 'gap-month'. It may be worthwhile considering something like this, or perhaps a longer trip if you've been made redundant or taken early retirement.

visit: www.gap-year.com

Heilwig Jones from Kaya Responsible Travel comments: "At Kaya we are seeing a great surge in older volunteers. Particularly for those who have retired, whose families have left home or who have more flexible working lives, volunteering is becoming more popular because of the cultural immersion it can provide, and because it is a great option for the single traveller as well. Older volunteers often have skills that can be used and are greatly valued by projects — and it is even more important to find a project that is the right match for them."

Many organisations that arrange places for people on overseas projects, have told us that more than half of their activity is now focused on helping place mature travellers and/or people who are taking a career break. Our friends at African Conversation Experience told us how the number of older gappers is increasing: "When African Conservation Experience started in 1999, it worked almost 100% with 'traditional' gap-year students — aged 17 or 18, and students during their university career. Now about 25% of our travellers are professionals aged 25+, including quite a few retirees!"

People are living longer and are also a lot healthier well into old age. Many, therefore, feel they want to continue to use their skills in places where they will do some good.

This, coupled with the issues of the retirement age being put back and worries about inadequate pension provision, has also prompted many older people to think about extending their working lives and perhaps also pursuing a different career altogether.

Taking a gap, perhaps to volunteer in another country, is one good way of identifying skills, wisdom and knowledge gained over a working lifetime, that may be useful in another sector and this could lead to a new career.

Time for a career break?

If you want to achieve more with your time out, we're looking for Volunteer Managers aged 25-75 to help lead our Expeditions and work overseas at the heart of sustainable projects that create lasting change.

Discover the world, have an adventure, wake up every day and do work that makes a real difference to the people around you.

Apply now for Expeditions in Nepal, Malaysian Borneo, Nicaragua & Costa Rica and Tanzania.

youth · energy · change

raleighinternational.org/expedition

Raleigh **Raleigh International**

Pre-travel checklist

Older travellers generally have different considerations from younger ones when making their plans. These include the effects of taking a gap on careers, what to do about the house and mortgage, financial issues and whether or not to take the children, if this applies.

This list covers the extra responsibilities older people might have to consider. It only covers the basics of what you might have to organise — but we hope it will be a useful start for you to cherry-pick what's appropriate and no doubt add your own extras!

Work:

· Talk to your employer about sabbatical/career break options

Career break:

· What do you want from it?

· What do you want to do?

· Where do you want to go?

Finance:

· Paying the bills

· Mortgage

· Financing and raising money for the trip

· Insurance

· Pensions and NI contributions

The house: Are you going to let it? If yes, you need:

· To talk to an accommodation agency

· Safety certificates

· Insurance

· To investigate tax exemption

Storage of possessions:

· What do you want to store? And can it be stored at home?

Children:

· Talk to the school(s) about taking them

· Find out about education possibilities where you're going

· If they're coming, how long will the trip be?

Safety precautions:

· Wills and power of attorney

Arranging a sabbatical

There is no legal obligation on employers to offer employees sabbaticals/career breaks. However, they are often regarded as an important part of an employee's career development, and may be granted for a variety of reasons including study research travel or voluntary work which can often be related to the employee's role.

Here's some useful things to know:

· Sabbaticals can help companies retain senior staff by giving them the chance to do something different, without leaving altogether.

· Employers who grant sabbaticals will usually attach various conditions to eligibility and what happens during the sabbatical.

· Sabbaticals are usually only available to employees at senior levels and those who have completed a specified number of years of continuous service.

· Some organisations do not even have sabbatical policies.

· Where an employer does grant sabbaticals, it must ensure that part-time employees are afforded the same benefits as equivalent full-time staff.

· Normally the employee will not receive pay or benefits for a sabbatical as the employee's contract is seen as suspended.

· It's important that a strategy for the return to work is agreed in advance of the sabbatical.

· The employer should take particular care to ensure that any guarantee of re-employment is worded clearly and unambiguously in order to avoid any disagreement or challenge at a later date.

What if you can't arrange a sabbatical?

Companies have no obligation to provide career breaks, so if you're turned down, you'll need to think about what to do. You may decide to resign. If not, you might want to consider how it will affect your future prospects there. It's a tricky one, and depends very much on both you and the company: your career goals, and their hopes and plans for you.

One option you might consider if you can't arrange a sabbatical and are wary of just quitting is arranging a job swap with someone from another country in a similar industry. You need to consider:

· Where do you want to travel?

· Do you speak a second, third or fourth language?

· Will you need housing?

· Do you need to be paid while away?

· How long do you want to be away for?

This may be easier in an international company where there may even be opportunities to transfer to the overseas office. Many such companies offer formal secondment programmes so it's always worth exploring these first.

If the above options are not possible, and you are prepared to resign, you could investigate whether your company might agree to guarantee you a job on your return.

visit: www.gap-year.com

Even if they don't guarantee a position for you, have regular contact with the key decision-makers whilst you are away by the occasional email *etc*. This will keep you in their minds and make it easier for you to approach them when you come back home, to see if they have any suitable job opportunities. Just remember, in job hunting, as in everything else, it's not *what* you know but *who*. So it's absolutely vital that you make the effort not to lose touch with your professional colleagues, networks and contacts whilst you are away. If you do, you'll regret it once you are back.

If you're not already signed up to LinkedIn, you might like to consider it. This website is the business world equivalent of Facebook. It's free to use and you can link to colleagues and business contacts and post recommendations about them and, importantly, get them to post recommendations about you. You can upload your CV, and indicate that you are open to job opportunities. It could also be useful to add your list of contacts gained *whilst* you're on your career break, thus adding extra value to your LinkedIn profile. Visit **www.linkedin.com** to create a profile.

No sabbatical? Take your chances

If you're willing to quit and take your chances, what about finding work when the break's over?

What the jobs market will be like when you return is anyone's guess; however, you'll have a faster and more productive job search if you work at it before you leave.

Think now about the job you should be aiming for after the gap. Your gap is likely to develop new skills and ambitions so you might want something different from the current role.

In the various sections in the book, you'll discover the vast range of things you can do on your gap; the skills you can learn and the places you can visit. Whatever you choose, it's likely you'll be boosting your CV in a number of ways — and not always those you'd expect.

the gap-year guidebook 2018

So, it's likely you'll return from your gap with new skills, a new sense of purpose, and a clearer idea of what you want to do in the future.

Your target job identified, talk to the people who'll help you find future vacancies. Research the specialist recruitment consultancies in that sector (*eg* Google them), then ask to talk to consultants with at least two years' experience of recruiting for the jobs that interest you. You want to know those consultants' best guesses about the likely state of that jobs market a year from now, what skills employers are most likely to look for in candidates and so on.

Stay in touch with the most useful of these recruitment consultants (*eg* by sharing snippets of your gap news with them). Keeping yourself at the forefront of their minds puts you on the inside track for news about developments in the jobs market. Similarly, stay in touch with ex-colleagues, university tutors and careers service advisors — they will often have huge networks for you to tap in to.

It's also a good idea to plan your career break around the natural hiring cycles of your industry. Recruitment activity tends to fall in December and early January, the Easter break and the weeks that coincide with the school summer holidays, for example. It may be harder to find jobs in these periods. The busiest times for recruitment tend to be the early spring and autumn.

Do update your CV before you go, ensuring it's ready for your return to employment. It's a good idea to keep it available on email so you can send it to interested parties while you're away, if an opportunity presents itself.

Finance

You've talked to your employer, perhaps also worked out what you hope to do — there are plenty of organisations to help you plan your chosen activities in the various sections in this book. The next crucial question is finance.

visit: www.gap-year.com

Obviously the amount of money you'll need depends on where you want to go, what you want to do, and how long you want to be away. At this point, drawing up a rough budget for how much it will cost would be a good idea. (See **Chapter 2 — Finance**, for a checklist). Once you have this it's worth talking to your building society or bank to see whether they have any schemes that can meet your needs.

While banks often have student and graduate advisers who can advise on what to do about everything from travel insurance to suspending direct debits and deferring loan payment, they don't seem yet to have reached the stage of having advisers *specifically* for career breakers. They are, however, increasingly aware of the trend to take a career break and may well be able to use their experience of advising younger gappers to help you think the finances through.

One recent survey amongst older people in the UK revealed that a large majority are extremely pessimistic or fearful about the quality of their lives in old age. A significant number were taking the view that, if their old age was going to be so grim, why not have one last adventure? Consequently, they were using annuities and equity release or lifetime mortgages to unlock money from their homes to boost their retirement income and pay for such adventures.

This might seem like a good plan. However, there have also been many reports of schemes offering to buy people's homes and allowing them to rent them back for their lifetimes, only for them to be evicted after a few months or to find 'hidden charges' that meant they saw little money at the end of it. So beware! Read the small print *very* carefully.

Some companies offer lifetime mortgages, where you can release the value of your home and live in it without paying anything until you die, when the company will recover its money from the sale of the home.

Individual circumstances vary and if you feel you are 'asset rich but cash poor' it may be tempting to consider such options. You should only consider such a scheme with a reputable company and if the scheme includes protection against negative equity. We would strongly advise that if you are thinking of doing something like this you consult an independent financial adviser.

Maximise your funds: the chance for a good clear out

Is the garage crammed, are every drawer and cupboard stuffed? Is it all 'file and forget' or 'might come in handy' but never has? Admit it, you're one of those people who hasn't touched any of this stuff for years and you've kept saying you'd do a massive clearout. But the more you add over the years, the more daunting it is and the easier it is to put off. We all do it. And how much houseroom do some of us give to all that stuff our children insist they have no space for but have sentimental attachments to?

Preparing for your year out is the perfect opportunity to de-clutter your life. Have a look at what you need to get rid of and turn into funding for your gap. Consider raising some cash by selling items through online auction sites, such as eBay, holding a garage sale or a car boot sale.

You'll create space to store your precious items (the things you want to keep but not leave lying about), you'll add some cash to your travel fund, and you'll come back to a well-organised home.

Imaginative fundraising

If you've already settled on the kind of project you want to do and it involves raising a specific sum, as volunteer projects often do, you can hold fundraising events to help you raise the cash — the options are as limitless as your imagination!

You have an untapped resource where you work — you could try asking for a contribution from your employer. It's good PR to have a link with someone doing something for a worthy cause.

If your employer agrees, what about baking cakes to sell at coffee time or holding competitions (guess the weight/number of objects in a container) or even asking colleagues to sponsor you? Even simple things like putting all those irritating bits of small change that weigh down pockets, and cram purses, into a large pot or jar can mount up surprisingly quickly.

Pensions and National Insurance contributions

If you have an occupational pension and are taking a sabbatical you should check with your employer to see if they offer a pension 'holiday' and what that might mean to your eventual pension, but it might be possible to stop or reduce your payments while you are away. If you have been with the company less than two years, it might be possible to arrange a refund of pension contributions.

For the state pension you might want to look at two issues: during the time you're away, you will be officially classified as living abroad and you won't be paying NI. However, you should check what that will do to your contributions' record and how it might affect your eventual state pension. You can find out if there are gaps in your record by calling the HMRC (HM Revenue and Customs) helpline (0845 915 5996) and for more information. People living abroad should call: 0845 915 4811.

Once you have that information it's worth talking to the DWP (Department for Work and Pensions). They have a help and advice service (Tel: 0845 606 0265) and you can find out what you can expect by way of state pension. A DWP adviser told us that, from 2010, to get the maximum state pension both men and women will have to have paid NI for at least 30 years.

However, another useful fact, if you're likely to reach retirement age during your gap and can afford it, is that there's an incentive for deferring your state pension. For every nine weeks you agree to defer (or five weeks if you reach state pension age before 6 April 2016), you get 1% added to your eventual pension. After a year, you can either take that as a taxable lump sum or have it incorporated into your regular pension payments. You can defer for more than a year and continue to add this interest to your eventual state pension.

The DirectGov website also has a useful page on pensions for people living abroad: **www.direct.gov.uk/en/BritonsLivingAbroad/Moneyabroad/DG_4000013**

Earning on your career break

It may even be possible to part-fund your career break by using your skills on volunteer and other projects.

United Nations Volunteers sometimes pay modest living or travel costs, for people with the skills they need for particular volunteer projects.

Have a look at their website: **www.unv.org/how-to-volunteer**

If you wanted a 'taster' before taking the big step of leaving the country, UNV also has a scheme for online volunteers, where you can become involved in worthwhile projects, using your computer in your spare time, at home: **www.onlinevolunteering.org**

There are also organisations that can help with funding for specific projects: the Winston Churchill Memorial Trust (WCMT) is one of them. It provides grants for people wanting to travel abroad and work on special projects that they cannot find funding for elsewhere and, crucially, then use the experience to benefit others in their home communities. Applicants must be British citizens, resident in the UK and must apply by October each year.

The Trust awards travelling fellowships to individuals of all ages wanting to pursue projects that are interesting and unusual. Categories cover a range of topics over a three-year cycle. Roughly 100 are awarded each year and they usually provide funds for four to eight weeks.

The Trust emphasises that fellowships are *not* granted to gappers looking to fund academic studies, attend courses or take part in volunteer placements arranged by other organisations.

The advice is to study the WCMT website for examples of projects that have been funded, as they are very wide-ranging and will help you come up with your own ideas.

To find out more you can contact the Trust, see **www.wcmt.org.uk**, where you can apply online.

Tax issues

If you go to live or work abroad, and become non-resident in the UK, you might still have to pay UK tax — but *only* on your income earned in the UK (savings, dividends, rental income *etc*). If you do need to pay, you may need to complete a self-assessment tax return.

This website explains the tax implications for all the circumstances in which you

GO BEYOND

TAKE YOUR SKIING OR SNOWBOARDING TO THE NEXT LEVEL

As the leading providers of instructor courses and season-long trips, we take hundreds of people over to Canada every year.

Learn to ski or snowboard like a pro in Canada's incredible powder and gain internationally recognised instructor qualifications.

Achieve more in a season than most will in a lifetime of winter holidays. Head home with new skills and opportunities.

- Teaching in your uni holidays and beyond
- Leadership and communication skills
- Make mates for life
- Experience traditional Canadian mountain living
- Enjoy a program of weekend activities and away trips
- Gain highly respected qualifications that look great on your CV
- All abilities welcome.

NONSTOP
Ski & Snowboard Coaching

THE #1 GAP YEAR SKI COMPANY
THE INDEPENDENT

CANADA | NEW ZEALAND | FRANCE

might be abroad, whether temporarily or permanently. It's particularly useful if you're thinking of renting out your home:
www.direct.gov.uk/en/BritonsLivingAbroad/Moneyabroad/index.htm

What about the house?

Some mortgage lenders may allow a payment holiday of up to six months without affecting your scheme.

Another option might be to rent out your house. You may need to check terms and conditions for subletting with your mortgage lender, but it can be a good way of covering the mortgage costs while you are away.

As it is your home and you need to be sure it will be looked after while you are away, the above reinforces our advice that, if you decide to rent, it's worth using an accommodation agent to take care of things and make sure you comply with all the regulations. It would also be wise to check with the Inland Revenue to see whether you are eligible for a tax exemption certificate (on your rental income), which should be given to the accommodation agent.

When letting a house there are some rules to abide by and some safety certificates you must have if you're going to take this route. Another must is to tell your insurance company what you're planning.

Another possibility is a house swap

Obviously you'd have to be careful in arranging this and in satisfying yourself that you're happy with the people you're planning to swap with, but we've found a couple of agencies that can help you. The following arrange holiday swaps in many countries around the world and have plenty of advice on how to go about it. You have to sign up as a member to access some information:

www.homelink.org — annual membership is £115. It has regional websites in 30 countries and has been operating for 50 years.

www.homebase-hols.com — annual membership is £49.

Household contents: storage

Two things to think about if you really want to clear your house before renting:

· Do you really want to add this to your list of 'things to do' before you go?

· Can you afford it?

You would need a 20ft container for the contents of an average house. Most containers are 'self-service' so you would have to pack, move and unpack yourself and therefore need to add the costs of van rental and transport to the container rental costs.

You would also have to arrange your own insurance, but normally you can extend your household contents insurance to cover property on secured sites.

National removals and storage companies also provide container storage on managed sites and can sell you the packing materials and boxes you might need as well. Prices vary according to the distance from the storage site, size of container and length of time and some self storage companies do not charge VAT on household storage, but others do. It is worth bearing in mind that storage alone for a year would come to over £1000.

the gap-year guidebook 2018

But remember, on top of that you have to add the packing, loading, removal and unloading costs at each end of your career break. On average the process can cost £300-£400 more than an ordinary house move and prices vary depending on whether your dates fall into peak season for house removals — such as children's school holidays and the peak times of year for house sales.

What about the kids?

There's some evidence that another growing trend is for families to take a gap together, particularly while the children are young.

Kaya Responsible Travel told us that the number of children joining them on their projects is increasing: "We have great success with our family volunteers. The ages of the children are the most important factor to consider. Teenage children can get stuck in to almost any work alongside their parents, where younger children might require more thought over the type of work they are involved in. Often working in projects where there are other children of the same age, they provide great opportunities for peer-to-peer learning. The children are always the responsibility of the parents and they work together on their projects, which might limit the work that the parent can take part in, but we have had families where one parent is working in a more professional capacity (for example in a hospital) while the other parent works with their children on a more family-friendly initiative (for example, in a child-care facility). What is important to identify is that volunteering together as a family is a great bonding experience that keeps the family busy while helping children better understand the privilege of their home lives. And the feedback we get from the kids is they have a lot of fun and make great new friends in the process."

The general view is that as long as the children are safe, have access to medical facilities and their education development is not harmed, family gap-years can have very beneficial outcomes. Some gap-year companies might have a minimum age limit of eight years and it's also important to clear the break with the children's school.

Whether to take the children out of school is really up to you as parents. Much will depend on the length of time you plan to be away and the point your children are at in their education.

Essentially you need to balance the effects of taking a child out of school against the benefits of the 'education' they will get from seeing something of the world.

You also need to think through health and medical issues, but that may mean nothing more than carrying essential medical supplies with you, as all travellers are advised to do when travelling abroad.

It's also possible that you can get your child into a local school for some of the time they are away, or you can organise some basic study for them with the help of their school while you are travelling.

The official view from the Department for Education is that, ultimately, it is down to the parents, but that they should talk it through with their child's school or local authority.

It is crucial that it's cleared with your child's school and headteacher, who has to authorise it, if you don't want to face court action by the local authority and a possible hefty fine for taking a child out of school during term time. But parents who have done it, even with very small children, say that it has been a very worthwhile experience and brought them closer to their kids. A few gap organisations are now providing family gap volunteer placements.

Safety precautions

You will find a great deal of advice on all aspects of planning your gap in **Chapter 1 – Tips for travellers**, as well as in-country advice and what to expect when you get back. Tips for travellers is relevant to all travellers, whatever their age. We also cover the importance of getting the right kind of travel insurance and the questions you need answered in **Chapter 2 – Finance**.

But there are some other issues that perhaps might be more important for older travellers to consider. You almost certainly have more in the way of assets than someone straight from school or university – things like a house, insurance and pension schemes; valuable personal property.

In the unlikely event of something going wrong, it makes sense to ensure your affairs are in order and to have someone you trust authorised to take care of your affairs until you can do so for yourself. It will make things that much easier for those back home, who may be coping with the trauma of a loved one in hospital overseas, if they have some idea of how you want your affairs to be handled.

You should consider two things – making a will and possibly appointing someone with legal power of attorney.

Making a will

It might seem a bit excessive to make your will before you go, but you can never be too sure what's going to happen. It's important to make a will before you leave to have things properly in order if the worst does happen. It will help put your mind at rest and those closest to you will know what your wishes are. Plus, wherever you are your will be processed under English law.

Points to remember when making a will:

· It doesn't have to be expensive

· It can be amended later if your circumstances change

· You can make it clear what you want to happen to your property

· It prevents family squabbles

· It allows you to choose executors you can trust

You should:

· Give yourself time to think

· Use a professional, preferably one experienced specifically with will preparation

· Make sure you can update it without large additional charges

· Make sure there's an opt out from executor or probate services if you don't need them — by the time the will is needed, which could be many years away, it may be that there is someone in the family, who was too young when you made it, that can deal with it

Power of attorney

Many people choose to make an informal arrangement with a family member to take care of things at home while they're travelling, but if you were to need someone authorised to pay bills at home or liaise with your travel insurance company, it might make sense to have a proper, formal arrangement in place before you go to give them the authority to act on your behalf.

You might be able to arrange with your bank to add them as a signatory to your account, in case it should be necessary, as long as you feel comfortable that the person you choose will make the right decisions about your money if you can't.

A more secure way is to appoint a power of attorney, but be warned it's a lengthy process, which can take up to five months to process. Until the documents are properly registered, whoever you appoint cannot act for you.

There's no fast track procedure on compassionate grounds and the Public Guardians' Office website says: "If there are no problems with the LPA (Lasting Power of Attorney) or application, we are typically returning the registered LPA in around nine weeks from the date of receipt. If there are any problems with the LPA or application, we are currently informing the applicant within two weeks of receiving the application."

Getting it right when there are at least 30 pages of forms per person is no joke; and, if you're a couple, each one of you has to fill out a set. So to avoid delays and mistakes (with possible charging of repeat fees) it makes sense to get professional advice from a specialist.

The process is administered by the Office of the Public Guardian, which charges a fee of £150. But compare that with having someone professional look after your property and personal welfare. It can cost as much as £1500 for a couple. To find out more about the new legislation go to: **www.publicguardian.gov.uk**

Please see the directory pages starting on page 271 for information on companies and organisations who are offering trips and opportunities for career breakers and older gappers.

visit: www.gap-year.com

Travelling and accommodation

Travelling and accommodation

Getting about

Planes

Booking flights, transport and accommodation for your trip can be easy and straightforward. But when you are on your travels think about what season you're travelling in — is it low or high season? This will affect prices and also how far in advance you need to book everything.

Heilwig from Kaya Responsible Travel, who offer volunteer opportunities across the world, gives us this advice: "We recommend people plan 3-6 months ahead for their projects. Flights are a lot cheaper to buy this far in advance, and it gives you enough time to get your vaccinations and prepare for your trip. Many of the most popular projects for summer can get fully booked by late February, so be sure to get in early to secure your space."

The internet is invaluable when searching for ticket information, timetables, prices and special offers, whether you're travelling by air, sea, train or bus.

Because the internet gives customers so much information to choose from, travel companies have to compete harder to get your business. The internet shows you what flexibility is possible, so you could find more opportunities available.

When booking flights, have a look at special offers for round-the-world tickets first, find out how far in advance you can book, and then plan your destinations to fit. A fantastic website for looking up internal and external flights is **www.skyscanner.com**, which searches all the companies for you to get the best price, and you can look over a whole month if your dates aren't fixed.

If one of your destinations has a fixed arrival and departure date — for example if you're signed up for a voluntary project — you could try asking for a route tailor-made for you using the prices you find on the web. Travel agencies can often find better deals and it takes some of the hassle away from you. Like Round the World Experts (part of the Flight Centre) but there's also the likes of STA Travel.

Make sure you check out the company making an offer on the web before you use internet booking procedures (does it have a verifiable address and phone number?). Remember, under EU law companies must publish a contact address on their website. So, unless the company in question is a household name, or you are able to locate a legitimate address via another source, think twice before handing over your hard-earned cash.

It's important — as ever! — to read the Terms and Conditions to see what you're paying for and whether you can get your money back before you agree to buy — just as you would outside the virtual world.

Once you have made a booking now is the time to be taking out your travel insurance. See **Chapter 2 — Finance** for more information.

visit: www.gap-year.com

What to watch out for

Once you've booked a flight online, especially if you do it through an agent such as **www.lastminute.com**, rather than direct with the airline, you may have to pay extra fees for rescheduling, not to mention date restrictions if you need to change the date. Unless you have a good, solid reason for cancelling — and most airlines define such reasons very narrowly — you also risk losing the money you've paid.

As we mention in **Chapter 1**, increasingly airlines are covering their additional fuel costs and taxes by adding charges for different services, like inflight baggage storage, airport duty, seats next to each other (if you're not travelling alone). You need to have your wits about you when you're going through the online booking forms as these extras can add a substantial amount to the final total, making that budget deal significantly more expensive than you originally thought (up to £100 at best and almost equalling the flight cost at worst).

Remember, the ads usually say 'flights *from* £XXX' and that's your clue to watch out for extras.

Bargain flights: scheduled airlines often offer discount fares for students under 26 so don't rule them out. Other cheap flights are advertised regularly in the newspapers and on the web. All sorts of travel agents can fix you up with multi-destination tickets, and student travel specialists often know where to find the best deals for gap-year students.

It's worth checking whether a particular flight is cheaper if you book direct with the airline — and if you are using a student travel card you may find that you have to do it this way to get the discount, rather than using one of the budget deal websites.

Above all, travel is an area where searching the internet for good deals should be top of your list — though it works best for single-destination trips rather than complex travel routes.

For example, make sure your tickets allow flexibility and know what the costs would be if you decided to change your plans.

See the real Australia

From the turquoise waters of the western coast to the wide open plains of the Outback, our tours are for those looking to develop a true-blue understanding of Australia's inner workings — and have a cracker of a time while they're at it! Complete with a knowledgeable guide and a crew of fellow adventurers, join us on an unforgettable road trip and see everything Australia has to offer.

Expert Local Guides

Cultural Experiences

Native Food Experiences*

*on select trips

FIND OUT MORE!

Adventure TOURS

0203 308 9761 • adventuretours.travel
reservations@adventuretours.com.au • #gdayata

Trains

Travelling by train is one of the best ways to see a country — and if you travel on an overnight sleeper it can be as quick as a plane. India's train network is world-famous and an absolute must experience! But don't think you can't use trains in other parts of the world. What follows is just a taster.

Inter-railing — Europe and a bit beyond

If you want to visit a lot of countries, one of the best ways to travel is by train on an InterRail ticket. With InterRail you have the freedom of the rail networks of Europe (and a bit beyond), allowing you to go as you please in 28 countries.

From the northern lights of Sweden to the kasbahs of Morocco, you can call at all the stops. InterRail takes you from city centre to city centre — avoiding airport hassles, ticket queues and traffic jams, and giving you more time to make the most of your visit. Passes are available for all ages, but you need to have lived in Europe for at least six months.

Overnight trains are available on most of the major routes, saving on accommodation costs, allowing you to go to sleep in one country and wake up in another.

The InterRail ticket also includes some ferry crossings as a deck passenger, you may be travelling outside on the top deck in open air but at least it's covered in your ticket and will be no extra costs. For example, you can choose an overnight ferry crossing from Italy to mainland Greece via lots of Greek islands for a spot of island-hopping on your ticket. You can also purchase a Thomas Cook InterRail timetable book republished every year to help plan your interrail trip: **www.europeanrailtimetable.eu**

Supplements apply so ask when you book. You will have to pay extra to travel on some express intercity trains or the Eurostar. Most major stations such as Paris, Brussels, Amsterdam and Rome have washing facilities and left luggage.

the gap-year guidebook 2018

The InterRail One Country Pass can be used for the following countries:

Austria, Belgium, Bulgaria, Croatia, Czech Republic, Denmark, Finland, France, Germany, Great Britain, Greece, Hungary, Italy, Luxembourg, Macedonia (FYR), Netherlands, Norway, Poland, Portugal, Republic of Ireland, Romania, Russia, Serbia, Slovakia, Slovenia, Spain, Sweden, Switzerland and Turkey.

The alternative choice is the InterRail Global Pass, which is valid in all participating InterRail countries. Available for several lengths of travel, it is ideal for gappers wanting to explore several, or even all, European countries in their year out.

One Country Pass prices

Second class prices vary by the country and range from £37 (under 26)/£50 (over 26) for three days in one month, to £95/£131 for eight days in one month in Bulgaria; to £205/£276 in France.

Belgium, The Netherlands and Luxembourg are combined as the InterRail Benelux Pass. For Greece you have the option to order a Greece Plus Pass, which includes ferry crossings to and from Italy.

Global Pass

For second class travel, over 22 continuous days, prices range from £330 (under 26) to £426 (over 26), there are also shorter passes available. For further details on prices and how to buy an InterRail pass, visit their website: **www.interrail.eu.**

Eurostar

The Eurostar train is a quick, easy and relatively cheap way to get to Europe. You can get from London to Calais or London to Paris from £45, and the trains are comfortable and run frequently. Tickets can be purchased online at **www.eurostar.com**, in an approved travel agency, or at any Eurostar train station.

Trans-Siberian Express

If you're looking for a train adventure — and you have a generous budget to play with — what about the Trans-Siberian Express? You could do a 14-day Moscow-Beijing trip. Do this as a 'full-on' or a 'no-frills' package.

You can also choose from a range of other trips lasting from nine to 26 days. On top of this you will need some money for food and drink, visas, airfare *etc.*

For China, Russia and Mongolia you'll need to have a visa for your passport to allow you into each country. Contact each relevant embassy to find out what type of visa you will need (*ie* visitors or transit). It's probably easiest to arrange for all your train tickets, visas and hotel accommodation through a specialist agency, about six months before you leave. Your journey will be a lot easier if you have all your paperwork in order before you leave — although it will cost you more to do it this way.

The trains can be pretty basic, varying according to which line you're travelling on and which country owns the train. On some trains you can opt to upgrade to first class. This should give you your own cabin with shower, wash basin and more comfort — however, although you'll be more comfortable, you may find it more interesting back in second class with all the other backpackers and traders.

If you're travelling in autumn or winter make sure you take warm clothes — the trains have rather unreliable heating. If you travel in late November/December you may freeze into a solid block of ice, but it will be snowing by then and the views will be spectacular. Travelling in September will be warmer and a bit cheaper.

If you want to read about it before you go, try the *Trans-Siberian Handbook* by Bryn Thomas. It's updated frequently and it has details about the towns you'll be passing through, and includes the timetables.

There are several websites you can look up, but **www.trans-siberian.co.uk** is one of the best out there. For cheaper options you could also try Travel Nation, which has a useful page of FAQs on the Trans-Siberian Moscow to Beijing rail trip: **www.travelnation.co.uk/blog/moscow-to-beijing-on-the-trans-siberian-train**

India and the rest of the world

Tell anyone you're going to India and you'll invariably be told you must try a train journey. Indian trains are the most amazing adventure — with all sorts of extras — like a meal included in the price on the Shatabdi Express intercity commuter trains, or the vendors who wander the length of the train with their buckets of snacks, tea or coffee, calling their wares "chai, chai, chai" as they go.

Indian trains get booked up weeks or months in advance, especially if you're planning to travel during any major public festival like Diwali, which is a national holiday. Be sure to book ahead, **www.cleartrip.com** is an excellent, secure site to do this through.

You need a seat or berth reservation for any long-distance journey on an Indian train; you cannot simply turn up and hop on. Bookings now open 90 days in advance.

the gap-year guidebook 2018

Reservations are now completely computerised and a tourist quota gives foreigners and IndRail pass holders preferential treatment. Go to: **www.irctc.co.in**

There's also a unique reservation system. After a train becomes fully booked, a set number of places in each class are sold as 'Reservation Against Cancellation' or RAC. After all RAC places have been allocated, further prospective passengers are 'wait-listed'. When passengers cancel, people on the RAC list are promoted to places on the train and wait-listed passengers are promoted to RAC.

If you want to try your hand at organising your own train travel in India you can get a copy of the famous Trains at a Glance from any railway station in India for Rs 35 (50p) or you can download it as a PDF from: **www.seat61.com/India.htm** But beware, it contains every train timetable (94 in all) for the sub-continent and it's very long.

Research the train network for your country as some countries have limited options, for example South America. However China has many great options. A great site to use for times there is: **www.china-diy-travel.com**. This site also shows you whether a train is selling out. It's pricey to book through the site so it's probably best to book at the train station itself. In China you always need to book in advance.

The Man in Seat 61 is possibly the most incredibly comprehensive train and ship travel website ever. It literally covers the world from India to Latin America, Africa and south-east Asia. It's not only about times, costs and booking, it goes into some detail about the kinds of conditions you can expect.

It's written by Mark Smith, an ex-British Rail employee and former stationmaster at Charing Cross. He has travelled the world by train and ship and it's a personal site run as a hobby, so he pledges it will always remain freely available: **www.seat61.com**

Buses and coaches

Getting on a bus or coach in a foreign country, especially if you don't speak the language, can be a voyage of discovery in itself. UK bus timetables can be indecipherable, but try one in Patagonia!

Get help from a local you trust, hotel/hostel staff, or the local police station if all else fails.

In developing countries, locals think nothing of transporting their livestock by public transport, so be prepared to sit next to a chicken! That said, some buses and coaches can be positively luxurious and they do tend to be cheaper than trains.

Be aware of the seasons when travelling; for example in South America, in low season (it's their winter) you can turn up a day before or on the day to buy bus tickets. There are lots of companies, so compare prices between each, and pick one. Most of the bus companies offer more or less the same, although there are luxury ones as well if you fancy being pampered.

Night buses are a favourite as they save you money on a nights accommodation. Look after your things when on buses — lock your bag up and tie it to your seat so you can sleep in peace. (Same advice for trains! Unfortunately sleeping travellers are a target for planned and opportunist theft.)

For buses that could be oversubscribed, book in advance either at the bus station (this gives you a good opportunity to familiarise yourself with the station), or through an agent/hostel in town. Usually there is an additional price for this.

Pure Exploration New Zealand, 46 Robins Road,
Queenstown 9300 New Zealand
T: +64 3 442 0735
E: explore@pureexploration.nz   W: www.pureexploration.nz

Adventure Guide Internships in New Zealand

Pure Exploration offer exciting 12 week outdoor adventure guiding internships in
Queenstown. Featuring climbing, hiking, kayaking & much more, interns will graduate
with world-recognised outdoor guiding qualifications, real job experience & a job offer for
a kiwi tourism operator.

On our internship, you'll find yourself on the top of the highest peaks, meandering down
enormous glacier-driven river valleys, exploring new golden sand beaches by kayak,
hanging from enormous rock faces with your new mates supporting you all the way.
New Zealand's diverse and spectacular outdoors will be your classroom, with lessons on
leadership, new outdoor skills and strategies to help in every area of life.

You'll also complete world-recognised outdoor adventure guiding certifications and gain
a front line adventure tourism job offer in legendary Queenstown!

What makes Pure Exploration different?

We are everyday Kiwis, helping you have extraordinary experiences. Real travel isn't just
about box-ticking guidebook recommendations or Instagram shots, it's about authentic
experiences spent with new friends who inspire you to think about the world and
yourself in new ways.

Our aim is to help young people develop all the skills necessary to attack their goals
in life and have confidence to move forward into their next level of education or
employment.

For more information on this internship, please visit www.pureexploration.nz

The 'Old Grey Dog'

Greyhound buses have air conditioning, tinted windows and a loo on board, as well as a strict no smoking policy. Greyhound offers Hostelling International members a discount on regular one-way and round-trip fares. They have a Discovery Pass, which allows seven, 15, 30 and 60 days unlimited travel. There's the usual 10% discount for ISIC and Euro 26 ID cardholders (go to **www.discoverypass.com**).

The bus company operates outside America too, with Greyhound Pioneer Australia (**www.greyhound.com.au**) and for South Africa there's Greyhound Coach Lines Africa (**www.greyhound.co.za**). Check out their websites or contact them for information about their various ticket options.

See also: **www.yha.com.au** (Australia)
www.norcalhostels.org (USA)
Greyhound Lines, Inc
PO Box 660691, MS 470, Dallas, TX 75266-0691, USA
Tel: 214-849-8966;
www.greyhound.com

Student gappers could also check out **www.anyworkanywhere.com** for useful information and advice on special travel deals and discounts — planes, trains, coaches and ferries. Other useful sources of information are:

www.statravel.co.uk
www.thebigchoice.com

Touring

Travelling as part of a tour — usually as part of a group of like-minded gappers, on a coach especially fitted out for the task — can prove a fun, action-packed adventure. It doesn't have to mean chugging around the tourist sights, staring at the wonders of

the world passing by your window. A tour can mean anything from full-on adventure trips across the desert to smaller, more intimate tours along a specific theme, such as vineyards or culinary hotspots. It's worth knowing that volunteering organisations will often include and organize all your travel and accommodation with your trip.

Booking a place on a tour can be a great way to meet new people and shouldn't be dismissed just because some backpackers see it as 'the easy option'. If you do your research and book with the right company, you'll find yourself with a small bunch of like-minded people and a tour leader who should know your destination's history and culture inside out.

A good leader will also have contacts in the local community and can get you into local hotels and restaurants — leaving you to enjoy your travels rather than worrying about finding a place to sleep for the night.

Scout around for long enough and you'll find a tour to suit most tastes, from smaller groups of travellers who are serious about getting off the beaten track to meet the locals and experiencing their way of life, to younger, noisier groups looking for a fun, sociable way to explore a country or region.

Overlanding

Overlanding involves travelling in groups on a rough-and-ready truck. Vehicles come fully equipped with a kitchen and tents — perfect for both seasoned backpackers and first-timers.

Overlanding isn't just about journeying overland and taking the time to experience the places you are passing through. These are adventurous trips that will take you off the beaten track. It might involve travelling in a truck which has been converted to carry passengers and, along the way, you may camp or stay in hostels. These trucks are usually self-sufficient and carry tents, cooking equipment and food. Everyone in the group throws in a bit of effort with cooking, shopping at local markets, collecting firewood and setting up camp. There are opportunities for overlanding all around the world.

Why overlanding?

Some places can be difficult or expensive to get to under your own steam and an overland trip can provide a cheaper, hassle-free way of getting there. Being on a self-sufficient truck can mean that you get to stop and spend a night in the Sahara Desert or on the Altiplano, instead of passing through to the next town. Overlanding is a good option if you don't want to travel on your own or are apprehensive about being away from home for the first time as you're travelling in a group.

Benefits of overlanding

As well as the usual benefits of travel (broadening your horizons and your mind, learning self-sufficiency) by the time you finish your overland trip you will have gained great experience of team working as well as living with a group of people in close quarters and generally learning consideration for others. Overland trips are not hand-held holidays — you may have to organise your own flights and accommodation before joining the trip as well as helping with the day-to-day running

visit: www.gap-year.com

of the trip which will prove your organisational skills. Great stuff for your CV!

Practical skills you may pick up include camp craft (where not to pitch your tent, fire lighting *etc*, cooking for a large group of people) and languages in Spanish or French speaking parts of the world.

There are plenty of opportunities to step outside your comfort zone on an overland trip. For many, just travelling to a new country with a group of 20 strangers is an adventure in itself but if that isn't enough, on a longer expedition you may spend the day digging the truck out of a huge, muddy pothole or carrying sandmats for the truck to drive over in the desert and then camp out in the bush with only a bucket of water for a shower!

Car

Another popular option is to travel by car. It means you have somewhere to sleep if you get stuck for a bed for the night, you save money on train fares and you don't have to lug your rucksack into cafés.

If you are considering it, you need to know the motoring regulations of the countries you'll be visiting — they vary from country to country. Check that you are insured to drive abroad and that this is clearly shown on the documentation you carry with you.

The AA advises that you carry your vehicle insurance and vehicle registration documents in the car and, of course, take both parts of your driving licence with you.

It is also advisable to take an International Driving Permit (IDP) as not all countries accept the British driving licence. In theory you don't need one in any of the EU member states, but the AA recommends having an IDP if you intend to drive in any country other than the UK — and it's better than getting into trouble and being fined for driving without a valid licence.

An IDP is valid for 12 months and can be applied for up to three months in advance. The AA and RAC issue the permits — you must be over 18 and hold a current, full, UK driving licence that has been valid for two years. You'll need to fill in a form and provide your UK driving licence, passport and a recent passport-sized photo of yourself, which you can take to a participating Post Office. Be warned, you need to allow at least ten working days for processing, so don't try and do this at the last minute.

It's a good idea to put your car in for a service a couple of weeks before you leave and, unless you're a mechanic, it's also worth getting breakdown cover specifically for your trip abroad. Any of the major recovery companies such as the AA, RAC or Green Flag offer this service. Remember, without cover, if you end up stuck on the side of the road it could be an expensive experience.

The RAC recommends taking a first aid kit, fire extinguisher, warning triangle, headlamp beam reflectors and spare lamp bulbs. These are all required by law in many countries and make sense anyway. **www.rac.co.uk**

The Foreign and Commonwealth Office has put together key tips for driving abroad:

1. Research — research the driving regulations for the country you will be driving through and check your insurance policy to ensure you are covered for breakdown recovery, medical expenses and driving overseas.

2. Prepare — prepare for driving abroad, research the regulations of what you are required to carry in your vehicle and ensure that your own or hired vehicle adheres to these. Remember these are often very different to the UK.

the gap-year guidebook 2018

my
gap-year
Cora, Alex, MJ, James & Jayleen

Being surrounded by nature in Zimbabwe's Matobo National Park was by far one of the best experiences of our lives

There's always more than one reason to gap, so Acacia Africa interviewed three of their recent overland travellers about their life-changing experiences in Africa.

Cora: 'I chose Acacia Africa, as I wanted to travel with a small group of people around my age and minimise my impact on the environment.'

'I loved that I was able to experience the true silence and beauty of camping in the middle of the Namibian desert, this vast sand swept expanse awaiting in the south out of my reach as a solo traveller.'

'My travels have made me realise, it's essential to see and do as much as possible outside of the strict framework of studying and home, so that you can figure out who you are, what you care about and what you want to do with your life.'

Alex & MJ: 'When we came to Africa, we really wanted to safari on the continent in the most authentic way possible and Acacia Africa delivered. Being surrounded by nature in Zimbabwe's Matobo National Park was by far one of the best experiences of our lives.'

'It makes you see that life's not meant to be stressful. Take it slow, relax, and go with the flow. Enjoy what's around you.'

James & Jayleen: 'Our Acacia Africa tour included so many life-changing experiences, perhaps the greatest being the camaraderie that forms when you travel across five countries from Cape Town to Johannesburg with 20 strangers from all over the globe.'

'We learned each other's likes and dislikes, shared in laughs, and empathised in frustrations. It's what being part of something bigger than yourself is all about. And make no mistake; an overland adventure is about something bigger than you. That's because you're forced to put aside creature comforts and pitch in as a team to make the most of exploring new destinations.'

For more information on Acacia Africa, please see their advert on page 106

3. Once on the road — expect the unexpected, drive with confidence and always wear a seatbelt. Be safe, don't drink and drive, don't overload your vehicle, and don't use your mobile, or get behind the wheel when you are tired.

Unless you're a very experienced driver, with some off-road experience, we wouldn't advise hiring a car and driving in many places in the developing world. South-east Asian, South Asian, South American and African roads are often little more than potholed tracks, and you really have to know what you're doing when faced with a pecking order decided purely by the size of your vehicle and the sound of your horn — not to mention negotiating wandering livestock, hand-pushed carts, overloaded local buses and trucks, and pedestrians with no road sense whatsoever.

But often you'll find you can hire a car and a driver pretty cheaply for a day or two and then you'll be an ethical traveller contributing to the local economy. In Australia, buying a cheap car to tour the country at your own leisure is a popular option. But attempting to drive around Australia in an old Ford Falcon or some clapped out old campervan is definitely a challenge.

Ships and boats

If you want to get to the continent, taking a ferry across to France or Belgium can be cheap — but why not set sail as a working crew member on ships? Take a short course beforehand to qualify as a deck hand or day skipper here, with a charity such as UKSA who offer professional maritime training courses alongside youth development programmes.

Or how about getting to grips with the rigging on a cruise yacht? There are numerous employers and private vessel owners out there on the ocean wave who take on amateur and novice crew. In this way you could gain valuable sailing experience and sea miles. You can also make some useful contacts on your way to becoming a professional crew member. And have the time of your life.

the gap-year guidebook 2018

Motorbike tours

If you're a keen biker and want to include your bike in gap travel plans, there aren't many places you can't go. There's an excellent website by UK couple Kevin and Julia Saunders who are double Guinness Book of Records winners for their bike expeditions around the planet. The site offers plenty of advice as well as the opportunity to join expeditions with guides and team leaders: **www.globebusters.com**

Bicycles

If you're feeling hyper-energetic, you could use your pedal-pushing power to get you around town and country. This is really popular in north Europe, especially Holland, where the ground tends to be flatter. Most travel agents would be able to point you in the right direction, or you can just rely on hiring bikes while you are out there — make sure you understand the rules of the road.

With a globally growing 'green awareness', there's been a real surge in promoting cycling in the UK and abroad. Weather and terrain permitting it's a wonderful way of seeing a city, or touring a region, be it Portugal, Sweden, Provence, Tuscany...

But why confine it to Europe? There are many places where bicycles can be hired and it's a great way of getting around. For example, you can hire bikes and a guide in Cambodia to visit the Angkor Wat Temple, you will see much more of the temples and surrounding forests and can pick your time to visit, thus avoiding the crowds.

You can also participate in some amazing gap-year programmes, such as cycling to raise sponsorship for worthwhile charities and community projects worldwide.

But charities aside, just get on your bike and enjoy a closer contact with nature and its vast range of spectacular scenery — getting ever fitter — for example, the USA's Pacific West Coast, Guatemala to Honduras, the Andes to the glaciers of Patagonia, Nairobi to Dar es Salaam, Chiang Mai to Bangkok, the South Island mountains of New Zealand...

Take a look at:

www.ride25.com a great way to see the world through their cycling holidays
www.responsibletravel.com for cycling and mountain biking holidays
www.imba.com the International Mountain Biking Association
www.nzcycletours.com Independent tours in New Zealand with worldwide links

Sustainable travel

Global warming, climate change and the world's depleting energy resources continue to be a serious concern, regardless of the economic climate, and increasingly people want to know how to be environmentally friendly on their gap travels. Nowhere is this likely to be more of an issue than in the types of transport you choose.

If you're hoping to travel to several destinations, time is inevitably an issue, so it may not be practical to avoid air travel altogether, but there are ways you can minimise your carbon footprint. If you're concerned about global warming, and want to do your bit, you can pay a small 'carbon offset' charge on your flight. If you want to know more try:

The site has a calculator so you can work out how much to pay for journeys by car, train or air. It also has some simpler options — for example £50 will offset one long-haul one-way flight from London to Australia. Your money goes towards sustainable development projects around the world and there's a complete list of all current projects on the website.

They are all managed by co2balance, but are also all independently validated and verified by international standards organisations. Projects include providing energy efficient woodstoves in east Africa, wind power in India and renewable energy projects in China.

The UK's Green Traveller website includes a list of the top ten fair trade holidays worldwide and lots more advice if you want your travel to be as environmentally friendly as possible: **www.greentraveller.co.uk**

To find out more about sustainable and responsible travel you could also look at the website of the International Ecotourism Society, which has a lot of tips for responsible travel both en route and in-country: **www.ecotourism.org**

Ethical travel

Thinking about the best way to get to and from your destination is one thing, but ethical travel means much more than that.

We asked Tourism Concern to explain further: "Tourism is an enormous industry and affects the lives of millions of people. Environments can be wrecked by irresponsible

and unregulated diving, climbing and other outdoor activities.

"Communities have been forcibly removed from their land to make way for tourism developments across the world, from Africa to Australia. Water used for swimming pools, golf courses and twice daily power showers can dwindle supplies for the local populations. Exploitation of local workers is a problem usually invisible to a visitor's eyes. When you start to look more closely, the issues can seem overwhelming, but the good news is that with the decisions you make today and while you're away, you are taking big steps to ensure that your trip benefits everyone."

Here are Tourism Concern's ten tips for ethical travelling:

1. Be aware: start enjoying your travels before you leave. Think about what sort of clothing is appropriate for both men and women. If the locals are covered up, what sort of messages may you be sending out by exposing acres of flesh? But use your guidebook as a starting point, not the only source of information.

2. Be open: something may seem bizarre or odd to you, but it may be normal and just the way things are done to 'them'. Try not to assume that the western way is right or best.

3. Our holidays — their homes: ask before taking pictures of people, especially children, and respect their wishes. Talk to local people. What do they think about our lifestyle, clothes and customs? Find out about theirs.

4. Giving constructively: giving sweets or pens to children encourages begging. A donation to a project, health centre or school is more constructive.

5. Be fair: try to put money into local hands. If you haggle for the lowest price, your bargain may be at the seller's expense. Even if you pay a little over the odds, does it really matter?

6. Buy local, behave local: look at the environment you're in, try to eat locally sourced foods and buy locally produced goods. Think about resources, don't shower for 20 minutes at a time in an arid zone, just because you might at home.

visit: www.gap-year.com

7. Ask questions: write a letter to your tour operator or venture manager about their responsible tourism policy.

8. Think before you fly: use alternative forms of transport where possible. The more and further you fly, the more you contribute to global warming and environmental destruction. Consider flying long-haul less often but staying longer when you're there.

9. Discover Tourism Concern: a charity that campaigns against exploitation in tourism and for fairly traded and ethical forms of tourism. Their website has a wealth of information on action you can take to avoid guilt trips. **www.tourismconcern.org.uk**

10. Be happy: by taking any, some or all of these actions you are personally fighting tourism exploitation. Enjoy your guilt-free trip!

If you also have concerns about ethical tourism, whether it is the company's environmental impact or the conditions of its workers, the Ethical Consumer website has a report on these issues, which can be viewed at **www.ethicalconsumer.org/buyersguides/traveltransport**

Arno Delport, from Acacia Africa, gave us a few tips on being an ethical traveller:

· Travel with a tour operator which has made a commitment to sustainable travel. Usually you will find more information on their website including a note on the ethical partners they support etc.

· Buy second hand gear to travel and if you are buying new, look at green, ethically designed backpacks

· Stay green on the road by reusing water bottles, dispose of your waste properly and leave the world as you find it

Accommodation

Traditionally, hostels are the first option that springs to mind, whenever gappers or backpackers are looking for cheap accommodation.

Today there are a range of hostels available, which offer clean, safe and reasonably priced accommodation, some even have 'luxury' extras, such as internet connection, games rooms and laundry facilities.

There are a number of good apps available for booking accommodation, including booking.com, hostelworld.com and TripAdvisor.

Use your common sense and always check where the fire exits are when arriving at a hostel, because it's too late to look if there's already a fire and you're trying to get out of the building.

If you do find you're staying in a basic, no frills-style hostel, it's wise to make sure there's some ventilation when you have a bath or shower — faulty water heaters give off lethal and undetectable carbon monoxide fumes and will kill you without you realising it as you fall gently to sleep, never to wake up again. For this reason, do consider taking a small carbon monoxide reader.

Use your instincts — if you think the hostel's simply not up to scratch and too risky, go and find another one.

Camping

If you're on a budget camping or caravanning can be worth considering though they're not options for some parts of the world and, particularly with camping, you need to think about whether you really want to carry all that extra equipment.

Many campsites are replacing tents with huts; usually they're in places close to areas where you can hike. You'll get a bed in a hut and use of other facilities so you only need a sleeping bag or sheet sleeping bag — no need to carry a tent.

Caravans, campervans and places to park them

Renting a caravan or travelling under your own steam with a camper van is another possibility — they call them motorhomes in the USA and it's easy to see why. They do have the advantage of giving you a secure place to leave your stuff and of not having to carry it all on your back but they're plainly not an option everywhere in the world.

Check out these websites:

www.campingo.com
www.internationalcampingclub.com
www.eurocampings.co.uk/en/europe
www.rentocamp.com
www.allstays.com/Campgrounds-Australia
www.familyparks.com.au
www.stayz.com.au

Temples and monasteries

Temples and monasteries are also an option worth exploring. The main consideration for deciding to stay in a monastery or temple guesthouse, should not be your budget, though there's no denying that it's affordable for the budget traveller. Indeed for anyone wanting some place to be able to relax and not be constantly on guard, or if you're seeking a peaceful sanctuary and simplicity, religious guesthouses are ideal.

Some places prefer that you have *some* link with their faith, even if only through a historic extended-family link, but there is a strong tradition of offering refuge, safety and peace in any religious community that isn't a closed order.

Historically, the religious communities and monasteries of many faiths have provided hospice and hospital services to their surrounding communities. Much of our early medical knowledge developed from here too.

Changing economics have also meant their costs have risen and many temples and monasteries have had to be practical about raising income for their communities and for the upkeep of buildings, whose antiquity makes them costly to maintain. Most are therefore open to guests regardless of faith.

Having said that, if you are considering this option, be prepared for rooms and meals to be simple, facilities to be austere and for the community to be quiet at certain times of the day. There will be daily rituals to the life of the community and, like anywhere else, it's only polite to respect their customs. Obviously it's not an option that would suit some gappers.

But a chance to think, to recharge the spiritual batteries, to learn more about oneself or a particular faith, maybe to learn yoga or meditation, is what some gappers are looking for and it can be worth considering this option as part of a gap programme. Respect traditions and be aware of your dress and manners as you could easily cause offence.

visit: www.gap-year.com

Hotels

If you've been on the move for several weeks and careful with the budget, you can find your spirits are flagging from coping with the often spartan conditions in budget hotels, hostels and the like.

A couple of days of comfort in a good hotel can be a worthwhile investment as a tonic, to give you time out to sort your stuff, get some laundry done, have a decent shower and sleep in a clean, comfortable bed before you set off again.

Most hotels around the world use the familiar one to five-star rating system, where five is luxury and one is likely to be a fleapit! But the symbols used can be anything from stars, diamonds and crowns to keys, suns, dots, rosettes and letters.

As with most things in life you get what you pay for, but prices will vary wildly depending on whether you're in peak tourism season or off-peak, currency rates and the costs of living in the country you're visiting, so you may be pleasantly surprised by the rates in some of the better hotels and find you can stretch your budget without reaching breaking point. (If you arrive late in the day don't forget to try to negotiate on fees. If rooms are empty you may get a discounted rate.)

But equally, hotel ratings are done by human beings, and they can vary wildly depending on who did them and which search engine you might have used. The best advice is to look for reviews or ratings from ordinary hotel guests who have actually stayed in the hotel — and slept in the beds!

There are several sources of independent information. Most of the travellers' guidebooks have lists of hotels within the different price ranges, but you have to bear in mind that, particularly in the tourism and hospitality industries, things can change between the time of printing and when you arrive.

If you want to check out a hotel while you're travelling, try **www.tripadvisor.com**

the gap-year guidebook 2018

What makes this site special is that it's all written by travellers from their own experiences and it pulls no punches. There are millions of posts on just about every place or topic you can think of, covering destinations all over the world — including some that might surprise you, like the Middle East, (Saudi Arabia, Jordan, United Arab Emirates to name a few). Useful websites for last-minute and affordable accommodation are:

'Bargain Rooms' — **www.roomauction.com** — you pay below the standard room rate by making the hotel a discreet offer, 'bidding' for the room.

www.laterooms.com — discount hotel rooms in UK and abroad; the low prices are genuine as they would rather see their rooms let out than not at all.

Lodging

Rental lodging has increased in popularity over the last few years due to the increase in websites such as **www.airbnb.co.uk**. The website allows you to search rooms and whole properties that are available to rent around the world. You could find yourself lodging with nature in a tree house in Costa Rica's rainforest, or lodging in a room with a view of New York's Times Square — the possibilities are endless.

The online booking system is easy to use and the extent of information and inspiring images available on each rental lodging listed makes booking accommodation via a service such as this very appealing.

Couch Surfing

This is the ultimate in finding free accommodation and, although there were safety concerns when this service first started, it's now had more than a million satisfied customers. But this not-for-profit organisation has a philosophy that's about more than that — it's about creating friendships and networks across the world.

visit: www.gap-year.com

Here's what couchsurfing.com say on the safety issue: "CouchSurfing has implemented several precautionary measures for the benefit of its surfers, hosts, and community. Every user is linked to the other users he or she knows in the system, through a network of references and friend links. In addition to the solid network with friend link-strength indicators and testimonials, we have our vouching and verification systems."

There's a lot more information on their website that should answer all your questions: **www.couchsurfing.com**

Luxury gap-years

Luxury gap-years are proving to be an increasingly popular cure to those Monday morning blues, with the traditional image of a student gapper rapidly being challenged by this new breed of travel-seeker.

Whether it's one month or twelve, these luxury breaks offer the chance to experience the thrill of a traditional gap-year with the added perks of plush accommodation, luxury travel options and custom made itineraries catering to a wide range of tastes and styles. Typically appealing to those aged 50 or over, these 'luxury gappers' are eager to quench their wanderlust with once-in-a-lifetime trips and experiences, often enjoying their travels with their partners or families.

A typical luxury gap-year could set you back anywhere from £5,000 to in excess of £20,000, dependent on your specific desires and requirements for your year out. In return for this, specialist providers can offer you unique opportunities ranging from spiritual yoga experiences and US road trips, to white knuckle adventures and opportunities to learn new languages. Additionally, many companies provide their customers with exclusive access to support systems and in-country links unavailable to the everyday explorer. For the ultimate stress free trip, accommodation and travel options can also be arranged by companies eager to make your year out an unforgettable experience.

Another popular choice for those planning on taking a luxury gap-year is to take a dip into the ever growing 'voluntourism' sector. Combining the chance to explore new lands with worthwhile activities in some of the world's most deprived communities and endangered environments, luxury gappers can return home brimming with the sense that their year out has not only improved their own well being, but, made a real difference to the lives and environments of others.

So, if you're looking for a career break, a pre-retirement celebration or simply a chance to fulfil that lifelong desire to see the world, then look no further than a luxury gap-year.

Please see the directory pages starting on page 275 for information on companies and organisations offering travel and accommodation services.

my
gap-year
Kristy

Kristy decided to take a break and head to Western Australia...

The overland journey covered the best of Australia's pristine beaches with some rugged outback terrain thrown in.

A nature-lover, Kristy's highlight for the trip was swimming with the whale sharks at Ningaloo Reef.

"Swimming with whale sharks or 'spotty fish' as they're

known, is something I've always wanted to tick off my bucket list. I had dreamed about doing it for a long time, and the experience didn't let me down — it was a humbling experience to be swimming next to such a massive, yet gentle and majestic creature.

"I had the honour of swimming alongside Zorro, one of the biggest males who is 7.5m long — and I'm only 1.5m tall to put that in perspective! He turned and swam directly toward me, so I was face-to-face with one of the biggest fish in the ocean! He looked me straight in the eye, it was amazing."

Kristy says one of the best things about the trip was getting away from the usual craziness of life at home.

"When we were camping in Karijini, we were completely off the radar. We had no phone service, no internet and just got to appreciate the beautiful night skies full of stars. It was so relaxing to reconnect with nature."

Her advice to anyone thinking of booking an Australian adventure is simply to "do it!"

"You get sun, surf, red dirt deserts, gorges, culture and history, stunning sunsets and sunrises, blue skies, nature, walking, climbing, swimming — you feel like a kid exploring the world again."

Kristy says the best thing about travelling on a small group tour is having built-in friends to share the experiences with.

"Everyone on the tour was genuinely amazing. It was so much fun meeting people from all over the world who have similar values to me and got to experience the same incredible moments I did."

For more information on Adventure Tours Australia, see their advert on page 102

Working abroad

Sponsored by

Why work a ski season?

When you decide to work a season, it isn't just a new job that you are taking on, but an entire lifestyle! You will be spending nearly six months in some of the most stunning scenery imaginable, creating memories and friendships that will last a lifetime!

There are many elements to take in to consideration when choosing where to go and who to work for; so with Work a Season the mixture of resort, nightlife, ski area and job role, leads to high demand for all of our positions across the French, Italian and Austrian alps. Everyone that you speak to about working a season will have their opinions of where you should go, but each year all 1600 of our seasonnaires take something from their season that no one else will have done.

Our Santa's Lapland program offers the opportunity to make every child and adults dream come true by visiting Lapland and meeting the big man himself! So if working a shorter winter season is something that would suit you better, then this six-week program could be just perfect, and it is the one place that every single one of our staff want to visit!

Our Ingham's program also has the chance to work in Lapland and help Santa but also has a ski/excursion program. Both giving you the rare chance of seeing the Northern Lights, experiencing reindeer sleigh rides and driving Huskies through the snow covered forests!

Recruitment Manager James Tait, who has worked for the company for the last ten years after commencing his career as a Chalet Host, has shared some of his experiences:

"Having finished university, I decided to follow my friends off to work this 'season' thing and flung myself head first into the unknown. I had never skied/snowboarded, experienced 'proper' snow or seen a real mountain, my closest experience was tobogganing three-inch slush in the Pennines as a delirious five-year-old growing up near Manchester.

I applied for several companies and found the one that I felt would provide me with the best experience and company culture that suited my personality. I immediately felt at home as soon as I went for the interview and never looked back. Three months later, I was headed to France with way too much in my suitcase and about to start my new adventure that would continue for the next ten years.

Like you, I had a burning desire to always work overseas, travel and speak another language, I chose France as my gateway. For myself I worked as a Chalet Host in

Les Gets in my first year. Catering, cleaning and skiing (or snowboarding in my case) was the name of the game. I loved every minute of it; I met interesting guests, locals, colleagues and, more importantly, had exposure to nationalities from all over the world, all united by the fluffy white stuff that fell a plenty all winter long.

I soon realised the opportunities that the travel industry offered and ten years and multiple seasons later finishing my time overseas as an Area

Operations Manager, I now work full time in our UK head office heading up the recruitment team and sourcing our future seasonnaires."

Do I require a Visa, work permit or local bank account?

Our positions across Europe do not require visa or work permits, however, you must be an EU national who has a UK National Insurance number, UK bank account and a European Health Insurance Card to complete the season. You will be paid in to your UK bank account.

What do I receive in return for working a season?

Packages are offered as accommodation, season lift pass, ski equipment, travel, food and insurance. You will also receive a wage and some roles will be subject to receiving bonuses and tips.

What job roles are there?

There really is a job for everyone — our job roles include Resort Drivers, Resort Assistants, Chalet Hosts, Hotel Assistants, Resort Representatives, childcare and catering positions too. We offer similar opportunities in Lapland where you can also be one of Santa's elves!

We also have a large array of management and supervisory positions. The company also look to promote from within and invest heavily in training and development.

Do I need a cookery course qualification to become a Chalet Host?

If you enjoy cooking at home and have plenty of experience in the kitchen it may not be needed. If you feel that you would like to have a little more confidence in the kitchen either in preparation for the season or to take to university with you, a cookery course can be very helpful.

Our Work a Season cookery course is designed to give you all the tools to tackle a season as a Chalet Host and we will discuss roles/resorts that you would like to visit as part of the assessments throughout the week.

To find out more about Work a Season, visit workaseason.com

Working abroad

Working abroad is a great option if you desperately want to go overseas, can't really afford it and the bit you have managed to save won't cover much more than air fare.

It's one of the best ways to experience a different culture; you'll be meeting locals and experiencing what the country is really like in a way that you can't do as a traveller passing through. Most jobs give you enough spare time, in the evenings and at weekends, to enjoy yourself, socialize and make friends.

You don't have to be tied to one place for your whole gap-year — you can work for a bit and save up for your travels. That way you can learn more about the place and get the inside information from the locals about the best places to see before you set off.

You cover at least some of your costs and, depending on what you do, the work experience will look good on your CV — but even if you're only doing unskilled seasonal work, prospective employers will be reassured that you at least know *something* about the basics like punctuality, fitting into an organisation and managing your time.

An internship with pay is a good way to get work experience if you already have an idea about your eventual career and will help in those early stages of the problem that affects many young people — when employers want experience but won't take you on so you can get it.

Working abroad on a gap-year is popular as it enables gappers to see different parts of the world and fund their travel through the work that they do overseas. It also looks great on the CV; it shows that you can can adapt, be resilient, live away from home, and hold down a job to help you live independently.

Arriving in a new place as a traveller can seem daunting and it may take time to find your way but as a paid worker you can join a team of staff and get taken under their wing straight away. You also get the chance to live as a local, living and working alongside them. Older gappers, too, may find that, despite the current global economic problems, their skills and experience are in demand, particularly in developing countries.

Key questions to get started

What kind of work do you want to do? There are some suggestions in this chapter but they're only a start.

- Is it to help pay your way on your gap?
- Is it to get work experience/enhance your CV?
- Where do you want to work?
- What skills and experience do you have?

It doesn't have to be work experience or education, don't forget hobbies and interests. If you can ride a horse, dance, draw, paint, or are good at a particular sport, you could use any of those skills as a basis for finding work.

visit: www.workaseason.com

Planning ahead

Choosing your destination

There are some jobs that always need to be done, whatever the state of the world, and if you're just looking at ways of funding your travel you could look for seasonal farm work.

In most cases, gappers intending to do seasonal work outside the EU need to have a job offer in order to get a visa. If you should find that, when you get there the job is no longer available, you can try elsewhere — but we would advise you to have a back-up plan before you set off on your travels (*eg* contacts, an emergency fund, names of companies that specialise in work overseas).

If you are a UK citizen, or hold an EU (European Union) passport, you can work in any other EU member country without a visa or work permit and there are countless jobs available to students who can speak the right languages. Not all European countries are EU members — go to the European Union website to check: **www.europa.eu**

Speaking English is always an advantage for jobs in tourism at ski resorts, beach bars and hotel receptions and if you have a TEFL (Teaching English as a Foreign Language) certificate there's always the option of paid teaching.

You could try using message boards to find out what other gappers have done and what it was like. If you want to be more adventurous and venture outside Europe, then check the Foreign Office website — **www.gov.uk/travelaware** — for important advice on your possible destinations.

Getting your paperwork sorted

Before you go, you should:

· Check whether you need to set up a job — you may need a confirmed work offer before you can get a work permit and visa — try **www.gap-year.com** for contact lists and more advice, or refer to the internship and graduate opportunities section in the directory of this guidebook.

· Check on the work permit and visa regulations for the country you plan to work in and make sure you have the right paperwork before you leave. Remember, you don't need a work permit or visa if you're an EU citizen and planning to work in an EU country.

· Check if there's any special equipment or clothing you'll need to take, *eg* sturdy boots and trousers for manual jobs, reasonably smart clothes for office internships *etc*.

· When you're getting your insurance, remember to check that you'll be covered if you're planning on working. Working can invalidate a claim for loss or damage to your belongings on some travel policies. If in doubt, ask.

· Make sure you understand all the regulations and restrictions. You can get into serious trouble if you work without the necessary documents — you don't want to be deported during your gap-year! The best place to get information is the relevant embassy in London — there's a link on **www.gap-year.com** to the Foreign and Commonwealth Office website, where you will find links to all embassies.

Finding a job

Finding a job may take time and effort. The more places you can send your CV to, the greater the chances of you getting a job. You can also register with international employment agencies but make sure you know what the agency fee will be if you get employment.

visit: www.workaseason.com

To find short-term jobs try:

www.workaseason.com
www.ozintro.com
www.transitionsabroad.com
www.pickingjobs.com
www.visitoz.org
www.anyworkanywhere.com
www.overseasjobcentre.co.uk

If you use an agency, always insist on talking to someone who has used it before — that way you'll really find out what the deal is.

Do a search to see if there's a website for a particular area you want to go to and then send or email your CV, with a short covering note, to any interesting local companies. Don't expect to be flooded with replies. Some companies are simply too busy to respond to every enquiry, though it always helps to enclose a stamped addressed envelope. It's also true that you may get lucky and have exactly the skills or qualifications they're looking for. Some companies will also advertise vacant posts on specialist employment websites, which often have an international section. You can register with the sites too, usually for free.

Tell everyone you know, including relatives and your parents' friends that you are looking for a job abroad — someone may know someone who has a company abroad who can help you.

Check the local papers and shop window notices. Lots of jobs are advertised in the local papers, or by 'staff wanted' notices put up in windows. So if you get there, and hate the job you've got, don't put up with it, or come running home — see if you can find something better. It's always easier to find employment when you're living locally.

Over the next few pages we've listed ideas on types of employment, and any companies we know about, that offer graduate opportunities or work experience, can be found in the directory. Always ask an employment company to put you in

the gap-year guidebook 2018

Au Pair Ecosse

Au Pair Ecosse, 6 Park Place, King's Park, FK7 9JR UK
T: +44 (0) 1786 474573
E: ruth@aupairecosse.com   W: www.aupairecosse.com

Spend a year in the USA as an au pair with a host family. If you have a genuine love of children you could be on your way to a fantastic experience. You will be provided with food and board and receive average pocket money of $199 a week, plus you will have the opportunity to study at an American college. The minimum period is 12 months with a possible extension of a further 12 months. Your return flight will be paid for and basic health insurance provided, so long as you stay for the 12 month period - the only cost to you will be the fee for the visa interview at the US Embassy (currently $160).

Applications have to be processed by a UK representative of the American agency. Ruth Campbell who runs Au Pair Ecosse has been working with Go Au Pair since she established her agency in 2005.

To find out more about Go Au Pair visit their website www.goaupair.com and to contact Ruth email her at ruth@aupairecosse.com or phone on (01786) 474573

contact with someone they have placed before — if they say no, then think twice about using them: they may have something to hide.

Au pairing

Being an au pair is a good way to immerse yourself in a different culture, learn a new language and hopefully save some extra cash. You don't need any qualifications to be an au pair, although obviously some experience with children is a bonus. However, au pairing is a hard job and a big responsibility and you may well have to pass the equivalent of a Disclosure and Barring Service (DBS) check.

In return for board, lodgings and pocket money, you'll be expected to look after the children and do light domestic chores like ironing, cooking, tidying their bedrooms and doing their washing, for up to five hours a day (six hours in France or Germany), five days a week, as well as spending two or three evenings a week babysitting. If you are asked to work more than this then technically you are not doing the work of an au pair, but of a mother's help (which pays more).

Remember that an au pair is classified as 'non-experienced', and you should never be left in sole charge of a baby. If the family gives you more responsibility than you can handle say so. If they don't stop — quit.

Our friends at Au Pair Ecosse give us some top tips for those looking to become an au pair:

· Be strong minded

· Understand that there will be bad days as well as the good but that the good days definitely make up for the bad days

· To be patient with finding the right family that fits your personality.

They also advised us on what to be wary on before signing up for an au pair position: "To make sure they find they right family and have the confidence to move away on their own. It is hard to move to a completely new country and have no friends, but if you are confident in doing so, it will be so worth it.

"Also making sure the family you match with is right for you. Different families have different requirements and personalities, take your time and find the right one for you."

Finding an au pair agency

It may be safest to look for a placement through a UK-based au pair agency. It's also better for the prospective family abroad, since they will be dealing with an agency (possibly working together with an agency in the family's own country) that has met you, interviewed you and taken up references; they will want reassurance before they trust you with their children.

What you should check:

· Does the agency you use have connections with another agency in the country where you'll be working?

· Can they give you a list of other local au pairs so you'll have support when you're out there?

· Take time finding a suitable family. The fewer children the better, and you should expect your own room.

· What is there to do in your free time? You don't want to spend every weekend in your bedroom because you're stuck in the middle of nowhere.

· Do you get written confirmation of the hours, duties and pay agreed?

· The number and address of the local British Consulate — just in case.

Check that the au pair agency is a member of either the Recruitment and Employment Confederation (which has a website listing all its members and covering au pair employment in many countries) or of the International Au Pair Association (IAPA), which has a list of its registered agencies in 38 countries around the world:

International Au Pair Association
WYSE Travel Confederation
174 Keizersgracht
1016 DW, Amsterdam
The Netherlands
Tel: +31 (0)20 421 2800
Enquiry: inquiry@iapa.org
www.iapa.org

There are, of course, perfectly good agencies that do not belong to trade associations, either because they are too small to afford the membership fees, or because they are well-established and have a good independent reputation.

You can also find information on au pair work worldwide by using the internet. Registration is usually free and your details will be matched to the families around the world that have registered on the site and that meet your specifications (but make sure you talk to both the agents, here and abroad, and the prospective family before you make your final decision).

However, if you are considering organising an au pair placement independently, you should be aware of the risks:

· High probability of unsuitable au pair or host family candidates.

visit: www.workaseason.com

- Absence of a written contract.
- Little or no experience in the au pair industry.
- Lack of professionalism or financial stability.
- Non-existent standards or guidelines.
- Insufficient references and/or medical certification.
- Danger of document falsification.
- No rematch policy (secondary placement) if the initial placement is unsuccessful.
- No local support during the placement.
- Limited understanding of national au pair and visa regulations.

Remember also that au pair agencies operating in the UK and sending au pairs abroad cannot, except under specified circumstances, charge for finding you a placement.

If you have a complaint against a UK agency it's best to take it up with the Department for Business, Innovation and Skills' Employment Agency Standards Helpline, Tel: +44 (0) 845 955 5105. It operates Monday-Friday 9.30am to 4.30pm.

Au pairing in Europe

There are EU laws governing the conditions in which au pairs can work:

- You must be 17 or over.
- You must provide a current medical certificate.
- You should have a written employment agreement signed by you and your host family; conditions of employment must be stated clearly.
- You should receive (tax exempt) pocket money.
- You should have enough free time to study.
- You should not be asked to work more than five hours a day.
- You must have one free day a week.

This is now the accepted definition for au pair jobs in the EU, but not necessarily in other countries. Some countries have different local rules.

Take a look at **www.conventions.coe.int/treaty/en/Treaties/Html/068.htm** for the details of the European Agreement and any local variations.

It's important to complete all the necessary paperwork for living and working in another country. Most agencies will organise this for you, and make sure the legal documents are in order before you leave.

You should listen to any legal advice you are given by the agency you use. Many also now require written references, police checks and other proof of suitability — which is as much a protection for you as it is for the parents of the children you might look after.

Here's an example. Most French agencies require a set of passport photos, a photocopy of your passport, two references (preferably translated into French), and your most recent academic qualifications, as well as a handwritten letter in French to your prospective family, which tells them something about you, your reasons for becoming an au pair and any future aspirations.

133

The agency may also ask for a medical certificate (showing you are free of deadly contagious diseases *etc*) dated less than three months before you leave, and translated into French. Au pairs also have to have a medical examination on arrival in France.

The French Consulate advises you to check that the family you stay with obtains a 'mother's help' work contract (*Accord de placement au pair d'un stagiaire aide-familiale*). If you are a non-EU citizen you are expected to do this before you leave for France, but British au pairs do not need to.

Au pairing in North America

Being an au pair in the USA is well paid. You'll receive $195 a week (£125 approximately), have your flight paid for, free health insurance, free food and lodging with your own room in the family house. You also get two weeks' holiday and a chance to travel for 30 days at the end of the year.

Au Pair Ecosse

Many American families need childcare help because both parents work. Childcare is very expensive in the USA and so a highly effective network of agencies has developed to supply international au pairs to US families.

The US Government regulates the au pair programme and in order to obtain the required J-1 au pair visa you must go though a local UK agency. The requirements are quite strict:

· Be aged 18-26.

· Be educated to minimum GCSE standard.

· Speak English well.

· Have no criminal record (including cautions) and obtain an enhanced CRB check.

· Have a minimum 200 hours of babysitting experience with non-relatives.

· Be able to drive and swim.

· Have no visible tattoos!

You also receive a $500 credit towards the college course of your choice.

The US Department of State website has all the up-to-date legislation on au pairing in the US. See: **j1visa.state.gov/programs/au-pair**

If you enjoy being with children, this is a great option for a year. UK agencies include:

www.gap360.com
www.culturalcare.co.uk
www.aupairinamerica.co.uk

If you want to combine au pairing with some study, the EduCare scheme in the US

visit: *www.workaseason.com*

places people with families who have school-aged children and who need childcare before and after school hours. Au pairs on the EduCare scheme work no more than 30 hours per week in return for roughly two thirds of the rates paid to au pairs.

You must complete a minimum of 12 hours of academic credit or its equivalent during the programme year (financed by the host family for up to US$1000).

Internships and paid work placements

· Are you at university?

· Are you a new graduate?

· Are you looking for work experience to land your dream job?

· Want to spend a year in another country?

Taking an internship abroad — either as part of a university course or not — is a good way to boost your CV, as well as getting away for a year and doing something useful.

Au Pair Ecosse

There is an increasing demand for paid work placements overseas and many gap-year companies now offer these. Paid work has always been popular as students seek to top up funds for the next stage of their travels. But in the current economic climate gaining work experience has become an important consideration when planning a gap-year and many gap-year organisations are now in a position to help secure suitable placements.

Some careers, the media for example, are extremely tough to get into, so using your gap-year to get relevant work experience may be a good plan. You'll have the benefit of something to put on your CV and also get an idea of what the job is actually like. Internships are not usually open to people pre-university. Many international companies offer internships but if you're thinking of the USA you should know:

1.   Internships in the USA can be difficult to get without paying for the privilege, unless you have personal contacts within the organisation you hope to work for.

2.   The USA has a strict job-related work permit system and won't hand out these permits for jobs that American nationals can do themselves.

3.   The USA authorities also need to be convinced that the work experience offered provides an opportunity to the UK student that he or she cannot get back home.

If the companies listed in our directory can't help you, try these websites:

www.cartercentre.org
www.summerjobs.com (enter internships in the search box)
www.internshipprograms.com
www.goabroad.com/intern-abroad
www.transitionsabroad.com

Before you sign up, make sure you're clear just what your placement will involve.

Canvas Holidays, East Port House, 12 East Port, Dunfermline KY12 7JG UK
T: +44 (0) 1383 629012
E: campingrecruitment@canvasholidays.com
W: www.canvasholidaysrecruitment.com

Canvas Holidays were the first company to offer package camping holidays, and over 50 years later we remain focused on providing customers the best holiday ever.

At Canvas Holidays we ensure that our customers return home having had the best holiday they have ever had. We believe that our staff at Canvas Holidays play a big part in achieving this.

We are looking for approachable, friendly, helpful and hardworking individuals to join our overseas team. Working for Canvas Holidays gives you an opportunity to see new places within Europe, create memories and make new friends.

Campsite Couriers (Part/Full Time): Single, Couple or Team Site Courier

You will be the face of Canvas Holidays and your duties will include delivering exceptional customer service, cleaning, preparing and maintaining customer accommodation for customer's arrival, welcoming them on to the campsite and ensuring that customers' needs are attended to during their stay. You will need to have initiative and be a quick thinker and be able to resolve problems efficiently and effectively. You will be responsible for the operation of your site and delivering the Canvas product.

Senior Courier / Site Manager:

Our Team Leaders ensure that every aspect of our customer's holidays is of the highest standard possible. All successful applicants must have previous managements/ supervisory experience, exceptional customer service, maintenance, problem solving, organisation and communication skills.

For more information please visit our website: www.canvasholidaysrecruitment.com or contact us on: 01383 629012 or email: Campingrecruitment@canvasholidays.com

my
gap-year
Lewis

When I applied to work for Canvas Holidays I was working full time in Scotland — which was great but it wasn't exciting and I needed a new adventure. I applied for Canvas Holidays as they were offering the opportunity to work abroad, which included accommodation and travel. With the job being seasonal, I knew it would enable me to go travelling over the winter months, which other jobs wouldn't enable me to do.

I knew of Canvas Holidays from when I was younger and went on holiday with my family and more recently in 2015, when my girlfriend and I went to Norcenni, Girasole, Italy — the year before we joined the Canvas team. We had an unforgettable time celebrating my birthday so Norcenni has to be my favourite campsite.

I chose to work for Canvas Holidays as from the day I applied they were 'on the ball'. I was really impressed with the recruitment team, the training team and then the management onsite. I also chose to work for Canvas Holidays as I would be able to go travelling at the end of the year, which is something I had been meaning to do for a long time but could never find the time.

I was then fortunate to be given a position and my Canvas Holidays journey began in 2016 on La Croix du Vieux Pont, Berny Rivière where I worked the full season. Berny Rivière is a huge site for Canvas Holidays and I worked under a great management team, which was perfect as they were always there to offer advice when needed.

This will be my 2nd season with Canvas Holidays and this year (2017) I have worked as a courier on Chenes Verts which is a small couple's site, in Dordogne, France. The best part about my job is that I love being able to manage myself and my workload knowing that I have the support from the Office, Maintenance team and Area managers to help me out if I ever need it.

I have absolutely loved this season. I have really enjoyed spending time with our customers — I have met some incredible and inspirational people from all walks of life. I have come across some real hidden gems that I would never have found without speaking to customers. The weather has been exceptional all season too. All in all, the highlight of the season was the season itself.

For more information on Canvas Holidays, see their advert on the opposite page

An internship should mean you are able to do interesting paid work related to your degree studies, current or future, for at least six months, but increasingly, even on some of the internship websites listed above, the distinction between a voluntary (unpaid) placement and an internship is becoming blurred so you may have to search for a while — or be creative and try a direct approach to companies in the fields that interest you.

Sport instructors

If you're already a qualified instructor in skiing, sailing, kayaking, diving, football, or any other sport for that matter, there are many places all around the world where you can use your skills — and many personal benefits.

Typical summer seasons run from the end of April to the beginning of November and winter seasons tend to run from the end of November until the end of April. That provides an opportunity for all-year round work, although it's worth noting that recruitment normally starts five months in advance. In some cases people can even get qualified and teach people to ski in the same season, such as in Oyster's Whistler Kids Instructor programme.

Here are a few websites worth having a look at:

Skiing:
www.oysterworldwide.com/gap-year/canada-whistler-blackcomb-ski-instructor-jobs
www.ifyouski.com/jobs/job/description/instructor
www.jobmonkey.com/ski/html/instructors.html

Football:
www.deltapublications.co.uk/soccer.htm — soccer coaching in the USA

General Sports:
www.adventurework.co.uk
www.campjobs.com

Skiing doesn't have to be in European resorts, don't forget there's the US and Canada,

visit: www.workaseason.com

but there are also ski resorts in the foothills of the Himalayas! For diving jobs you can go pretty much go anywhere there's water and water sports. Football's popular throughout Africa and Latin America, and there are now several football academies in India looking for help to spread the message of the 'beautiful game'. But whichever sport is your passion, you can use it as part of your gap-year plan.

We have much more on the opportunities available for teaching and playing sport abroad in **Chapter 8**.

Teaching English as a Foreign Language (TEFL)

TEFL is one of the most popular ways of earning (and volunteering) when you travel, but you need to have a recognised qualification and it does help in getting a post abroad. It also has the advantage that, if you were thinking of teaching as a career, it's a good chance to find out if you like it before you begin your teacher training.

The two best-known British qualifications are:

· TESOL (a certificate from Trinity College, London).

· CELTA (Cambridge University certificate).

The USA has its own qualification and there are many private schools and colleges who offer their own certification. There are a great many colleges around the UK that offer TEFL courses but, ideally, you should check that the certificate you will be working for is one of these two.

It is worth doing your TEFL training within an accredited training centre, as most will help you find a placement once you qualify and face to face training can be more beneficial.

One word of warning, if you were hoping to get a job with one of the many well-known language schools around the world, some will insist that you undertake your TEFL training with them first. It's always worth checking this out, and deciding how you wish to use your training, before you sign up for a course. for more info, visit: **www.tefl.org.uk**

How to find TEFL work

The availability of work for people who can teach English can vary, particularly outside the EU. In most countries it is possible to give private lessons. As stated before, if you wish to work for a language school or academy, find out what their requirements are before you begin your training.

Most professional employers will expect you to have had some teaching practice before they will employ you. You should also find out more about the country you hope to find work in before you go. The contact details of the relevant embassies in the UK can be found on the FCO website — **www.gov.uk/travelaware** — and you should be able to obtain up-to-date details of visas, salaries, qualifications needed and a view about the availability of work in your chosen country. Rates of pay and conditions of employment will vary greatly from country to country and will most likely depend on your own education, training, experience and expertise.

In the UK, TEFL jobs are advertised in:
The Times Educational Supplement.
The Guardian.
In the education section of *The Independent.*
The EL Gazette.

visit: www.workaseason.com

www.oysterworldwide.com/projects/tefl
www.tefl.org.uk/tefl-jobs-centre
www.eslbase.com/jobs
www.cactustefl.com
www.eteach.com
www.esljobfeed.com

You could also check out the various 'blacklists' that have appeared on the internet in recent years. These list schools to avoid or watch out for. These are informal sites run by people with experience of TEFL teaching. They should be a good place to find out about language schools around the world and whether or not it's worth your time pursuing a vacancy there.

The most popular destinations for TEFL teachers are China, Hong Kong, Japan, Thailand and, of course, Europe. As the EU grows, so does the demand for English teachers, and the advantage of securing a job within the EU is that the UK is a member. This will give you some protection and should involve far less paperwork than if you applied to work further afield.

In China, you are more likely to find work in a private school, rather than the state schools system, as the latter is controlled by the Department of Education in Beijing.

Hong Kong is an obvious choice as it was once a British Colony and English is a second language for nearly everyone there. The added advantage for those with no Chinese language skills is that all the road signs, public transport and government information are in English as well as Chinese and most of the shops, agencies and essential services (such as police, doctors *etc*) employ English speakers.

There is also a daily English language newspaper, *The South China Morning Post* and it may well be worth checking their online jobs section for vacancies: **www.cpjobs.com/hk**

If you want to take your skills and use them in Japan you should check out **www.jet-uk.org**. This is the Japanese Government's website for promoting their scheme to improve foreign language teaching in schools. You do have to have a

Bachelor's degree to qualify though. The *Japan Times* (which is online) also lists job vacancies in English: **www.jobs.japantimes.jp**

There is a great demand for English speakers in Thailand and so if you are taking your gap in that country, and wish to earn money whilst there, TEFL could well be the answer, particularly as you will be unable to find work in a country where foreigners are forbidden from taking most unskilled occupations. The *Bangkok Post* lists job vacancies, including those for English teachers, in their online jobs section: **www.bangkokpost.net**

Teaching English in private lessons

If you decide to supplement your income in-country by giving private lessons, you can put notices in schools, colleges, newspapers and local shops but there are some basic safety precautions you should take:

1. Be careful how you word your ad — *eg* 'Young English girl offering English lessons' is likely to draw the wrong kind of attention.

2. If you arrange one-to-one tuition, don't go to your student's home until you've checked out how safe it would be.

visit: www.workaseason.com

3. Equally, if you're living alone, don't give classes at home until you've got to know your student.

4. Arrange classes in public, well-populated locations, which will also help as teaching aids (coffee bars, restaurants, shops, markets *etc*).

5. Make sure you're both clear about your fee (per hour) and when it should be paid (preferably these should both be put in writing).

Usually, you'll be inundated by friends of friends as word gets round there's an English person willing to give private lessons.

Cookery

Cooking jobs are available abroad as well as in the UK, particularly during the summer months. Gaining some cooking skills is a great way to boost your CV and opens up new possibilities.

Families will often look for a young person to help *eg* during the long summer months — animal/child-friendly and an ability to drive are good skills combinations along with basic cooking skills to provide all-round household support. Some families have holiday homes abroad and in the traditional English holiday locations so there can be a chance to get to know a new area.

You can also look at Ski Resorts or other holiday resorts. Most of these will need extra staff during peak seasons to help feed their guests. Mountain Cookery School not only gives you a week cookery course, but their graduates can go on to get a job within a resort.

Seasonal work in Europe

Working in Europe offers endless possibilities — from fruit picking to hospitality and tourism, leading nature trips to teaching English (for more on this see our TFFI section on the previous pages). Some non-EU members need work permits so you should check the regulations in the country you want to go to.

Companies offer a variety of roles working with children at locations across the UK, France and Spain for as little as 12 weeks, to a maximum of ten months with the option to return the following year.

Jobs on offer include children's group leaders, activity or watersports Instructors, French-speaking tour leaders or administrators and Spanish-speaking roles. Non-guest-facing roles include support team positions: catering assistants, chefs, drivers, retail, housekeeping and maintenance. Some roles do not require qualifications or previous experience — in fact there are opportunities for a comprehensive training programme including apprenticeships and coaching awards so you may even have the opportunity to gain an additional qualification for life at no cost to yourself.

To find other short-term jobs try:

www.oysterworldwide.com/projects/paid-work
www.transitionsabroad.com
www.pickingjobs.com

visit: www.workaseason.com

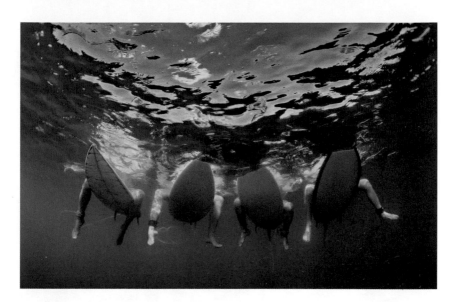

Seasonal work in North America

Probably the most popular seasonal job for gappers in the US is working on a summer camp. The US has strict regulations on visas and work permits but summer camps are a well-established way of working for a short time.

US work regulations are very complicated, and specific, and this is one time where it would help to use a placement organisation to help you through the paperwork, but make sure you check out the small print about pay, accommodation and expenses.

Each year thousands of young British and European students apply to join the summer camp programmes in the US as counsellors. Note, though, that programmes can only be arranged with specialist organisations.

If you don't fancy summer camp there are lots of other possibilities, from working on a ranch to cruise ship jobs. Have a look at: **www.jobmonkey.com**

It covers all sorts of work from fishing jobs in Alaska, to working on a ranch, to casino and gaming clubs and cruise work. But check with the US embassy to make sure you can get a visa or a work permit for the job you fancy. See: **www.usembassy.org.uk**

There are plenty of opportunities for working holidays in Canada, most commonly at hotels and restaurants, and ski and summer resorts. Canada has a limited supply of work permits. These are released once a year and run out very fast, so it's very important to plan ahead. "Canadian Immigration changed the application process for the International Experience Canada Working Holiday Program in late 2015. The new system requires candidates to complete a short application to enter a pool of candidates. Each candidate is given a reference number and then, a bit like a lottery, numbers are randomly selected by Immigration. Once a number has been selected, that candidate is invited to apply for the full work permit."

No company can truly guarantee you a work permit for Canada. Whether you are organising your own independent travel, or joining an organised programme, you will be responsible for making your own application. Our friends at Au Pair Ecosse,

advise those who wish to become an au pair in America that: "You will need proof of childcare experience, a police check, a DS2019 form and visa and insurance documentation." With this in mind, it's best to plan well ahead of time in case any of the checks end up taking longer than originally thought.

Seasonal work in Australia and New Zealand

Periods of working and travelling in Australia and New Zealand are a very popular option and you can do everything from fruit picking to helping Amnesty International. However, you don't have to stick to the traditional backpacker temporary work — fruit picking, bar work or call centres. If you have a trade, such as IT skills or a nursing qualification they're also good for finding work.

Australia has a well worked-out system to allow you to work and travel. It's called the working holiday visa (subclass 417). You can qualify for any specified work and UK passport holders can apply online. Specified work is work, whether paid or unpaid, in certain specified industries or postcodes — for more details have a look at: **www.immi.gov.au/visitors/working-holiday/417/specified-work.htm**

visit: www.workaseason.com

The main points are:

· You must be between 18 and 30.

· It costs around £210 (AU$440).

· You will also be required to have a health certificate before you apply for your visa.

What you can do:

· Enter Australia within 12 months of the visa being issued.

· Stay up to 12 months.

· Leave and re-enter Australia any number of times while the visa is valid.

· Work in Australia for up to six months with each employer.

· Study or train for up to four months.

The Australian working holiday visa is currently under review. They will be looking at potentially increasing the age limit from 30 to 35, as well as potentially introducing a working holiday income tax. We advise you check the government website for updates: **www.border.gov.au/Trav/Visa-1/417-**

Or call the High Commission in the UK:
Australian High Commission,
Australia House, Strand, London WC2B 4LA
Tel: 020 7379 4334
uk.embassy.gov.au

To find seasonal work try:
www.oysterworldwide.com/destinations/australia
www.visitoz.org
www.seasonalwork.com.au/index.bsp
www.workaboutaustralia.com.au

Successful applicants should allow about three weeks to find work, although it may

the gap-year guidebook 2018

well come quicker than that. The average rate of pay for temporary staff is at about A$15 to A$21 an hour, enabling a good standard of living that can help fund travels.

Joanna Burnet, of Visitoz, told us: "Our participants go to the job of their choice on their ninth day in Australia. Those searching for work in the cities should allow at least six weeks to find a job; those looking for fruit picking work should allow longer than that. A lot of people run out of money in these six or eight weeks and have to return home. It is always the best to book with an organisation that (a) guarantees you a soft landing in Australia and gets all your ready-to-work paperwork done for you and (b) guarantees a job."

New Zealand has a similar working visa scheme for either 12 or 23 months — and also a health certificate requirement. To qualify you must:

1. Usually be permanently living in the United Kingdom — this means you can be temporarily visiting another country when you lodge your application.

2. Have a British passport that's valid for at least three months after your planned departure from New Zealand.

3. Be at least 18 and not more than 30 years old.

4. Not bring children with you.

5. Hold a return ticket, or sufficient funds to purchase such a ticket.

6. Have a minimum of NZ$350 per month of stay in available funds (to meet your living costs while you're there).

visit: *www.workaseason.com*

7. Meet New Zealand's health and character requirements.

8. Satisfy the authorities that your main reason for going to New Zealand is to holiday, not work.

9. Not have been approved a visa permit under a Working Holiday Scheme before.

The regulations for British subjects are very clearly laid out on the NZ Government website:
www.immigration.govt.nz/migrant/stream/work/workingholiday/ unitedkingdomworkingholidayscheme.htm

And here are a few websites to check for seasonal work in New Zealand:

www.picknz.co.nz
www.seasonaljobs.co.nz
www.backpackerboard.co.nz/work_jobs/seasonal_jobs_new_zealand.php

Working holiday

A working holiday is exactly what it sounds like; a holiday that you fund by working. If you haven't been able to save up much money, or decided to take a holiday last minute this might be the way to go. Once you get to your chosen destination, the next step is to find a job in order to fund your stay. If this sounds a bit nerveracking, there are companies that will help you find a job.

There are many benefits to a company helping you find a job abroad. This includes that many of them have strong relationships with employers in the resorts that they operate in and year on year continue to help provide them with seasonal or long-term employees. They are familiar with them and know very well how the process works so can guide you through it.

One of the main benefits of a working holiday is that the upfront costs are very small. You will need to book flights and travel as well as your first few weeks accomodation (until your first pay check arrives), but from then on you will be living off your wages to fund your activities.

149

Applying for a working holiday visa

Individuals can apply for working holiday visas themselves or use an agency to prepare the paperwork for you. UK agencies for this include:

www.oysterworldwide.com
www.visabureau.com
www.realgap.com

If you are not British you should check the websites to see if your citizenship allows you to obtain the visa.

The sort of work that you can obtain is not restricted, but in most cases you are only allowed to work for the same employer for six months. The idea is that it is a holiday being supported by working, rather than work being the prime reason for travelling.

Please see the directory pages starting on page 305 for information on companies and organisations offering working abroad opportunities.

Volunteering
abroad

6 Volunteering abroad

Pod Volunteer

Voluntary work abroad can be one of the most rewarding ways to spend all, or part, of your gap-year. You could find yourself working with people living in unbelievable poverty, disease or hunger. It can be a humbling and hugely enriching experience and it can make you question all the things you've taken for granted in your life. It's no exaggeration to say it can be life-changing.

Some people who have done it have ended up changing their planned course of study at university or even their whole career plan. Year Out Group's members, who are all gap providers, report that volunteering is the top gap choice among all age groups and had risen by 20% in the last full year for which they carried out research.

Teaching and working with children are the most popular options and interestingly women gappers outnumber men, and women are also more likely to choose volunteering and expeditions rather than courses or cultural exchanges.

Who goes volunteering?

It's clear from speaking to gap providers that students still make up most of the market, but the picture is changing.

Our friends from African Conservation Experience told us: "We have definitely seen an increase of more mature volunteers. When African Conservation Experience started in 1999, it worked almost 100% with 'traditional' gap-year students — aged 17 or 18, and students during their university career. Now about 25% of our travellers are professionals aged 25+, including quite a few retirees!"

visit: www.gap-year.com

Why volunteer?

We think our friends at Kaya Responsible Travel answer this question rather well:

"Justifying you travels for your CV: Whether you are a student or a career-breaker, when employers see a gap in your CV, they will want to know what you did with that time. Demonstrating that you participated in a structured program that contributed something tangible is seen in a positive light and enables you to talk about your experiences in the context of certain soft-skills than enhance your employability

"To experience greater cultural immersion: Travellers often struggle to experience the local perspective on their visits. A volunteer program working alongside local people within the community opens a window to real life in a country that is otherwise difficult to achieve.

"To make you a better global citizen: Volunteers working on any project will learn about the issues and challenges that are encountered in tackling that particular problem. Having a local context on global issues gives you a real perspective which will hopefully influence your opinions and behaviours back at home in the future.

"To meet new people: Volunteering is the best way that a single traveller can ensure they keep busy and meet people — both locals and other volunteers from around the world. And volunteering generally doesn't incur any of those single-person supplements either!

"Because there is so much to learn: All the best volunteers tell how much they learned from their experience. Sometimes it's language skills, from Spanish and Thai to Siswati; or a practical skill — like building a clean-burning stove, or tracking an elephant; sometimes it is a soft skill — like how to control a class of children, or present to a community group; and sometimes it is learning something about themselves — like how they don't need to be connected to the internet at all times, or how easy they found to connect with someone so different to themselves. It is true that as a volunteer you gain as much as you give when you join a great project."

Our friends at Richmond Vale Academy say that you should volunteer "because even if you search the internet and watch TV with your eyes wide open, you never get the bigger picture of the world before you leave your own country — getting out of your comfort zone and meeting reality is the best teacher in the world."

On an organised voluntary project you often live amongst the local community and tend to get closer to daily life than you do as an independent traveller. By taking part in an organised voluntary work project you can learn about a different culture, meet new people and learn to communicate with people who may not understand your way of life, let alone your language.

Our friends at Pod Volunteer tell us that: "Volunteering overseas is a wonderful opportunity to travel, experience new cultures, make lifelong friends all the while making a real a difference! Volunteering overseas enables you to experience new cultures and fully immerse yourself in them, make lifelong friends with likeminded people all whilst doing something good and adding to your CV!"

You will come away with an amazing sense of achievement and (hopefully) pride in what you have done. Career breakers have also found that a volunteer gap has not only been a satisfying experience but given them new ideas and attitudes too. A structured volunteer placement can also give a new dimension to the skills you can highlight on your CV.

Change your view, go somewhere new

Looking for your next step? We need volunteers aged 17-24 to...

- Work overseas at the heart of sustainable projects that create lasting change
- Live with local families in remote communities
- Be submerged in biodiverse landscapes and test their limits on an adventure trek
- Be part of an international team and make lifelong friendships

Raleigh Expedition is a fantastic way to develop skills for future career or education and see new parts of the world.

Apply now for Expeditions in Nepal, Malaysian Borneo, Nicaragua & Costa Rica and Tanzania.

youth · energy · change

raleighinternational.org/expedition

Kaya Responsible Travel

Being realistic, voluntary work can be tough. You may be out in the middle of nowhere, with no western influence to be seen; food, language, accommodation — the entire culture is likely to be totally different from what you're used to and there might not be many English speakers around: so you may have to cope with culture shock or feeling lonely, isolated and homesick at first, but if you stick with it you'll usually find those feelings will go as you get more involved in what you're doing.

Are you going for the right reasons?

Sounds like a silly question, doesn't it? But volunteering requires people who really want to make an impact and so something to help others, rather than those interested in a round-the-world jolly.

Our friends at Kaya Responsible Travel told us: "The most important thing to think about when you volunteer is not how much you can achieve, or how much you can give, but rather, how much can I learn from those with whom I will work. Those who come open and eager to learn about their project, the local culture and the work they are joining become the people who can make the greatest difference on a project."

Stefan Wathan of the Year Out Group agrees the right attitude is very important: "Volunteers also need to question their own motives and expectations. Yes, you will learn and develop but you are volunteering primarily to support a worthwhile cause so it's important to consider if you are prepared to put in the time and effort to really make a difference. There is a danger that you simply use a small piece of volunteering to shore up a CV. Short programmes (one week or so) are available and over the course of a year tens or hundreds of volunteers can have a big impact but make sure you ask what this greater benefit is and perhaps focus on something that will count as a genuinely worthwhile experience."

RICHMOND VALE
ACADEMY

Richmond Vale Academy, Saint David, Chateaubelair Post Office, Saint Vincent And The Grenadines
T: +1 784 458 2255
E: info@richmondvale.org   W: www.richmondvale.org

Become a Climate Activist in the Caribbean

There is no doubt that climate change is hitting poor countries the hardest.

Saint Vincent is one of the poorer island nations in the Caribbean and one of the world's most disaster prone countries.

Global warming means longer periods without rain. Only 7% of the farms in St. Vincent have irrigation systems. Water reservoirs need to be built and water conservation measures need to be taken to secure food production in the future.

Climate change means more flooding and hurricanes. In 2013 extreme weather hit St. Vincent and left thousands without public water, with heavy destruction of roads, bridges and houses and left hundreds in shelters. The damages from 2014 disasters alone equaled 17% of the small developing island nation's GDP.

Climate activists with Richmond Vale Academy stand side-by-side with the poor and plant trees to prevent landslides, keep rivers and drains clear to prevent flooding, start organic home gardens to promote food security and teach people how to be more prepared for climate change.

Join a 6 month intensive program with studies, courses and actions to make the small island nation of St. Vincent and the Grenadines ready for climate change meaning energy, food and disaster secure.

Study and Teach Organic and Perma Culture techniques * Organize Tree planting Campaigns * Stop Pollution * Protect Biodiversity * Create Organic Homegardens with families.

Experience community living, cooking, cleaning, harvesting food, garden farming and develop skills needed to become a self-sufficient leader who can do anything he or she puts her mind to. Train to become an environmental activist who is able to take a stand to the future of this world.

The volunteers come from all over the world with different ages and background ranging students taking a gap-year, environmental engineers, lawyers, carpenters etc.

my gap-year
Malte

I'm going to keep it short, but it will have everything you would want to know about the 6 months I spent with Richmond Vale Academy (RVA).

My English and my ability to understand other people grew immensely, I also got to make so many new friends and it really was life-changing.

Before I went to RVA, I was lost with what I should do with my life, even though I had plenty of opportunities.

Being at RVA and having my teammates with me for 6 months opened my eyes in many ways. Being almost 18 by the time I arrived, I was still a child in many ways. I didn't really understand what it meant to work as a team, to work together on a big project, to share work and duties and to communicate and rely on one another.

Through the day-to-day interactions with my team and the school teacher, I learned a lot about being a responsible adult. I now can enjoy life more than ever, since I see so many things in my everyday life that I never really appreciated before.

Our team helped the local community a lot and we created many bonds and friendships. It made me really happy to see that my work was appreciated.

I honestly wish many more young people would join some international volunteer projects to experience another side of life. It is an invaluable experience that everyone should have. It helps them and it helps you.

In my point of view, my team got to experience how to build up relationships and trust, how to make new projects and encourage others to continue our work.

I hope whoever is reading this can feel the happy memories and feelings I put into this.

I can't wait to visit RVA again!

For more information on Richmond Vale Academy, see their advert on the opposite page

Pod Volunteer

What would you like to do?

There are a huge amount of options, as you'll see in this chapter and the directory section, so you need to make sure you find the best fit for you. All of the companies we speak to come back with the same advice: make sure you do your research!

Our friends at Kaya Volunteer gave us this advice: "There are many options open to gappers who want to volunteer. Within community settings there are projects focussed on aspects of education, women's empowerment, sports development, building, childcare, entrepreneurship, skills development, communications and fundraising, to name a few. Then for those interested in issues of conservation there is work researching and protecting forests, savannahs and marine areas, supporting sustainable agriculture, and working with animals both in sanctuaries and in the wild. Identifying a project that you have an interest in is very important to ensure you really enjoy and commit to the work at hand.

"The most popular option depends on that person's personal preferences, and what is right for one person might be wrong for another. We interview each and every volunteer to make sure they are matched with a placement that suits their interests. Some people prefer outdoor work, working with animals or something in a rural location. The most popular placements for these people will be different to those for people who want to work in a community or prefer an urban environment, for

A Broader View Volunteers, 236 Glen Place, Elkins Park PA 19027 USA
T: +1 215 780 1845
E: volunteers@abroaderview.org   W: www.abroaderview.org

Volunteer Abroad with A Broader View Volunteers, a highly rated USA based non-profit organization with over 10 years' experience specializing in volunteer travel, internship abroad and Gap Year programs.

With ABV you can confidently travel with a purpose by participating in one of our 245 worthwhile service abroad projects.

Volunteer abroad programs are available in Latin America, Asia and Africa.

We offer overseas voluntary work & study abroad placements including:

- Medical, Nurse, Dental Program
- Orphanage, Child Care
- Sea Turtles Conservation
- Teaching

and much more

With A Broader View Volunteers:

- You select your own project start and end dates.
- You decide the length of your commitment
- You become part of the ABV network of international volunteers
- You can tax deduct your program expenses*

Our USA based non-profit organization was founded in 2007. With a decade of experience, A Broader View specializes in affordable, safe, quality volunteer travel programs worldwide.

Travel with us and gain a broader view of the world!

Reef Conservation International (ReefCI)

example. It is important to find a project that is right for you, in order for you to be a useful volunteer for that project and ensure you have a good experience. A happy volunteer who genuinely cares about the issues they are working with always works harder and contributes more to the work at hand!"

Independent or go with an organisation?

Quite often people think that whilst going with a large organisation might be the easy option but comes with an inflated price tag. This is not always the case, organisations will know the local area better. They will know the most breathtaking sights, the cheapest hostels and the tastiest restaurants (if there are any!). Our friends at The Leap give us this advice to help you decide if you can go it alone, or it an organisation is more suitable:

"Friends. All veteran travellers will say 'you'll meet loads of people when you travel' which is very true and travellers really are a friendly, chatty bunch but it's one to think about... how comfortable would you be with arriving in a hostel and sparking up conversation with total strangers? If you think 'not easy', then look at an organisation where you can join a team of 'ready-made-friends'... it'll still be a bunch of total strangers BUT they are all on the same page and as keen to make friends as you are.

"Adventure. Obviously you want to explore, get the adrenaline pumping and create a repertoire of life changing stories to keep your friends on their toes. White-water rafting, bungee jumping, mountain biking, 4x4 driving all spring to mind and readily available to those travelling independently or with an organisation. But what if you want to do a bit more adventure which involves heading way off the beaten track? Hunting out with a local tribe in the Amazon, tracking endangered rhino through the bush? This is best accessed if you go with an organisation who have the contacts and logistics in place to make it happen.

"Arriving in a country and thinking you want to venture off into the wilderness will take a lot of planning, dedication and luck. Of course it's possible but how much of a challenge do you want? If you have booked the project from home and its way off the beaten track then you need to know that you will be able to cope with the tough logistics in getting there. All possible — just consider your limitations.

"Quality of Project Work. Research is key here to work out the quality of projects; their hosts, whether the communities actually need your help, that they are well organised *etc.*

"Remember you get what you pay for in life and it is no different when looking at volunteering. All projects will involve you having to pay for the privilege as you have to cover your food, accommodation, project materials and transport. The Year Out Group or American Gap Association are good places to start for reputable feedback as they complete in depth studies on the quality of their member's projects.

"Safety. This is a topic for the whole family to consider. When you venture off, how are you going to communicate with home, how relaxed are your parents and if you get into trouble who is going to help?

"Cost per day. You will undoubtedly spend more per day via an organisation, but you'll be surprised that it's not a lot more than travelling independently when you drill down."

Current trends

The most popular voluntary work activity is working as a teacher or teaching assistant. Teaching placements may include sports coaching, teaching assistants, pastoral care outside the classroom or taking a class.

Voluntary work on community and conservation projects also remain popular. Community projects, such as building a school room or a dam, vary in type and length and tend to be done in teams and be of shorter duration than teaching or caring placements.

the gap-year guidebook 2018

Reef Conservation International (ReefCI), Placencia, Belize
T: +1 513 334 9393
E: anthony@reefci.com   W: www.reefci.com

© FELKER FILMS

Feel the thrill of swimming with a whale shark, the excitement of spearing the invasive lionfish, and the satisfaction in helping the marine environment. Reef Conservation International (ReefCI) offers an all-inclusive diving and marine conservation gap-year experience on a private Caribbean island in Belize. ReefCI trips are a unique opportunity to protect the reef ecosystem by directly participating in our ongoing marine conservation projects! The diving is incredible and the conservation work we do is meaningful!

ReefCI is an exceptional opportunity to learn about coral reefs and marine species and to help protect and conserve this precious resource while having a fun gap year adventure. Our trips are for both certified divers and those who wish to become certified. We certify new divers on the island, so everyone contributes regardless of their background and experience. The majority of people who volunteer with us are passionate about coral reefs, the ocean, and marine life and want to do their part in protecting it. Our volunteers are the change they wish to see in the world and ReefCI makes that possible.

ReefCI is a non-profit marine conservation organization and has been protecting our oceans for over 12 years. ReefCI is a fantastic way to experience real world conservation efforts, while having an unforgettable journey! You will get hands-on experience in marine conservation work and gain real world insight on what it is like to work in the field of marine conservation.

Come to our private Caribbean island for a gap-year experience of a lifetime! Reserve your spot at www.reefci.com.

The most popular destinations for volunteering include South Africa, Tanzania, Thailand, Cambodia, Madagascar, Nepal and India. You will have read a little more about these locations — and the Year Out Group's explanation of their popularity — in **Chapter 1**.

Our friends at Kaya Responsible Travel told us: "Countries go through phases of popularity, due to news stories, changing perceptions of a location and other factors. Ebola affected the popularity of Africa for some time, and that has now moved on, with projects in Southern African countries now very popular again. We work in two locations that were affected by recent natural disasters — The Philippines was badly hit by Hurricane Hiyan in 2013 and Nepal experienced devastating earthquakes in 2015 — the attention these received in the news make these two of our most popular destinations to this day. But long-term development is as important as immediate aid and the work we are involved with, even at these locations, work to long-term sustainable goals."

One exciting new development — and one that comes highly recommended by the NUS — is the government-funded International Citizen Service (ICS) programme. **www.volunteerics.org**

It seeks to put young people at the forefront of the fight against global poverty and over the next three years 7,000 young people from the UK will work in partnership with young people in developing countries, on projects to fight poverty where help is needed the most.

The scheme follows a hugely successful pilot year and aims to offer a transformative experience for 18-25 year olds. The programme is designed to deliver three outcomes: to have a real and lasting development impact on sustainable development projects; to help the volunteers both from the UK and from developing countries learn key life skills such as teamwork, leadership, communication and project planning: and to instil in these volunteers a life-long commitment to development and to becoming active citizens, engaged in their communities back in the UK.

my
gap-year
Amanda

Feel the thrill of swimming with a whale shark, the excitement of spearing the invasive lionfish, and the satisfaction in helping the marine environment with Reef Conservation International...

I was looking for something a bit different than the standard gap-year experience. I love the ocean and love volunteering with non-profits around the world. This was my 5th placement — I have done everything from animal conservation in Africa to inner city green initiatives in South America. This was without a doubt my most rewarding and favourite experience to date. ReefCI is a unique non-profit marine conservation organization that enables volunteers like me to help in conservation efforts in protecting the ocean and coral reefs from invasive species that are devastating the reef.

I learned all about the invasive lionfish and how they have no natural predators in the Caribbean and how they decimate the native reef ecosystems. It was so fun and rewarding to spear and remove these invasive intruders from the reef! And then we eat! Lionfish is so delicious — baked, fried, ceviche — it was all so good. Linda is the best authentic Mayan cook in all of Belize.

I was a complete dive novice before my ReefCI experience. Prior to my trip, I knew absolutely nothing about diving. I have always loved the ocean and couldn't pass on this opportunity to learn to dive in the Caribbean on a private island. I was a bit nervous getting my PADI Open Water Certification but I am so thrilled I did it. It was everything I had ever hoped for. The ReefCI instructors were great: I had a bit of anxiety but they let me go at my own pace — a special shout out to Frank!

Diving is like exploring another planet right here on earth. Seeing all the biodiversity and scope of life opened a whole new world to me. Thanks ReefCI for all the great memories, the conservation work you do on the reef is inspiring. It was a truly unforgettable four-week experience.

For more information about Reef CI, see their advert on page 164

Only you can decide what's most important to you, it depends on whether you're more into plants, animals and the environment, in which case you'd be happier on a conservation project. If you're a people person you might do something that helps disadvantaged people, whether they're children, adults, and disabled or able-bodied.

Whichever you feel is right for you there's a huge range of companies and types of voluntary placements to choose from.

Even if you are straight from school or university and haven't yet had much experience of work-related skills you shouldn't underestimate the skills and qualities you may have, and take for granted, that can be far less accessible to disadvantaged people in places where such things as access to education or to communications are not universally available.

How much time do you want to spend?

This is about how committed a volunteer you want to be. Would you feel more satisfied spending two weeks on a building project providing homes for people displaced by a natural disaster? Or are you the kind of person who wants to get stuck into a long-term project, where the results you see will be more gradual?

Because voluntary work is so popular with gappers, commercial companies offering volunteering packages exist alongside the more traditional not-for-profit organisations and the idealism associated with voluntary work, though still there, has come under some commercial pressure.

Kaya Responsible Travel

AFRICAN CONSERVATION EXPERIENCE

Make a difference as a conservation volunteer

Have you dreamt of tracking predators through the bush, working alongside a wildlife vet, observing dolphins or hand rearing rhino?
Come and share our passion for Africa!

"Learning about conservation in Africa I gained a lot of self confidence and knowledge while having an amazing time" **Rachel Bragg**

"I got to work with such a wide variety of animals and got loads of hands on experience that will no doubt be valuable at vet school." **Kirsty Giles**

OUR PROJECTS

- Shadow an experienced **Wildlife Vet** in South Africa
- Care for injured and orphaned animals at a **Wildlife Rehabilitation Centre**
- Assist **Game Rangers** and **Field Researchers** with wildlife surveys, reserve patrols and game capture and relocation
- Study dolphins and whales on **Marine Conservation Projects**

Info@ConservationAfrica.net

www.conservationafrica.net

T. +44 (0)1454 269 182

A.C.E RESPONSIBLE TRAVEL

HOW DOES IT WORK?

Placements are available throughout the year and our team will help you choose the right project. You can volunteer for only 2 weeks or up to 3 months - it's up to you. Placement costs start from £2,600, including return flights from London, transfers, accommodation, meals, in-country support and the financial contributions to the projects.

WORK WITH THE WILDLIFE

Some companies offer two to four-week holidays combined with some voluntary work, but equally there are many organisations still committed to the idealism of volunteering, offering placements from a few months to up a year or more.

However, you may not want (or be able) to offer more than a few weeks or months of your time, so the combined holiday/short volunteering option might be for you. There's no point in committing yourself to a whole year only to find that, after a few weeks, you hate it and want to go home early. The two to four-week option may also be a good 'taster' experience to help you decide whether to commit to something more long-term.

Our friends at Kaya Responsible travel tell us more: "You can participate in volunteering for any length of time. Some projects have longer minimum periods, but most Kaya projects have a 2 week minimum — or 4 weeks minimum for internships. However, it is important to remember that the longer you stay the more you will learn and the better relationships you can develop, which means the more you can do (the more you will be trusted to do) and the more you can help your project achieve. 6-8 weeks is the average time our participants sign up for, but the most consistent feedback we receive, across all projects, is that people wish they had stayed longer."

So, it's a good idea to be honest with yourself about what you want — there's nothing wrong with wanting to travel and have a good time. But, whatever you choose, make sure you are clear about what you will be doing *before* you sign up and part with your money.

Kaya Responsible Travel, Arch 30, North Campus,
Sackville Street, Manchester M60 1QD UK
T: +44 (0) 161 870 6212
E: info@kayavolunteer.com   W: www.kayavolunteer.com

Africa

Botswana	Namibia	Zambia
Ghana	South Africa	Zimbabwe
Kenya	Swaziland	
Mozambique	Tanzania	

Asia-Pacific

Australia	Borneo	Philippines
Cambodia	India	Thailand
China	Indonesia	
New Zealand	Nepal	

Latin America

Belize	Costa Rica
Bolivia	Ecuador
Brazil	Peru

Proud gold medal winners of "The Best Volunteering Organisation", at the British Youth Travel Awards 2016 and 2014 (and awarded silver in 2015 and 2013).

For quality, ethical volunteer and internship placements that are individually matched to make the most of your skills and interest, Kaya Responsible Travel is a leader in the field.

With over 150 projects in 28 countries across Asia, Africa and Latin America, Kaya's expert team of advisors can identify an immersive, supported and sustainable project that is the right fit for you.

Sign up to projects from 2 weeks to 12 months, working with local people on issues affecting their communities and environments.

Kaya conservation initiatives include wildlife sanctuaries, breeding programs and habitat research, marine conservation on coral reefs, fair trade sustainable agriculture, reforestation and many other projects improving and protecting the environment and animals of the world.

Community initiatives include work with English teaching, child-care, sports development, women's empowerment, building, cultural restoration, all areas of health, therapy and medical work and much more.

Kaya have volunteers from 16-80, from all around the world, joining projects all year-round, travelling as individuals, with friends, groups and even as a family, always matching each volunteer to a project that is right for them.

Whether you join a volunteer or an internship placement, the structured program offered by are an excellent way to help build your CV, while taking part in something truly worthwhile.

To make your gap travels really count, Kaya offer you a world of choice, so you can make a world of difference on your journey, whilst discovering the real cultures in the heart of local communities. Contact the Kaya Placement Advice team to find the best project for you.

my
gap-year
Lawrence

Here is a short interview with one of our volunteers about his experience volunteering abroad in Swaziland on our Help Build Family Homes project

What have you achieved?

· Helped World Challenge with giving water access to a community

· Built pit latrines for a pre-school and bases for jojo stands (giant water butts)

What have you learnt?

· My Siswati is very good (Sarah the Project/Volunteer Manager also confirmed that Lawrence has done very well)

· It has been an eye opening experience

· I was independent before but I have learnt to be more independent especially with budgeting money for food and activities

What went well?

· I had no culture shock

· Orientation when I arrived put me at ease. I was feeling scared on the plane as I had never been away by myself but the day after I arrived I just thought, "everything is sweet!"

What has been the highlight?

· Learning about the local culture from the local building project manager who made it come to life, not just gave me the information.

· I have enjoyed working in the rural areas.

· It has been great meeting other volunteers and making friends from all around the world.

What were your motives for extending?

· I wanted to spend more time here and get more out of the experience.

What tips would you give to other people volunteering abroad?

· Look after yourself but go out and get involved.

· Try to learn the language as it is helpful and goes a long way when building relationships with local people.

To find out more about Kaya Responsible Travel, see their advert on the opposite page

Kidogo Adventure
T: +44 (0)7725 996434
E: info@kidogoadventure.com   W: www.kidogoadventure.com

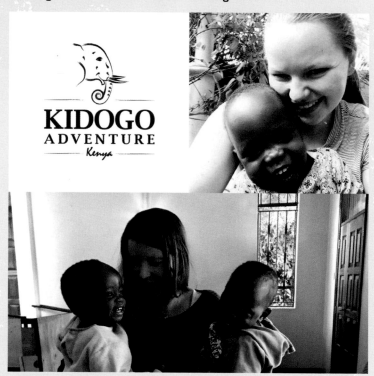

Kidogo Adventure is a small, personally-run organisation that enables travel and adventure through volunteering. The projects are based in Kenya and are currently child-focused (baby homes, orphanages and schools).

Placements are short-term with a typical duration of two weeks. As well as volunteering, you will get the chance to see a bit more of the country through visits to the elephant orphanage, the giraffe centre and other local attractions. Also included is a short safari.

To make your trip run as smoothly as possible, Kidogo Adventure will organise all aspects of your stay including accommodation, food, in-country transport, activities, a short safari - and of course your volunteer placement.

Come and join us for your own adventure - please visit our website (www.kidogoadventure.com) or contact us on info@kidogoadventure.com for more information. Karibu Kenya!

When to start applying

Applications can close early, particularly for expeditions and conservation projects needing complex funding or for those tied in with international government programmes. If you'd like to go on one of these projects, planning should start about a year ahead, usually in the autumn term of the academic year.

Our friends at Kaya Responsible Travel also agree that it is best to book well in advance. Not only are the flights cheaper, but you are more likely to get your first choice of placement. Some companies can cater for those who book last minute, but you might not get exactly what you wanted.

Others can be taken up at very short notice. In fact, some organisations can take in applications during the August period and book you on a project that starts in September. If you don't have much time before your gap starts (maybe you didn't get the grades you expected, or you've made a last-minute decision to defer university for a year, or your company has offered you a sabbatical or made you redundant) it is always worth contacting a voluntary organisation about a project you're interested in. They may have had a last-minute cancellation.

The application process

As more people are becoming motivated by the almost daily media reports on poverty in the developing world and on various global threats to the planet's climate, ecology and environment, to go out and do something, the competition for places can be fierce. Companies can afford to be picky — you may find you have to prove to them that you should be selected to go before they will accept your money!

They have a point. Increasingly NGOs and volunteers are trying to make sure both sides benefit from the experience, so placement organisations put a lot of effort into checking and briefing as well as getting you out there and providing in-country support. If you can't stick it, everyone loses out — including the person who could have been chosen instead of you.

Intrepid Travel

Pod Volunteer

Our friends from African Conservation Experience told us about their application process: "We have an online application form, which is usually the starting point. The application is not competitive though: There is no deadline for submitting the form and we don't compare applicants with each other. The form is far more important for getting to know a potential gapper a little bit, as we then have a personal chat with them. In this chat we talk in detail about the projects they are interested in and together we make a plan as to which project — or projects — are the best choice, when they want to go and how much time they will spend there. Only then do we set up a placement and ask the traveller to commit to their trip."

What is the cost?

It varies hugely — some companies just expect you to pay for the air fare — others expect you to raise thousands of pounds for funding. It can be hard to combine raising money with studying for A-levels or with work, but there are a lot of ways to do it.

As usual, the earlier you start, the easier it will be. The organisation that you go with should be able to give advice, but options include organising sponsored events, writing to companies or trusts asking for sponsorship, car boot sales, or even just getting a job and saving what you can.

Stefan Wathan from The Year Out Group says that "some people will question why volunteering placements cost anything at all and often as much as other programmes. Quite simply, volunteering is never cost free. In the UK many charities will spend huge sums of money supporting and developing their volunteer base

visit: www.gap-year.com

but they don't charge the volunteer. Overseas, the organisations that require volunteer support have very little funding, so some of the fee (or donation) will be used to help them administer and manage their volunteer programmes and some of the fee will cover the cost of a UK based organisation managing your recruitment, training and covering the costs of insurance and staff."

If approached, many local newspapers will do a short article about your plan if it's interesting enough — but it's better to ask them during the quieter news spells, like the summer holiday months, when they'll be more likely to welcome an additional story.

The last resort is to go cap-in-hand to your parents, either for a loan or a gift, but this can be unsatisfying and they may simply not be able to afford it. If your parents or relatives do want to help, you could ask for useful items for Christmas or birthday presents — like a rucksack.

Before you opt for a what seems like a bargain gap-year make sure you know what is covered and what isn't. African Conservation Experience gives us this advice: "There are no doubt cheaper options out there, but I would urge volunteers to consider both how much support they will receive (Will they be met at the airport? Do they need to find their own way to a project? Is there a 'real person' to look after them in country or just an emergency phone number?) — and how much support the money they pay can generate for the project. If you only pay $200 / week, and that includes food and accommodation, how much funding can be left over for conservation or community development?"

Stefan Wathan from The Year Out Group advises that: "Organisations should be able to give you a breakdown of where your money goes and its worth comparing profit making companies, with not-for-profits and charities to see how they differ. Don't assume one type of company is 'better' than any other, do your research and find a company that speaks to similar values as yours and again, don't just rely on impressive looking websites."

Career breakers will have different considerations. There's more on this in **Chapter 3 - Career breaks and older travellers**, but if you work for a large organisation it's worth asking whether they have any links to projects, or run their own charitable foundation, which might offer placements to employees.

What to expect

Placements range from a couple of weeks to a whole academic year, but most provide only free accommodation and food — a very few provide pocket money. You'll need to be resourceful, be able to teach, build, inspire confidence, communicate and share what you know. Physical and mental fitness, staying power and the ability to get on with people are essential.

Are there ethical concerns?

The debate continues about the ethics of volunteering, and covers a variety of issues:

· Is it environmentally sustainable?

· Does it really benefit the people or is it creating a dependency culture?

· What's the 'benefit balance' between volunteer satisfaction and the community being helped?

The 'volunteering industry' has in the past few years become just that — an industry, with different organisations giving different levels of importance to the benefit for the projects, the experience for the volunteer and the profit for the company.

Our friends at Pod Volunteer tell us: "Unfortunately not all volunteering companies are set out with the right intensions and may have more negative impacts than positive on the host community, so it is important that you research to ensure that your chosen project is ethical and has the right intensions."

Ethical volunteering is incredibly important. Here are a few things to watch out for:

· Unethical organisations just wanting to make a profit out of disadvantaged people/ children in need (example: 'fake' orphanages that just exist to take money from volunteers)

· Wildlife breeding programs in Africa that are actually selling their offspring into canned hunting

· 'Fake' animal protection efforts, where so-called endangered animals are put in cages so that volunteers can pet them *etc.*

· Organisations not giving enough money to the institutions they work in, compared to the profit they make

Dont let this put you off. "Volunteering really can make a difference," says African Conservation Experience. It is a great way to generate funding, awareness and ongoing global support for a huge number of very worthwhile projects. A lot of initiatives would not exist without the support of international volunteer travellers."

Tourism Concern is an independent, non-industry based UK charity that fights exploitation in tourism. They believe that it is vitally important for volunteer organisations to demonstrate that they have attained a recognised level of responsibility in the way they recruit volunteers, find placements and manage the volunteering process, and they have developed the Gap-year and International Volunteering Standard (GIVS). International Volunteering Organisations in the UK are now being assessed under GIVS and Tourism Concern advises you look for the GIVS kitemark in order to ensure that you sign up to worthwhile and rewarding placements.

GIVS assesses organisations on eight key principles:

1. Purpose: achievable objectives that have been identified by host partners and communities.

2. Marketing: marketing and imagery that is consistent with good practice.

3. Recruitment: fair, consistent and transparent recruitment procedures.

4. Pre-placement Information: clear and accurate information on the sending organisation, their partners, programmes and volunteer placements.

5. Pre-placement training: appropriate preparation, training and induction.

6. Volunteer support: ongoing support appropriate to the placement and volunteer.

7. Risk Management: ensuring protection, safety and well being of volunteers and those they work with.

8. Monitoring & Evaluation: ongoing monitoring and evaluation in order to improve performance and ensure work remains relevant.

For more information go to **www.tourismconcern.org.uk**

How to be an Ethical Traveller

Here are some easy steps to follow from Tourism Concern to help you be a more ethical traveller — and your experience will be richer as a result.

1. Your holiday, their home: your travel destination is a place where people live; people who may have different values and sensibilities to your own. Opening your mind to new cultures and traditions is part of the joy and adventure of travelling. Be respectful but don't be afraid to ask questions. Getting to know the local people is the best way of learning about a place.

2. Switch off and relax: whilst your visit may provide some economic benefits to local people, it can also use up scarce natural resources. Water is in short supply in many tourist destinations, and one tourist can use as much water in one day as 100 people in a developing country would in a year. Keep this in mind when using water or electricity on holiday.

3. Keep children smiling: it is best never to give anything directly to children (not even sweets) as they may think there is no need to go to school (and hassle other travellers). Donating to a local school, hospital or orphanage will have a lasting impact. Tragically more than one million children are sexually abused by tourists every year. Help protect children by telling your hotel manager if you see something suspicious.

visit: www.gap-year.com

4. Haggle with humour: try to keep your money in the local economy; eat in local restaurants, drink local beer or fruit juice rather than imported brands and pay a fair price when you're buying souvenirs and handicrafts. Bargaining can be great fun, so haggle with humour — but remember that if you bargain too hard, sheer poverty might make a craftsman accept a poor price just so that he can feed his family that day. Pay what something is worth to you.

5. Support Tourism Concern: Tourism Concern — 'the voice of ethical tourism' — is a UK charity that campaigns against exploitation in tourism and for fairly traded and ethical forms of tourism. The website has a wealth of information on action you can take to avoid guilt trips. **www.tourismconcern.org.uk**

Our friends at Kaya Responsible Travel also advise the following to be a more ethical traveller: "For community initiatives, ask your program provider how the initiative they are offering is set up, whether it is led by local people, how it is sustainable and what support is provided to the participants and the organization when they receive volunteers. Good organisations should be able to easily provide information about these issues. For wildlife projects, ask about the long-term goals and general operations of the initiative. Also whether captive animals work towards long-term release. And for health projects challenge the understanding of medical ethics — if you are told that you can participate in treatment which you are unqualified for, stay well-away!"

Some other points worth emphasising

Big organisation or small specialist? You might feel safer going with a big voluntary organisation because they should be able to offer help in a nasty situation. Experience is certainly important where organisations are concerned. But often a small, specialist organisation is more knowledgeable about a country, a school or other destination.

Size and status have little bearing on competence. A charity can be more efficient than a commercial company. Conversely a commercial company can show more sensitivity than a charity.

There are few general rules — talk to someone who's been with the organisation you're interested in. Organisations vary as to how much back up they offer volunteers, from virtually holding your hand throughout your stay and even after you come back, to the 'sink or swim' method.

You need to know yourself if you're going to get the most out of your volunteering gap. If you feel patronised at the slightest hint of advice then you might get annoyed with too much interference from the organisation.

Though do bear in mind that they probably know more than you do about the placement, what sort of vaccinations you're going to need, what will be useful to take with you, and how to get the necessary visas and permits. Equally if you're shy or nervous it might be as well to go with an organisation that sends volunteers in pairs or groups. There's nothing wrong with either type of placement — it's about choosing what's right for you.

Talk to a few organisations before you decide which one to go with — and, probably even more useful, talk to some previous volunteers. They'll be able to tell you what it's really like; don't just ask them if they enjoyed it, get them to describe what they did, what they liked and why, what they didn't like and what they'd do differently.

Pod Volunteer, 3 Crescent Terrace, Cheltenham GL50 3PE UK
T: +44 (0)1242 241 181
E: info@podvolunteer.org   W: www.podvolunteer.org

Awarded Best Volunteering Organisation, we have been arranging ethical and inspiring volunteer placements around the world since 2001. Whether you want to want to help care for elephants, be part of ground-breaking research, learn to dive and contribute to reef conservation or support children and education around the world, then Pod Volunteer has the project for you! Volunteers are needed for 1-12 weeks to help work with animal care and rescue, conservation initiatives, building projects and disadvantaged children and communities in Belize, Cambodia, Costa Rica, Ghana, India, Madagascar, Namibia, Nepal, Peru, South Africa and Thailand.

We are a leading non-profit organisation working with long term projects that we visit personally so we can answer any questions you might have about them. We are focussed exclusively on overseas volunteering, it's all we do and what we are passionate about and we're driven by the needs of the projects we support. We only offer sustainable volunteering projects that have lasting and positive impact on the local community.

As a Pod Volunteer you will have a dedicated specialist who will help you to choose the right project for you, and then support you all the way through the process, including 24/7 back up support. Our friendly team has a wealth of overseas volunteering and travel experience. We have all volunteered overseas and pride ourselves on our project and location knowledge.

"Pod Volunteer is extremely organized and takes phenomenal care of their volunteers. There was always an open line of communication, very thorough information packet and support throughout the entire process." - Kayleigh, 2017

my
gap-year
Alexandra

21-year-old Alexandra decided to join the Pod Volunteer Elephant Care project in Thailand as part of her gap-year! Here she talks about her experience:

This volunteer experience for me was life changing. The whole time I was there I was constantly learning and gaining new skills that are applicable to many aspects of life. Working with the elephants in itself was truly amazing, they are such beautiful animals and being up close to them and feeding them was very special. I am already trying to plan for another trip back, it was so hard to leave!

This volunteer experience also gave me the opportunity to work closely in teams, which were different every day, allowing me to meet and connect with so many different and interesting people from across the world. Some of those people I can confidently say will be lifelong friends and I'm going to visit later in the year!

I chose Pod Volunteer because I read excellent reviews about them online and because they are a not-for-profit organisation so I know my money was going to a good place. Pod Volunteer made this experience so incredibly easy! With great communication and information they went above and beyond what I expected. I would definitely recommend Pod Volunteer to anyone planning a volunteer trip.

I would advise others to just book it and go! Be open and be yourself, learn as much as you can and throw yourself at every opportunity. You absolutely will not regret it and you have nothing to lose.

For more information on Pod Volunteer, see their advert on the opposite page

Remember, wherever you're sent, you can't count on much. Regardless of the organisation, you will be going to poor countries where the infrastructure and support services can be minimal — otherwise why would they need volunteers?

Expect to be adaptable. Regardless of the reputation of the voluntary work organisation you choose, or the competence of voluntary work coordinators in a particular country, it's about your skills and human qualities and those of the people you'll be with so there's bound to be an element of chance as to whether the school you are put in, for example, really values you or whether you get on with the family you stay with. It's worth checking first what training is given and what support there is in-country, but be aware that you may not get what you expect — you need to be adaptable and make the most of whatever situation you find yourself in.

Safety first

If you're going with a good organisation they shouldn't send you anywhere too dangerous — but situations change quickly and it's always worth finding out for yourself about where you're going.

Check out the Foreign Office's travel advice pages on **www.gov.uk/travelaware** The Foreign Office site also has lots of advice on visas, insurance and other things that need to be sorted out before you go, and advice on what to do in an emergency abroad. There's much more on all this in **Chapter 1 — Tips For Travellers**.

Also, make sure you have proper insurance cover and that it is appropriate for where you're going, the length of time you'll be away and for any unexpected emergencies.

Stefan Wathan at The Year Out Group tells us: "Our best advice for volunteers looking to support worthwhile projects is not to rely solely on website imagery and descriptions but to ask the company concerned how they have developed their project and why they consider it to be necessary. The Year Out Group website can help you but we'd also recommend reading up about Fair Trade Volunteering and Tourism Concern which will help you to understand the possible issues."

Our friends at Kaya Responsible Travel advised us: "Volunteering is often a great way to stay safe, as you join a well-structured program with an in-county support system and local staff who can advise you on how best to recognise the local dangers and avoid them. With that, remember to read the information you are provided, listen to local advice and remember to be more vigilant, more careful and take less chances than you might at home, because as a foreigner you will generally stick out."

Please see the directory pages starting on page 317 for information on companies and organisations offering opportunities to volunteer abroad.

7

Learning abroad

Sponsored by

It doesn't have to mean more exams and lecture theatres

What we do

Established in 1985, a gap-year course with Art History Abroad is more than just a study abroad programme — it's a headfirst dive into European culture. With trips of anywhere between two and twelve weeks, AHA uses art and architecture as a springboard to understand how the history of Western civilization shapes societies around the world today. Our insider's knowledge of the countries we visit ensures you see both the major landmarks and exciting off-the-beaten-track gems, taking in a fantastic spectrum of cultural and culinary highlights.

How it works

AHA provides the ideal bridge between school and university study: without homework or exams, the emphasis is on discursive, seminar-style education. All of our teaching sessions take place outside of the classroom and in front of the masterpieces themselves, at Europe's most important museums, galleries and historical sites. Our expansive curriculum moves across disciplines, variously touching on philosophy, literature and politics to explore the wide-ranging history of Western Civilization. Lively discussion and debate is our hallmark, and the magic of an AHA course is that there are no wrong answers: every student is encouraged to express themselves with confidence and enthusiasm.

What you need

No prior experience in Art History is necessary: we simply ask for an enquiring mind and a willingness to learn. Our tutors are all from a wide range of academic backgrounds, and many are respected curators, lecturers and arts journalists outside of their work for AHA. Their aim is to bring the works we see to life — and their flexibility ensures that whether you're completely new to the world of art, or it's already a lifelong passion, everyone is offered a stimulating experience and no student is left behind.

Who we are

Our tutors are experts in their field and fully trained in pastoral care: they stay and travel with the students, and accompany them for most meals, meaning everyone gets an unrivalled amount of contact time to share their thoughts and opinions on the day's learning. Most students agree that the tutors are the highlight of their trip with their energy, erudition and sense of humour, they make every work of art and architecture relevant to our lives today.

Day to day

This leads on to one of our favourite parts of the courses: no visit to Italy would be complete without exploring its culinary heritage. We know the very best (and best-value) restaurants in every city, and make sure that there's enough delicious Italian food to satisfy even the most prodigious eater. Nothing beats an evening spent discussing the day's art over spaghetti alle vongole with fresh mussels from the Venetian lagoon, or savouring a traditional wood-fired pizza in a lively Neapolitan piazza. We even include a traditional five-course Tuscan cooking class, where you learn to make your own pasta and gain a deeper understanding of the Italian art of gastronomy.

Get creative

For those of a creative bent, all courses include optional drawing and creative writing sessions, allowing students to make the most of their time with the masterpieces of Western Art, and use them as a starting point for their own creative endeavours. We also ensure there is time off in each city for students to explore at their leisure. It's an opportunity to get lost in the back streets of Venice, to wander down the boulevards of Paris (Semester course only), or just to rest and recuperate after taking in all of the greatest sights each city has to offer.

Broadening horizons

In the words of our founder, Nicholas Ross, the thrill of an AHA course is "to be excited by knowledge, and to make the most of our faculties of sight and intellect." While our priority is for students to leave the course with an educated eye and an increased intellectual confidence and maturity, the benefit of taking this rite of passage through Europe with expert tutors is often difficult to articulate (although that hasn't stopped our students from trying — for verified testimonials from alumni, check out our reviews at gooverseas.com).

Of course, we hope that our students come away with a passion for European culture, and a deeper appreciation for the importance of the arts. But nothing can rival the experience of seeing these seminal artworks in the company of like-minded peers, and the legacy of an AHA trip extends to the life-long friendships formed with fellow students from across the globe. After taking an AHA course, our students can enter a museum or gallery anywhere in the world and find something to be enriched and enlightened by. Perhaps the best summary of an AHA course is our motto, 'broadening horizons' — we hope to continue expanding our students' worldview, as we have done for thousands of young people across three decades.

Check out more about Art History Abroad on page 188

Learning abroad

While your gap-year will inevitably be about personal growth, because of all the new things you experience and see you could build on this by using it as an opportunity to combine living and studying abroad. This might not seem appealing if you've just 'escaped' from a period of intense study and exams, but consider this:

· The learning doesn't have to be goal-oriented or laden with exam stress, you could learn a new skill and gain a qualification.

· You could pursue an interest, hobby or passion you haven't had time for before.

· You'll be able to explore and enrich your knowledge in your own way, rather than following a curriculum.

· You could also find you've added another dimension to your CV.

· You'll meet like-minded folk and have a lot of fun.

These are some of the things you could do: learn a language in-country, do a sports instructor course, music or drama summer schools, explore art, music, culture and learn about conservation. If you're not jaded with study or are at a time of life when a postgraduate qualification would be useful, and a career break possible, you could go for an academic year abroad. Another option for those of you who want to try to earn while you travel is to do a TEFL course.

Here's a good link for courses abroad: **www.studyabroaddirectory.com**

visit: www.arthistoryabroad.com

An academic year abroad

A good way of getting to know a place and its people in depth is to spend a whole academic year at a foreign school, either in Europe, the USA, or further afield. One possibility is an academic year before university:

· French Lycée

· German Gymnasium

· School in Spain

· Spanish-speaking school in Argentina

The most relevant EU education and training programmes are Comenius, Erasmus and Leonardo. For more information see:

Comenius: **www.britishcouncil.org/comenius.htm**

Erasmus: **www.britishcouncil.org/erasmus**

Leonardo: **www.leonardo.org.uk**

A scheme called Europass provides trainees in any EU country with a 'Europewide record of achievement for periods of training undertaken outside the home member state'. So it's important to ask the school: "Is this course recognised for a Europass?"

University exchange

If you want to spend up to a year abroad at a European university as part of the European Union's Erasmus (European community Action Scheme for the Mobility of University Students) scheme, you'll need to have some working knowledge of the relevant language — so a gap-year could be the time to start, either studying overseas or in Britain. Information about Erasmus courses is usually given to students in their first year at university. To apply for Erasmus you must be an EU citizen. When you spend your time abroad, you continue to pay tuition fees or receive loans or grants as if you were at your university back home. For more information visit: **www.britishcouncil.org/erasmus**

The scheme is also open to teaching and non-teaching staff at higher education and HE/FE institutions, as long as your home higher education institution has a formal agreement with a partner in one of the eligible countries. It must also have an Erasmus University Charter awarded by the European Commission.

Postgraduate MA/visiting fellowship/exchange

Several universities in the UK have direct links to partnership programmes with others around the world, but if you want to widen your search, the Worldwide Universities Network (WUN) **(www.wun.ac.uk/about)** is a good place to start looking for exchange, overseas study and funding for research projects. It's a partnership of 16 research-led universities from Asia, Australia, Asia, Europe and North America.

WUN's Research Mobility Programme funds a period of study overseas, for senior postgraduates and junior faculty, to establish and cultivate research links at an institutional and individual level between the partners in Europe, North America, South-East Asia and Australia. It is also intended to encourage the personal and academic development of individuals early in their research careers.

Arts and culture

Art

If you want to go to art school, or have already been, no matter which art form interests you, travelling and soaking up the atmosphere is a good way to learn more and give you ideas for your own work. It's also a great opportunity to add to your portfolio.

You don't have to be an art student or graduate to enjoy the beauty of art and artefacts produced by different cultures. Most courses listed in this guidebook are open to anyone who wants to explore the arts in a bit more depth.

For example, have a look at the courses offered by Art History Abroad: **www.arthistoryabroad.com**

Culture

It's a cliché, but also true, that travel broadens the mind and you'll absorb much about the culture of the places you visit just by being there. However, if you want to develop your understanding in more depth, maybe learn a bit of the language and discover some of your chosen country's history, then you could go for the cultural component of some of the language courses listed in the directory.

Alternatively, you might like to try something like The John Hall Venice Course, which gives an insight into Western culture and achievements and features time spent in London, Venice, Florence and Rome. To find out more visit **www.johnhallvenice.com**.

John Hall Venice

JOHN HALL VENICE

John Hall Venice, 9 Smeaton Road, SW18 5JJ UK
T: +44 (0)20 8871 4747
E: info@johnhallvenice.com   W: www.johnhallvenice.com

The John Hall Venice Course is an epic gap-year experience and one that you will never forget. It is a nine-week introduction to some of the finest and most thought-provoking achievements in the Western world, from the classical past to today.

There are lectures and visits by a team of world-class experts and the course includes painting, sculpture, architecture, music, world cinema, literature and global issues. There are practical classes in studio life drawing and portraiture, as well as classes in photography, Italian language and cookery.

The course consists of a week in London, six weeks in Venice, a week in Florence and a week in Rome. The heart of the experience is Venice - to be in the historic and uniquely beautiful city of Venice, living more like a resident than a tourist, is a life-changing experience.

Students come from around the world - UK, America, Africa, Europe and Asia, creating a cosmopolitan collegiate atmosphere that leads to friendships and connections for life. There are many privileged private visits throughout the course, including an unforgettable night visit to St.Mark's in Venice.

The John Hall Venice Course gives a foretaste of a university style of living and learning. It will leave you with not only some lifelong friendships, but also with a seriously improved CV.

Design and fashion

Every year, when the new season's collections are shown on the world's fashion catwalks, it's clear that the designers have 'discovered' the fabrics, or decoration or style, of one region or another.

So for those with a passion for fashion a gap-year is a great opportunity to experience the originals for themselves. Wandering the streets in other countries, and absorbing the street style can be an inspiration.

Then there's the opportunity to snap up, at bargain prices, all kinds of beautiful fabrics that would cost a fortune back home.

But if you wanted to use part of your gap to find out more about fashion and design you could also join a fashion summer school in one of Europe's capitals, take a look at a few we've listed below:

IFA Paris Fashion School: **www.ifaparis.com**

Ecole supérieure d'art Françoise Conte: **www.fconte.com**

Paris American Academy: **www.saiprograms.com/paris/paa**

Pauline Fraisse Art & Culture: **www.paulinefraisse.com**

Or why not India? The country's National Institute of Fashion Technology in Delhi runs summer schools for fashion stylists — here's the link: **www.nift.ac.in**

SACI
STUDIO
ARTS
COLLEGE
INTERNATIONAL

COLLEGE OF ART & DESIGN
FLORENCE, ITALY

Take time off to pursue your passion in a U.S.-accredited arts program at the oldest and most prestigious American art school in Florence. We offer programs in studio art, design, photography, conservation, art history, and more.

saci-florence.edu

Film, theatre and drama

If you're thinking of a short course in performing arts, the USA is one of the most obvious places to go — most famously the New York Film Academy, which has a very useful page for international students:

www.nyfa.edu/admissions/international_student.php

The Academy runs summer schools in London, Paris, Florence, Colombia, China, Japan and South Korea.

We also recommend Met Film School who run courses at their studios in Berlin, incorporating writing, producing, directing and editing.

You can find out more at: **www.metfilmschool.de**

For a wider search try: **www.filmschools.com**

If you want dance as well, the world is your oyster. You can learn salsa in Delhi (as well as in South America) and the traditional Indian Kathak dance in the USA.

And then, of course, there's Bollywood. There are courses in film direction, cinematography, sound production and editing at the Film and Television Institutes of India, in Pune (south-west of Mumbai), which runs a number of courses for overseas students: **www.ftiindia.com**

Music

Whether you're into classical or pop, world music or traditional, there are vibrant music scenes all over the world.

From the studios that have sprung up in Dakar, the West African capital of Senegal, to the club scenes of Europe, to more formal schools, check out the opportunities

my gap-year
Brooke

Brooke jointed Art History Abroad on a summer combination course in the summer of 2017 and is now studying at Princeton University...

I heard about Art History Abroad (AHA) completely by chance after striking up conversation on a train with a college student who was going home for winter break. She said that one of her friends had spent a semester in Italy studying art history with AHA and described it as one of the best experiences she ever had.

I was a four-sport varsity letter winner in high school, so from the age of twelve onwards, I spent the entirety of my summers training, practicing, and competing on playing fields. I had always wanted to take summer courses or go abroad during the summer but knew it wouldn't be logistically possible. After spending four weeks studying art history with AHA, I am so happy that I decided to try something different (and can't believe I spent all those years sweating on a field in New Jersey when I could have been studying Michelangelo and Caravaggio!)

The course was the perfect way to cap off my senior year of high school due to the passionate tutors, the sights we saw, and the people I met. I hadn't taken an art history course before the trip but quickly learned that it wasn't necessary as the tutors used concise yet evocative and thought-provoking language to describe not only individual paintings but entire time periods. The art and architecture we saw gave a whole new dimension to the European history I learned in school; it is undoubtedly worth seeing in person.

To top it off, I was travelling with an intelligent, diverse and fun group of peers. I had a fantastic time with both groups and made friends that I still keep in contact with and hope to keep in contact with long term. Overall, my experience with AHA was intellectually and socially enervating and fantastic.

For more information on Art History Abroad, see their advert on page 188

to combine your interest with travel and maybe learn to play an instrument, if you don't already, or another one if you do.

We've checked online for short music courses, since the UNESCO site no longer offers a directory, and although there are plenty out there, it's a case of searching by location.

Here's one for all UK summer schools, including music: **www.summer-schools.info**

Media and journalism

Although the print media has been suffering from the rise of online material there are, of course, other options.

You may want to get into media/journalism but you're not the only one, so do thousands of others and the competition is intense.

The skills you'll need could include media law, shorthand, knowledge of how local and national government works and, not least, the ability to construct an attention-grabbing story!

To get a job you may need to do more than gain a media studies degree or have on-the-job training in a newsroom. It's therefore, always a good idea to demonstrate your commitment and a gap is a good time to do this. You can try contacting your local paper for a work experience placement, though don't expect to be paid!

Plus, if you search the internet there are plenty of internships in newsrooms — many of them in India, where there's still a lot of attachment to local and national newspapers. We Googled 'journalism placements and internships' and found possibilities around the world. These websites may also be useful:

www.gorkanajobs.co.uk
www.tigweb.org/resources/opps
www.internews.org

Many large media organisations have Twitter pages specifically for jobs and internships, following those that interest you and keeping an eye out may be a good way to discover placements.

Photography

Travelling offers you the chance to develop your skills as a photographer — after all almost everyone takes pictures to remember their travels. But if you've always dreamed of turning professional, it's a chance to practice.

You could be innovative by contacting a local newspaper or magazine and asking if they'll let you accompany one of their photographers on assignments. You won't be paid but you'll learn a lot and it might give you pictures to add to your portfolio.

Cookery

Learning to cook abroad can be a popular path to take for those who want to become a wizard in the kitchen. There are numerous benefits that come with taking a cooking adventure abroad, including the opportunity to learn authentic cuisines in their home countries, the chance to expand your palate, open your mind up to a wealth

Istituto di Lingua e Cultura Italiana Michelangelo,
Via Ghibellina 88, Florence 50122 Italy
T: +39 055 240 975
W: www.michelangelo-edu.it

Michelangelo Institute

Founded in 1975, the Institute is open all year round, welcoming students of all nationalities who wish to begin, improve or perfect their knowledge of Italian.

The Institute is housed in Palazzo Gherardi, a XV century building in the old sector of Florence, in close proximity to the National Museum, the National Library, the Church of Santa Croce, and the House of Michelangelo.

Living, Language and Culture

Traditionally, the Institute has always offered its students every opportunity to make themselves at home with Italian life and culture. Besides regular courses, visits to museums, concerts, excursions, movies, dinners in restaurants, visits to markets, and evening entertainment are organised by the Institute staff, who gives a special attention to student 'get-togethers'.

Courses

- The Italian Language courses, offered in six levels, all year round, enables the progressive learning of Italian.
- The Specialisation course, is thought for teachers of Italian, to those in possession of the Michelangelo Diploma, and to those who, having complete mastery over the language, wish to take a 'refresher course'.
- The one-on-one courses, offered in several 'options', are addressed to those who must reach a good level of Italian knowledge and fluency in a short time.
- The Art History course outlines, analyses and offers an historical overview of the Italian artistic heritage.
- The Italian Culture courses are a wide range of subjects to be examined under the guidance of teachers specialised in the various fields proposed.
- The Art Courses are totally practical in nature, inviting students to develop and to improve their artistic aptitudes in our wonderful ateliers.
- The Italian Cooking course is a pleasant and interesting way to learn about our culinary culture and to prepare some of the most typical dishes from the rich Italian gastronomic tradition.

of different cultures and tastes, and meet a host of different people from different backgrounds and countries..

Our friends at Lynda Booth's Dublin Cookery School tell us that: "This is a fantastic opportunity to meet a group of like-minded people who all get to bond over their love of cookery. Whether you are coming from near or afar, being able to share different food cultures, and explore what Ireland has to offer, will generate a wonderful 'once in a lifetime' experience. Many of our past students have made strong lasting friendships, travelling overseas together, keeping each other up to date with amazing job opportunities both at home and abroad, and who knows where their paths will lead them in the future."

Languages

You learn a language much more easily and quickly if you're living in the country where it's spoken, but there's more than one reason to learn a new language. There's more to a language than just words: most language courses will include local culture, history, geography, religion, customs and current affairs — as well as food and drink.

Students often study abroad for lots of different reasons. For example, many are on their gap-years before university and want to get a head start before reading languages, or just want to learn a new skill while they have the time. Other gappers are already well into their careers and need to brush up on their language skills for work, or are just taking time out for themselves. There are also some who are enjoying retirement and finally learning the language they had always wished they could speak but never quite got round to!

There are also a great number of benefits that always seems to surprise students. This includes how the understanding of their own language improves when they begin to work through the grammar rules of a new one. What's more, students take so much pleasure in being able to make friends from all over the world — it opens up so many possibilities. Learning a language is also said to improve the functionality of the brain.

the gap-year guidebook 2018

my gap-year
Becca

I have always known I wanted to take a GAP year, but that's more because I knew I didn't want to head straight to university. I couldn't say I've ever had a burning desire to do something in particular with my year. I had played with various ideas in my head about what I could do but I wasn't particularly enthralled by any of them. I've known of CESA Languages for years now, as they are based very close to where I l live and are part of a biennial GAP Year Fair at the school I used to attend.

After a quick browse on CESA's website and an exchange of a few emails with the staff, I knew I wanted to go. CESA had organised everything so that it was all as simple as possible for me, I stepped out of arrivals and was met with a transfer straight to the student house, given my new house key and even walked to the door!

I was immediately met by a friendly face (in the form of a Dutch girl named Elizabeth), giving me the wifi code and offering to show me the easiest route to the school the next morning. It was a totally unfamiliar and slightly nerve wrecking situation but I settled into my room quickly and managed to get a good night's sleep.

The school itself is right in the centre of Munich, a few minutes' walk away from Marienplatz. It is quite a small building as there is no accommodation on site, but it is very modern, with a lot of classrooms as well as a communal area and a kitchen. You find out your class and level on the first day and are then shown to your classroom and introduced to your teacher and fellow students.

It is inexplicably wonderful to know a city in more depth than just on an average tourist level. Knowing where to actually get the best Weisswurst in the city definitely makes you feel involved in the Bavarian culture. The museums and galleries are also a must around the city, but personally I think it's much more fun to find little bars that only the locals know about, sit and have a couple (or a few) Augustiner's and talk to anyone and everyone in German, with your best Bavarian accent...

All around the trip was amazing and definitely a worthwhile way to spend a GAP year! CESA were incredibly helpful and I could not fault them! I definitely would go back again, and actually I did about a month after a finished the first course I went back out there, with CESA again, and continued what I had been previously doing.

Vielen Dank CESA!

For more information on CESA Languages Abroad, see their advert on the opposite page

Think laterally about where you want to study. Spanish is spoken in many countries around the world, so you could opt for a Spanish course in South America, rather than Spain, and then go travelling around the country, or learn Portuguese in Brazil, where it's the main language, or perhaps French in Canada.

Be aware though that if you learn a language outside its original country you may learn a particular dialect that is only spoken in a specific region of the country as a whole. It may even be considered inferior by some people (or not understood) elsewhere in the country.

CESA Languages offer some advice for gappers thinking about learning a language abroad: "Stay open minded. Be realistic about what can be achieved on a language course. If you are studying for two or three weeks you will make progress, but you won't become fluent. If you are on long term course you can really improve significantly but you need to stay focused and avoid reverting to your native tongue if at all possible. The more disciplined you are about only using the target language throughout the stay, the greater your progress will be."

Finding the right place to learn

Universities often have international summer school centres or courses for foreign students, or there's the popular network of British Institutes abroad. And there are hundreds (probably thousands) of independent language colleges to choose from, either directly or through a language course organiser or agency in the UK.

The advantage in dealing with a UK-based organisation is that, if something goes wrong, it is easier to get it sorted out under UK law.

Choosing a course provider

There are a number of companies that you can choose to take your language course with. Do make sure you get as much information from them as possible before making your choice.

Art History Abroad

my gap-year
Chloe

In my opinion, SACI has found the perfect balance between size of classes and number of course offerings. This is a rare combination, one that provides the perfect environment to try previously unknown courses of study, exactly what I believe to be the purpose of a gap-year.

Coming from a relatively small high school, I had few choices in terms of what art forms I could pursue. Before I even arrived in Florence, I was exposed to techniques that I had never heard of, just by browsing the SACI course catalogue. My impromptu decision to enrol in serigraphy turned out to be one of the best decisions I have ever made. After the spring term finished, I ended up staying the summer in Florence, helping to develop SACI's social media platforms and working at Fuji Studios, the printshop that SACI is affiliated with. Now at Columbia University, I spent this past summer interning at the LeRoy Neiman Center for Print Studies as well as completing an independent study with Tomas Vu Daniel, the director of the printshop.

The extension of my time in Florence also speaks to the close community that SACI has developed. I cannot speak more highly of the students and professors that I engaged with at SACI. Although I was one of the youngest students at SACI, I never felt excluded from my classmates, most of whom were juniors in college. Working and living with my peers also helped to ease the transition to Italy and challenge me creatively.

I can say with complete sincerity that my time at SACI altered the course of my future. While I have always been passionate about art, it is because of my time in Florence that I am now an Art History major, with a Visual Arts concentration.

For more information on SACI Florence, see their advert on page 192

Live Languages Abroad offer some excellent options. Their website can be found at: **www.livelanguagesabroad.co.uk**

These pages are also worth at look:

www.cesalanguages.com
www.esl.co.uk
www.europa-pages.co.uk — for language courses in European countries.
www.ialc.org (International Association of Language Centres)

Living with a family

If enrolling on a language course sounds too much like school, another way of learning a language is staying with a family as an au pair or tutor (giving, say, English or music lessons to children) and going to part-time classes locally.

Language courses

Courses at language schools abroad can be divided into as many as ten different levels, ranging from tuition for the complete beginner to highly technical or specialised courses at postgraduate level. The usual classification of language classes, however, into 'beginner' or 'basic', 'intermediate' and 'advanced', works well. Within each of these levels there are usually subdivisions, especially in schools large enough to move students from one class to another with ease.

When you first phone a school from abroad or send in an application form, you should indicate how good your knowledge of the language is. You may be tested before being allocated your class, or you may be transferred from your original class to a lower or higher one, as soon as they find you are worse or better than expected.

Different schools will use different methods of teaching: if you know that you respond well to one style, check that is what your course offers. Foreign language lessons are often attended by a variety of nationalities, so they are almost always conducted in the language you are learning, forcing you to understand and respond without using English. In practice, however, most teachers can revert to English to explain a principle of grammar if a student is really stuck.

The smaller the class the better, though the quality of the teaching is most important — at more advanced levels, well-qualified graduate teachers should be available. Language schools and institutes show a mass of information, photographs and maps on their websites, so it's easy to find out if the school is near to places that interest you, whether it's in a city centre or near a coastal resort. The admissions staff should be happy to give you references from previous students.

In the directory, you'll find some of the organisations offering language opportunities to gappers, from formal tuition to 'soaking it up' while you live with a family. We've split the organisations according to the languages they offer: Arabic, Chinese, French, German, Greek, Indonesian, Italian, Japanese, Portuguese, Russian and Spanish. Here's a quick look at each:

Arabic

Arabic is the language in which the *Quran* is written and, although there are translations into the local languages of Muslims around the world, there's also a lot of argument about the way they're translated. This has led to differences about what Islam means.

It's all a matter of interpretation of the roots of words and what's more there are two main versions of Arabic: Fousha — Modern Standard Arabic; and Aameya — Egyptian Colloquial Arabic.

Chinese

As Chinese enterprises become global, the language is becoming a popular choice in UK schools, with as many as 400 state schools now offering lessons.

There are two main dialects. Cantonese is the language of most Chinese people living abroad, from Singapore to Europe and the USA. Cantonese is also spoken widely in the Guangdong and Guangxi provinces of mainland China and in Hong Kong and Macau.

Mandarin is the official language of government, international relations and much education in China is undertaken in Mandarin. It is the more formal language and most students are advised to learn it.

Both languages are tonal (the same sound said in a different tone will change the meaning of a word) and therefore can be quite difficult for English speakers to learn. The different tonal pronunciation, vowels and consonants effectively turn Mandarin and Cantonese into two different languages, although both use the same written characters. There are many, many other Chinese dialects, including Hokkien, Hakka, Wu and Hui.

You can find course information at: **www.mandarinhouse.cn/chinesecourses.htm**

It has a choice of 12 different courses in Chinese, including one for expatriates, in Beijing or Shanghai.

visit: www.arthistoryabroad.com

French

Languages have changed over time as they have been introduced to other parts of the world from their home countries and then developed in their own directions. Then there are the local dialects. French covers French as it's spoken in France, but then there's also Swiss French, Belgian French and Canadian French.

There's a busy French community in the UK, a large French Lycée in London and more than one teaching institute run by French nationals, so there are plenty of opportunities to carry on developing your French language skills when you return to the UK.

German

German has many very strong dialects (particularly in Austria, Switzerland and much of South Germany), and it is important to bear this in mind if you want to study German academically, or use it for business, in which case you may need to be learning and practising *Hochdeutsch* (standard German).

Many universities in Germany, Austria and Switzerland run summer language schools for foreign students.

Contact:

German Embassy
23 Belgrave Square
Cultural Department
London SW1X 8PZ
Tel: +44 (0) 20 7824 1300.

Their website has a section on studying in Germany: **www.london.diplo.de** There's also a lively German community in the UK and many courses run by the Goethe Institut (**www.goethe.de/ins/gb/lon/enindex.htm**).

Greek

The thoughts of the great philosophers such as Socrates and Aristotle, upon whose ideas the foundations of western values were built, were written in ancient Greek.

Democracy, aristocracy, philosophy, pedagogy and psychology are just some of the many Greek terms that are part of our culture and language.

Modern Greek is spoken by ten million Greek citizens and by about seven million others spread around the world.

Indonesian

Based on the Malay trade dialect, Bahasa Indonesia is the national language of the Republic of Indonesia. In a country of more than 230 million people, who speak over 580 different dialects, having a national language makes communication easier, in much the same way as Hindi does in India.

There's no general greeting in Indonesian; there are different words specific to the time of day. But it's said to be an easy language to learn and Indonesia is such a popular backpacker destination it's likely to be worth making the effort. Here's a web link to get you started: **www.expat.or.id**

Italian

Schools vary from the very large to very small, each with its own character and range of courses in Italian, Italian culture, history, art, cooking and other subjects. As in language schools across most of Europe, the language is often taught in the morning

visit: www.arthistoryabroad.com

with extracurricular activities in the afternoon. If you want to do a course from March onwards it is advisable to get in touch with them at least two months in advance, as courses and accommodation get booked up early.

Most schools can fix you up with accommodation before your trip, either with a family, bed and breakfast, half-board, or even renting a studio or flat. If you're part of a small group, you might prefer to arrange accommodation yourself through a local property-letting agent, but this can be tricky unless you have someone on the spot to help.

Japanese

If you can get to the Japanese Embassy in London you can look up a comprehensive guide in its large library called Japanese Language Institutes (based in Japan). The library also has material on learning Japanese and stocks Japanese newspapers including the English-language *Japan Times*, which runs information on jobs in Japan.

There's information about studying in Japan on the embassy website, with guidance on the type of visa you will need if you want to teach English as a foreign language or do other types of work there.

www.uk.emb-japan.go.jp/en/embassy

Dublin Cookery School, 2 Brookfield Terrace, Blackrock, Co. Dublin, Ireland
T: +353 1 210 0555
E: info@dublincookeryschool.ie   W: www.dublincookeryschool.ie

Want to spend your winters on the slopes, summers on a yacht and be in demand anywhere your adventures may take you?

Lynda Booth's Dublin Cookery School is an award-winning, well-established cookery school in Ireland, and the only school offering a 3 month certificate cookery course in Dublin.

Our tutors are selected for their teaching skill, energy and experience gained from working in top restaurants around the world. We challenge students, but always with an eye for fun and a focus on boosting the student's confidence. With a maximum of 24 students per course, we are able to help you learn, regardless of the level at which you arrive.

The days are varied with hands-on cooking, interspersed with inspiring visiting chefs, and experts from small food businesses. The whole group bonds together through trips (foraging, artisan producers) or facing the monthly challenge of running a pop-up restaurant evening which gives them a great sense of progress.

Our intensive professional 3 Month Certificate course balances a relaxed, hands-on atmosphere with modern cooking techniques, which will allow you ultimately to breeze into your local market, pick-up something fresh and know exactly what to do with it - that means, you'll be in demand.

We are happy to help organise accommodation. Dublin is a fun, vibrant city and the airport (just half an hour from our door) makes it easy for your friends and family to come and visit. Don't let your gap year slip by - have a great time and learn a lifelong skill that will enable you to earn money during the holiday months.

Like the look of the course but don't have 3 months to spare? Why not get in touch and ask about our 1 Month Certificate cookery course?

my
gap-year
Shane

Shane discusses his experience on the three-month certificate course at Dublin Cookery School...

I always had a passion for food and a desire from a young age to explore and experiment with the many flavours and shared experiences it can bring.

I needed a cookery school where the focus was on hands-on cooking; where I could be free and confident enough to experiment with food; be taught by tutors from a diverse range of culinary backgrounds and to be surrounded by passionate, fun and dedicated students.

I found all of this and much more at Dublin Cookery School. From foraging, visiting artisan producers, being exposed to Michelin-star chefs, getting advice on how to set up a food business and running pop-up restaurant nights - this experience really stood me well when it came time for me to join a professional kitchen. The school staff has remained in regular contact and have continued to provide me with a whole host of new job opportunities both at home and abroad.

I had an absolutely wonderful experience at Dublin Cookery School, the level of experience was so broad and rich that I felt it was a remarkably good investment of my time, effort and money. It opened up many doors for me and introduced me to so many great people. Whether you want to do this as a career or simply take this as an opportunity to learn a whole set of eternally useful life-skills during your gap year, like me, I would highly recommend it.

Working in a kitchen is not just about cooking, it teaches you about teamwork, effective communication, interpersonal skills, time management, working under pressure and creative problem solving.

What future employer would not admire such a list of personal qualities?

For more information on Dublin Cookery School, see their advert on the opposite page

my
gap-year
Henry

It took me a while to work out what I wanted to do on my gap-year, my goal was to find an academically enriching experience that would simultaneously allow me to have a good time and meet new people. The John Hall Venice course fulfilled these aims and offered so much more.

The incredible talks and tours given by world-leading experts were interwoven with the opportunity to explore Venice, Florence and Rome in our own time. I have been left with memories that will last a lifetime: from a private viewing of the beautiful mosaics of St Mark's narrated by Lord Ture's dulcet tones, to evening celebrations in Messner; from Nigel McGilchrist's egg tempura demonstration, to two Hallers' use of David to

demonstrate the perfect bum; from reclining in the beautiful gardens of the Villa Gamberaia high above Florence, to reclining on the sofas of Piccolo Mondo in the early hours of the morning.

For nine weeks, John, who has run the course since its inception in 1965, and Charlie, who has been both student and leader on the course, looked after us, sharing their insider knowledge of these beautiful cities, scolding us for lateness, loudness and general loutishness. Their care, but also their desire for us to have our freedom, is what makes the course truly special, an opportunity we will eternally relish having taken.

Above all else, sharing this experience with so many like-minded people has seen me form friendships that I'm sure will last a very long time. When we meet today we reminisce about moon lit walks on the Zattere, daily congregations in Campo Santa Margherita and life drawing at Geoffrey Humphries'.

I'm sure I will be back very soon, as we have all truly fallen in love with Venice.

For more information on John Hall Venice, see their advert on page 190

Portuguese

Being the 6th most common language, Its not surprising that many people choose to learn Portuguese. You don't have to go to Portugal to learn Portuguese — it's the main language of Brazil too, so if you're heading for Latin America on your gap, try: www.esl.co.uk/en/learn-portuguese-in-brazil.htm

Russian

We suggest you check with the Foreign & Commonwealth Office before making any plans to travel to Russia to study.

That said, both CESA and Live Languages Abroad offers Russian language lessons in Russia:
www.livelanguagesabroad.co.uk/category/russian/russian-in-russia
www.cesalanguages.com/learn-russian-in-russia

Spanish

Spanish is the third most widespread language in the world after English and Mandarin Chinese. Over 400 million people in 23 countries are Spanish speakers — Mexico and all of Central and South America (except Brazil) designate Spanish as their official language.

Forms of Spanish can also be heard in Guinea, the Philippines and in Ceuta and Melilla in North Africa. But if you go to a language school inside or outside of Spain, you will probably be learning formal Castilian.

For information about universities and language courses, try:

Spanish Embassy, Education Department, 20 Draycott Place, London SW3 2RZ
Tel: +44 (0) 20 7727 2462
If you want to learn it in Latin America try:
www.expanish.com
www.spanish-language.org

Multi languages

There are companies offering courses in many different languages. When you're getting references, make sure they're not just for the company — but specifically for the country/course you're interested in.

TEFL

Recent research has revealed that within the next ten years roughly half the world will be using English, so there's never been a better time to do a TEFL course. Like having a sports instructors' certificate, a TEFL qualification is useful if you want to earn a little money for expenses on a gap and it's a passport that will get you into many countries around the world and in close contact with the people. For more information on getting a TEFL qualification go to **Chapter 5 - Working Abroad**.

Please see the directory pages starting on page 347 for information on companies and organisations offering opportunities for learning abroad.

8

Sport

 **Sport**

Travelling abroad doesn't mean that you have to stop playing the sports that you love — sports coaching projects are also a great way to give something back to a community on a gap-year or career break abroad. If you are looking to join a sports volunteer project, there are many different projects and destinations available.

Lots of companies offer you the chance to live, play, train and coach many different sports all over the world. Whether your chosen sport is football, cricket, rugby, netball, tennis, sailing or even polo, you can use your skills to enrich the lives of others by becoming a volunteer coach or use your time to improve your own skills for a career in your chosen sport.

And a sporting placement abroad can seriously boost your personal development — showing your commitment, teamwork and leadership skills to prospective employers. So whether you want to use your football skills to become a coach teaching children in South Africa, join a cricket club for the season in Australia, experience the challenge of playing rugby in New Zealand or learn how to sail and dive in Thailand, there is definitely a placement out there for you.

Training to be an instructor

There are many options to consider, but three of the most popular and well-established areas for gap-year students are skiing, snowboarding and scuba diving.

There are well-established routes for training as a professional and choices of courses tailored to gap-years. Specialist gap-year training companies will take care of all organisation and train you through national governing body sports coaching qualifications.

There are lots of options out there, with all the northern hemisphere courses running from December to March and the southern hemisphere's winter season, June to October.

The instructor lifestyle is hard work but a lot of fun, although entry-level jobs are not too highly paid. On the plus side, you work on the sea or the slopes and have plenty of time to improve your own skills and enjoy your favourite sport.

Watersports instructor courses are also amongst the most popular for those interested in learning a new sport on their gap-year. In addition to diving, you will also find plenty of courses to qualify you to teach windsurfing, yachting and sailing, canoeing, kite surfing, kayaking — any activity on or around water, you can teach!

Volunteering as a sports coach

There are hundreds of sports-based volunteer programmes available, from coaching cricket to underprivileged children in India to coaching football in inner cities in the UK.

visit: www.gap-year.com

Gap-years can be spent doing practically every sport you can think of, from hockey to netball and from basketball to football. There's also a range of countries you can go to.

As a sports-coaching volunteer, you will have the opportunity to help build communities through sport. For example, in working with a local football academy in Ghana, you will be able to establish relationships with young players who often have a fantastic talent and profound love of the game — but have been unable to progress because of a lack of physical training, emotional guidance and financial support. Giving them the opportunity to develop both their skills and their character can be a life-changing experience.

Even without formal coaching qualifications, you can offer them constructive advice and new ideas on tactics, skills and their mental approach to training and competition, simply by arriving with enthusiasm, imagination and a general understanding of the game.

Development may not simply be about coaching. It may also involve education to understand how and why their ideas count, perhaps even some time as an English language teacher. On the best placements, you'll find yourself contributing to community development, in sport and beyond.

The attributes you need depend on the activity you go for. If it involves teaching kids, you'll obviously need to have empathy with children, and if it involves a lot of hardcore activity, you'll need to be reasonably fit and resilient.

Even if the sport has nothing to do with your future career path, it will boost your CV. Better still, if in an interview you can make an energetic case for why you did it, it will make you stand out above others who have sat around on their bums in the summer. It can only impress a future employer.

215

In the developing world, sport is often more than just competition or idle pastime. Often sport can have a real impact at the heart of communities, and play a pivotal role in the health and prosperity of the people.

Getting a job

Once you have earned your qualification, the world is your oyster for potential jobs.

Make sure you write a good covering letter with your CV. This is particularly important for jobs overseas where an interview might not be practical.

If you do have an interview, make sure you ask about the things that matter to you — terms and conditions of service, accommodation, feeding arrangements, insurance and equipment requirements, days off, daily routine, annual leave, flights home, *etc*. And don't forget about money — how do you get paid? And what are the career opportunities? Is there a job specification available? Why not go back to the company that trained you and ask if they have any vacancies? It can be a great way to continue doing what you love, and make money doing it.

Playing sport on your gap

More and more people are looking to take a sports gap-year with a purpose, so they are using their time out to play a season of sport abroad: for example cricket in Australia, or rugby in New Zealand or South Africa.

Placements on these 'academy programmes' will usually mean you are matched with a club abroad at a suitable level for your standard, for whom you play at the weekends whilst perfecting your game throughout the week with coaching, fitness

training and sports psychology from local coaches.

You may be set a specific training regime to stick to, which might include things like:

· Gym fitness work and flexibility training.

· Sport-specific fitness training.

· One-on-one sessions to develop specific skills.

· Video analysis.

· Group training sessions with other academy players.

· Club practice sessions.

· Sessions with players of a higher standard, perhaps even professionals.

Of course, you don't have to be looking at improving your skills to a semi-professional standard. You can also use your gap-year to take up a completely new sport. Perhaps you are interested in learning jiu-jitsu in Brazil, or polo in Argentina — you can certainly find placements to cover most sports in a huge range of countries.

Xtreme sport

Taking a gap-year gives you a once in a lifetime opportunity to do something amazing — the things that you just can't do at home and are likely to never forget. To some adventurous types, this means really exciting stuff, activities and adventures that get the butterflies going and gives you very sweaty palms.

There are companies that organise adrenaline-pumping activities in various locations around the world. These include adventures that really test your metal on a gap-year, which can have positive consequences when you return home.

That could mean bungee jumping or skydiving, scuba diving, swimming with whalesharks in Thailand or learning to surf in Australia. It would certainly pay to book before you go — you can organise things in-country but why take the chance of missing out? Also bear in mind that such activities are expensive - so make sure you have planned your budget in advance.

There is also merit in the idea of taking a qualification in an extreme sport — which might even help you stay for longer in certain countries.

Don't forget to make sure your travel insurance covers extreme sports. It's always better to be safe than sorry, so make sure you check the activities you wish to do are included in your cover. If you are struggling to find insurance why not phone up the company organising your trip/activity, it's a problem they've probably dealt with many a time before.

Snowsports

Some of the most popular sports to do on your gap-year take place on the snowy slopes, skiing being the most popular of these. A majority of people choose to get a qualification to get something out of their time on the slopes and something extra for their CV, however you can also take part in skicamps, or training courses.

The British Association of Snowsport Instructors (BASI) is the official UK organisation with responsibility for the training and grading of snowsports instructors and provides official BASI Gap 10-week courses through its licensed ski school providers, ICE and New Generation, that operate in the world's premier ski resorts — Val d'Isere, Courchevel, Meribel and La Tania.

visit: www.gap-year.com

You should already be a capable skier to be able to keep up with the course progression. Ideally, you should be able to confidently link turns on at least a European red run, although different countries may use different difficulty ratings. It is recommended that you are fit before you start a course to become a snowsport instructor.

"Furthermore, it's worth getting fit before you start, especially working on your legs and core. 11 weeks of intense on-snow training is going to take a lot out of you, and your legs need to be strong enough to handle it. You'll develop leg strength and stamina very quickly during a course, however being fit beforehand helps a lot!"

Once qualified as a level 2 ski instructor, your most likely first job would be teaching at a resort ski school. There is plenty of employment for newly qualified instructors, as long as you arrange your work visa in advance.

With a season's experience you are likely to be more in demand as an employee. Italy, Switzerland, Germany, Austria, Croatia, Spain, Andorra, USA, Canada and Japan are among the countries with established ski industries in the northern hemisphere.

Your opportunities in France can still be limited, though. The French snowsports authorities have traditionally made it difficult for non-French nationals to work in the Alps.

The biggest problem for a new instructor looking for a job is the lack of experience — and so any opportunity to gain experience should be grabbed with both hands.

A good idea may be to apply to ski schools for part-time work during the busy holiday weeks of Christmas/New Year, half-term and Easter. It may well lead to more work.

the gap-year guidebook 2018

In the southern hemisphere New Zealand is famous for its mountains, but don't overlook Australia, which has several winter resorts too. Some schools in Australia and New Zealand employ new instructors from early season hiring clinics: you are expected to attend a short period of in-house training and if you measure up you get a job

Sailing

If you fancy taking the to waters you can easily turn your love of sailing into a gap-year to remember. You can take part in courses to pick up and improve your existing skills and gain new qualifications, or just take part in a voyage cross the world with likeminded people.

Jubilee Sailing Trust takes crew members of any age, experience and physical ability and tells us the benefits of taking a gap-year on the open sea: "Life on-board our tall ships can be tough, but it'll give you skills you can use for life! You'll learn how

visit: www.gap-year.com

to exercise self discipline and resilience in challenging situations, develop empathy and mutual respect for other team members and adapt to new environments and cultures. You really will be a fully fledged member of our crew!"

Diving

If you would rather go under the waves, another popular choice for gap-years is going swimming with the fish, going diving. The most popular choice is taking part in marine conservation, helping with research into coral reefs and the factors contributing to their decline.

Our friends at Blue Ventures told us this: "People choose to partake in marine conservation and diving on their gap-year for a number of reasons. However, I'd say the main one is a passion for the underwater world and these projects provide people the opportunity to advance their diving skills, to explore diving in a more meaningful way or to gain practical conservation skills to apply in their future careers."

They usually provide all the diving equipment you need, plus accommodation. Not only do you get the chance of a lifetime to get up close with the endangered coral reefs, but you are giving something back to the environment.

See the directory pages starting on page 371 for information on companies and organisations offering gap-year opportunities

9

Working in
the UK

9 Working in the UK

Why work on a year out?

If you're not working to raise money for gap travel and you've just finished school or university, you might want a break from study and take a deep breath or two for a while. But even though work doesn't seem too appealing, just try going through the complex claiming procedure for the Jobseekers' Allowance and then living on it for a few weeks, and you'll soon see that working has its advantages.

But there are plenty of much better reasons to use a gap for work:

Saving money for university

Going to university is an expensive thing to do. Today, the vast majority of graduates are heavily in debt and this burden will be with them for many years to come.

Graduate debt is rising sharply as temporary jobs dry up and tuition fees, rent and travel costs increase.

Studies suggest students in the UK typically spend £12,000 a year on living expenses, including nearly £5000 on rent, £1900 on groceries, £1200 on socialising, £1700 on travel and £500 on books, equipment and field trips.

With tuition fees at £9000 a year, total debt for a three-year course could break the £60,000 barrier.

Even so, earning just a little bit now could really help your bank balance in the future.

Showing commitment

If you're attracted to a career in popular professions like the media, medicine and law, which are incredibly competitive and hard to get into, it could well prove necessary to grab any experience you can, paid or unpaid. It might make all the difference down the line when you have to prove to a potential employer that you really are committed.

Work experience

Another consideration is the frequency with which people applying for jobs report being rejected at interview 'because of a lack of work experience'. A gap-year is a great time to build up an initial experience of work culture as well as getting a foot in the door and getting recognised; in fact many students go back to the same firms after graduation.

Not sure what you want to do?

If your degree left you with several possible options and you couldn't face the university final year/graduate 'milk round' or you're undecided what career direction you want to head in, then a gap could be a great time to try out different jobs and to get a feel for what you might want to do in the future.

Whatever your reasons for working during a gap, you should start looking early to avoid disappointment.

visit: www.gap-year.com

Writing a CV

Fashions change in laying out a CV and in which order you arrange the various sections.

The advice is that a CV should be no more than two A4 pages and also that it should be tailored to the sector you're applying for.

The thing to remember is that employers are busy people, so they won't have time to read many pages, especially if they're trying to create a shortlist of maybe six interviewees from more than 100 applications for just the one job.

If you're at the start of your working life, there's a limit to how much tailoring you can do. A good tip is to put a short summary of your skills, and experience to date, at the top so the recruiter knows what you can do. It can either be a bullet point list or a short paragraph, but remember that it's essentially your sales pitch explaining why you're useful to the company. It should only be a short summary of what's contained in the sections that follow.

There are a number of online CV-writing advice sites and templates that can help you, but do check for any fees before you start.

Here's a selection:
nationalcareersservice.direct.gov.uk/advice/getajob
www.alec.co.uk/cvtips
www.soon.org.uk/writing-a-cv-resume/writing-cvs.html

Here's a list of headings for the details your CV should include:

- Personal details: name, address, phone number and email. You do not have to include gender, age, date of birth, marital details or nationality nor send a photograph, in fact some employers actively discourage photos for fear of being accused of bias in selecting people for interview.

- Short skills paragraph or key skills bullet points (see above).

- Work experience and skills: in order with most recent first. You can include part-time working that you've combined with education, as well as any voluntary work you've done, but if neither is directly within the job sector you're applying for, you need to focus on the transferable skills you got from it *eg* familiarity with office routines, record keeping, filing, if you've been in an office, or people skills if you worked in a shop.

- Achievements: have you been on any committees? (student council?), organised any events or fundraisers? Again, concentrate on what you learned from it, such as organisational skills, persuading companies to donate prizes for a raffle, planning catering and refreshments.

- Other skills: such as the Duke of Edinburgh's Award Scheme, workshops you've attended, hobbies *etc*.

- Education: again most recent first, with subjects studied and grades.

- References: you usually need two, one of them a recent employer, the other from school or university, though on a CV you only need to say 'references can be supplied'.

Getting the job

How do you get that first job with no prior experience? What can you offer?

The key is creativity. Show the company you're applying to that you can offer them something that nobody else can and do this by giving them an example. Be creative: If you're applying to an advertising firm, for instance, then mock up some adverts to show them.

Want to go into journalism? Write some sample articles and send them to local newspapers. Write to the editor and ask whether you could volunteer to help out in the newsroom to get a feel for the environment and the skills you'll need — a kind of

visit: www.gap-year.com

extended work experience to add to what you should have had via school.

You could try this with companies in other fields you're interested in. Be proactive and persevere. It will show you have initiative and commitment and whatever your eventual career it will also help you to learn the basics of acting professionally in a professional environment.

Do the research: Whatever your chosen field, find out about the company and show your knowledge about the industry. If you are going for an industry, such as medicine or law, then showing that you are more than competent and willing is all that you can really do. Saying this, you have to make sure that you stick out from other applicants.

Contacts

In the directory of this guidebook we list some companies that specifically employ gap-year students or offer graduate opportunities. But take this as a starting point — the tip of the iceberg — there are hundreds of other companies out there waiting to be impressed by you.

Research is crucial. Tailor your approach towards that specific company and never just expect to get a job; you have to work at it. The general rule is that nobody will call you back — be the one who gets in contact with them.

Job surfing

You don't get the personal touch from a website that you do by going into a local branch and getting advice, or registering face-to-face, but recruitment websites are really useful if you know what you want to do and you have a 'skills profile' that one of their customers is looking for. Some of them are aimed at graduates and students, others at a general audience, others at specific areas of work (IT, for example).

Here are a few to start with:

Student summer jobs

www.activate.co.uk
(This one contains gap-jobs, summer jobs, internships and jobs for new graduates.)

Graduate careers:

www.milkround.com
jobs.guardian.co.uk

General vacancies:

www.indeed.co.uk
www.reed.co.uk
www.jobsite.co.uk
www.monster.com
www.totaljobs.com

Technology specialists:

www.agencycentral.co.uk/jobsites/IT.htm

Finance:

www.exec-appointments.com

the gap-year guidebook 2018

On spec

If you can't find what you're looking for by using contacts, advertisements, agencies or the internet there is always DIY job hunting. You can walk into shops and restaurants to ask about casual work or use a phone directory (*eg Yellow Pages*) to phone businesses (art galleries, department stores, zoos…) and ask what is available.

Ring up, ask to speak to the personnel or HR manager and ask if and when they might have jobs available and how you should apply. If they ask you to write in, you can do so after the call. If you go in, make sure you look smart.

Remember, opportunities in the big professional firms are not always well publicised.

Temporary jobs (except agency-filled ones) are often filled by personal contact. If you have a burning desire to work for an architects' or lawyers' firm, for example, and you find nothing advertised, you could try making a list and phoning to ask if work is available.

Think about people you might already know in different work environments and ask around for what's available.

Banking: approach local branches for work experience. Also, try: **www.hays.com**

Education: most educational work experience is tied in with travelling abroad, to places like Africa or Asia, mostly to teach English. However, there are ways of gaining experience back home in England.

A very popular way is to see if the school that you have just left would like classroom helpers, or perhaps they need help in teaching a younger sports team. The key to this is to ask around and see what might be available.

But remember, for any work with children you will have to have a DBS (Disclosure and Barring Service) check. These were previously known as CRB (Criminal Records Bureau) checks. For more information, see: **www.gov.uk/disclosure-barring-service-check**

As well as straight teaching, any experience with children can be very useful, so try looking at camps and sports teams that may need help — there are a few contacts for camps within the Seasonal Work section.

Legal and medical: it's well known that studying for these two professions is lengthy and rigorous, so any amount of work experience could prove very useful. There's plenty available, but lots of competition for the places so you need to start looking early.

Nearly all NHS hospitals look for volunteer staff. So, if you can't find a worthwhile paid job, just contact the HR manager at your local hospital.

Try also: **www.jobs.nhs.uk** (for all NHS jobs)
www.lawgazettejobs.co.uk (for law jobs, including trainee positions)

Media, publishing and advertising: working on television or the radio is a favourite and it is no surprise that, because of this, the media is one of the hardest industries to break into.

Work experience is highly recommended. Many companies are very willing to try out gap-year students as trainees, as raw talent is such a limited commodity they want to nurture it as much as possible — plus it's cheap.

There are many websites dedicated to media jobs, but a good place to look for publishing vacancies is **www.thebookseller.com**

visit: www.gap-year.com

Theatre: many theatres provide work experience for gap-year students, so it's definitely worthwhile contacting your nearby production company. This industry recognises creativity and application probably more than any other, so starting out early and fiercely is the only way to do it.

Try also: **www.thestage.co.uk/recruitment**

Internships

Graduates cannot rely on the safety net of the traditional internship or graduate job this year. A survey by the Higher Education Statistics Agency last year found that nearly 1 in 10 students were believed to be unemployed six months after graduating from UK universities. Applicants for jobs are expected to have more skills, better grades and some form of industry experience as a minimum. In such turbulent times it is essential to make your CV stand out and rise above the competition of the near 400,000 graduates leaving the UK's 168 universities every year.

Check out **www.ratemyplacement.co.uk** for ideas about some of the opportunities that are out there.

There's also some good information at: **www.allaboutcareers.com/careers-advice/internships**

Interviews

Once your persistence has got you an interview, you need to impress your potential employers.

Attitude — confidence and knowledge are probably top of the list for employers, so that is what you must portray, even if you're a bag of nerves and haven't got a clue. They want to know you're committed.

229

Dress — make sure you are dressed appropriately (cover tattoos, remove nose piercings etc, don't show too much flesh, have clean and brushed hair — all the stuff that your teachers/parents tell you and really annoys you). If you're going for a creative job (advertising, art, etc) then you can probably be a little more casual — when you phone the secretary to confirm your interview time and venue, you can ask whether you'll be expected to dress formally. Alternatively, you could go to the company's offices around lunchtime (usually 1pm) and have a look at how people coming out are dressed.

Manner — stand straight; keep eye contact with the interviewer and smile. Be positive about yourself — don't lie, but focus on your good points rather than your bad ones.

Be well prepared to answer the question: "So, why do you want this job?" Remember they'll want to know you're keen, interested in what they do and what benefit you think you can bring to their company.

Gap-year specialists

If you would like to get a work placement from a gap-year specialist, the contacts listed in the directory sections in this guidebook are a good starting point for organisations to approach.

Another option is the Year Out Group, the voluntary association of gap specialists formed to promote the concept and benefits of well-structured year out programmes and to help people select suitable and worthwhile projects. The group's member organisations are listed on their website and provide a wide range of year out placements in the UK and overseas, including structured work placements.

Year Out Group members are expected to put potential clients and their parents in contact with those who have recently returned. They consider it important that these references are taken up at least by telephone and, where possible, by meeting face-to-face. See **www.yearoutgroup.org**

Gap-year employers

In the directory we've listed companies that either have specific gap-year employment policies or ones that we think are worth contacting. We've split them into three groups: festivals, seasonal work and graduate opportunities and work experience.

This isn't a comprehensive list, so it's still worth checking the internet and your local companies (in the *Yellow Pages*, for example).

Festivals

Whether musical, literary or dramatic, there are all kinds of festivals taking place up and down the country every year. You need to apply as early as possible, as there aren't that many placements. Satellite organisations spring up around core festivals; so if you are unsuccessful at first, try to be transferred to another department. The work can be paid or on a voluntary basis. Short-term work, including catering and stewarding, is available mainly during the summer. Recruitment often starts on a local level, so check the local papers and recruitment agencies.

It's also worth having a look at this site: **www.festaff.co.uk/jobs-at-festivals**

visit: www.gap-year.com

Seasonal and temporary work

A great way to make some quick cash, either to save up for travelling or to spend at home, is seasonal work. There are always extra short-term jobs going at Christmas: in the Post Office sorting office or in local shops. In the summer there's fruit or vegetable picking for example. There's a website that links farms in the UK and worldwide with students looking for holiday work: **www.pickingjobs.com**

Another option, if you have reasonable IT skills, is to temp in an office. July and August are good months for this too, when permanent staff are on holiday. You can register with local job agencies, which will almost certainly want to do a simple test of your skills. Temping is also a great idea if you're not at all sure what sector you want to work in — it's a good chance to find out about different types of work.

Pay, tax and National Insurance

You can expect to be paid in cash for casual labour, or by bank transfer (weekly or monthly) for small or large companies. Always keep the payslip that goes with your pay, along with your own records of what you earn (including payments for casual labour) during the tax year: from 6 April one year to 5 April the next. You need to ask your employer for a P46 form when you start your first job and a P45 form when you leave (which you take to your next employer). If you are out of education for a year you are not treated as a normal taxpayer.

Personal allowances — that is the amount you can earn before paying tax — are reviewed in the budget each year in April. To find out the current tax-free personal allowance rate call the Inland Revenue helpline or go to: **www.hmrc.gov.uk/nic**

231

Minimum wages, maximum hours

In the UK, workers aged 16 and 17 should get a 'development rate' of £4.05 an hour; 18 to 20-year-old workers should receive £5.60 an hour; workers aged 21 to 24 should received £7.05 per hour; and anyone aged 25 or over should get £7.50 an hour.

To check on how the National Minimum Wage applies to you, go to the Department for Business, Enterprise and Regulatory Reform (formerly called the DTI) website: **www.gov.uk/national-minimum-wage**

Alternatively, phone the National Minimum Wage Helpline on 0845 6000 678.

If you think you are not being paid the national minimum wage you can call this helpline number: 0800 917 2368.

All complaints about underpayment of the National Minimum Wage are treated in the strictest confidence.

The UK also has a law on working hours to comply with European Union legislation. This says that (with some exemptions for specific professions) no employee should be expected to work more than 48 hours a week. Good employers do give you time off in lieu if you occasionally have to work more than this. Others take no notice, piling a 60-hour-a-week workload on you. This is against the law and, unless you like working a 12-hour day, they must stop.

Please see the directory pages starting on page 389 for information on companies and organisations offering opportunities to work in the UK on your gap-year.

10

Volunteering in the UK

# Volunteering in the UK

Volunteering doesn't have to be done in a developing country, amongst the poorest on the planet, to bring a sense of satisfaction. There are many deserving cases right on your doorstep. You might also find that, if you do voluntary work close to home, it will make you more involved in your own community.

What's more, the global recession has prompted a greater need for volunteers, as charities have had to cut back on paid staff in the wake of reduced donations.

Some charities have also reported a huge increase in the numbers of potential volunteers. Arguably this reflects the numbers of graduates coming out of university unable to find work as well as high numbers of reported redundancies.

Benefits of UK volunteering

You can:

· Do some things you couldn't do abroad. Good examples are counselling, befriending and fundraising, all of which need at least some local knowledge.

· Have more flexibility: you can do a variety of things rather than opting for one programme or project.

· Combine volunteering with a study course or part-time job.

· Get to know more about your own community.

· Get experience before committing to a project abroad.

· Develop career options – a now well-accepted route into radio for example is to do a volunteer stint on hospital radio.

If you choose to spend at least some of your gap doing something for the benefit of others here in the UK, you'll get the same satisfying sense of achievement as volunteers who have been on programmes elsewhere.

To get the most out of volunteering during your gap-year, you must consider what you would like to achieve. Try asking yourself about your interests, skills and experience to define what type of volunteering role you are looking for.

Volunteering in the UK has other benefits too: it is usually cheaper and it can provide a tangible benefit to your local community. For example student volunteers contribute over £42 million to the economy each year through their activities (*National Student Volunteering Survey*) and many people go on to find jobs as a direct result of their volunteering.

Research has also proved that those who do voluntary work, or are helped by volunteers, adopt healthier lifestyles, can cope better with their own ill-health, have greater confidence and self-esteem, have an improved diet and even have a higher level of physical activity.

To find out more about volunteering you can visit Volunteering Matters' website **https://volunteeringmatters.org.uk**, where you can find your nearest volunteer opportunities.

https://do-it.org/ or **www.ncvo.org.uk** also list volunteering opportunities online.

Wherever you are, volunteering is an opportunity to learn about other people and about yourself.

If you're just starting out on a career path and are unsure what you want to do, volunteering can be an opportunity to gain relevant work experience. If you know, for example, that you want a career in retail, a stint with Oxfam will teach you a surprising amount. Many charity shops recognise this and offer training. Careers in the charity sector are also extremely popular and can be quite hard to get into, so a period of voluntary work will demonstrate your commitment and willingness to learn.

Volunteering for a while can also be useful for those who are maybe thinking of a career change or development. For example you could use your skills to develop a charity's website, or perhaps you have experience of marketing or campaigning.

While you're volunteering your services you can also use the time to find out more about the organisation's work, whom to talk to about training or qualifications and about work opportunities within the organisation.

What can you do?

Before contacting organisations it is a good idea to think about what you would like to do in terms of the activity and type of organisation you would like to work for. There's good advice on this at: **www.volunteernow.co.uk/volunteering/get-involved**

The UK has its share of threatened environments and species, homeless people and the economically disadvantaged, and those with physical disabilities or mental health problems.

the gap-year guidebook 2018

In some ways, therefore, the choices for projects to join are no different in the UK from the ones you'd be making if you were planning to join a project abroad.

Cash-strapped hospitals are always in need of volunteers – Great Ormond Street Children's Hospital in London is a good example. They look after seriously ill children and need volunteers to play with the children and make their stay less frightening. It also runs a hospital radio station – Radio Lollipop – in the evenings and on Sundays, for which it needs volunteers.

Or you could help with a youth sports team, get involved in a street art project, or with a holiday camp for deprived inner-city youngsters – there are many options and there are any number of inner-city organisations working to improve relations between, and provide/identify opportunities for, people from different ethnic groups, faiths and cultures.

Remember, though, that any volunteer work you do that puts you directly in contact with young people and other vulnerable groups, such as people with mental health problems, or care of the elderly, is likely to mean you'll need a CRB (Criminal Records Bureau) check for both their protection and yours. In some cases, you'll have to pay for this yourself.

Where to start?

Your own home town will have its share of charity shops on the high street, and they're always in need of volunteers. But you could also try local churches or sports groups. Check your local paper for stories on campaigns, special conservation days and other stories about good causes close to home that you might be able to support.

As with most opportunities, don't forget the internet is another good place to look. Just be sure to do your homework to make sure the company you're applying to is actually contributing to the community, and not just someones pocket.

visit: www.gap-year.com

What qualities does a good volunteer need?

The Samaritans is one organisation that's reported an upsurge in calls to its confidential helpline as a result of the recession – and if you've been in the position of losing your job, and are maybe thinking of volunteering to help others, it would be a good idea to think hard about whether you're able to offer what's needed.

Here's what the Samaritans have to say: "Samaritans volunteers need to be able to listen. They are not professional counsellors. They can also:

· question gently, tactfully – without intruding;

· encourage people to tell their own story in their own time and space;

· refrain from offering advice and instead offer confidential emotional support; and

· always try to see the other point of view, regardless of their own religious or political beliefs."

Go to this section on the Samaritans website: **www.samaritans.org/volunteer-us**

You can find out more here on the training and support you will be given before you are taken on.

ChildLine too has good advice for volunteers on its website and sees them as the essential basis of ChildLine's service. They need volunteers to speak to children and young people on their helpline, to work with them in schools, and to support fundraising, administration and management.

the gap-year guidebook 2018

The charity provides full training and support, and has centres in London, Nottingham, Glasgow, Aberdeen, Manchester, Swansea, Rhyl, Leeds, Belfast, Exeter and Birmingham.
Follow this link for more information:
www.nspcc.org.uk/what-you-can-do/volunteering-nspcc-childline/

There's a need for volunteers to help with disadvantaged people of all ages and if you're older, and considering volunteering, your work skills could come in handy. Many charities may need professional advice from time to time. If you have expertise in accountancy, administration, construction and maintenance, the law, psychiatry or treasury you might be able to help.

Helping refugees

The International Red Cross has a long history of helping traumatised and displaced people around the world, from being the first port of call in an emergency to monitoring the treatment of political prisoners, it is often trusted as the only impartial authority allowed access to detainees.

The British Red Cross has a specific scheme dedicated to helping refugees adjust to life in the UK. Trained volunteers provide much needed support to thousands of people every year, helping them to access local services and adjust to life in a new country. The Red Cross's services provide practical/emotional help to vulnerable asylum seekers and refugees. This includes offering orientation services to help refugees adapt to life in the UK, providing emergency support for large-scale arrivals, providing emergency provisions for those in crisis and offering peer-befriending support to young refugees.

You can volunteer to help out in charity shops or with fundraising. To find out more about volunteering with the Red Cross go to: **www.redcross.org.uk**

Conservation

Perhaps you're more interested in getting close to nature and doing some conservation work? The British Trust for Conservation Volunteers is a good place to start. It offers short (and longer) training courses that are informal and designed to be fun – including practical skills such as building a dry stone wall, creating a pond or a wildlife garden. It also has a number of options for volunteer schemes you can join: **www.tcv.org.uk/volunteering**

The Wildlife Trusts also offers regular volunteering opportunities from hedge laying to Wildlife Watch groups. They have hundreds of locations all over the UK, so there bound to be something near you. **www.wildlifetrusts.org/**

Not only do you get to give back to your local community, you can meet new people too. Plus it will look good on your CV.

Animals

Volunteer jobs with animal welfare organisations can vary from helping with kennel duties, assisting with fundraising events, carrying out wildlife surveys, to working on specific projects.

You can start off by contacting your local veterinary practises, zoos and animal rescue charities too see if they are in need of volunteers.

Animal Jobs Direct has information on paid work with animals but it also has a section for volunteers, as well as courses you can take part in – perfect for anyone looking for the edge to get them into veterinary college.

The web address below gives direct links to animal welfare and rescue charities that offer a variety of different and interesting volunteering opportunities –there are an amazing range of voluntary jobs available. Remember, many animal charities exist on limited funds and therefore voluntary workers are much needed and appreciated.

To find out more, visit: **www.animal-job.co.uk/animal-volunteer-work-uk.html**

Help with expenses

While giving your time for free is part of the definition of volunteering, financial help is often available and organisations shouldn't leave you out of pocket. Many charities will reimburse your expenses such as travel tickets and lunch costs.

For some long term volunteering placements, different rules apply and as well as having your basic expenses covered, you may be given a 'subsistence allowance' to cover living costs like heat, light, laundry and food. You may also be given free accommodation – for example if you are volunteering for several months in a care home.

If you are interested in volunteering with an organisation, ask whether they cover volunteer expenses and find out what they will reimburse.

In the directory we list the contact details of a number of charities and organisations that are grateful for volunteers. If you can't find anything that interests you there, then there are a number of organisations that place people with other charities or that have a wide national network of their own – an internet search should give you a good list.

The following websites provide useful links and information about volunteering:
www.do-it.org.uk
www.ncvo-vol.org.uk
www.timebank.org.uk

Please see the directory pages starting on page 395 for information on companies and organisations offering volunteering opportunities in the UK.

11

Learning
in the UK

Learning in the UK

You don't have to spend your gap-year travelling the globe if that doesn't appeal to you. The point about taking a gap is to try out new experiences that leave you feeling refreshed and stimulated, to learn something new and possibly come up with some new ideas about where you want your life to head next. So if you're frustrated that hardly anything you were taught at school seems relevant to your life, why not use your gap-year to learn new skills that you choose yourself? You can make them as useful as you want.

There are plenty of evening classes available at local colleges, though usually only in term time, and, if you're thinking of training that doesn't involve university or are looking for ways to expand your skill set as part of a change of career direction, check out the Skills Funding Agency and the Young People's , which exists to promote lifelong learning, with the aim of young people and adults having skills to match the best in the world. There's lots of information on what's available, including financial help, on: **https://www.gov.uk/government/organisations/education-and-skills-funding-agency.**

A gap is also a good opportunity to explore interests that may, up to now, have been hobbies; here are some suggestions:

Archaeology

Do relics from the past fascinate you? Would you love to find one? You could get yourself on an actual archaeological dig. One good place to start is with your local county council's archaeology department, which may know of local digs you could join. Nowadays, whenever a major building development is going through the planning application process, permission to build often includes a condition allowing for archaeological surveys to be done before any work can begin; so another source of information could be the planning departments of local district councils.

Art

If you're seriously interested in painting, sculpting or other artistic subjects, but don't know if you want to carry it through to a full degree, there is the useful option of a one-year art foundation course. These are available from a wide variety of art colleges.

A foundation course at art college doesn't count towards an art degree, in the sense that you can't skip the first year of your three-year degree course, but it can help you find out whether you are interested in becoming a practising artist, maybe an illustrator, an animator, a graphic designer, or are more interested in things like art history, or perhaps working in a gallery or a museum or in a field like interior design. If you do want to go on to do a three-year art school degree, most colleges will require you to show them a portfolio of your work during the interview process. A foundation course would help you build up a portfolio of work and prepares you for a three-year degree.

visit: www.gap-year.com

Cookery

A cookery course is a great way of learning a fundamental skill that can change your life, whether it leads to professional cooking jobs in your time off allowing you to pay your way while travelling, or simply sets you up with skills to cook for yourself and friends throughout university and beyond.

With just a few tips and tricks, sharp knife skills and plenty of ingredient know-how, learning basic cooking skills can transform the way you eat, shop and cook.

Offering four, six or ten-week courses in which students learn through demonstration and practical sessions, certificate cookery courses generally comprise a thorough understanding of basic cooking skills and techniques, a certificate in health and hygiene, as well as a basic grounding in pairing food with wine.

Cookery schools tell us that the majority of those who want to work after doing a cookery course do find cooking work. What's involved in being a chalet cook depends on what a ski company or employer wants. Usually the day starts with a cooked breakfast for the ski party, then possibly a packed lunch, tea and cake when hungry skiers get back, possibly canapés later, and a three or four-course supper. The food does need more than the usual amount of carbohydrates.

Ski companies expect high standards and may ask for sample menus when you apply for chalet cooking jobs. Sometimes the menus are decided in advance and the shopping done locally by someone else; sometimes the cook has to do the shopping.

Perhaps surprisingly, ski companies and agencies rarely ask about language skills – the cooks seem to manage without.

Here's a list of highly recommended cookery schools for you to check out:

www.ashburtoncookeryschool.co.uk
www.cookeryschool.co.uk
www.leiths.com
www.tantemarie.co.uk

ROYAL CENTRAL
SCHOOL OF SPEECH & DRAMA

UNIVERSITY OF LONDON

STUDY ACTING IN LONDON

> CENTRAL'S PART-TIME GAP YEAR DIPLOMA

Auditions from February for **October 2018 course start**
Register interest at **www.cssd.ac.uk/course/gap-year-diploma**

CSSDLondon

Drama

There are plenty of amateur dramatic and operatic societies in small towns across the UK. If you've always had a hankering to tread the boards, they're a great way to find out more about all the elements of putting on a production. You may be able to volunteer at your local theatre and gain valuable experience that way. Ring them up or check out their website to see if they have a bank of volunteers.

Our friends at Peer Productions tell us that: "Often graduates find that they have gained performance confidence and organisational abilities. There is a focus on improving communication and a greater understanding of theatre, both theatrically and practically within the industry. Cohesive team work, creative problem solving and working under pressure are key attributes that our graduates leave with. Importantly, our course offers real world experience and thus helps young actors decide whether the performance route is one they wish to follow and we aim to support those who find it is not what they wish to do."

"87% of our graduates have gone on to drama school or university after completing our course. Others have pursued non performance-based routes including sound production, stage make-up, project management and teaching. We do our utmost to support a student in whichever direction they decide to go after studying with us."

Then there are short courses and summer schools. This site lists a wide range of programmes available over the summer holidays: **www.summer-schools.info**

Driving

There may be a lot of pressure to minimise car use in an effort to reduce carbon emissions and tackle global warming, but there are still plenty of good reasons for learning to drive.

First, unless you're intending to live in an inner city indefinitely, you may need a driver's licence to get a job; secondly, it will give you independence and you won't have to rely on other people to give you lifts everywhere. Even though you might not be able to afford the insurance right now, let alone an actual car, your gap-year is an ideal time to take driving lessons.

245

The test comes in two parts, theory and practical: and you need to pass the theory test before you apply for the practical one. However, you can start learning practical driving before you take the theory part, but to do that you need a provisional driving licence. You need to complete a driving licence application form and a photocard application form D1 – available from most post offices. Send the forms, the fee and original documentation confirming your identity such as your passport or birth certificate (make sure you keep a photocopy) and a passport-sized colour photograph to the DVLA.

You also need to check that you are insured for damage to yourself, other cars or other people, and if you are practising in the family car, your parents will have to add cover for you on their insurance.

The DSA (Driving Standards Authority) is responsible for driving tests. However, to avoid duplication, all information on learning to drive, including fees, advice on preparing for the test and booking one has been moved to the Government services website: **www.gov.uk/browse/driving/learning-to-drive**

Theory

The theory test is in two parts: a multiple-choice part and a hazard perception section. You have to pass both. If you pass one and fail the other, you have to do both again.

The multiple-choice is a touch-screen test where you have to get at least 43 out of 50 questions right. You don't have to answer the questions in turn and the computer shows how much time you have left. You can have 15 minutes' practice before you start the test properly. If you have special needs you can get extra time for the test – ask for this when you book it.

In the hazard test, you are shown 14 video clips filmed from a car, each containing one or more developing hazards. You have to indicate as soon as you see a hazard developing, which may necessitate the driver taking some action, such as changing speed or direction. The sooner a response is made the higher the score. Test results and feedback information are given within half an hour of finishing. The fee for the standard theory test is currently £23.

Your driving school, instructor or local test centre should have an application form, although you can book your test over the phone (0300 200 1122) or online at: **www.gov.uk/book-a-driving-theory-test**

Practical test

You have two years to pass the practical test once you have passed the theory part. The practical test for a car will cost £62, unless you choose to take it in the evening or on Saturday, in which case the cost will increase to £75. On top of this you will usually have to pay for the use of the driving instructors car.

It's more expensive for a motorbike and the test is now in two modules – module 1 is £15.50 for both evenings and weekends, module 2 is £75 for weekday and £88.50 for weekend and evening tests.

You can book the practical test in the same way as the theory test. The bad news is that the tests are tough and it's quite common to fail twice or more before a pass. The practical test lasts around 40 minutes, and is divided into 5 parts: eyesight check; 'show me, tell me' questions, driving ability, reversing your vehicle and independent driving. You'll fail if you commit more than 15 driving faults.

Once you pass your practical test, you can upgrade your provisional licence for a full licence.

visit: www.gap-year.com

Instructors

Of course some unqualified instructors (including parents) are experienced and competent, as are many small driving schools – but some checking out is a good idea if a driving school is not a well-known name. You can make sure that it is registered with the Driving Standards Agency and that the instructor is a qualified Approved Driving Instructor (ADI). AA and BSM charges can be used as a benchmark if you're trying other schools. There's information about choosing an instructor and what qualifications they must have if they're charging you here: **www.gov.uk/find-driving-schools-and-lessons**

Film

For those wanting to forge a career in the filmmaking industry it can be difficult to navigate the world of film school and to decide whether it is the right option for you.

To gain access to the industry it is important to have as much practical experience on your CV as possible. There are many options available, from working as a runner and camera trainee to gaining experience in post-production houses and internships in feature film production companies.

You can also spend your gap-year making your own films and learning from industry professionals to develop the skills needed for a career in filmmaking.

Language courses

Even if the job you are applying for doesn't require them, employers are often impressed by language skills. With the growth of global business, most companies like to think of themselves as having international potential at the very least.

If you didn't enjoy language classes at school, that shouldn't necessarily put you off. College courses and evening classes are totally different – or at least they should be. If in doubt, ask to speak to the tutor, or to someone who has already been on the course, before you sign up.

And even if you don't aspire to learn enough to be able to use your linguistic skills in a job, you could still take conversation classes so you can speak a bit of the language when you go abroad on your holidays. It is amazing what a sense of achievement and self-confidence you can get when you manage to communicate the simplest things to a local in their own language: such as ordering a meal or buying stamps for your postcards home.

You can now get very comprehensive language courses on CD-ROM, which include booklets or pages that can be printed off. The better ones use voice recognition as well, so you can practise your pronunciation. These can also be found in bookstores.

The internet itself is also a good source of language material. There are many courses, some with free access, some that need a very healthy credit card. If all you want is a basic start, then take a look at: **www.bbc.co.uk/languages**

This site offers you the choice of beginner's French, German, Italian, Mandarin, Portuguese, Greek, Spanish, Japanese, Urdu and some other languages, complete with vocabulary lists to download, all for free.

As well as courses, there are translation services, vocabulary lists and topical forums – just do a web search and see how many sites come up. Many are free but some are extremely expensive so check before you sign up.

The best way to improve your language skills is to practice speaking; preferably to a native speaker in their own country. But if you don't have the time or the money to go abroad yet, don't worry. There are plenty of places in the UK to learn a wide variety of languages, from Spanish to Somali. We've listed some language institutions in the directory, but also find out what language courses your local college offers, and what evening classes there are locally.

Practice makes perfect

When you need to practise, find out if there are any native speakers living in your town – you could arrange your own language and cultural evenings.

Terrestrial TV stations run some language learning programmes, usually late at night. If you have satellite or cable TV you can also watch foreign shows though this can be a bit frustrating if you're a beginner. It's best to record the programmes so you can replay any bits that you didn't understand the first time round.

Once you get a bit more advanced then you can try tuning your radio into foreign speech-based shows from the relevant countries. This is also a good way to keep up-to-date with current affairs in your chosen country, as well as keeping up your listening and understanding skills. Subjects are wide-ranging, and there's something to interest everyone.

Most self-teach language tapes have been well received by teachers and reviewers, but can be a bit expensive for the average gap-year student. So, you might be glad to hear that, if you have iTunes, you can download language podcasts from the store. Most of these are free and you have the option of subscribing so that new podcasts are automatically downloaded next time you log on.

my
gap-year
Philip

What sparked your interest in performing arts?

My interest in performing began when I started secondary school. It was a great way to make new friends and made me feel like a part of something. It also gave me an opportunity to express myself and the feeling of people watching me perform was just exhilarating!

What made you take up the gap-year and choose The Royal Central School of Speech and Drama?

I found the gap-year course when I was nearing the end of my first year of applying for drama schools, I really wanted to get into a routine and although I would have liked to do a foundation course it would have been a very costly investment. I also wanted time to enjoy the freedom from full-time education in order to allow myself to find my feet as a 'young adult'.

As a result, the schedule on the gap-year course was perfect for me. As well as that, Royal Central is such a renowned school and the ability to be able to train here has been amazing.

What have you learnt over the course of the last year?

The course teaches you so much in such a short amount of time, we explored screen, stage and radio all the while being taught by visiting lecturers and professionals that were so knowledgeable in their field. The course emphasised the importance of group work and we were constantly collaborating with each other to create exciting work within the fantastic facilities that we had access to throughout the week which was definitely helpful when searching and preparing.

What your next adventure is and has the diploma helped?

My next step is actually on the BA (Hons) Acting course at Royal Central, which I have been fortunate enough be offered a place on. It's really one of those dream come through things and I can't thank the teachers on the diploma enough who were always there to offer support and advice. The diploma gave me an opportunity to meet some truly fantastic people and to learn the necessary skills needed to start the next chapter of my journey, which I will never forget.

For more information on the Royal Central School of Speech and Drama, see their advert on page 244

Music

Perhaps you always wanted to learn the saxophone, but never quite got round to it? Now would be an ideal time to start. If you're interested, your best bet is to find a good private tutor. Word of mouth is the best recommendation, but some teachers advertise in local papers, and you could also try an online search engine like **www.musicteachers.co.uk**

If you already play an instrument, you could broaden your experience by going on a residential course or summer school. These are available for many different ability levels, although they tend to be quite pricey. There's no central info source on the net, as there is for drama courses, but we searched the internet for residential summer music schools and found loads of individual schools offering courses, so there are bound to be some near you. See the directory for more information.

Online learning

There are plenty of online learning courses for those who are welded semi-permanently to their computers. Some will grant recognised qualifications at the end of the course, others will award you their own award.

Here are a few websites that cover a variety of subjects, although there are hundreds out there, so search what you want to learn and take your pick from what's on offer. Be sure to have a look through the course summary to make sure you will be learning about the aspects of the subject you're interested in.

www.open.ac.uk/courses
www.futurelearn.com
www.reed.co.uk/courses
www.shawacademy.com

Photography

There are lots of photography courses available, from landscape photography to studio work. Don't kid yourself that a photography course is going to get you a job and earn you pots of money, but there's nothing to stop you enjoying photography as a hobby or sideline.

If you do want to find out more about professional photography you could try contacting local studios and asking about the possibility of spending some time with them as an assistant. Wedding photographers quite often take along a second photographer for the big day and although shooting a whole wedding can be quite exhausting (and daunting!), it will give you some valuable experience working alongside a professional. Another option is to contact your local paper and ask if you can shadow a photographer, so you can get a feel for how they work and perhaps start building a portfolio of your own.

Sport

After all that studying maybe all you want to do is get out there and do something. The same applies if you've been stuck in an office at a computer for most of your working life. If you're the energetic type and hate the thought of spending your gap-year stuck behind a desk, why not get active and do some sport?

There are sports courses for all types at all levels, from scuba diving for beginners to advanced ski instructor qualification courses. Of course if you manage to get an instructor's qualification you may be able to use it to get a job (see **Chapter 8 – Sport**).

TEFL

Teaching English as a Foreign Language qualifications are always useful for earning money wherever you travel abroad. The important thing to check is that the qualification you will be gaining is recognised by employers. Most courses should also lead on to help with finding employment. There's more on TEFL courses in **Chapter 5 – Working Worldwide**.

X-rated

For a real adrenalin rush, go for one of the extreme sports like sky boarding, basically a combination of skydiving and snowboarding – you throw yourself out of a plane wearing a parachute and perform acrobatic stunts on a board.

Or, if you like company when you're battling against the elements, then you could get involved in adventure racing: teams race each other across rugged terrain without using anything with a motor, *eg* skiing, hiking, sea kayaking. Team members have to stay together throughout the race. Raid Gauloises (five person teams, two weeks, five stages, half the teams don't finish!) and Eco-Challenge (ten days, 600km, several stages and an environmental project) are the two most well-known adventure race events.

If you want to get wet, then try diving, kayaking, sailing, surfing, water polo, windsurfing, or white-water rafting.

And if those don't appeal then there's always abseiling, baseball, basketball, bungee jumping, cave diving, cricket, fencing, football, golf, gymnastics, hang gliding, hockey, horse riding, ice hockey, ice skating, jet skiing, motor racing, mountain biking, mountain boarding, parachuting, polo, rock climbing, rowing, rugby, running, skateboarding, skating, ski jumping, skiing, skydiving, sky surfing, snowmobiling, snowboarding, squash, stock car racing, tennis or trampolining! If the sport you are interested in isn't listed in our directory then try contacting the relevant national association (*eg* the LTA for tennis) and asking them for a list of course providers.

Please see the directory pages starting on page 405 for information on companies and organisations offering learning opportunities in the UK.

Being Safe

A Squadron Ltd
UK

trainingwing@a-sqn.com

+44 (0)7762 507 146

www.a-sqn.com

A Squadron is a UK company offering military, security and survival training; related corporate and bespoke entertainment events; and historical lectures.

Adventure Expeditions
UK

info@adventure-expeditions.net

+44 (0) 1305 813107

www.adventure-expeditions.net

Outdoor First Aid training with ITC Certification - a nationally recognised qualification that fulfils training requirements for insurance purposes and those stipulated by training bodies.

Adventure First Aid
UK

info@adventurefirstaid.co.uk

0800 999 2716

www.adventurefirstaid.co.uk

Travel first aid and crisis management courses, delivered by experienced professional trainers.

British Red Cross
UK

information@redcross.org.uk

0844 871 1111

www.redcross.org.uk

The Red Cross (Charity No. 220949) offers first aid courses around the UK lasting from one to four days depending on your experience and the level you want to achieve.

Consularcare
UK

info@consularcare.com

+44 (0)20 3198 1890

www.consularassist.com

From a lost or stolen passport to liaising with authorities and family back home in the event of an incident, we'll be there for you; so you can sleep easy.

DS-48
UK

info@ds-48.com

UK: +44 (0)203 745 5877; US: +1 (713) 4894172

www.ds-48.com

DS-48 offers discreet, intelligence-led risk management, advisory and resolution services. Wherever you are in the world, we keep you from harm, provide assistance when needed and grant you peace of mind.

Free European Health Insurance Card

UK

0191 218 1999

www.nhs.uk

The European Health Insurance Card (EHIC) enables access to state-provided healthcare in all European Economic Area countries at a reduced cost or sometimes free of charge.

Healthy Travel

UK

enquiries@healthy-travel.co.uk

www.travelwithcare.com

Healthy Travel stock a range of health products and travel products suitable for all types of outdoor activities, from a walk in the country to trekking in the jungle.

InterHealth Worldwide

UK

info@interhealth.org.uk

+44 (0)20 7902 9000

www.interhealth.org.uk

InterHealth provide clinics and travel health advice, eg on immunisations.

Intrepid Expeditions

UK

nigel@intrepid-expeditions.co.uk

0800 043 2509

www.intrepid-expeditions.co.uk

Runs many different survival courses, including a first aid course, ranging from two to 14 days.

MASTA

UK

enquiries@masta.org

020 7291 9333

www.masta-travel-health.com

MASTA healthcare provide travel clinics across the UK offering professional advice to travellers about their specific travel health needs including anti-malarials, vaccinations and disease prevention.

Objective Travel Safety Ltd

UK

office@objectiveteam.com

01788 899 029

www.objectivegapyear.com

A fun one-day safety course or personalised safety courses for travellers, designed to teach them how to think safe and prepare for challenges they may face.

Pacsafe

China

info@pacsafe.com

+852 3664 8300

www.pacsafe.com

Pacsafe® offers a range of travel security products to keep travellers one step ahead of the game and their gear secure from opportunistic thieves. Pacsafe® gives travellers the peace of mind they need to get on and get out there on the road less travelled.

RYA

UK

admin@rya.org.uk

023 8060 4100

www.rya.org.uk

The RYA is the national body for all forms of boating and offers courses specialising in the technique of sea survival at training centres across the UK.

Safe Gap Year

UK

Info@safegapyear.co.uk

0845 602 55 95

www.safegapyear.co.uk

Safe Gap Year is a training and consultancy company specialising in Independent Travel Safety and Cultural Awareness.

St John Ambulance

UK

+44 (0)8700 104950

www.sja.org.uk

The St John Ambulance Association runs first aid courses throughout the year around the country. Courses last a day and are suitable for all levels of experience.

Taurus Insurance Services

Gibraltar

team@taurus.agency

+350 0207 183 6081

www.taurus.gi

Taurus Insurance Services provides gap year and working holiday travel insurance.

The Royal Life Saving Society

UK

info@rlss.org.uk

+44 (0) 1789 773 994

www.rlss.org.uk

Contact The Royal Life Saving Society for information about qualifications in life saving, lifeguarding and life support.

TravelPharm

UK

info@travelpharm.com

+44 (0)115 951 2092

www.travelpharm.com

Provides travellers with a range of medication and equipment at very competitive prices to make your journey both healthier and safer!

TripTogether

UK

support@triptogether.com

www.triptogether.com

Find a travel companion for any trip you have planned – from a city break to a month of backpacking.

Ultimate Gap Year

UK

info@ultimategapyear.co.uk

www.ultimategapyear.co.uk

Personalised safety training suitable for anyone embarking on a gap-year. Training held at homes throughout south-east England.

Communication

0044 Ltd

UK

+44 (0)1926 332153

www.0044.co.uk

Their global SIM card could save you money on international calls.

Aether Mobile Ltd

UK

customersupport@aether-mobile.com

www.aether-mobile.com

Get your SIM now and cut your mobile phone calls by up to 90% when abroad and get free incoming texts and calls in all countries.

ekit

UK

shout@ekit.com

0800 028 2402/0800 376 2370

www.ekit.com

ekit is a global provider of integrated communications, mobile, VOIP and Internet services, designed to keep travelers in touch.

255

EuroCallingCards.com

UK

contactus@eurocallingcards.com

+44 (0) 208 099 5899

www.eurocallingcards.com

Leading online supplier of international phone cards.

Go Sim

UK

0800 376 2370

www.gosim.com

Supplier of pre-paid international mobile SIM cards for travellers wishing to make phone calls abroad.

My UK Mail

UK

contact@my-uk-mail.co.uk

0845 838 1815

www.my-uk-mail.co.uk

UK based company providing a mail holding and forwarding service to international destinations including permaneant and temporary addresses.

NobelCom

Bermuda

help@NobelCom.co.uk

0800 652 1979

www.nobelcom.co.uk

Supplier of pre-paid phone cards for international long distance calling that can be tailored to travellers needs.

O2

UK

0800 230 0202

www.o2.co.uk

Provider of international broadband dongles enabling travellers to connect to the internet by simply plugging their broadband dongle into their laptop.

Orange

UK

0800 079 0409

www.orange.co.uk

Provider of international broadband dongles enabling travellers to connect to the internet by simply plugging their broadband dongle into their laptop.

PocketComms Ltd

UK

sales@pocketcomms.co.uk

+44 (0)1635 799484

www.pocketcomms.co.uk

A manual pocket sized universal language system in pictorial form to help travellers communicate through language barriers.

Talkmobile

UK

0870 071 5888

www.talkmobile.co.uk

Talkmobile provides monthly or pay as you go international mobile SIM cards for travellers wishing to make phone calls abroad.

Virgin Broadband

UK

0845 650 4500

www.virginmedia.com

Provider of international broadband dongles enabling travellers to connect to the internet by simply plugging their broadband dongle into their laptop.

Planning the route

Gap Advice

UK

info@gapadvice.org

07973 548316

www.gapadvice.org

Independent gap year travel advice, information, help and ideas on projects and placements.

Go Overseas

USA

marketing@gooverseas.com

www.gooverseas.com

Explore Programs: Simplify your search by comparing programs side by side. Read Reviews: Learn what to expect on your trip by reading reviews from travelers who have been there. Start Planning: Read articles to get answers to all of your pre-departure questions.

HyperDia

Japan

hyperdia.vz@ml.hitachi-systems.com

www.hyperdia.com

www.hyperdia.com features a search engine which provides information on routes and timetables for trains and flights in Japan. HyperDia also offer an app, 'Hyperdia by voice' which can be dowloaded via the App Store and makes it even easier for you to plan your travel routes.

iGapyear

UK

info@igapyear.com

+44 (0)845 643 9338

www.igapyear.com

iGapyear.com helps you do your prep work and make sure you arrange your perfect gap year. Choose from jobs, courses, placements and trips.

Japan Rail Pass

Japan

www.japanrailpass.net

Japan Rail Pass offer a pass covering all six companies which make up the Japan Railways Group, with tickets valid for seven, 14 or 21 days of travel.

The Bus Station

UK

www.busstation.net

www.busstation.net is a website which provides an extensive database of links to bus, tram and trolleybus operators and providers from across the world.

Working Holiday Store

UK

+44 (0) 1737 887556

www.workingholidaystore.com

An independent company that aims to provide travellers with an online resource, enhancing their planning and prep for the adventure of a lifetime.

YearOutWork

UK

www.yearoutwork.co.uk

YearOutWork is dedicated to helping you plan your time out... whatever you choose to do.

What to take

Ardern Healthcare Ltd

UK

info@ardernhealthcare.com

01584 781777

www.ardernhealthcare.com

Ardern Healthcare Ltd specialise in offering travellers a suitable insect repellent, in the form of sprays, wipes and creams, whatever their age or destination.

Blacks

UK

customercare@blacks.co.uk

0844 257 2078

www.blacks.co.uk

Blacks has 90 UK stores and provides a wide range of outdoor equipment and clothing from leading brands including The North Face, Berghaus and Craghoppers.

Brunton Outdoor

USA

support@bruntongroup.com

+44 (0) 2392528711

www.brunton.com

Compact personal power device, from the Brunton freedom range, which recharges devices like MP3 players, smart phones, digital cameras and more via car or sun ray.

CEWE Photoworld

UK

+44 (0)1926 463 107

www.cewe-photoworld.com

From printing your holiday snaps to producing your wedding photo book, printing greeting cards to creating a special gift, we make items you'll treasure from the memories you love.

Cotswold Outdoor Ltd

UK

customer.services@cotswoldoutdoor.com

+44 (0) 844 557 7755

www.cotswoldoutdoor.com

Cotswold Outdoor Limited have stores across the UK and provide camping equipment, clothes, maps, climbing gear and footwear from brands such as Osprey, Scarpa and Solomon.

Craigdon Mountain Sports Edinburgh

UK

sales@craigdon.com

+44 (0)1467 629394

www.craigdon-edinburgh.com

Craigdon Mountain Sports Edinburgh is an independent outdoor retailer with its flagship store based on Biggar Road, Edinburgh. They stock a wide range of clothing and equipment.

Field and Trek

UK

www.fieldandtrek.com

Field & Trek has stores all over the UK and supplies outdoor equipment and performance clothing ranges from brands such as Berghaus, The North Face, Mountain Equipment, Merrell, and Lowe Alpine.

Gap Year Travel Store

UK

0113 8715 880

www.gapyeartravelstore.com

Online store selling quality travel kit and equipment to backpackers and independent travellers.

Go Outdoors

UK

enquiries@gooutdoors.co.uk

+44 (0)844 387 6800

www.gooutdoors.co.uk

Go Outdoors operates from 41 retail stores across the UK and offers a wide choice of outdoor accessories and equipment from brands such as Hi Gear, Ragatta, North Ridge and Outwell.

Go Travel

UK

sales@design-go.com

+44 (0)208 906 8505

www.go-travelproducts.com

Go is the most widely distributed range of travel accessories in the world. It still remains a UK family business and it is just as committed to bring innovative products to market as it was over 30 years ago.

Knowles Travelgoods

UK

info@bagsandaccessories.co.uk

+44 (0)1905 22019

www.bagsandaccessories.co.uk

Knowles Travelgoods stocks a wide variety of luggage such as suitcases, hand luggage, holdalls and backpacks.

Lifesaver Systems

UK

info@lifesaversystems.com

0808 1782799/+44 (0) 1206 580999

www.lifesaversystems.com

All-in-one filtration system, in a bottle, which will turn the foulest water into safe drinking water without the use of chemicals, allowing for much lighter packing.

Lifeventure

UK

+44 (0)118 981 1433

www.lifeventure.com

When you're on your travels, whether you're going solo or in a group, it's vital you have reliable and practical accessories by your side. Life Venture know how to make kit that's right for the job.

Millets

UK

customercare@millets.co.uk

0161 393 7060

www.millets.co.uk

Millets, with over 150 stores, is one of the UK's largest travel and outdoor retailer. Brands include Berghaus, Eurohike, Merrell, North Face and Peter Storm.

Mountain Warehouse

UK

info@mountainwarehouse.com

+44 (0)20 3828 7700

www.mountainwarehouse.com

At Mountain Warehouse we have been developing the very best outdoor gear for all the family since 1997.

Nikwax Ltd

UK

info@nikwax.com

+44 (0)1892 786400

www.nikwax.com

To clean and waterproof all your gear, extend its life and maintain high performance with low environmental impact - Nikwax it!

Nomad Travel & Outdoor

UK

orders@nomadtravel.co.uk

+44 (0) 845 260 0044

www.nomadtravel.co.uk

As well as the usual stock of clothing, equipment, books and maps their 8 travel stores also hold medical supplies.

Outdoor Megastore

UK

admin@outdoormegastore.co.uk

0151 944 2202

www.outdoormegastore.co.uk

Online store for all your outdoor equipment.

Outdoor Spirit

UK

info@outdoor-spirit.co.uk

+44.1387 252891

www.outdoor-spirit.co.uk

Online shop offering a rangre of out door clothing, including Dr Martens shoes and boots.

Powertraveller

UK

sales@powertraveller.com

+44 (0)1420 542980

www.powertraveller.com

Power traveller products give the end user freedom to pursue an active outdoor lifestyle by keeping essential lines of communication open whilst they are "off-grid".

Simply Hike

UK

info@simplyhike.co.uk

0844 567 7070

www.simplyhike.co.uk

Simply Hike - dor camping gear, outdoor clothing and accessories.

Snow and Rock

UK

manager.direct@snowandrock.com

01483 445335

www.snowandrock.com

Snow & Ice have stores across the UK offering a wide choice of outdoor clothing and equipment including Arc'teryx, Merrell, The North Face and Salomon.

Steri Pen

USA

support@steripen.com

+1 207 374 5800

www.steripen.com

Steripen is a portable, fast and easy way to ensure water is safe to drink through harnessing the power of ultraviolet light.

Student Money Saver

UK

info@studentmoneysaver.co.uk

0207 183 4671

www.studentmoneysaver.co.uk

Established by graduates in 2010, Student Money Saver is a website all about living large and spending little. We're here to save students money, source the best student deals and student discounts and give the best student finance tips.

Total Backpacking

UK

contactus@totalbackpacking.com

www.totalbackpacking.com

Total Backpacking sells a range of travel essentials, including backpacks, tents, sleeping bags, portable electronics and first aid equipment.

Trespass

UK

+44 (0) 141 568 8089

www.trespass.com

Trespass is an outdoor clothing, footwear and equipment manufacturer and retailer with over 200 stores throughout the UK. It also operates an e-commerce website for purchasing online.

Urbane Traveller

UK

info@urbanetraveller.com

+44 (0)117 973 4053

www.urbanetraveller.com

Urbane Traveller source beautifully made & stylish travel accessories and fashionable travel clothing, bringing these products together under a premium and stylish online emporium.

Vango

UK

info@vango.co.uk

01475 744122

www.vango.co.uk

Evergrowing range of tents, sleeping bags, rucsacks and outdoor accessories.

Weldricks Pharmacy

UK

customerservices@weldricks.co.uk

0845 402 4409

www.weldricks.co.uk

Our UK based online pharmacy has a great range of travel medicines, insect repellents, sun care and travel accessories at great prices. Our online Doctor can assist with travellers requiring Prescription Only malaria prophylaxis.

Yeomans Outdoors

UK

01246 477 513

www.yeomansoutdoors.co.uk

With over 90 stores across the UK, Yeomans Outdoors stocks a wide range of tents, camping equipment and out-door clothing from brands such as Vango, Trekmates, Easycamp and Karrimor.

Finance

Credit Cards

Advanced Payment Solutions Ltd
UK

0871 277 5599

www.mycashplus.co.uk

Produce the Cashplus Card, a pre-paid card which ensures you do not go overdrawn, incure interest or fall prey to credit card fraud.

Cash Passport
UK

cardservices_prepaid@mastercard.com

0800 056 0572

www.cashpassport.com

Cash Passport can carry many different currencies at one time meaning you can travel or shop freely from one country to the next. You can even use it online to avoid hidden charges.

Caxton FX
UK

info@caxtonfxcard.com

www.caxtonfx.com

Caxton FX provide a prepaid currency card usable wherever you see a MasterCard symbol. They also offer an app which allows you to transfer money to the card.

Escape Prepaid
UK

customerservices@escapeprepaid.co.uk

0871 220 6420

www.escapeprepaid.co.uk

With the 'Escape Travel Money Prepaid MasterCard' you can withdraw cash from over 1.5 million ATMs worldwide, usually without having to pay a fee.

FairFX Plc
UK

enquiries@fairfx.com

+44 (0)20 7107 1206

www.fairfx.com

FairFX offer a free chip and PIN secure card when you load £50 or more, which can be used in over 220 countries.

H&T
UK

0800 838 973

www.handt.co.uk

H&T specialises in a variety of financial services, including fast-turnaround foreign exchange. They have over 180 stores across the UK.

my Travel Cash
UK

0845 867 6496

www.mytravelcash.com

my Travel money offer the pre-paid multi currency card which allows travellers to withdraw cash in any currency without ATM fees.

Patchwork Present Ltd
UK

hello@patchworkit.com

+44 (0)20 8617 8487

www.patchworkit.com

Patchwork offers a fun and creative way of funding your gap year by creating a wish-list and sharing it with friends and family, making keeping track of donations much simpler.

Revolut
UK

+44 (0)203 322 83 52

www.revolut.com

Revolut is a Global Money App, it allows you to exchange currencies at perfect interbank rates, send money through social networks and spend with a multi-currency MasterCard®.

T24 Black Card
UK

support@t24blackcard.com

+44 (0) 20 7281 6090

www.t24blackcard.com

Offers a USD-denominated prepaid card that comes with complimentary premium travel insurance and standard Priority Pass membership, giving you access to 850+ airport lounges worldwide.

Travel Money Card Plus
UK

0344 809 4564

www.postoffice.co.uk/travel-money/card

Travel Money Card Plus is a prepaid MasterCard. You can manage your account from anywhere via an app, online or even by text message.

Travelex UK
UK

www.travelex.co.uk

Whether you're going to Andorra or Zambia, we've got you covered. With a choice of over 45 currencies and a range of Cash Passports™, we'll make it easy for you to get your travel money.

Virgin Money
UK

info@virginmoney.com

0845 089 6278

http://uk.virginmoney.com

Offers a 'Pre-paid Travel Money Card' enabling travellers to budget more easiliy and spend abroad with greater security.

WeSwap
UK

support@weswap.com

+44 (0)203 053 6610

www.weswap.com

WeSwap let travellers around the world swap currency with each other with no hidden costs, so that everyone gets the fairest rate and has more to spend.

Insurance

ACE European Group Ltd
UK

ace.traveluk@acegroup.com

0800 028 2396

www.aceinsure.com/backpacker

Offers gap year/backpacker/student traveller insurance to anyone aged 14-44 and traveller plus insurance for those aged 45-55 years.

Adventures Travel Insurance
UK

contact@adventuresinsurance.co.uk

02392 419 070

www.adventuresinsurance.co.uk

Adventures is a tailor-made insurance for almost any activity or occupation including amateur sports, manual work and hazardous pursuits. With a wide range of activities to choose, from Abseiling to Zorbing, Adventures travel insurance can cover you for peace of mind travel.

Alpha Travel Insurance

UK

website@alphatravelinsurance.co.uk

0203 829 6764

www.alphatravelinsurance.co.uk/gap-year-travel-insurance

Alpha Travel Insurance provides backpacker and gap year travel insurance for up to 24 months, including over 100 sports and activities free of charge.

American Express

UK

0800 028 7573

www.americanexpress.com

Provide cover 18-49 year olds wishing to take a gap year, sabbatical, or career break up to 24 months.

Big Cat Travel Insurance

UK

info@bigcattravelinsurance.com

0333 003 3161

bigcattravelinsurance.com

Big Cat specialises in affordable Worldwide Travel Insurance for Backpackers and Adventure Travellers. Our Activity Packs provide cover for various activities whether you'll be trekking, mountain biking, scuba diving, bungee jumping, sky diving, kayaking and lots more...

For further information see page 70

Blue Insurance

Ireland

info@blueinsurance.ie

+353 0818 444449

www.blueinsurance.ie

Multitrip.com is a domain name of Blue Insurances, offering competitive prices to anyone less than 45 years of age on back-packer insurance for trips up to 12 months in length .

Boots UK Limited

UK

+44 (0) 845 125 3810

www.bootstravelinsurance.com

The Boots UK Limited website has an area dedicated to gap-year insurance and offers policies to 18-34 year olds for 3-12 months.

British Mountaineering Council (BMC)

UK

office@thebmc.co.uk

+44 (0)161 445 6111

www.thebmc.co.uk

BMC travel insurance covers a range of activities and is designed by experts to be free from unreasonable exclusions or restrictions, for peace of mind wherever you travel.

Campbell Irvine Ltd

UK

info@campbellirvine.com

+44 (0)20 7938 1734

www.campbellirvinedirect.com

Campbell Irvine specialises in arranging travel insurance for the adventurous traveller. We provide cover for over 75 activities including trekking, safaris, sports and overseas volunteering work.

Citybond Suretravel

UK

info@citybond.co.uk

www.citybond.co.uk

Citybond Suretravel offer a Young Traveller policy for people planning to travel the world or study abroad, with cover available for temporary return trips home, computer equipment and course fees. It also covers you for over 120 sports and activities and jobs including office work, bar/restaurant work and fruit picking.

Columbus Direct

UK

admin@columbusdirect.com

0845 888 8893

www.columbusdirect.com

Columbus Direct offer backpacker insurance for anywhere in the world for 2-12 months. Also offer sports and activities cover.

Consularcare

UK

info@consularcare.com

+44 (0)20 3198 1890

www.consularassist.com

From a lost or stolen passport to liaising with authorities and family back home in the event of an incident, we'll be there for you; so you can sleep easy.

Cover-More Insurance Services Ltd

UK

enquiries@covermore.co.uk

01245 272408

www.covermore.co.uk

Cover-More have been a travel insurance specialist for 30 years, and globally insure over 2.2 million travellers each year. Our service, commitment and experience make us a top choice for travel companies and affiliates.

Direct Travel Insurance

UK

info@direct-travel.co.uk

+44 (0) 845 605 2700

www.direct-travel.co.uk

Direct Travel Insurance provide basic or comprehensive insurance cover to 18-36 year olds for 3-12 months.

Dogtag Ltd

UK

enquiries@dogtag.co.uk

+44 (0) 8700 364824

www.dogtag.co.uk

Dogtag Ltd offer insurance cover for 'action minded' travellers aged 18-55 for up to 18 months.

DU Insure

UK

travel@duinsure.com

+44 (0) 800 393 908

www.duinsure.com

Save up to 60% on High Street prices plus a further 10% discount if you book online. Comprehensive travel insurance for the adventurous traveller. Working holidays covered plus over 80 adventurous sports or activities. Medical emergency and money back guarantee.

For further information see page 24

Endsleigh Insurance Services Ltd

UK

+44 (0) 800 028 3571

www.endsleigh.co.uk

Endsleigh has tailored gap-year cover to suit travellers for up to 12 months, with over 100 sports and activities covered as standard.

Essential Travel Ltd

UK

customerservices@essentialtravel.co.uk

08713602720

www.essentialtravel.co.uk

Special backpacker travel insurance for anyone aged betwen 19-45 years old.

Globelink International

UK

globelink@globelink.co.uk

+44 (0)1353 699082

www.globelink.co.uk

Globelink provides coverage for almost any type of journey and age group (up to 84). Our Globetrekkers travel insurance provides excellent cover for student, gap year travellers, backpackers and over 65 travel insurance.

Holidaysafe

UK

website@holidaysafe.co.uk

0845 658 0570

www.holidaysafe.co.uk

Holidaysafe is a travel insurance provider based in Kent, UK. They have a range of cover options such as backpacking, sports, and long stay.

Insure and Go

UK

+44 (0) 844 888 2787

www.insureandgo.com

Insure and Go provide backpacker travel insurance for up to 18 months. Free cover for many sports and activities.

insurewithease.com

UK

help@insurewithease.com

0330 024 9295

www.insurewithease.com

insurewithease.com provides backpacker travel insurance for travellers planning trips of 12 months or less, including a baggage and personal possessions cover of up to £500.

Jackson Lees

UK

enquiry@jacksonlees.co.uk

0151 282 1700

www.jacksonlees.co.uk/services/wills-probate/traveller-insurance-package

Whatever form your gap year is going to take, whether it be working abroad, volunteering or travelling, we have a TIP for you. Our Traveller Insurance Package can provide a sense of relief should anything happen whilst you are away.

LetUsFixIT

UK

contactus@letusfixit.co.uk

0800 032 3499

letusfixit.co.uk

LetUsFixIT provides a computer protection service that allows you to safeguard up to three devices against accidental damage, theft, and mechanical failure, as well as access 24/7 remote technical support.

MB&G Direct

UK

enquiries@mbgdirect.com

0191 258 8199

www.mbgdirect.com

MB&G Direct offers car breakdown cover that gets you back on the road quickly and efficiently, whether you're in the UK or elsewhere in Europe.

Mind The Gap Year

UK

+44 (0) 845 180 0059

www.mindthegapyear.com

Mind The Gap Year offers a low cost economy package or the fully inclusive standard package back packer insurance cover.

MoneySuperMarket

UK

0333 123 1983

www.moneysupermarket.com/travel-insurance

MoneySuperMarket are a price comparison website enabling consumers to compare policy prices from a range of travel insurance providers.

Navigator Travel Insurance Services Ltd

UK

sales@navigatortravel.co.uk

0161 973 6435

www.navigatortravel.co.uk

Navigator Travel Insurance Services Ltd offer specialist policies for long-stay overseas trips with an emphasis on covering adventure sports. These policies also cover casual working.

P J Hayman & Company Ltd

UK

info@pjhayman.com

02392 419 050

www.pjhayman.com

With over 20 years experience in travel insurance, we have created specific products to cater for specific needs. Whether you require cover for a medical condition, hazardous activities, round the world trip, Gap year, etc., we have a policy for you.

Post Office Travel Insurance

UK

0800 294 2292

www.postoffice.co.uk/travel

Provides cover to 18-35 year olds wishing to take a career or study break.

ROCK Insurance Group

UK

info@rockinsurance.com

+44 (0)333 202 5670

www.rockinsurance.com

We provide smart and agile travel, gadget and commercial insurance products through our own direct brands and leading brands of our Affinity partners. We're fast growing and developing a reputation for doing things differently and that's why we say, you're better with us.

Round the World Insurance

UK

info@roundtheworldinsurance.co.uk

+44 (0)1273 320 580

www.roundtheworldinsurance.co.uk

Round the World Insurance provide specialist travel insurance designed for people on round-the-world or multi-stop trips.

Sainsbury's Travel Insurance

UK

0800 316 1453

www.sainsburysbank.co.uk/insuring/ins_extendedtrip_trv_skip.shtml

Sainsbury's Extended Trip Travel Insurance have a policy tailored to those between 16 and 45, providing cover for up to 12 months.

Snowcard Insurance Services Limited

UK

enquiries@snowcard.co.uk

0844 826 2699

www.snowcard.co.uk

An all-round activities insurance covering winter, general mountain and water sports as well as the standard travel risks. The unique 'Snowcard' gives 24 hour access to Assistance International.

SportsCover Direct Ltd

UK

contact@sportscoverdirect.com

01494 484800

www.sportscoverdirect.com

Whether you need to protect your income, are travelling abroad or wanting protection at home, we cover for most eventualities. Our products are tailored to amateurs or semi-professionals taking part in sports and activities including competitions.

STA Travel

UK

0333 321 0099

www.statravel.co.uk

As well as offering fantastic travel opportunities, STA also provide single trip insurance policies from 37p a day, or annual multi-trip policies from 22p a day

Taurus Insurance Services

Gibraltar

team@taurus.agency

+350 0207 183 6081

www.taurus.gi

Taurus Insurance Services provides worldwide travel insurance.

Top Dog Insurance

UK

info@topdoginsurance.co.uk

0800 093 6686

www.topdoginsurance.co.uk

Providing gap year travel insurance which covers many extreme sports and activities, including bungee jumping, scuba diving etc. The flexible policy allows you to return home for short periods of time.

Travel Insurance Direct

UK

info@travel-insurance.net

0800 652 9944

www.travel-insurance.net

The Discovery policy is designed for anyone travelling on a budget, backpacking or travelling light. Whilst being a low cost option it still maintains excellent levels of medical insurance, including vital medical emergency repatriation cover.

Travel Insured

UK

0800 092 4383

www.travelinsured.co.uk

Travel Insured offer a backpacking and young traveller insurance policy for 16-45 year olds, covering non-manual work, sports and recreation, and innocent incarceration/kidnap.

Travelinsurance.co.uk

UK

Information@travelinsurance.co.uk

0844 888 2757

www.travelinsurance.co.uk

Provides cover for up to 18 months travelling. Cover can be arranged for medical expenses, personal accident to repayment of student loan.

True Traveller Insurance

UK

insurance@truetraveller.com

0333 999 3140

www.truetraveller.com

True Traveller offer Single Trip and Backpacker Insurance from 1 day to 2 years, as well as Multi-Trip Insurance, and you can take out cover if you're already travelling.

For further information see page 66

Voyager Insurance Services

UK

enquiries@voyagerins.com

01483 562 662

www.responsibletravelinsurance.co.uk

Voyager's Responsible long stay travel insurance policy gives you cover for up to 18 months, so it can be ideal if you're a backpacker, or if you're planning a gap year or sabbatical.

World First Travel Insurance

UK

info@world-first.co.uk

0345 90 80 161

www.world-first.co.uk

We are the worldwide travel insurance specialists and have 40 years of experience providing holiday insurance cover for all kinds of people, going to all kinds of places and doing all kinds of wonderful things.

World Nomads Ltd

UK

+44 (0) 1543 432 872

www.worldnomads.com

World Nomads Ltd offer an insurance package specifically targeted at independent travellers under the age of 60 for up to 18 months.

Worldtrekker Travel Insurance

UK

info@preferential.co.uk

0843 208 1928

www.preferential.co.uk/worldtrekker

World Trekker Travel Insurance offers four levels of cover from Standard to Ultra to UK resident travellers up to the age of 45 years.

Career breaks and older gappers

Career Breaks

Africa in Focus
UK

info@africa-in-focus.com

01803 770 956

www.africa-in-focus.com

A travel agency which offers overland travel tours throughout East and Southern Africa with more comfort and innovative facilities.

African Conservation Experience
UK

info@conservationafrica.net

+44 (0) 1454 269182

www.conservationafrica.net

African Conservation Experience offer volunteering opportunities at wildlife conservation projects in southern Africa. You can count on our full support and more than 10 years experience. See our main advert in Conservation.

Audley Travel
UK

01993 838 020

careers.audleytravel.com

Audley Travel offers a wide range or holidays and destinations for every traveller. From luxury hotels to wildlife safaris and city tours, Audley Travel can offer a tailor-made experience.

Experience Travel
UK

info@experiencetravelgroup.com

020 3468 3029

www.experiencetravelgroup.com

Travel agent specialists which can arrange tailor made travel to Vietnam, Thailand, Cambodia, Sri Lanka, The Maldives and Laos.

Globalteer
UK

0117 2309998

www.globalteer.org

Globalteer is a registered UK charity offering career breakers affordable, sustainable volunteer placements within community and conservation projects overseas.

Inspire
UK

info@inspirevolunteer.co.uk

0800 032 3350

www.inspirevolunteer.co.uk

Inspire offers meaningful volunteer opportunities in Africa, Asia, South America & Europe. Share skills and change lives on teaching, childcare, conservation & business programmes overseas.

Inspired Breaks
UK

info@inspiredbreaks.co.uk

01892 701881

www.inspiredbreaks.co.uk

Company specialising in career breaks and volunteer work for the over 30s, hundreds of programmes in over 20 countries from two weeks to 12 months.

JET - Japan Exchange and Teaching Programme UK

UK

ukjet@ld.mofa.go.jp

+44 (0)20 7465 6668

www.jet-uk.org

The JET Programme, the official Japanese government scheme, sends UK graduates to promote international understanding and to improve foreign language teaching in schools for a minimum of 12 months.

Nonstop Adventure

UK

info@nonstopsnow.com

+44 (0)1225 632 165

www.nonstopsnow.com

Nonstop Adventure provide action sport instructor courses and improvement camps around the world. Their courses are ideal for a gap year, career break or career change.

For further information see page 94

Pod Volunteer

UK

info@podvolunteer.org

+44 (0)1242 241 181

www.podvolunteer.org

PoD (Personal Overseas Development) is a leading non-profit organisation arranging ethical, inspiring and supported volunteering opportunities around the world.

For further information see page 180

Projects Abroad Pro

UK

info@projects-abroad-pro.org

01903 708300

www.projects-abroad-pro.org

Projects Abroad Pro is an arm of Projects Abroad, designed to encourage professionals on a career break and retired seniors to take part in voluntary work in a developing country.

Raleigh International

UK

info@raleighinternational.org

+44(0) 20 7183 1270

www.raleighinternational.org

Develop new skills, meet people from all backgrounds and make a difference on sustainable community and environmental projects around the world.

For further information see page 86

Secret Compass

UK

info@secretcompass.com

UK: +44 (0)20 3239 8038; USA: +1 347 8900182

www.secretcompass.com

Secret Compass is a pioneering exploration, expedition and adventure travel company. Its teams aim to achieve the extraordinary in the world's wildest places.

It was founded in 2010 by two former commanders in the UK Army's Parachute Regiment, Tom Bodkin and Levison Wood. Secret Compass is based in Bristol and London.

Sunvil Traveller

UK

020 8758 4774

www.sunvil.co.uk/traveller

A travel agency which can arrange long stay travel across Latin America.

The Book Bus Foundation

UK

info@thebookbus.org

+44 (0) 208 0999 280

www.thebookbus.org

The Book Bus provides a mobile service and actively promotes literacy to underpriviledged communities in Zambia and Ecuador.

Undiscovered Destinations Ltd
UK

info@undiscovered-destinations.com

0191 296 2674

www.undiscovered-destinations.com

An adventure travel agency dedicated to providing truly authentic experiences, through small group tours or tailormade trips, to some of the world's most exciting regions.

VentureCo Worldwide
UK

01822 616 191

www.ventureco-worldwide.com

VentureCo provides the ideal combination for career break travellers who want to explore off the beaten track, learn about the host country and give something back to the communities they stay with.

Visitoz
Australia

info@visitoz.org

+61 741 686 106

www.visitoz.org

Visitoz provides training and guarantees work for young people between the ages of 18 and 30 in agriculture, hospitality, child care and teaching all over Australia.

3 Career breaks and older gappers

Travelling and accommodation

Accommodation

Agoda
Singapore
+44 (0)20 3027 7900
www.agoda.com
Agoda is one of the world's fastest-growing online hotel platforms. It offers thousands of accommodation options around the globe, from budget hostels to luxury hotels and more.

Airbnb
USA
+1 855 424 7262
www.airbnb.co.uk
Whether a flat for a night, a castle for a week, or a villa for a month, Airbnb connects people to unique travel experiences, at any price point, in more than 34,000 cities and 190 countries. And with world-class customer service and a growing community of users, Airbnb is the easiest way for people to monetise their extra space and showcase it to an audience of millions.

An Óige - Irish Youth Hostel Association
Ireland
info@anoige.ie
+353 01 830 4555
www.anoige.ie
The Irish YHA consists of more than 20 hostels throughout Ireland. They have a range of hostels, from large city centre buildings to small hostels in rural settings. Online booking available.

Base Backpackers
Australia
info@stayatbase.com
AU: 1800 24 22 73; NZ: 0800 22 73 69
www.stayatbase.com
At Base it's all about the traveller! Modern, central and fun backpacker hostels located throughout Australia & New Zealand.

Booking.com
UK
www.booking.com
Booking.com lists the best prices for every type of property, from small, family-run bed and breakfasts to executive apartments and five-star luxury suites. It is available in more than 40 languages, and offers over 1 million active properties in 225 countries and territories worldwide.

Campingo
France
www.campingo.co.uk
Our fast, easy and efficient guide helps you find the perfect campsite for your holidays. Use our selection of 160 search criteria and our 319 reviews, to find the campsite that really suits you. Fancy a change of air? Campingo gives detailed descriptions of 8341 campsites in 85 countries!

Gap Year Hostel
Singapore
info@gapyearhostel.com
+65 6297 1055
www.gapyearhostel.com

Inspired, designed and managed by backpackers, Gap Year hostel is a well-equipped modern hostel offering easy access to the heart of Singapore. Features include CCTV and key-cards for security, air-con and high-speed fibre optic wifi for leisure, and complimentary breakfast and tea/coffee for comfort.

HomeAway
UK
+44 (0)208 827 1971
www.homeaway.co.uk

HomeAway connect property owners and managers with holidaymakers looking for the perfect accommodation to share their dream holidays together with families and friends. The beautiful homes on our sites feature more space, privacy, and amenities than hotels, often for less than half the cost per person. We are dedicated to helping holidaymakers create unforgettable experiences by staying together.

HomestayWeb
USA
support@homestayweb.com
www.homestayweb.com

The Homestay Web allows you to search for hundreds of host families worldwide and post requests for accommodation on the message board.

Hostelbookers.com
UK
support@hostelbookers.com
+44 (0) 207 406 1800
www.hostelbookers.com

Youth hostels and cheap accommodation in over 3500 destinations worldwide, with no booking fees.

Hostelling International
UK
info@hihostels.com
01707 324 170
www.hihostels.com

Research, plan and book your trip online with Hostelling International. HI hostels are a great way to travel the world safely - explore new cultures and meet friends.

Hostelling International - Canada
Canada
info@hihostels.ca
+1 613 237 7884
www.hihostels.ca

Contact details for the Canadian branch of this worldwide hostel service.

Hostelling International - Iceland
Iceland
info@hostel.is
+354 575 6700
www.hostel.is

Hostelling International Iceland has 36 hostels all around the country, offering comfortable, budget accommodation which is open to all ages.

Hostelling International - USA
USA
+1 240 650 2100
www.hiusa.org

Hostelling International USA has a network of hostels throughout the United States that are inexpensive, safe and clean.

Hostelworld.com

Ireland

customerservice@hostels.com

+353 (0)1 5245800

www.hostels.com

Hostelworld.com is an online booking site which operates a network of over 27,000 hostels in more than 180 countries. Provides confirmed reservations at a selection of youth hostels, independent hostels and international hostels.

Housing Anywhere BV

Netherlands

+31 090 30 39 23

www.housinganywhere.com

Housing Anywhere is an international student housing platform where you can book or rent out a room. All advertisers are verified and bookings are made over a secure booking system.

Italy Bike Hotels

Italy

business@italybikehotels.com

+39 0541 307531

www.italybikehotels.com

Italy Bike Hotels was founded in 2000 by a group of hoteliers passionate about cycling and is dedicated to providing accommodation and facilities for all cycling enthusiasts.

KAYAK

USA

www.kayak.co.uk

KAYAK provides a price comparison site for hotels and flights all around the world, helping you to easily compare hundreds of travel sites with one search.

Koyasan Sankei-Koh

Japan

+81 (0)736 56 2616

eng.shukubo.net

Provides details on sightseeing, Buddhist experiences and lodging options in the Koyasan area of Japan, including an alphabetised list of local temples open to overnight guests.

Love Home Swap

UK

info@lovehomeswap.com

+44 0800 131 0000

www.lovehomeswap.com

Love Home Swap helps set you up with over 80,000+ homes in the world's most popular destinations just waiting for you to visit. Choose either a direct swap or use the clever Swap Points and you'll find yourself in your dream holiday house in no time.

Nomads Hostels

Australia

bookings@nomadsworld.com

1800 666 237

www.nomadsworld.com

With great locations, awesome activities and friendly staff, Nomads hostels offer budget backpacker accommodation across Australia & New Zealand.

Roomlala

UK

communication@roomlala.com

+44 (0)203 514 7775

www.roomlala.com

Roomlala is an user-friendly online platform that puts people with spare rooms in touch with people who need somewhere to stay. We have more than 1.3 million members in over 40 countries.

Scottish Youth Hostel Association

UK

info@syha.org.uk

01786 891400

www.syha.org.uk

There are over 70 SYHA hostels throughout Scotland. You can book online but you must be a member - you can join at the time of booking. Registered Charity No. SC013138.

Stay4free.com

USA

www.stay4free.com

Stay4free.com enables people from all corners of the globe to arrange home exchanges for their next vacation. Best of all: no money changes hands and accomodation is free!

Swiss Youth Hostels

Switzerland

contact@youthhostel.ch

+41 (0) 44 360 1414

www.youthhostel.ch

They have 52 hostels, ranging from traditional Swiss chalets, to modern buildings, large historic houses and even one or two castles.

TalkTalkBnb

France

www.talktalkbnb.com/en

TalkTalkBnb connects travellers with hosts wanting to improve their language skills. Find free accommodation in exchange for speaking your mother tongue with your host!

The Hospitality Club

Germany

info@hospitalityclub.org

www.hospitalityclub.org

The Hospitality Club is a global collection of members who assist each other with travelling opportunities, be it with a roof for the night or a guided tour through town.

The Tasty Ski Company

UK

info@thetastyskicompany.co.uk

+44 (0)7538 761 767

www.thetastyskicompany.co.uk

The Tasty Ski Company has a selection of catered ski chalets in Morzine and Le Grand Massif. Our prices include our lovely house wines, beer and soft drinks. This is an unlimited service not just confined to meal times.

Uxlabil Eco Hoteles

Guatemala

+502 2366 9555; +1 305 677 3107

www.uxlabil.com

Experience Guatemala at affordable prices. Uxlabil offers three unique hotels in Atitlán, Antigua and Guatemala City, each fully equipped with modern facilities and providing breathtaking views.

VIP Backpackers

Australia

info@vipbackpackers.com

+61 (0) 2 9211 0766

www.vipbackpackers.com

VIP Backpackers is the largest independent backpacker accommodation network in the world, with over 1,200 hostels across 80+ countries, and counting.

Warm Showers

USA

wsl@warmshowers.org

+1 720 259 9684

www.warmshowers.org

The Homestay Web has over 900 host families registered worldwide and waiting for you. You can search for a Homestay Host family open your own home up to others.

Youth Hostel Association New Zealand

New Zealand

info@yha.co.nz

+64 (0)3 379 9970

www.yha.co.nz

Budget accommodation in New Zealand. Hostels open to all ages. Book online before you go.

Youth Hostels Association of India

India

contact@yhaindia.org

+91 (011) 2611 0250

www.yhaindia.org

Youth Hostel Association in India, with hostels which can be booked online through their website.

Car Hire

Auto Europe

UK

customerservice@auto-europe.co.uk

0800 358 1229

www.auto-europe.co.uk

Auto Europe can provide travellers with a vast selection of vehicles for hire in over 8,000 locations around the world.

AVIS

UK

0844 581 0147

www.avis.co.uk

AVIS worldwide can provide travellers with car hire from 4,000 locations in 114 countries.

Budget International

UK

0844 444 0002

www.budgetinternational.com

Budget International can provide travellers with car hire from 3,400 locations in 128 countries.

Europcar UK Ltd

UK

reservationsuk@europcar.com

0371 384 1087

www.europcar.co.uk

Europcar and its alliance partner Enterprise can provide travellers with car hire from more than 13,000 locations in about 150 countries.

Hertz

USA

0843 309 3099

www.hertz.co.uk

Hertz Global Holdings is an American car rental company providing a wide range of options for car hire around the world.

International Motorhome Hire

UK

enquiry@rv-network.com

01780 482 565

www.international-motorhome-hire.com

International Motor Home are an agency that organises the hire of motor homes, on behalf of travellers, throughout the world.

4 Travelling and accommodation

Motorhome International
USA
info@motorhome-international.com
+1 847 531 1454
www.motorhome-international.com
Motorhome International provide RV Rentals and Motorhome Hire in the USA, Canada, Europe, New Zealand Australia & South Africa.

Spaceships
New Zealand
info@spaceshipsrentals.co.nz
+64 9 526 2130
www.spaceshipsrentals.co.nz
Company offering campervan rentals in New Zealand and Australia.

Travellers Auto Barn
Australia
info@travellers-autobarn.com.au
+61 2 9360 1500 (outside Australia) 1800 674 374 (within Aus
www.travellers-autobarn.com.au
No cheaper way to travel around Australia than in any of our campervans or stationwagons - we have offices all around Australia and all our rentals come with unlimited KM, free insurance, special discounts.

Travel Companies

Adagio
UK
info@adagio.co.uk
01707 386700
www.adagio.co.uk
Adagio offers holidays with character. Whether your interest is in culture, cuisine, history or sightseeing, Adagio will help you have a calm, stress-free holiday where you can move at your own pace.

Africa Odyssey
UK
info@africaodyssey.com
UK: +44 (0)20 8704 1216; USA: +1 866 356 4691
www.africaodyssey.com
We are experts in travel to Africa and the Indian Ocean. We arrange memorable experiences and adventures for our clients whilst supporting eco-tourism and travel.

ATG Oxford
UK
trip-enquiry@atg-oxford.com
+44 (0)1865 315678
www.atg-oxford.co.uk
ATG organises escorted and independent walking trips for trekkers of all abilities. Keep fit whilst enjoying the beautiful scenery and breathtaking views of Europe. Relax in comfortable accommodation, enjoy tasty food and good company.

Aurora Expeditions
Australia
+61 2 9252 1033
www.auroraexpeditions.com.au
Aurora Expeditions offer cruise expeditions to all corners of the globe. From the frozen Arctic and Antarctica to the hot savannahs of Africa, explore new landscapes and participate in exciting activities that will make your trip one to remember.

Bamboo Travel
UK
info@bambootravel.co.uk
+44 (0)20 7720 9285
www.bambootravel.co.uk

Discover Asia with Bamboo Travel. Explore the local culture and see the sights with a classic holiday, or enjoy a more action-packed trip with an active and adventure holiday. Special interest trips are available for those with a particular passion, and bespoke trips can be arranged to personalise your experience. Whether you're an individual adventurer seeking new experiences, a couple looking for a romantic honeymoon or a family wanting a trip which everyone can enjoy, Bamboo has you covered.

Best Gap Year
UK
01743 277150
www.bestgapyear.co.uk

Search a huge range of gap year courses, paid working holiday, paid jobs and volunteer placements from around the world. Travel abroad with leading providers of paid and volunteer gap year projects.

Best Served Scandinavia
UK
enquire@best-served.co.uk
020 7838 5956
www.best-served.co.uk

Best Served Scandinavia is an independent, tailor-made tour operator specialising in adventure holidays to Scandinavia, Canada and the Nordic and Baltic regions.

Beyond BA LATAM
Argentina
latamtravel@beyondba.com
+54 11 4766 8255
latam.beyondba.com

We provide tailor-made trips to Argentina, Chile and the Antarctic region. Our Team will design a trip around you and our guides will show you the highlights in a different light.

Bookme Australia
Australia
info@bookme.com.au
+61 450 458 730
www.bookme.com.au

50% Off fun things to do in Australia? Bookme offers easy online booking, amazing last-minute and pre-booking deals, as well as latest traveller reviews & photos.

Bookme Fiji
Fiji
info@bookme.co.nz
+64 21 565 577
www.bookme.com.fj

The largest online resource for fun things to do in Fiji. Offering amazing last-minute, and pre-booking deals as well as latest traveller photos & reviews.

Bookme New Zealand
New Zealand
info@bookme.co.nz
+64 21 565 577
www.bookme.co.nz

The largest online resource for fun things to do in NZ. Offering amazing last-minute, and pre-booking deals (50% Off +) as well as latest traveller photos & reviews.

Buffalo Tours

Vietnam

info@buffalotours.com

+84 4 3828 0702

www.buffalotours.com

Choose from a range of holidays, focusing on local culture, adventure or luxury trips, or opt for something different with a variety of day trips and short breaks, or even a cruise holiday.

Classic Journeys

UK

info@classicjourneys.co.uk

+44 (0)1773 873497

www.classicjourneys.co.uk

Classic Journeys operates tailor-made, quality adventure holidays. Specialising in the area of Asia, a friendly, informal and relaxed trip will provide travellers with memorable and meaningful travel experiences, in addition to supporting educational, healthcare and environmental projects in local communities.

Connoisseur Travel

UK

info@connoisseurtravel.co.uk

01403 272143

www.connoisseurtravel.co.uk

We offer each and every one of our clients their own unique tailor made experience. We provide the finest in location and accommodation. Our personalised service takes care of all your arrangements right down to the most tedious of details.

Country Walks

UK

info@country-walks.com

+44 (0)207 233 6563

www.country-walks.com

Country Walks offers high-quality walking experiences through both guided and self-guided walking holidays. Trips provide beautiful landscapes and natural environments, cultural interest, accommodation, food and will give you an enhanced sense of wellbeing, leaving you re-energised and rejuvenated.

Cox & Kings

UK

cox.kings@coxandkings.co.uk

020 7873 5000

www.coxandkings.co.uk

Cox & Kings offer a variety of holidays to a number of destinations all around the world, whilst also promoting responsible tourism.

Cuba Solidarity Campaign

UK

tours@cuba-solidarity.org.uk

020 7490 5715

www.cuba-solidarity.org.uk/tours

Cuba Solidarity Campaign offers brigades to Cuba to meet local people involved in healthcare, community projects, education and culture, and work alongside Cuban farmers.

Discover the World Education

UK

travel@discover-education.co.uk

01737 218 807

www.discover-the-world.co.uk

From Iceland to New Zealand, Scandinavia to Antarctica then back to the High Arctic, as well as Alaska and Canada, our complete collection of holidays features imaginative itineraries that will ensure your time away exceeds expectations.

Expert Africa
UK

+44 (0)20 8232 9777

www.expertafrica.com

Expert Africa is a travel company which organises safaris and holidays for all types of travellers. Team members have travelled extensively in Africa, providing advice and guidance from ﬁrst-hand experience to offer you the best possible trip.

Gapwork.com
UK

info@gapwork.com

+44 (0)1133 230759

www.gapwork.com

Gapwork is an independent information provider specialising in gap years, gap year jobs, gap year vacancies, activities and voluntary work either in the UK or abroad.

Goa Way
UK

sales@goaway.co.uk

0207 258 7800

www.goaway.co.uk

Goaway specialises in organising travel to Goa and Kerala. You can book flights, hostels or even package tours.

Goolets Ltd - Croatia Luxury Gulet
Slovenia

info@goolets.net

+44 (0)20 3318 1079

www.croatialuxurygulet.com

Selection of the top luxury gulet yachts in Croatia. Let the world's number 1 gulet expert organize for you the best cruise of your life in Croatia.

Goolets Ltd, Gulet expert
Slovenia

info@goolets.net

+44 (0)20 3318 1079

www.guletexpert.com

Find your perfect gulet for your dream vacation in Croatia, Italy, Greece, Turkey, Indonesia... With our free assistance, we will help you organize your cruising itinerary, food preferences, activities, and excursions.

Greyhound Lines Inc
USA

ifsr@greyhound.com

+1 214 849 8966

www.greyhound.com

The most famous and largest bus company in America. Book online and join the millions of others who travel across America on the 'old grey dog'.

HighLives Travel
UK

info@highlives.co.uk

+44 (0)20 8835 7034

www.highlives.co.uk

HighLives is a specialist in travel to the Andes and wider Latin America and the Caribeean, working in Bolivia, Peru, Ecuador, Colombia, Chile, Argentina, Brazil, Guyana, Costa Rica, Cuba and more.

Holiday Architects
UK

mail@holidayarchitects.co.uk

01242 253073

holidayarchitects.co.uk

Holiday Architects specialises in organising awe-inspiring trips to South Africa, Jordan, Oman, Burma, India, Vietnam, Cambodia, Namibia, Laos, Zambia and Sri Lanka.

4 Travelling and accommodation

Journey Latin America
UK

sales@journeylatinamerica.co.uk

0208 747 3108

www.journeylatinamerica.co.uk

Journey Latin America is the UK's major specialist in travel to Central and South America. Learn a new skill with their 'Learn to ... ' holidays.

KE Adventure Travel
UK

info@keadventure.com

+44 (0)17687 73966

www.keadventure.com

KE Adventure Travel is one of the world's leading independent adventure travel specialists. Whether you seek to walk amongst the world's highest peaks, explore untamed wilderness areas, or witness first hand the wildlife or culture of far-off lands, we have the perfect adventure for you.

laterallife
UK

info@laterallife.com

+44 (0)207 607 1943

www.laterallife.com

Whether you are looking for remote beaches, an Arctic adventure, a gorilla safari or a sailing trip through the Galapagos Islands, laterallife has plenty to offer to ensure your trip is truly unforgettable.

Llama Travel
UK

mail@llamatravel.com

020 7263 3000

www.llamatravel.com

One of the UK's leading tour operators to Latin America, Llama Travel provides high quality holidays at the lowest possible prices. All of our staff have either lived in Latin America or know the countries well. Choose from 63 itineraries or design your own holiday by choosing where you would like to visit.

Mirya Yachting
Canada

+1 604 547 3220

www.miryayachting.com

Mirya Yachting is a global yacht charter and brokerage firm specializing in private gulet charter and gulet sales in the Eastern Mediterranean.

Oasis Overland
UK

info@oasisoverland.co.uk

+44 (0) 1963 363400

www.oasisoverland.co.uk

Oasis Overland provide exciting and adventurous tours and expeditions in Africa, South America and Central Asia. You'll take an active involvement in the day to day running of the trip with like-minded travellers as you explore different cultures and regions.

Odyssey Overland Ltd
UK

info@odysseyoverland.co.uk

+44 (0)20 8123 3544

www.odysseyoverland.co.uk

Odyssey Overland is an overland tour travel agency specialising in the big overland tours available around the world from 1 to 6+ months. With 25 years experience, Odyssey can help you find your perfect gap year overland tour!

visit: www.gap-year.com

One World 365

UK

+44 (20) 8123 8284

www.oneworld365.org

Interested in travelling, working, volunteering, teaching, interning or studying abroad? Search thousands of trips, programs, jobs & courses worldwide.

Outward Bound Costa Rica

Costa Rica

info@outwardboundcr.org

+506 2278 6058

www.outwardboundcostarica.org

Outward Bound Costa Rica challenges participants to live bigger, bolder lives. Embark on a life-changing journey through our rigorous programs in Costa Rica and Panama, expanding capacity in leadership, intercultural competence, Spanish language, self-awareness, and life skills.

OzIntro

Australia

office@introtravel.com

+61 2 9664 7000

www.ozintro.com

OzIntro help 18-35's travel and work in Australia, starting with pickup at the airport and a week of group activities in Sydney.

Peter Sommer Travels

UK

info@petersommer.com

+44 (0)1600 888220

www.petersommer.com

Peter Sommer Travels provide inspirational trips, stimulating & enlightening expert-led tours and relaxing & beautiful gulet cruises. On offer are a range of archaeology tours, food tours and walking holidays by land and sea. Our escorted tours in Turkey, Greece and Italy will take you to some of the world's best preserved ancient and historic sites.

Pettitts Tailor Made Tours

UK

info@pettitts.co.uk

+44 (0)1892 250500

www.pettitts.co.uk

Pettitts is an independent travel company that for over 27 years has specialised in arranging private and unique tours, journeys and itineraries for travellers' worldwide. We are one of the UK's leading tailor-made holiday experts and our central aim is to create the perfect holiday by combining our vast knowledge and experience

Pure Exploration New Zealand

New Zealand

explore@pureexploration.nz

+64 3 442 0735

www.pureexploration.nz

Gap Year, Summer And Winter Semester Programs And Adventure Tourism Guide Training In Queenstown, Nz – The Adventure Capital Of The World!

For further information see page 108

Quark Expeditions
USA
+1 802 227 7303
www.quarkexpeditions.com

Explore the mysteries of the Artic and Antartic with Quark Expeditions. Discovery trips offer the opportunity to visit some of the most secluded locales, experience genuine Inuit cultures and see a vast array of native wildlife. Alternatively, adventurous trips will let you try your hand at camping, mountaineering, skiing, kayaking and paddleboarding.

Rainforest Expeditions
Peru
sales@rainforest.com.pe
+51 9935 12265
www.perunature.com

Rainforest Expedition is a Peruvian Ecotourism company. Since 1989 our guests and lodges, have added value to standing tropical rain forest turning it into a competitive alternative to unsustainable economic uses.

Regent Holidays
UK
regent@regentholidays.co.uk
0203 553 3240
www.regent-holidays.co.uk

Regent Holidays has been pioneering travel experiences to a wide range of unique and off-the-beaten-track destinations since 1970. Our travel experts are passionate about creating the perfect tailor made holiday or group tour for you, whether you want to visit the northern lights in Iceland, enjoy a city break in Poland, take a fly drive through Croatia or embark on the journey of a lifetime on the Trans Siberian Railway.

Responsible Travel
UK
rosy@responsibletravel.com
+44 (0)1273 823700
www.responsibletravel.com

Responsible Travel offers a wide range of destinations, from picturesque villas in Italy to cultural experiences in japan, all whilst promoting respectful and considerate tourism.

Round The World Experts
UK
+44 (0)203 056 7993
www.roundtheworldexperts.co.uk

Round the World Experts are the tailor-made specialists of the Flight Centre Travel Group. Our experienced team are experts at creating amazing and authentic travel experiences all around the globe.

Rug&Rock Adventures Ltd
UK
info@rugandrock.com
+44 (0)8 4444 123 12
www.rugandrock.com

Rug&Rock is an exciting company founded by and for enthusiastic travellers from a variety of different backgrounds. We have many years experience of adventure travel, mountaineering and sport and most of us have also taken part in social projects overseas, especially in Morocco.

Sail in Greece
UK
info@sail-ingreece.com
+44 (0)203 239 9253
www.sail-ingreece.com

Sail in Greece specializes in cruises and adventures around Greece and as we are specialized in one country we are good at it! We have the same passion as if we join every cruise we make and our fellow travelers are our close friends. Our experiences are enormous and our desire is to pass them on to the world!

School Of All Relations (SOAR)

Greece

school.of.all.relations@gmail.com

+30 2297 026885

www.schoolofallrelations.com

School Of All Relations (SOAR) offers a residential educational program for international youth aged 18-26, based on the Greek Island of Aegina.

Smaller Earth UK

UK

uk@smallerearth.com

+(44) 0151 702 6808

www.smallerearth.com

Smaller Earth is one of the UK's leading gap year travel providers, sending thousands of travellers abroad every year. Whether you're looking to volunteer in Africa, earn money in Australia or party in Bangkok, we've got the perfect collection of travel programmes for you.

STA Travel

UK

0333 321 0099

www.statravel.co.uk

This company has branches or agents worldwide and a Help Desk telephone service, which provides essential backup for travellers on the move.

Student Universe

UK

marketing@studentuniverse.co.uk

0808 234 4107

Whether you're looking for a great deal on round the world flights, arranging a work abroad placement in Australia or a volunteering trip to Africa, StudentUniverse can handle every aspect of your gap year travel.

ThaIntro

UK

enquiries@thaintro.com

+44 (0)845 3700 499

www.thaintro.com

Travel to Thailand and meet like-minded travellers. Explore wondrous Thai temples and beautiful national parks, relax on the warm beaches or try your hand at snorkelling in the sparkling clear waters, and enjoy an up-close experience with elephants in the jungle. Thaintro offers a great stepping stone into Thailand.

The Luxury Cruise Company

UK

enquire@theluxurycruisecompany.com

020 7838 5991

www.theluxurycruisecompany.com

The Luxury Cruise Company offers ocean, river and exploration-style cruises worldwide and specialises in organising personalised cruise itineraries aboard the world's finest vessels.

The Luxury Holiday Company

UK

enquire@theluxuryholidaycompany.com

020 7590 0770

www.theluxuryholidaycompany.com

With over 210 years of collective travel specialist experience, The Luxury Holiday Company team are passionate about creating tailor-made holidays that live long in the memory.

Tourdust Ltd

UK

help@tourdust.com

+44 (0)203 291 2907

www.tourdust.com

Tourdust specialises in adventurous holidays for independent minded travellers, combining down-to-earth adventures with carefully selected boutique hotels. They partner closely with local guides and hotels to offer high quality & great value holidays.

Tracks Safaris

UK

sue@trackssafaris.co.uk

+44 (0)1386 830264

www.trackssafaris.co.uk

Whether you are looking for a lodge safari, a tented safari, a self drive safari, a mobile safari, a walking safari, a flying safari, or a safari for the whole family, let Tracks Safaris give you some ideas and inspiration.

Travel Talk

UK

info@traveltalktours.com

+44 (0)20 8099 9596

www.traveltalktours.com

UK adventure and cultural tour operator, whom design tours especially for fun-loving and motivated people aged between 18 and 39.

Travelbag Ltd

UK

0871 703 4698

www.travelbag.co.uk

Book flights, hotel, holidays and even find insurance on their website.

TrekAmerica

UK

0208 682 8920

www.trekamerica.co.uk

With year round departures and over 50 unique itineraries from 3 to 64 days in length TrekAmerica tours are the ideal way to explore North America.

Tru Experience Travel

UK

travel@truexperiencetravel.co.uk

01494 526163

truexperiencetravel.co.uk

Tru Experience Travel provides the opportunity to get involved through volunteer programs and internships from 2 weeks up to one year.

USIT

Ireland

info@usit.ie

+353 (0)1602 1906

www.usit.ie

Irish travel agents offering cheap flights from Dublin, Cork and Shannon specifically aimed at students.

Venture Uganda

Uganda

info@ventureuganda.org

+256 (0)393 20 20 33

www.ventureuganda.org

Venture Uganda is an independent, Ugandan tour operator offering specialist holidays and educational visits to Uganda.

Vietnamese Private Tours

Vietnam

inspire@vietnameseprivatetours.com

+84 917 951100

www.vietnameseprivatetours.com

Vietnamese Private Tours specializing in tailor made private tours within Vietnam, Cambodia, Laos and Myanmar. Our services start from Vietnam visa, to hotel, cruises and more.

Warriors

South Africa

marketing@warriors.co.za

+27 83 737 2892

www.warriors.co.za

Warriors offers a variety of programs to participate in a range of experiences that are designed around the 5 core values of emotional fitness, social skills development, adventure & eco-tourism, entrepreneurship and work readiness and health & fitness to support the transition of entering adulthood.

Wexas Travel

UK

travel@wexas.com

020 7590 0610

www.wexas.com

Established for over 45 years, Wexas is one of the UK's most respected travel companies, specialising in luxury tailor-made travel to destinations across all seven continents.

Wild Frontiers Adventure Travel Ltd

UK

+44 (0)20 3930 4296

www.wildfrontierstravel.com

Wild Frontiers is committed to producing the most innovative and ground-breaking holidays on the market. Whether you are looking for serious adventure, or a more relaxing and luxurious experience, we have always strived to offer something different and memorable.

Wildlife Worldwide

UK

sales@wildlifeworldwide.com

01962 302 088

www.wildlifeworldwide.com

Wildlife Worldwide has been organising tailor-made wildlife tours since 1992. We provide tailor-made Indian & African safari holidays, whale watching holidays, wildlife cruising and Antarctic & Arctic voyages.

Younique Travel Adventures

UK

fiona.simpson@yoproject.co.uk

01793 680545

ytauk.co.uk

Younique Travel Adventures are experts in group travel and work specifically in Kenya & India.

Travel Companies

Amtrak

USA

+1 800 872 7245

www.amtrak.com

Operating in North America, Amtrak operates with 300+ trains a day across 21,000 miles of track. They also offers over 350 unique rail travel packages to choose from.

Cheap Flights

UK

www.cheapflights.co.uk

This useful website does not sell tickets but can point you in the right direction to get the best deal.

EasyJet Plc

UK

www.easyjet.com

Offers cheap flights to European destinations with further reductions if you book over the internet.

ebookers.com

UK

www.ebookers.com

Cheap flights can be booked through their website.

Eurail.com

Netherlands

customerservice@eurail.com

www.eurail.com

Get around Europe with the most hassle-free and comfortable travel option: the European rail pass. No airport check-in lines or being confined to your seat. Your Eurail Pass is an all-in-one train ticket for Europe, so you can enjoy every moment of your journey

Florence by Bike

Italy

info@florencebybike.it

+39 055 488992

www.florencebybike.it

Scooter, motorbike and bike rental company in Florence. Also sells clothing and accessories as well as bike parts.

International Rail

UK

sales@internationalrail.com

+44 (0)871 231 0790

www.internationalrail.com

InterRail Pass provides unlimited travel on the sophisticated European Rail network. The pass is very flexible allowing you to choose either one country or all 30 countries.

Kiwi Experience

New Zealand

+64 9 336 4286

www.kiwiexperience.com

Extensive bus network covering the whole of New Zealand. Passes valid for 12 months.

megabus.com/megatrain.com

UK

enquiries@megabus.com

+44 (0)141 352 4444

uk.megabus.com

megabus.com offers services from as little as $1 between 120 city centres across North America through their fleet of luxury single and double decker buses.

Ryanair

UK

www.ryanair.com

Low cost airline to European destinations.

Stray Ltd

New Zealand

enquiries@straytravel.co.nz

www.straytravel.com

Stray is New Zealand's fastest growing backpacker bus network - designed for travellers who want to get off the beaten track.

Thomas Cook
UK

www.thomascook.com

General travel agent with high street branches offering flights and late deals.

Travellers Contact Point
Australia

+61 2 9211 7900

www.travellers.com.au

A specialist travel agency for independent and working holiday travellers. We have shops in Australia, New Zealand and the UK.

Voyages-sncf.com
UK

0844 848 5848

www.voyages-sncf.com

Specializes in selling tickets and passes for travel throughout Europe by train. Available to buy online, at our London Travel Centre or via our call centre.

Travel Companies

AA Safaris and Tours Ltd
Uganda

info@gorillas-safaris.com

+256 392883831

www.gorillas-safaris.com

AA Safaris and Tours Ltd is a safari company that organizes affordable safaris in Uganda and Rwanda. All our members provide advice from first-hand experience.

Acacia Adventure Holidays
UK

info@acacia-africa.com

+44 (0) 20 7706 4700

www.acacia-africa.com

Acacia offers exciting and affordable overland tours and small group safaris across Africa. Enjoy game viewing, desert adventures, beach breaks, dive courses or trekking!

For further information see page 106

Adventure Tours Australia
Australia

admin@adventuretours.com.au

+61 (0)3 8102 7800

www.adventuretours.travel

Adventure Tours Australia is an award winning company specialising in small group nature-based tours for the active traveller.

For further information see page 102

Adventure Tours NZ
New Zealand

reservations@adventuretoursnz.co.nz

+64 9 526 2149

www.adventuretours.com.au

Adventure Tours NZ offer specialised small group nature-based tours for the active traveller on a budget. Go off the beaten track, see unique scenery and wildlife.

Adventure Travellers Club P Ltd
Nepal

info@nepaltravellers.com

www.nepaltravellers.com

Offers trekking and adventure tours in Nepal, Tibet, Bhutan and Indian regions. Includes peak climbing, jungle safaris, river rafting and much more.

Afreco Tours Ltd
UK
info@afrecotours.com
+44 (0) 845 812 8222
www.afrecotours.com

Afreco Tours specialises in African safari ranger training and wildlife adventures – from seven days to one year.

Africa Travel Centre
UK
info@africatravel.co.uk
+44 (0)20 7843 3500
www.africatravel.co.uk

Africa Travel is a specialist dealing with travel to Africa, a boutique, owner-run company with personal connections.

Africa Travel Co
South Africa
cpt@africatravelco.com
+27 21 3851530
www.africatravelco.com

Specialists in trips around Africa ranging from three to 56 days.

African Horizons
Zambia
safariplans@gmail.com
+877 256 1074
www.africanhorizons.com

Provides quality African travel not only to the savvy globetrotters among us but also to those who have never experienced the thrill of an African safari or wildlife tour.

AITO – Association of Independent Tour operators
UK
info@aito.com
+44 (0) 208 744 9280
www.aito.com

Expert, independent tour operator specialising in offering an unrivalled collection of affordable holidays to every corner of the globe.

Alaska Heritage Tours
USA
info@AlaskaHeritageTours.com
+1 907 777 2805
www.alaskaheritagetours.com

At Alaska Heritage Tours we strive to give you the best of Alaska, the way you want it - with pre-packaged Alaska vacations and itineraries. Explore Alaska's top destinations.

Alpine Exploratory
UK
info@alpineexploratory.com
+44 (0) 1729 823197
www.alpineexploratory.com

Alpine Exploratory specialises in self-guided walking and trekking tours in Europe. Full programme of guided tours also offered, as well as bespoke holidays.

Andean Trails
UK
info@andeantrails.co.uk
+44 (0) 131 467 7086
www.andeantrails.co.uk

Andean Trails is an owner run specialist adventure travel company organising small group tours to Peru, Bolivia, Ecuador, Cuba, Guyana and Patagonia.

Artstur Ltd
UK
artstur@gmail.com
+44 (0)207 591 0312
www.artstur.com
Specialist in Italian Art and Culture through lectures, tours to Italy and short courses for students between Sixth Form and University.

Backpacker Travel Auctions
Australia
info@safaripete.com
www.safaripete.com
Safari Pete can offer you directions to the best deals on tours around Australia and New Zealand.

Back-Roads Touring Company Ltd
UK
info@backroadstouring.com
+44 (0)208 987 0990
www.backroadstouring.com
With over 25 years' experience in small group and tailor-made tours across the UK and Europe, Back-Roads Touring is truly the original small group touring company.

Bicycling Empowerment Network
South Africa
andrew@benbikes.org.za
+27 21 788 4174
www.benbikes.org.za
BEN, a non-profit organisation, promotes the use and sale of refurbished bicycles. They conduct Bicycle Township Tours empowering local people and winning International Responsible Tourism Awards.

Black Feather - The Wilderness Adventure Company
Canada
info@blackfeather.com
+1 705 746 1372
www.blackfeather.com
Company offering canoeing and kayaking trips and expeditions to remote arctic locations. Offer women only trips and will do a customized trip for groups of four or more.

Borderlands Travel
UK
info@borderlandstravel.com
+44 (0)1913 082201
www.borderlandstravel.com
Borderlands offer escorted group tours in beautiful destinations in Europe and tailor-made itineraries for individuals and small groups. Take a cultural journey through cities steeped in history, visit UNESCO World Heritage Sites and travel through some dramatic scenery, all whilst under the guidance of an expert escort.

Borneo Anchor Travel & Tours/ Sabah Divers
Malaysia
sabahdivers2u@yahoo.com
+60 88 256 483
www.borneoanchortours.com
They offer various wildlife, nature and adventure packages all over Sabah, Malaysian Borneo.

BridgeClimb Sydney
Australia
admin@bridgeclimb.com
+61 (0) 2 8274 7777
www.bridgeclimb.com
BridgeClimb provides the ultimate experience of Sydney, with guided climbs to the top of the world famous Sydney Harbour Bridge. Climbers can choose between The Express Climb, The Bridge Climb or The Discovery Climb.

Cape York Motorcycle Adventures

Australia

adventures@capeyorkmotorcycles.com.au

+61 (07) 4059 0220

www.capeyorkmotorcycles.com.au

Motorcycle tours in north Queensland from one to eight days duration. Private charter also available. They have their own motorbikes and a support vehicle that accompanies the longer excursions.

Cordillera Blanca Trek

Peru

info@cordillerablancatrek.com

+51 (0) 43 427 635

www.cordillerablancatrek.com

Offers treks in Machu Picchu, a volcanco tour and more.

Do Something Different

UK

contact-us@dosomethingdifferent.com

+44 (0)208 090 3890

www.dosomethingdifferent.com

Want to dog sled in the Rockies? Take a Hong Kong Island or helicopter tour? Or climb Auckland Harbour Bridge?

Dolphin Encounter

New Zealand

info@dolphin.co.nz

+64 3 319 6777

www.dolphinencounter.co.nz

Swim or watch dolphins in Kaikoura. You do need to book in advance as there is a limit to how many swimmers are allowed per trip.

Dorset Expeditionary Society/ Leading Edge Expeditions

UK

dorsetexp@gmail.com

www.dorsetexp.org.uk

Dorset Expeditionary Society promotes adventurous expeditions to remote parts of the world. Open to all. May qualify for two sections of the Duke of Edinburgh's Gold Award.

Dragoman

UK

info@dragoman.co.uk

+44 (0)1728 861133

www.dragoman.com

Overlanding is stil the most authentic and accessible way of discovering new countries, their people and culture. Join us in Africa, America and Asia.

Eco Trails Kerala

India

mail@ecotourskerala.com

+91 48125 24447

www.ecotourskerala.com

This tour company provides budget holiday tour packages in the Kumarakom and Alleppey Backwater areas.

Equitours - Worldwide Horseback Riding Adventures

USA

+1 307 455 3363

www.ridingtours.com

With over 30 years experience, Equitours offer tested and tried horseback tours on six continents. Rides from three to eight days (or longer) for riders of all experience.

Explore Worldwide Ltd

UK

res@explore.co.uk

01252 884223

www.explore.co.uk

Company organising special tours in small groups. Types of worldwide tours available are walking holidays, dog-sledding, wildlife and railway tours amongst others.

Fair Dinkum Bike Tours

Australia

dave@fairdinkumbiketours.com.au

+61 0()7 4053 6999

www.fairdinkumbiketours.com.au

Offer a range of tours using local guides to cater for all levels.

Flying Kiwi

New Zealand

info@flyingkiwi.com

+64 3 547 0171

www.flyingkiwi.com

Flying Kiwi bus tours around New Zealand offer a unique and fun experience. Camping or cabin options are available in exciting locations and usually meals are included.

Fräulein Maria's Bicycle Tours

Austria

biketour@aon.at

+43 650 3426297

www.mariasbicycletours.com

Maria's Bicycle tours take you to the main attractions from the film The Sound Of Music! The tour lasts three hours with stop points along the way and operates between May and September.

G Adventures

Canada

travel@gadventures.com

+1 416 260 0999

www.gadventures.com

G Adventures offers one of the widest selection of affordable small-group tours, safaris and expeditions across the world.

Go Differently Ltd

UK

info@godifferently.com

+44 (0) 1273 732236

www.godifferently.com

Company offering small-group, short-term volunteering and tailor-made holidays based on the appreciation and respect of the local environment and people.

Goyo Travel

UK

info@goyotravel.com

+44 (0)1869 866520

www.goyotravel.com

Goyo Travel provides a variety of group and private trips to beautiful Mongolia. Whether you are looking for adventure or a more cultural experience, there is plenty on offer.

Grand American Adventures

UK

03339 997965; +44 208 682 8921

www.grandamericanadventures.com

Grand American Adventures specialises in tours to the Americas, with unrivalled knowledge and experience we are committed to bringing you the finest small group adventures available. Enjoy spectacular natural sights, challenging and rewarding activities and encounters with some of the world's most colourful cultures and wildlife.

Grayline Tours of Hong Kong
China
sales@grayline.com.hk
+852 2368 7111
www.grayline.com.hk
Special sightseeing day tours around Hong Kong and Macau.

Haka Tours
New Zealand
info@hakatours.com
+64 3 980 4252
www.hakatours.com
Haka Tours represents the ultimate in New Zealand adventure holidays, from small group adventures to New Zealand snow tours exploring the impressive Southern Alps and the active volcanoes of the North.

High Places Ltd
UK
holidays@highplaces.co.uk
+44 (0)845 257 75
www.highplaces.co.uk
Independent specialist trekking company organising tours to 22 countries.

Highland Experience Tours
UK
info@highlandexperience.com
+44 (0)131 226 1414
www.highlandexperience.com
Travel company offering one day and private tours around Scotland, such as a two day highland tour, a whisky tasting tour, or a tour of Scotland personalised to your own requirements.

In the Saddle Ltd
UK
rides@inthesaddle.com
+44 01299 272 997
www.inthesaddle.com
Specializes in horse riding holidays all over the world, catering for all levels of experience. From ranches in the Rocky Mountain states of Montana and Wyoming, to expeditions in remote and unexplored parts of the world.

Inside Japan Tours
UK
info@insidejapantours.com
+44 (0)117 370 9751
www.insidejapantours.com
Specialist company offering tours of Japan, including small group tours and individual, self-guiding tours. You can also book a Japan Rail Pass online here.

International Wilderness Leadership School
USA
info@iwls.com
+1 800 985 (4957)/ +1 907 766 3366
iwls.com
An outdoor school specialising in the highest quality guide training, outdoor leadership training, wilderness education and technical instruction.

Intrepid Travel
UK
islington@intrepidtravel.com
0800 781 1660
www.intrepidtravel.com
For travellers with a yearning to get off the beaten track, Intrepid opens up a whole new world of adventure travel.

Intro Travel
UK

enquiries@introtravel.com

0800 133 7007

www.introtravel.com

With epic adventures in Australia, Thailand, Bali & Vietnam, an Intro Travel trip includes advice and support before you go, an awesome Group Leader from the moment you arrive, an instant group of friends, an amazing itinerary and all the important stuff sorted so you can relax and enjoy your experience.

Irish Gap Year
Ireland

info@Irishgapyear.com

+00 353 83-198-4288

www.irishgapyear.com

Why not travel to Europe and experience the magic of Ireland! On the western edge of Europe, along the wild Atlantic you'll meet the friendliest people, explore untouched nature and immerse yourself in the Irish culture. Develop leadership and communication skills, volunteer with the local community and immerse yourself in nature.

Jungle Surfing Canopy Tours
Australia

info@junglesurfing.com.au

+61 7 4098 0043

www.junglesurfing.com.au

Night walks in a tropical rainforest or jungle surf through the Daintree Rainforest.

Kande Horse Trails
Malawi

info@kandehorse.com

+265 (0) 8500416

www.kandehorse.com

Experience the Malawi bush on horseback. All ages and riding abilities catered for.

Killary Adventure Company
Ireland

adventure@killary.com

00 353 (0) 95 43411

www.killaryadventure.com

We specialise in adventure activities that range from bungee jumping to kayaking on Irelands only fjord and much more in between. Whether you are a soft adventurer or after the extreme adrenaline thrill we have something for you.

Kivu Gap Year
USA

andy@kivugapyear.com

970-403-6016

www.kivugapyear.com

The KIVU Gap Year is designed to guide you into a year of travel, internship, and home stay experiences around the world. A purposeful program designed to guide you on the journey into young adulthood.

KT Adventure
Vietnam

info@vivutravel.com

+84 4 36740486

www.vivutravel.com

KT Adventure, part of Vivu Travel, offer specialised tours in Vietnam, from adventure tours to motorbiking.

Live Travel
UK

phil.haines@live-travel.com

+44 (0) 208 894 6104

www.live-travel.com

Personalised travel plans offered as well as group tours.

4 Travelling and accommodation

M. Trek and Tour
Morocco
info@moroccotrek.co.uk
00212 524330597
www.mtrekandtour.com
Trekking trips, tailormade tours, group holidays and specialised activity weeks in Morocco.

Melbourne Street Art Tour
Australia
booking@melbournestreettours.com
+61 (03) 9328 5556
www.melbournestreettours.com
Melbourne Street Art Tours, led by one of Melbourne's elite street art stars, gives you an overview of the Melbourne underground street art scene.

Mountain Kingdoms Ltd
UK
info@mountainkingdoms.com
+44 (0)1453 844400
www.mountainkingdoms.com
Himalayan Kingdoms is the UK's foremost quality trekking company, running treks and tours to the great mountain ranges of the world.

My Odyssey Tours
China
inquiry@myodysseytours.com
+86 156 9773 0073
www.myodysseytours.com
Focusing on Asia and Middle East, our expertise in private & custom travel can make your gap-year a lifetime experience at your most comfortable pace.

Natural World Safaris
UK
sales@naturalworldsafaris.com
+44 (0)1273 691 642
www.naturalworldsafaris.com
Natural World Safaris is a small specialist company offering the best safari holidays with a focus on viewing some of the worlds greatest animals.

NOLS
UK
admissions@nols.edu
800-710-6657 / 307-332-5300
www.nols.edu/en
NOLS is a nonprofit school that seeks to help you step forward boldly as a leader.

It's our role to provide the environment and training to help you discover your full potential. We do that in classrooms close to home and in remote wilderness areas around the world.

Olympic Bike Travel
Greece
info@olympicbike.com
+30 283 1072 383
www.olympicbike.com
A variety of bike tours available for all ages. From a ride down the highest mountain in Greece, to bike and hiking tours.

On The Go Tours
UK
info@onthegotours.com
0207 371 1113
www.onthegotours.com
Special tours such as solar eclipse tours and railways of the Raj can be arranged.

Oyster Trekking

UK

trek@oystertrekking.com

www.oystertrekking.com

Take the trek of a lifetime in the stunning Himalayas, with full Oyster support and a fair price. Adventurous treks include Everest Base Camp. The Langtang, Ghale Guan and Annapurna Base Camp.

Oyster Worldwide Limited

UK

anne@oysterworldwide.com

+44 (0) 1892 770 771

www.oysterworldwide.com

Take the trek of a lifetime in the stunning Himalayas, with full Oyster support and a fair price. Adventurous treks include Everest Base Camp. The Langtang, Ghale Guan and Annapurna Base Camp.

Palmar Voyages

Ecuador

gerencia@palmarvoyages.com

+593(9) 9 480 2268

www.palmarvoyages.com

Tailor-made programmes for tours in Ecuador, Peru, South America, the Andes and the Galapagos Islands.

Pathfinders Africa

Zimbabwe

info@pathfindersafrica.com

+263 4 870 573

www.pathfindersafrica.com

Pathfinders Africa is an African-based expedition company that operates from Zimbabwe. Developed to meet the needs of the adventurous traveller, Pathfinders' over-riding philosophy is of friendliness and individuality.

Peregrine Adventures Ltd

UK

travel@peregrineadventures.co.uk

+44 0844 736 0170

www.peregrineadventures.com

Peregrine offer small group adventure tours worldwide. They offer a vast range of tours from polar expeditions to trekking the Himalayas.

Peru Trip Advisors

Peru

info@peru-tripadvisors.com

+51 1 241 7429

www.peru-tripadvisors.com

Explore Peru, from the Inca Trail to Machu Picchu with an inclusive and personalised tour.

Pioneer Expeditions Worldwide

UK

info@pioneerexpeditions.com

01202 798922

www.pioneerexpeditions.com

High and Wild plan some of the most unusual and exciting adventures to destinations worldwide.

Pura Aventura

UK

info@pura-aventura.com

01273 961928 / +44 1273 961 921

www.pura-aventura.com

Various beautiful tailor-made tours in exotic locations. Career break to fulfil a long held dream or a special diversion on your gap-year perhaps?

4 Travelling and accommodation

the gap-year guidebook 2018

Rickshaw Travel
UK

info@rickshawtravel.co.uk

+44 (0) 1273 322 399

www.rickshawtravel.co.uk

Rickshaw Travel is a UK based ABTA/ATOL bonded travel operator, that uses locally owned accommodation with an authentic feel that is a cut above the usual backpacker haunts.

Ride With Us
UK

sales@ridewithustours.co.uk

+44 (0)1582 840 621

www.ridewithustours.co.uk

Organised motorcycle holidays around western and eastern Europe that offer something for everyone regardless of their touring experience.

Saddle Skedaddle
UK

info@skedaddle.co.uk

+44 (0)191 265 1110

www.skedaddle.co.uk

Some say there is no better way to see a country, its culture, its wildlife and its people, than by bike! This company offers off-road, road or leisure cycling.

Safari Par Excellence
UK

+44 (0) 1548 830 059

www.zambezi.co.uk

Safari company with a 'no fuss or frills' ethos. They cover Zimbabwe, Zambia, Botswana, Namibia and other countries in Africa.

SAS Travel Peru
Peru

info@sastravelperu.com

+51 984 652 232

www.sastravelperu.com

SAS organize a huge variety of tours in Cusco and Peru, from Adventures trips, Treks, Amazon Jungle Trips and Packages in Peru to MachuPicchu tours, Inca Trail hikes and many more.

Scenic Air
Namibia

windhoek@scenic-air.com

+264 61 249 268

www.scenic-air.com

Scenic Air caters for individual travellers, families as well as groups. They offer flights to all of the popular tourist destinations in Namibia.

Selective Asia
UK

contact@selectiveasia.com

+44 (0) 1273 670001

www.selectiveasia.com

Selective Asia offers a range of unique, privately guided tours and adventure holidays in Cambodia, Laos, Vietnam and Thailand.

Specialtours Ltd
UK

info@specialtours.co.uk

+44 (0) 20 7386 4690

www.specialtours.co.uk

International art and cultural tours. Access wonderful private houses, art collections and gardens. Most tours are accompanied by an expert lecturer.

Suntrek
UK
0800 781 1660
www.intrepidsuntrek.com
Adventure tours arranged in the USA, Mexico, Alaska, Canada, Central and South America and Australia.

Sunvil
UK
+44 (0) 20 8568 4499
www.sunvil.co.uk
A range of active holidays/trips available including sailing holidays around the world.

The adventure company
UK
0845 287 6541
www.adventurecompany.co.uk
Offers inspirational holidays and trips worldwide that venture off the well trodden tourist trails.

The Bundu Safari Company
UK
0800 781 1660
www.intrepidbundu.com
The Bundu Safari Company has teamed up with Intrepid Travel to offer exciting safari adventures.

The Dragon Trip Pte Ltd
UK
info@thedragontrip.com
0203 817 5974
thedragontrip.com
The Dragon Trip is a provider of affordable holidays in China in the form of backpacking trips.

The Imaginative Traveller
UK
online@imtrav.net
0845 287 2908
www.imaginative-traveller.com
Individual, escape and volunteering tours available.

The Oriental Caravan
UK
info@theorientalcaravan.com
+44 (0)1424 883 570
www.theorientalcaravan.com
The Oriental Caravan is a truly independent adventure tour operator specialising in escorted small group travel in the Far East.

The Russia Experience
UK
expert@trans-siberian.co.uk
0345 521 2910
www.trans-siberian.co.uk
The Trans-Siberian is a working train covering 9,000 km, 10 time zones, 16 rivers and some 80 towns and cities. A once in a lifetime experience.

The Unique Travel Company
UK
info@theuniquetravel.co.uk
01264 889 644
www.theuniquetravel.co.uk
We provide a personal, affordable Sri Lankan experience that gives you a truly unique experience knowing that you are also putting money back into the island to help it grow and prosper - we feel this is what responsible tourism is about.

Timberline Adventures
USA
timber@earthnet.net
+1 800 417 2453
www.timbertours.com
Hiking and cycling tours in the USA.

Topdeck
UK
info@topdecktravel.co.uk
0845 257 5212; +44 (0)20 8987 3305
www.topdeck.travel

Providing unforgettable travel experiences for 18 to 30 somethings. Extended trips, festivals, ski and sailing in Europe, holidays in Egypt, Morocco, Jordan and Israel, safaris in Africa, adventures in Australia and New Zealand.

Tour Bus
Australia
questions@tourbus.com.au
www.tourbus.com.au

If you are looking for Tour Bus options within Australia or around the world you will likely find some great resources here.

Tourism Queensland
UK
44 20 7367 0981
www.experiencequeensland.com

Explore the many beautiful destinations Queensland has to offer.

TransIndus
UK
enquiries@transindus.com
0844 879 3960
www.transindus.co.uk

TransIndus provides opportunities to discover both the must-see sights and off-track gems where you can gain an authentic taste of rural as well as urban India, beyond the reach of more conventional tourist trails with holidays which are both comfortable and relaxing, and culturally stimulating.

Travel Nation
UK
+44 (0)1273 320580
www.travelnation.co.uk

Independent specialist travel company providing expert advice and the best deals on round-the-world trips, multi-stop itineraries, overland/adventure tours and Trans-Siberian rail journeys.

Travel The Unknown
UK
+44 (0)20 7183 6371
www.traveltheunknown.com

Travel The Unknown offers small group (up to 12 travellers) and tailormade tours to various locales throughout Afica, Asia, Europe, Latin America and the Middle East.

Travellers Connected.com
UK
info@travellersconnected.com
www.travellersconnected.com

A totally free community site for gap-year travellers. Register and contact travellers around the world for to-the-minute advice on the best places to go and best things to do.

Tribes Travel
UK
enquiries@tribes.co.uk
+44 (0)1473 890499
www.tribes.co.uk

A Fair Trade Travel company with lots of exciting tours for you to choose from, such as budget priced walking safaris to the more expensive once in a lifetime trips.

Tucan Travel

UK

+44 (0)800 804 8435

www.tucantravel.com

Tucan Travel are an adventure tour operator, specialising in group tours in South and Central America, Asia, Europe and Africa

Veloso Tours

UK

travel@veloso.com

020 8762 0616

www.veloso.com

Veloso Tours specialise in trip to various countries in South America. Experience an authentic approach to travel, personalised around you from inspiration to implementation with our specialists advisors, high-quality service, expert local guides and professional organisation.

Vietnam Tour Pedia

Vietnam

hamid@vietcenter.vn

+84 4 6281 6212

www.vietnamtourpedia.com

Vietnam Tour Pedia is a Hanoi based travel agency offering tailor-made tours within Vietnam and Indochina with attention to gap year offers.

Vodkatrain

UK

+44 (0) 20 8877 7650

www.vodkatrain.com

Experience the Trans-Mongolian railway and the Silk Road, travelling with local people, sampling local food and travel at local prices.

Walks Worldwide

UK

sales@walksworldwide.com

0845 301 4737

www.walksworldwide.com

Walks Worldwide is a leading independent specialist for trekking and walking holidays, offering a wide choice of walking holidays to all the world's great trekking and walking destinations, many of which are unique to Walks Worldwide.

Wendy Wu Tours

UK

info@wendywutours.co.uk

0800 9888 209

www.wendywutours.co.uk

Visit some of Asia's most beautiful locations with tailormade trips and tours from Wendy Wu Tours. From the Great Wall of China to the Taj Mahal in India, indulge yourself in a new culture and discover the wonders Asia has to offer.

Winterline Global Education

UK

1-888-737-4226

www.winterline.com

Whether you spend a year or a week on a Winterline program, you will visit extraordinary places, experience new cultures, learn new skills and find out something important about yourself.

World Expeditions

UK

enquiries@worldexpeditions.co.uk

+44 (0)20 8545 9030

www.worldexpeditions.com

Adventure travel company offering ground breaking itineraries on every continent. They offer exciting all inclusive adventures and challenges worldwide.

Au Pairing

Au Pair Ecosse
UK
ruth@aupairecosse.com
+44 (0) 1786 474573
www.aupairecosse.com

Au Pair Ecosse places au pairs with families in Scotland and sends British au pairs to families in Europe and America using established, reputable agent partners.

For further information see page 130

Au Pair in America (APIA)
UK
info@aupairamerica.co.uk
0207 581 7322
www.aupairamerica.co.uk

Whether you're looking for a year out or a legal cultural exchange opportunity, APIA's au pair programs give you plenty of free time to explore, study, travel and make new friends, complete with support throughout your stay.

AuPairCare
USA
customercare@aupaircare.com
+1 800 428 7247
www.aupaircare.com

As the premier au pair agency, we are dedicated to matching families in the United States with international au pairs who provide live-in childcare.

Bunters Au Pair Agency
UK
office@aupairsnannies.com
+44 (0)1327 831144
www.aupairsnannies.com

Bunters offers various au pair positions in the UK and Europe.

Childcare International Ltd
UK
office@childint.co.uk
+44 (0)20 8731 4551
www.childint.co.uk

Childcare International, together with their partner agencies abroad, arrange au pair placements across Europe, Australia, New Zealand, Canada and the US.

Gap 360
UK
info@gap360.com
01892 527392
www.gap360.com

Gap 360 is an exciting travel company offering an amazing range of affordable gap year adventures.

Planet Au Pair
Spain
info@planetaupair.com
+34 91 546 6605
www.planetaupair.com

Company placing au pairs throughout Europe and the USA.

Total Nannies
UK
+44 (0)207 0601213
www.totalnannies.com

This company places nannies and au pairs worldwide.

305

Internships & Paid Work Placements

African Conservation Experience
UK
info@conservationafrica.net
+44 (0) 1454 269182
www.conservationafrica.net

African Conservation Experience offer volunteering opportunities at wildlife conservation projects in southern Africa. You can count on our full support and more than 10 years experience. See our main advert in Conservation

Animafest Experience
Spain
info@animafestexperience.com
+34 93 765 39 69
www.animafestexperience.com

Online platform for students all over the world. We find them internship places in Spain. Free service for students.

BUNAC
UK
enquiries@bunac.org.uk
+44 (0) 333 999 7516
www.bunac.org

BUNAC the work and travel expert offers exciting work abroad, volunteering abroad programmes and gap year opportunities.

Bushwise
South Africa
+27 (0)87 754 6287
www.bushwise.co.za

Bushwise specializes in running professional FGASA accredited courses and Hospitality Course and Work Placement programmes. Both the organisation, as well as our graduates, are highly recognized in the hospitality industry due to our high standards and excellent reputation.

China Study Abroad
China
info@chinastudyabroad.org
+86 10 8468 3799
www.chinastudyabroad.org

Club Med
France
+33 1 53 35 35 53
www.clubmedjobs.co.uk

Club Med offers a wide range of job opportunities at resorts all around the world for those interested in a career in hospitality, catering, sports, leisure and luxury provision.

Connect-123
UK
info@connect-123.com
+44 (0)207 096 1201
www.connect-123.com

Connect-123 develops and administers volunteer, internship and study abroad programs in Barcelona, Buenos Aires, Cape Town, Dublin and Shanghai.

Gap 360
UK
info@gap360.com
01892 527392
www.gap360.com

Gap 360 is an exciting travel company offering an amazing range of affordable gap year adventures.

Gi2C
China
info@gi2c.org
+86 10 52889011
www.gi2c.org

Our goal is to help students and young professionals not only get into China but also to help them understand China and Chinese business culture. We provide tailor-made opportunities for interns to work for companies based in China.

Global Choices
UK

+44 (0) 20 8533 2777

www.globalchoices.co.uk

Offers internships and working holidays in USA, Australia, Canada, UK, Ireland, Brazil, Argentina, Spain, Greece and Italy.

Global Nomadic
UK

contact@globalnomadic.com

+44 (0)207 193 2652

globalnomadic.com

Global Nomadic was founded in 2009 to connect grassroots NGO's from around the world with students eager to gain hands-on experience and further their careers!

Initiative Auslandszeit
Germany

info@initiative-auslandszeit.de

+49 (0)5242 4054340

www.initiative-auslandszeit.de

INITIATIVE auslandszeit is the leading network in Germany for young people willing going abroad after school or before studying.

InterExchange
USA

info@interexchange.org

+1 212 924 0446

www.interexchange.org

InterExchange offers J-1 & H-2B visa programs throughout the US. Options include au pair, internship, seasonal work and travel and summer camp positions.

International Exchange Programme UK (IEPUK)
UK

ws@iepuk.com

+44(0)1572 823 934

www.iepuk.com

Based in the United Kingdom IEPUK is offering a wide range of international exchange programmes and educational packages to support study and work experience abroad.

IST Plus
UK

info@istplus.com

020 7788 7877

www.istplus.com

Internships in the USA, Australia, New Zealand. Summer work in the USA. Summer camp in the USA. Gap-year work in Australia, New Zealand. Volunteer in Thailand. Teach in Thailand, China (for graduates).

Leave UR Mark
USA

info@leaveurmark.com

+1 516 998 6615

www.leaveurmark.com

Work on personal and professional goals by gaining hands on experience in a variety of fields that help provide new skills, networking, and new perspectives.

Lucasfilm
USA

jobs.lucasfilm.com

As you can imagine, internships with Lucasfilm are few and far between. They are also quickly filled. See their website for further details.

Mountbatten Institute
UK

info-uk@mountbatten.org

0845 370 3535

www.mountbatten.org

Grab a whole year's worth of paid work experience through the Mountbatten Programme and enhance your CV.

Start Me Up
UK

startmeup.careers

Learn start up skills while you travel the world. Get matched with hard-to-find startup internships across three continents.

TeachVietnam
Vietnam

will@teachvietnam.co.uk

+84 90 365 4596

teachvietnam.co.uk

Teach Vietnam is a British company that organizes rewarding positions for graduates wanting to teach in Ho Chi Minh City, Vietnam. In a supportive professional environment, Tutors learn to teach in a variety of settings, including: academic tutoring across a range of subjects, assisting with international NGOs that work with vulnerable children and local people and English teaching in local schools.

The Career Break Site
UK

info@thecareerbreaksite.com

www.thecareerbreaksite.com

On The Career Break Site you'll find tons of career break opportunities, like ski instructor courses, TEFL, working abroad and volunteering.

The New England Wild Flower Society & Garden in the Woods
USA

information@newenglandwild.org

+1 508 877 7630

www.newenglandwild.org

The oldest plant conservation organization in the USA and a leader in regional plant conservation programmes and native plant studies. They have volunteering and internship opportunities.

Twin Work & Volunteer
UK

0208 297 3278

www.workandvolunteer.com

Work and volunteer programmes listed. Also offers a travel insurance package.

V2 Volunteer & Vacation
UK

info@v2volunteers.com

+44 (0)203 289 4611

www.v2volunteers.com

Join us for an amazing volunteering experience on the islands of Jamaica or Trinidad and Tobago.

Visitoz
Australia

info@visitoz.org

+61 741 686 106

www.visitoz.org

Visitoz provides training and guarantees work for young people between the ages of 18 and 30 in agriculture, hospitality, child care and teaching all over Australia.

WE ARE SNO
UK

hello@wearesno.com

wearesno.com

WE ARE SNO provide ski and snowboard instructor courses at resorts around the globe. All courses come with guaranteed paid work for winter!

Work and Traveller
Germany
info@work-and-traveller.de
+49 (0)5242 5810090
www.work-and-traveller.de
Innovative Operator for Working Holidays especially Work and Travel in Australia, New Zealand, Canada, Chile & Japan.

Work the World Ltd
UK
info@worktheworld.co.uk
+44 (0) 1273 974 634
www.worktheworld.co.uk
Organises healthcare and community development projects that provide maximum benefit to both the participants and the overseas communities they support.

Seasonal work

Acorn Adventure
UK
info@acornadventure.co.uk
+44 (0)1384 398870
www.acornadventure.co.uk
Acorn Adventure specialises in trips for schools and youth groups nationwide. A wide range of adventurous activities are available at natural outdoor environments such as mountains, lakes, rivers and caves in France, Italy, Spain and South Wales.

Air Pro
UK
support@air-pro.co.uk
+44 (0)1695 511 61
www.air-pro.co.uk
Air Pro is an informative jobs website, helping those wanting to work abroad to find their perfect job in resorts like Ibiza, Zante, Magaluf or Ayia Napa.

Alpine Elements Group
UK
jobs@alpineelements.co.uk
0844 770 4070
jobsite.alpineelements.co.uk
Alpine Elements is a specialist Ski and Summer Holiday Company in France, Austria and Greece offering exciting jobs vacancies, both full and part time, in both the summer and winter.

AmeriCamp
UK
info@americamp.co.uk
0161 312 3640
www.americamp.co.uk
We offer people around the world the chance to work in the USA at a summer camp and become an AmeriCamper. We pay at least $1500 and you make memories that last a lifetime! Join the AmeriCamp Revolution!

BUNAC
UK
enquiries@bunac.org.uk
+44 (0) 333 999 7516
www.bunac.org
BUNAC the work and travel expert offers exciting work abroad, volunteering abroad programmes and gap year opportunities.

Camp America
UK
enquiries@campamerica.co.uk
0207 581 7373
www.campamerica.co.uk
Camp America sends over 7,500 people to work on summer camps in the USA every year with up to 4 weeks independent travel after camp!

Camp Leaders In America
UK
uk@campleaders.com
+44 (0) 151 708 6868
www.campleaders.com

For those aged between 18 and 25 who love fun, adventure and are passionate about a sport, hobby or interest and want to get paid for enjoying it, look no further than Camp Leaders. Combine life-changing cultural experiences with the perfect summer job abroad.

Camp Thailand
UK
info@summercampthailand.com
0161 222 3780
www.summercampthailand.com

Here at Camp Thailand we've combined the best that Thailand has to offer! Teach English as a foreign language and run sporting activities for local children, help out in the Elephant Conservation Village, and many other exciting activities whilst making new friends.

Camp Vietnam
UK
info@camp.co.uk
0161 222 3780
www.campvietnam.com

Have you ever dreamed of going to Vietnam? Have you ever thought about working in a summer camp? We have planned the perfect experience for you with Camp Vietnam Adventures! We have combined the best that Vietnam has to offer with a Camp experience.

Canvas Holidays
UK
campingrecruitment@canvasholidays.com
+44 (0) 1383 629012
www.canvasholidaysrecruitment.com

We have paid positions at over 100 campsites across Europe. We require a minimum of eight weeks commitment for July and August.

For further information see page 136

Castaway Resorts
Thailand
+66 (0)831 387 472 / +66 (0)811 707 605
www.castaway-resorts.com

Castaway Resorts invite enthusiastic active young people on a gap year to join our friendly teams at one of our tropical beach resorts in Thailand.

CCUSA
UK
info@ccusa.co.uk
0208 874 6325
www.ccusa.com

Work in summer camps in beautiful locations in America. You don't need any experience or qualifications but you do need to be at least 18 years old. Also available, a range of worldwide programs including winter seasons in Canada.

Changing Worlds
UK
info@changing-worlds.com; media@changing-worlds.com
+44 (0)2081 238702
www.changingworlds.co.uk

We offer a range of gap year placements in: Australia, China, Fiji, Ghana, India, Indonesia, South Africa, Thailand and many more. So, if you like the idea of travel, meeting like-minded people and don't mind working hard, then this is for you!

Château Beaumont

UK

holidays@chateau-beaumont.co.uk

+44 (0)1388 741370

www.chateau-beaumont.co.uk

Chateau Beaumont is a small friendly language and activity centre based in the Normandy region of France.

Crewseekers Ltd

UK

info@crewseekers.net

+44 (0)238 115 9207

www.crewseekers.net

We offer a personal service assisting people of all ages and experience levels looking for the opportunity to build up some sea miles, find professional sailing work and paid delivery jobs, gap year adventures, sailing weekends and holidays, or simply to go sailing with like minded sailors.

Gap 360

UK

info@gap360.com

01892 527392

www.gap360.com

Gap 360 is an exciting travel company offering an amazing range of affordable gap year adventures.

Go Workabout

Australia

info@goworkabout.com

+61 (0)8 6226 9979

www.goworkabout.com

Arranges work in Australia for working holiday makers before they travel.

Good Teachers Union

China

esljobsinchina@outlook.com; tina@goodteachersunion.org

+86 138 3635 8190

www.goodteachersunion.org

Good Teachers Union began in 2009 and has helped over 1000 teachers from all around the world find teaching jobs in China. Our primary objective is to not only provide you with a suitable job in China but also help you have a positive and memorable China teaching experience. Using Good Teachers Union to help you find a job makes your life easier.

Ibiza Intro

UK

info@ibizaintro.com; liam@ibizaintro.com

0844 409 6474

www.ibizaintro.com

If you're coming to work in Ibiza, then come and see why 1000's of workers choose Ibiza Intro for jobs, accommodation and packages.

Immigration New Zealand

UK

09069 100 100 (premium rate number)

www.immigration.govt.nz/branch/londonbranchhome

New Zealand government website offering details on working holidays for visitors to the country.

Jetsetter Jobs

UK

info@jetsetterjobs.com

+44 (0)7792 284780

www.jetsetterjobs.com

The GO-TO platform connecting youth travellers and students with temporary paid work in foreign countries. English teaching, ski seasons, hospitality, volunteering, childcare and more!

Leiths List, Agency for Cooks
UK
info@leithslist.com
+44 (0) 1225 722983
www.leithslist.com
Find short term cookery jobs such as chalet and holiday home work. Once qualified (see cookery section), you can earn money in your gap year or university holidays.

Mark Warner Ltd
UK
recruitment@markwarner.co.uk
0207 761 7020
www.markwarner.co.uk/recruitment2
Leading independent tour operator with opportunities all year round in ski and beach resorts. Variety of hotel positions and fully inclusive benefits package on offer.

Mountain Cookery School
UK
0330 102 8001
www.themountaincookeryschool.co.uk
Are you looking to work in the mountains as a chalet host? Or flying the nest for the first time? Then how about a week in Tignes to master the art of cooking, and learn a bunch of invaluable life skills? Chuck in a great social scene and a chalet-load of mountain activities, and you've got yourself a cracking week away from home.

Natives.co.uk
UK
info@natives.co.uk
+44 (0)1772 639604
www.natives.co.uk
Seasonal recruitment website for ski or summer resorts.

Neilson Holidays
UK
recruitment@neilson.com
01273 666130
www.neilson.co.uk
This company offers a selection of worldwide sporting holidays, all year round.

Oyster Worldwide Limited
UK
anne@oysterworldwide.com
+44 (0) 1892 770 771
www.oysterworldwide.com
Oyster is the specialist gap-year provider offering paid work projects abroad. Whether you're a ski nut or budding jackaroo, you'll get excellent, personal support throughout.

PGL
UK
recruitment@pgl.co.uk
0333 3212 123
www.pgl.co.uk/jobs
As the UK's market-leading provider of residential activity holidays and educational courses for children, PGL have an immense variety of Gap Year Jobs to offer for your Gap Year: and we pay you!

PlayaWay Abroad Ltd
UK
info@playawayabroad.com
UK: 0871 288 4412;
Non UK: +34 922 79 31 93
www.playawayabroad.com
Offering seasonal bar and club work at resorts such as Ibiza, Malia, Zante and Magaluf.

Season to Season Employment
UK

enquiries@seasontoseasonemployment.
com

0117 214 0769

www.seasontoseasonemployment.com

Season to Season Employment is a recruitment agency offering a bespoke service in both seasonal and permanent contracts within the hospitality business.

SeasonWorkers.com
UK

info@seasonworkers.com

0845 6439338

www.seasonworkers.com

Season Workers is one of the busiest and most informative sites of its kind. Search and apply online for your dream job or to get news, information and advice for Seasonal Work and Gap Year placements Worldwide.

Skiworld
UK

recruitment@skiworld.co.uk

0330 102 8003

www.skiworld.co.uk/recruitment

Skiworld offers skiing holidays in the top snow sure resorts in Europe and North America, ensuring we have a long season from late November until mid April, offering the possibility of crowd free skiing at great prices.

The Travel Visa Company Ltd
UK

info@thetravelvisacompany.co.uk

+44 (0) 1270 250 590

www.thetravelvisacompany.co.uk

The Travel Visa Company Ltd specialises in obtaining all types of visas for destinations right across the world including Australia, USA, India, Russia, China and Sri Lanka.

Visas Australia Ltd
UK

sales@visas-australia.com

+44 (0)1270 250 590

www.visas-australia.com

Visas Australia Ltd specialises in processing and issuing all types of visas, particularly suited to gap-year travellers. Their service is approved by both the Australian Tourist Board and Australian High Commission.

Visitoz
Australia

info@visitoz.org

+61 741 686 106

www.visitoz.org

Visitoz provides training and guarantees work for young people between the ages of 18 and 30 in agriculture, hospitality, child care and teaching all over Australia.

Workaseason
UK

recruitment@workaseason.com

01483 791010

www.workaseason.com

Workaseason offers a wide range and variety of jobs in the Alps - from Resort Reps, Hospitality Management, Chefs, Bar Staff and Childcare to name just a few - all based in top class countries and resorts.

For further information see pages 124-125

Xtreme Gap
Netherlands

info@xtremegapyear.co.uk

+44 (0)20 32867065

www.xtremegapyear.co.uk

Gap company offering extreme sporting adventures.

Adventure Alternative

UK

office@adventurealternative.com

+44 (0) 28 708 31258

www.adventurealternative.com

Teaching and volunteering in needy schools and orphanages in Kenya and in schools in Kathmandu (includes Himalayan trek).

i-to-i TEFL

UK

tefl@i-to-i.com

+44 (0)113 205 4610

www.i-to-i.com

TEFL (Teaching English as a Foreign Language) is all about exploring the world while learning new skills and getting useful experience for 'real life'. LoveTEFL offer internationally recognised TEFL training, and unique teaching/travel adventures and internship.

Link Ethiopia

UK

chris@linkethiopia.org

+44 (0)20 8045 4558

www.linkethiopia.org

Experience Ethiopia and teach basic English to small groups on a very inexpensive three-month placement with us. Registered Charity No. 1112390.

Oyster Worldwide Limited

UK

anne@oysterworldwide.com

+44 (0) 1892 770 771

www.oysterworldwide.com

Highly motivated university graduate? We can organise a top quality TEFL course followed by a well-paid job teaching English in China or Thailand.

SEE TEFL

Thailand

info@seetefl.com

seetefl.com

Located in Chiang Mai, Thailand, SEE TEFL is now in its 11th year of TEFL Teacher Training with 1,200+ TEFL graduates from 40+ countries on 6 continents.

Our graduates teach English as a Foreign Language across Thailand and throughout the world.

Shane Global Language Centres

UK

sales@shaneglobal.com

+44 (0)14 2471 2000

www.shaneuk.com

If you don't yet have your TEFL qualification, Saxoncourt runs full time four-week courses in London and Oxford, leading to either the Trinity TESOL diploma or the Cambridge CELTA qualification.

Syndicat Mixte Montaigu-Rocheservière

France

anglais@sm-montaigu-rocheserviere.fr

+33 (0) 2 51 46 45 45

www.gapyear-france.com

Receives local government funding to teach English in primary schools, offering five posts annually - and it also employs a sixth person to work as a language assistant in a local college and lycée.

TEFL Heaven

UK

teachabroad@teflheaven.com

+44 (0)20 8133 3885

www.teflheaven.co.uk

TEFL Heaven offers guaranteed paid teaching positions in some of the most breathtaking and exciting locations in Asia, Latin America and Europe.

The English Teacher Training College

Austria

admissions@abci-english.at

+43 7614 51400 18

www.english-teacher-college.at

Teach, study and travel in Austria with a non-profit organisation! Earn an internationally recognised TEFL qualification while making a difference in the lives of children.

The Language House

France

info@teflanguagehouse.com

+33 (0)6 84 83 85 59

www.teflanguagehouse.com

TEFL/TESOL programme available. Also courses in French, Arabic, Spanish or Italian. Small classes.

Volunteering Abroad

Conservation

A Broader View Volunteers
USA
volunteers@abroaderview.org
+1 215 780 1845
www.abroaderview.org

A Broader View Volunteers offers a variety of conservation, humanitarian and medical volunteering opportunities across Latin America, Africa and South East Asia.

For further information see page 160

Adventure Under Sail
UK
enquiries@adventureundersail.com
+44 (0)1305 858274
www.adventureundersail.com

TS Pelican of London is a unique square rigger that sails thousands of miles each year with a voyage crew of young people and the young at heart!

African Conservation Experience
South Africa
info@conservationafrica.net
+44 (0) 1454 269 182
www.conservationafrica.net

African Conservation Experience offer volunteering opportunities at wildlife conservation projects in southern Africa. You can count on our full support and more than 10 years experience. See our main advert in Conservation.

For further information see page 168

African Conservation Trust
South Africa
talk@projectafrica.com
+27 33 342 2844
www.projectafrica.com

The mission of ACT is to provide a means for conservation projects to become self funding through active participation by the public.

African Wildlife Protection Fund Leadership (AWPF)
South Africa
info@awpf.co.za
+27 (0)23 004 0074
www.awpfleadership.co.za

AWPF offers learners the opportunity to develop leadership and survival skills such as team work, community work & development, animal tracking, self-reliance skills and survival/bush craft skills whilst visiting some of the largest private game reserves in South Africa, providing great sight-seeing experiences.

All Out Africa
Swaziland
info@alloutafrica.com
+268 2416 2260
www.alloutafrica.com

All Out Africa offers various volunteering opportunities in Africa, from marine conservation to studying the savannah and its native species. Make a difference whilst absorbing the beauty and culture of Africa.

Amanzi Travel
UK

info@amanzitravel.co.uk

+44 (0) 117 253 0888

www.amanzitravel.co.uk

Amanzi Travel offers tailor-made volunteer opportunities in Africa or Asia. Perfect for a career break, gap year or holiday, get involved with wildlife conservation, marine, medical, teaching, orphan care and sustainable community programmes. There are also opportunities to join world famous courses where you will learn to be a game ranger as well as adventure overland tours - a great way to explore more of these beautiful continents.

For further information see page 158

Andaman Discoveries
Thailand

info@andamandiscoveries.com

+66 (0) 87 917 7165

www.andamandiscoveries.com

Tours allow visitors to experience the traditional culture and ecology of rural coastal Thailand. Volunteer, stay with a family or partake in an eco-project.

Big Beyond
UK

hello@bigbeyond.org

0800 644 6203

bigbeyond.org

With Big Beyond, you will volunteer your time, experience and skills in some of the world's most breath-taking and remote destinations. Put your personal skills and passions to work on relevant, high-impact projects in the fields of conservation, education, gender, health and community development.

Biosphere Expeditions
UK

uk@biosphere-expeditions.org

0870-4460801

www.biosphere-expeditions.org

Biosphere Expeditions is an international non-profit wildlife volunteer organisation, founded in 1999, that runs conservation expeditions for environmental volunteers all across the globe.

Blue Ventures
UK

info@blueventures.org

+44 (0) 20 7697 8598

www.blueventures.org

Blue Ventures runs award-winning marine research projects for conservation, education and sustainable development. Volunteers participate in diving and terrestrial activities in partnership with local communities.

BUNAC
UK

enquiries@bunac.org.uk

+44 (0) 333 999 7516

www.bunac.org

BUNAC the work and travel expert offers exciting work abroad, volunteering abroad programmes and gap year opportunities.

Camps International Limited
UK

info@campsinternational.com

+44 (0)1425 485390

www.campsinternational.com

Gap-year volunteer holidays available. Spend time in community and wildlife camps and still have the time and opportunity to trek mountains and dive in the ocean.

Comunidad Inti Wara Yassi
Bolivia
info@intiwarayassi.org
+591 4 413 6572
www.intiwarayassi.org

CIWY is always looking for volunteers to help care for rescued wildlife and the day-to-day running of their three reserves in Bolivia. Volunteers help care for and interact with numerous animals including pumas, jaguars, monkeys, tapirs, tortoises, exotic birds and more, whilst helping to improve their lives and raise awareness of poaching and illegal animal trade.

Concordia International Volunteers
UK
info@concordiavolunteers.org.uk
01273 422 218
www.concordiavolunteers.org.uk

Concordia offers the opportunity to join international teams of volunteers working on short-term projects in 60 countries in Europe, North America, Latin-America, Africa and Asia.

Conservation Volunteers Australia
Australia
info@conservationvolunteers.com.au
+61 (0) 3 5330 2600
www.conservationvolunteers.com.au

Conservation Volunteers Australia offers projects across Australia, including tree planting, wildlife surveys, track building, year-round. Contribution for meals, accommodation and travel applies.

Conservation Volunteers New Zealand
Australia
info@conservationvolunteers.com.au
+61 (0) 3 5330 2600
www.conservationvolunteers.com.au

Conservation Volunteers New Zealand offers projects year-round, including habitat restoration, tree planting, track building. Contribution for meals, accommodation and travel applies.

Coral Cay Conservation
UK
info@coralcay.org
0207 620 1411
www.coralcay.org

Volunteer with award-winning specialists in coral reef and rainforest conservation expeditions. Scuba dive or trek in tropical climes and work with local communities to aid long-term conservation efforts.

Crees Foundation
Peru
Peru: +51 (0)84 262 433 / UK: +44 (0)20 7581 2932
www.crees-manu.org

Crees Foundation offers various volunteering opportunities in Peru, ranging from 1 week to 12 weeks duration. Live and work in the heart of the Amazon rainforest. Help support sustainable development and conduct conservation research.

Discover Nepal
Nepal
stt@mos.com.np
+977 1 4413690
www.discovernepal.org.np

The aim of Discover Nepal is to provide opportunities for the involvement in the development process, and to practically contribute towards the socio-economic development of the country.

Dyer Island Cruises

South Africa

bookings@whalewatchsa.com

+27 (0)82 801 8014

www.whalewatchsa.com

Dyer Island Cruises offer volunteering opportunities, in addition to activities such as shark cage diving, boat-based whale and bird watching and plane-based wildlife viewing.

Earthwatch Institute

UK

info@earthwatch.org.uk

01865 318 838

www.earthwatch.org.uk

Work alongside leading scientists around the world and help solve pressing environmental problems. With expeditions on over 25 research projects to choose from, conduct hands-on conservation research in stunning locations whilst having an experience of a lifetime.

Ecoteer

UK

contact@ecoteer.com

+44 (0)1752 426285

www.ecoteer.com

Community-based placements in countries around the world and most are free! Volunteer with us and make everlasting friends across the whole world!

Ecoteer (Malaysia)

Malaysia

explore@ecoteer.com

+6 012 217 3208 (Malaysia)

www.ecoteerresponsibletravel.com

With Ecoteer Responsible Travel you will help communities and wildlife at our various projects across Asia.

Edge of Africa

South Africa

info@edgeofafrica.com

+27 (0) 443820122

www.edgeofafrica.com

Edge of Africa offer volunteer programmes to suit your personality, preference and budget. Give the edge and volunteer in Africa.

Enkosini Eco Experience

South Africa

info@enkosini.org

www.enkosini.org

Enkosini Eco Experience offers self-funding volunteers a unique opportunity to work abroad at leading wildlife conservation, rehabilitation and research programs in South Africa, Namibia and Botswana.

Essential Croatia

UK

info@essentialcroatia.com

www.essentialcroatia.com

Join the Griffon Vulture and nature protection programme. Volunteer opportunities available year round on the beautiful and upspoilt island of Cres-Croatia.

Fauna Forever Tambopata

Peru

www.faunaforever.org

Volunteer researchers needed for wildlife project in the Peruvian Amazon. Fauna Forever Tambopata is a wildlife monitoring project based in the Amazon rainforest of Tambopata in south-eastern Peru.

FirstStep.me

South Africa

contact@firststep.me

www.firststep.me

FirstStep.me is an information and reference based online magazine.

Flooglebinder

UK

info@flooglebinder.co.uk

+44 (0) 7772 689 811

www.flooglebinder.co.uk

Flooglebinder are an educational travel specialist that offer students and volunteers conservation and community projects in Europe, South Africa and Asia, whilst promoting the importance of sustainable travel.

Forest Animal Rescue

USA

+1 352 625 7377

forestanimalrescue.org

The perfect opportunity to learn about the welfare of big cats, bears, wolves, monkeys, bats and more while helping the staff and interns of a wild animal sanctuary to provide them with lifetime care.

Friends of Conservation

UK

focinfo@aol.com

+44 (0) 20 7348 3408

www.foc-uk.com

There are some opportunities to volunteer on overseas projects such as the Namibian based Cheetah Conservation Fund. Volunteers are also needed in the UK and at their head office in London. Registered Charity No. 328176.

Fronteering

Canada

+1 604-831 7725

fronteering.com

Fronteering takes you off the beaten path to volunteer with wildlife, conservation, communities or internships.

Frontier

UK

info@frontier.ac.uk

+44 (0) 20 7613 2422

www.frontier.ac.uk

With 250 projects around the world Frontier offers volunteers the chance to get involved in an array of activities from wildlife and marine conservation to trekking and biodiversity research, teaching and community development.

Galapagos Conservation Trust

UK

gct@gct.org

0207 399 7440

www.savegalapagos.org

The Galapagos Conservation Trust has two aims: to raise funds to support the expanding conservation work and to raise awareness of the current issues the islands face. Registered Charity No. 1043470.

Gapforce

UK

info@gapforce.org

0207 736 2769

www.gapforce.org

Gapforce has established itself as a leading provider for enjoyable gap adventures worldwide including volunteering. It is the parent company of Trekforce and Greenforce.

Gili Shark Conservation

Indonesia

sharks@gilisharkconservation.com

+62 812 4676 8517

www.gilisharkconservation.com

Gili Shark Conservation project is a small conservation and data collection course/program seeking enthusiastic people who want to live and study in paradise while making a difference on their holiday.

Give a Fig Volunteering

Sri Lanka

enquiries@giveafigvolunteering.com

+44 (0) 2032907392

www.giveafigvolunteering.com

Give A Fig Volunteering provide fantastic fully supported Sri Lanka volunteering and internship opportunities for you to make a difference.

Global Action Nepal

UK

info@gannepal.org.np

+44 (0) 7941 044063

www.gannepal.org.np

Global Action Nepal projects are always closely in harness with grass roots level needs, focusing on community-led, participatory development. Registered Charity No. 1090773.

Global Nomadic

UK

contact@globalnomadic.com

+44 (0)207 193 2652

globalnomadic.com

Global Nomadic was founded in 2009 to connect grassroots NGO's from around the world with students eager to gain hands-on experience and further their careers!

Global Vision International (GVI)

UK

info@gviworld.com

01727 250 250

www.gvi.co.uk

With unparalled in-country support, GVI volunteers benefit from exceptional training and a Careers Abroad job placement scheme.

Global Volunteer Network

New Zealand

info@volunteer.org.nz

+64 0800 032 5035

www.globalvolunteernetwork.org

Volunteer through the Global Volunteer Network to support communities in need around the world. Volunteer placements include schools, refugee camps, wildlife sanctuaries and nature reserves.

Greenforce

UK

info@greenforce.org

+44 (0) 20 7384 3028

www.greenforce.org

Greenforce is a not-for-profit organisation offering voluntary and paid work overseas. With ten years experience and a range of opportunities, Greenforce will have a programe to suit you.

International Volunteer HQ (IVHQ)

New Zealand

info@volunteerhq.org

NZ: +64 6 758 7949; UK: 0808 234 1621

www.volunteerhq.org

IVHQ offers volunteer programs in more than 30 different locations worldwide including: Africa, Asia, Central & South America, The Pacific and Europe. Programs have many different start dates and a wide range of volunteer work opportunities including: Medical & Healthcare, Arts & Music, Education, Conservation and Construction.

322

Intrax/ProWorld

USA

info@globalinternships.com

+1 877 429 6753

www.globalinternships.com/us/social-development-internships

Projects offered: conservation, health care, education, human rights, journalism, and business projects. Programmes start every month of the year.

InvAID

UK

info@invasion.com

01612121051

www.invasion.com

We offer people around the world the opportunity to volunteer in countries such as Brazil, The Maldives and Thailand. Not only do you get the Invasion experience, but you get to make a real difference in people's lives whilst being based in some of the most rewarding locations in the world.

Kaya Responsible Travel

UK

info@kayavolunteer.com

+44 (0) 161 870 6212

www.kayavolunteer.com

Kaya offer over 200 volunteer projects worldwide working with local communities and conservation initiatives from 2 weeks to 12 months. Placements are tailored to specific needs and skills of students, career breakers', retirees, families or groups.

For further information see page 170

Kevin Richardson Wildlife Sanctuary Pty Ltd

South Africa

info@lionwhisperer.co.za

www.lionwhisperer.co.za

Kevin Richardson Wildlife Sanctuary offers unique opportunities for volunteers to play an important role in the maintenance, care, management and enrichment of all the animals at the sanctuary.

For further information see page 162

Local Ocean Trust : Watamu Turtle Watch

Kenya

+254 717 57 87 23

www.watamuturtles.com

There's so much at the Local Ocean Trust for you to get involved in, with programmes such as turtle nest protection, turtle rehabilitation centre, turtle net release and research and data entry. There is also an education and community outreach programme for those interested in giving humanitarian aid.

N/a'an ku se Foundation

Namibia

volunteer@naankuse.com

+264 (0)81 261 2709

www.naankuse.com

Help to preserve and conserve the Namibian ecosystem by volunteering with N/a'an ku se. With projects ranging from 2 weeks to 3 months and no experience or qualifications necessary, there is something for everyone.

Natucate
Germany
info@natucate.com
+49 241 - 91 99 43 57
www.natucate.com/en/
NATUCATE takes you to fascinating corners of our earth, whose amazing beauty and uniqueness and whose ecological integrity needs to be sustainably protected. By taking an active part in animal protection and nature conservation, you are making a valuable contribution towards this objective.

Nature Guide Training
South Africa
lee@natureguidetraining.com
+27 73 468 9267
www.natureguidetraining.com
Situated on a private game reserve three hours drive from Johannesburg, Nature Guide Training offer a series of programmes in nature guiding and other tailor-made courses.

On African Soil
South Africa
julia@onafricansoil.com
+27 78 820 3353
www.onafricansoil.com
Become an On African Soil Volunteer and take part in wildlife conservation and social upliftment projects.

On Track Safaris (Ingwe Leopard Research Program)
UK
carol@ontracksafaris.co.uk
www.ontracksafaris.co.uk/styled-28/vol.html
Our project allows volunteers to join us in our own private research reserve in South Africa in which they will learn the different concepts of conservation such as wildlife identification, bush senses, bush craft, data input and analysis, tracking ect.

Orangutan Foundation
UK
+44 (0) 20 7724 2912
www.orangutan.org.uk
Participate in hands on conservation fieldwork that really makes a difference and see orangutans in their natural habitat.

Outreach International
UK
info@outreachinternational.co.uk
+44 (0)1903 746 900
www.outreachinternational.co.uk
Outreach International offers a personal service to committed volunteersworking in ethical projects in Cambodia, Nepal, India, Mexico, Ecuador, Galapagos, Costa Rica, and Kenya.
For further information see page 176

Oyster Worldwide Limited
UK
anne@oysterworldwide.com
+44 (0) 1892 770 771
www.oysterworldwide.com
Oyster is a specialist gap-year provider offering genuine opportunities with endangered or abused animals. Vets, zoologists and animal lovers all welcome. Excellent, personal support throughout.

Pacific Discovery
New Zealand
info@pacificdiscovery.org
+64 3 5467667
www.pacificdiscovery.org
With programmes blending meaningful and challenging travel, cultural immersion, volunteer and community service project, Pacific Discovery offers inspiring summer, semester and gap-year educational travel programs abroad.

visit: www.gap-year.com

Pod Volunteer

UK

info@podvolunteer.org

+44 (0)1242 241 181

www.podvolunteer.org

PoD (Personal Overseas Development) is a leading non-profit organisation arranging ethical, inspiring and supported volunteering opportunities around the world.

For further information see page 180

Rangers Survivalcraft

South Africa

info@rangerssurvivalcraft.com

+27 (0)23 004 0074

www.rangerssurvivalcraft.com

A non profit organisation based in the Western Cape of South Africa, Rangers Survivalcraft offers a 2 week or up to 5 week mini-gap programme for young people. Help build a private nature reserve, develop leadership and survival skills or help make a difference in the lives of people by working with disadvantaged youth and communities through the Young Rangers programme.

Real Gap Experience

UK

info@realgap.co.uk

01892 277 040

www.realgap.co.uk

Real Gap offers a wide and diverse range of programmes. These include: volunteering, conservation, adventure travel and expeditions, sports, teaching English, round the world, paid working holidays and learning.

Reef Conservation International (ReefCI)

Belize

anthony@reefci.com

+1 513 334 9393

www.reefci.com

ReefCI offers a unique one-of-a-kind marine conservation diving experience. We offer an all-inclusive Monday-Friday diving and marine conservation trip on a small private island surrounded by turquoise coral seas situated on the Belize Barrier Reef.

For further information see page 164

ReefDoctor Org Ltd

UK

volunteer@reefdoctor.org

+44 (0)208 788 6908

www.reefdoctor.org

Become a volunteer ReefDoctor and contribute to marine research, education, conservation and sustainable community development alongside our team of local and international scientists.

Rempart

France

contact@rempart.com

+33 (0)1 42 71 96 55

www.rempart.com

Rempart, a union of conservation associations organises short voluntary work in France. The projects are all based around restoration and maintenance of historic sites and buildings.

SEED Madagascar
UK

info@seedmadagascar.org

0208 960 6629

www.madagascar.co.uk

SEED Madagascar (Sustainable Environment, Education & Development in Madagascar) operates in the south-east of Madagascar, and manage a wide range of sustainable development and conservation projects.

Starfish Ventures Ltd
UK

info@starfishvolunteers.com

+44 (0)3300 010807

www.starfishvolunteers.com

Starfish has a volunteer placement for you, whatever your skills, they can be put to good use in our various projects in Thailand.

Sumatran Orangutan Society
UK

+44 (0)1235 530825

www.orangutans-sos.org

SOS is looking for committed, energetic volunteers to support our small team. The roles will involve fundraising, campaigning, and raising awareness about orangutans and the work we do in Sumatra.

Sunrise Volunteer Programmes
UK

info@sunrint.com

+44 (0) 121 5722795

en.sunrint.com

Specialist for volunteer projects in China, offering volunteer opportunities in social, environment, education, medical, journalism and community areas around China.

The British Exploring Society (BSES Expeditions)
UK

info@britishexploring.org

+44 (0)20 7591 3141

www.britishexploring.org

BSES Expeditions organises challenging scientific expeditions to remote, wild environments. Study climate change whilst mountaineering or kayaking in the Arctic, measure biodiversity in the Amazon or investigate human interaction with the environment in the Himalayas.

The Career Break Site
UK

info@thecareerbreaksite.com

www.thecareerbreaksite.com

On The Career Break Site you'll find tons of career break opportunities, like ski instructor courses, TEFL, working abroad and volunteering.

The Great Projects
UK

info@thegreatprojects.com

+44 (0)208 885 4987

www.thegreatprojects.com

We, The Great Projects, specialise in wildlife volunteering projects and currently have 38 projects and 17 Tours throughout Africa, Asia, Europe and South America.

The Leap Overseas Ltd
UK

info@theleap.co.uk

01672 519922

www.theleap.co.uk

Team or solo placements in Africa, Asia or South America. Volunteer to get stuck into our unique mix of eco-tourism, community and conservation projects. Connect with local people.

The Mighty Roar

UK

hello@themightyroar.co.uk

01233 720676

www.themightyroar.co.uk

The Mighty Roar provide structured, safe and affordable volunteer abroad programmes to make a positive impact in the conservation, research and protection of some of the worlds amazing animals along with helping in the local communities.

TrekFORCE

UK

info@trekforce.org.uk

+44 (0) 207 384 3028

www.trekforce.org.uk

TrekFORCE offers expeditions in Bornea, Central America, Nepal and Papua New Guinea. Learn survival skills, jungle training and work on conservation and community projects. Expedition leadership training also available.

Tropical Adventures Foundation

Costa Rica

info@tropicaladventures.com

+506 8868-0296

www.tropicaladventures.com

Provides volunteer tour packages for individuals, families and groups interested in exploring the culture, language and natural beauty of Costa Rica.

UNA Exchange

UK

info@unaexchange.org

02920 223 088

www.unaexchange.org

Registered charity that supports people to take part in international volunteer projects in over 50 countries across the world. Each project is organised by one of our international partner organisations, based in the country of the project. Projects cover a large range of themes including; social, environmental, construction and cultural projects.

V2 Volunteer & Vacation

UK

info@v2volunteers.com

+44 (0)203 289 4611

www.v2volunteers.com

Join us for an amazing volunteering experience on the islands of Jamaica or Trinidad and Tobago.

Volunteer Latin America

UK

info@volunteerlatinamerica.com

+44 (0)20 7193 9163

www.volunteerlatinamerica.com

Volunteer abroad for free or at low-cost in Central and South America via the greenest volunteer advisor on the planet.

Volunteer World

Germany

helpcenter@volunteerworld.com

+49 211 41 60 49 83

www.volunteerworld.com

Volunteer World helps grassroot projects and interested volunteers worldwide to get in touch. Volunteers can compare and apply for the social projects while local NGOs receive the support they need to fulfill their great cause.

Wild Animal Volunteers
South Africa
info@wildanimalvolunteers.com
+27 (0) 44 272 5593
www.wildanimalvolunteers.com
We are a very special zoological facility like no other in Africa! Since inception we have worked tirelessly to create a place where our resident animals' care and love is at the highest level.

Wilderness Awareness School
USA
wasnet@wildernessawareness.org
+1 425 788 1301
www.wildernessawareness.org
The school, a not for profit environmental organisation, offers courses for adults in tracking, wilderness survival skills and a stewardship programme.

Wildlife PACT
India
wildlifepact@gmail.com
+91 99 10 586006
www.wildlifepact.org
Wildlife PACT offers volunteering opportunities to students of wildlife, ethnology, anthropology, conservation and environment studies. Short and long term projects available.

WorkingAbroad
UK
victoria.mcneil@workingabroad.com
+44 (0)1273 479047
www.workingabroad.com
Choose from a range of volunteering opportunities, including marine and terrestrial wildlife conservation, environmental education, language teaching, childcare and healthcare. Caters for all ages, gap years up to seniors, professionals taking sabbaticals and students wanting to gain field experience.

Worldwide Experience
UK
+44 (0) 1483 860 560
www.worldwideexperience.com
Worldwide Experience specialises in volunteer gap-year placements in conservation, marine and community projects throughout Africa.

WWOOF (World Wide Opportunities on Organic Farms)
UK
www.wwoof.net
Join WWOOF and participate in meaningful work that reconnects with nature, share the lives of people who have taken practical steps towards alternative, sustainable lifestyles.

Humanitarian

A Broader View Volunteers
USA
volunteers@abroaderview.org
+1 215 780 1845
www.abroaderview.org
A Broader View Volunteers offers a variety of conservation, humanitarian and medical volunteering opportunities across Latin America, Africa and South East Asia.

For further information see page 160

Action Aid
UK
supportercare@actionaid.org
+44 (0)1460 238000
www.actionaid.org.uk/experiences
Take part in ActionAid's First Hand Experience and change lives, including your own. ActionAid is offering volunteering opportunities in South Africa and Nepal, working alongside local people to build homes and centres to benefit whole communities for the better.

Africa & Asia Venture

UK

av@aventure.co.uk

+44 (0)1380 729009

www.aventure.co.uk

Established in 1993 AV specialises in community, sports coaching and teaching volunteer projects in Africa, Asia and Latin America. We offer group based projects from 3 weeks to 5 months, including designated travel time.

African Impact

South Africa

info@africanimpact.com

0800 098 8440

www.africanimpact.com

African Impact is a volunteer travel organisation providing meaningful interactive volunteer programs throughout Africa for a positive and measurable impact on local communities and conservation efforts.

All Out Africa

Swaziland

info@alloutafrica.com

+268 2416 2260

www.alloutafrica.com

All Out Africa offers various volunteering opportunities in Africa, from caring for orphans to teaching the disadvantaged. Make a difference whilst absorbing the beauty and culture of Africa.

Alliance Abroad Group

USA

+1 (512) 457 8062

www.allianceabroad.com

Alliance Abroad is a non-profit organisation that provides international teaching, work and volunteer placements. Our services include guaranteed placement and 24/7 personal assistance.

Amigos de las Americas

USA

lkelley@amigosinternational.org

+1 (713) 782 5290 (Ext:149) ; +1 (800) 231 7796 (Ext:149)

www.amigosinternational.org

AMIGOS offers cultural immersion gap semester and gap year opportunities for participants in Nicaragua, working a volunteer internship and living with a host family.

ATD Fourth World

UK

atd@atd-uk.org

+44 (0)20 7703 3231

www.atd-uk.org

ATD Fourth World is an international voluntary organisation working in partnership with people living in poverty worldwide.

Balloon Ventures

UK

www.balloonventures.com

Balloon Ventures brings exceptional people from around the world to developing countries to volunteer for 6 weeks with budding local entrepreneurs and lead sustainable economic development.

BERUDA

Cameroon

berudepservices@gmail.com

+237 67760 1407; +237 67732 3407

www.berudep.org

BERUDA's vision is 'to eradicate poverty and raise the living standards of the rural population of Cameroon's North West province'. They rely on volunteers to help them achieve this.

BMS World Mission
UK

+44 (0) 1235 517700

www.bmsworldmission.org

BMS World Mission is a Christian organisation which sends people in teams and as individuals or families to 34 countries worldwide.

Brathay Exploration Trust
UK

01539 433 942

www.brathayexploration.org.uk

BET has taken around 10,000 people on over 700 expeditions designed to broaden knowledge and help the planet. We are an environmental and cultural education charity that builds partnerships to provide UK and worldwide exploration opportunities to young people. From measuring the depths of Lake District tarns to glacial surveying in Norway, BET specialises in going the extra distance.

Bruce Organisation
Peru

info@bruceorg.org

www.bruceperu.org

Our mission is to help as many of the poorest children in the third world as we can to receive as good an education as their circumstances permit.

Cameroon Association for the Protection and Education of the Child (CAPEC)
Cameroon

info@capecam.org

+237 22 03 01 63

www.capecam.org

Volunteer to teach children in Cameroon. See website for vacancies and details of programmes available.

Camphill Association of North America
USA

info@camphill.org

+1 802 472 1102

www.camphill.org

Each year many people come to live and work in one of our Camphill Communities in North America for a Gap Year experience. Whether you are taking a break after high school, during your college studies or you are just looking for a new perspectives your life and your work, Camphill has plenty of gap year opportunities for you.

Camphill Communities of Ireland
Ireland

info@camphill.ie

+353 045 483 735

www.camphill.ie

Camphill Communities of Ireland is part of an international charitable trust working with people with intellectual disabilities and other kinds of special needs.

Volunteers live, work and share their lives with the community for periods of time between 3 months and two years, helping to make a difference.

Challenges Worldwide
UK

info@challengesworldwide.com

+44 (0)131 225 9549

www.challengesworldwide.com

Volunteers with professional skills and experience are needed to work on Challenges Worldwide's many projects.

Changing Worlds

UK

info@changing-worlds.com; media@
changing-worlds.com

+44 (0)2081 238702

www.changingworlds.co.uk

We offer a range of gap year placements
in: Australia, China, Fiji, Ghana, India,
Indonesia, South Africa, Thailand and
many more. So, if you like the idea of
travel, meeting like-minded people and
don't mind working hard, then this is for
you!

Chase Africa

Kenya

alice@chaseafrica.org

www.chaseafrica.org

CHASE Africa is a grassroots organisation
working to empower and educate
communities through sustainable
volunteering programmes.

China Study Abroad

China

info@chinastudyabroad.org

+86 10 8468 3799

www.chinastudyabroad.org

For over a decade CSA has been helping
people come out to China, always with the
goal to expand peoples' understanding of
China. The China Experience programme
offers a combination of interning,
traveling, studying and volunteering
that happens over a period of about six
months.

Cicerones de Buenos Aires
Asociación Civil

Argentina

contacto@cicerones.org.ar

+54 11 5258 0909

www.cicerones.org.ar

Volunteering in Argentina: Cicerones
in Buenos Aires works in a friendly
atmosphere ensuring contact with local
people, experiencing the city the way it
should be!

Connect-123

UK

info@connect-123.com

+44 (0)207 096 1201

www.connect-123.com

Connect-123 develops and administers
volunteer, internship and study abroad
programs in Barcelona, Buenos Aires,
Cape Town, Dublin and Shanghai.

Cross-Cultural Solutions

USA

0845 458 2781

www.crossculturalsolutions.org

Cross-Cultural Solutions operates
volunteer programmes in 12 countries in
partnership with sustainable community
initiatives. CCS brings people together
to work side-by-side with members
of the local community while sharing
perspectives and cultural understanding.

Cultural Canvas Thailand

USA

info@culturalcanvas.com

www.culturalcanvas.com

Cultural Canvas Thailand offers unique
and meaningful volunteer experiences
in Chiang Mai, Thailand. Placements
are available in the following areas: hill
tribe education, women's empowerment
and Burmese refugee education and
assistance.

331

Development in Action
UK

info@developmentinaction.org

www.developmentinaction.org

Development in Action is a youth and volunteer led development education charity, whose main aim is to engage young people in global issues and promote global citizenship.

Discover Adventure Ltd.
UK

01722 718444

www.discoveradventure.com

Discover Adventure Fundraising Challenges are trips that are designed to be challenging, to push your limits. They are not holidays! They involve preparation in terms of fundraising and improving fitness.

Dragonfly Community Foundation
Thailand

martin@thai-dragonfly.com

+66 087 963 0056

www.dragonflycommunity.org

Volunteering programs are currently arranged through Dragonfly Volunteer Projects.

Ecuador Volunteer
Ecuador

+593 2 255 7749

www.ecuadorvolunteer.org

Ecuador Volunteer Foundation, is a non-profit organization that offers volunteer work opportunities abroad.

Education & Health Nepal
Nepal

wayne@ehn-nepal.org

+977 9803719037

ehn-nepal.org

EHN is a UK registered charity & Nepali NGO that works to improve the levels of education & health in rural Nepal.

EIL (Experiment for International Living)
UK

info@eiluk.org

01684 562 577

www.eiluk.org

Offers a diverse range of programmes in the UK and worldwide, including volunteering, individual homestays and group learning.

Embrace Tanzania
Tanzania

info@embracetanzania.org

+255 772744588

embracetanzania.org

Embrace Tanzania was established under two very simple premises; to support and assist East African communities in need of basic services and to provide placements for people in search of ethically minded volunteer projects within this truly wondrous part of the world. Volunteers will assist with teaching and caring for young children in selected schools in Zanzibar.

Foundation for Sustainable Development (FSD)
USA

info@fsdinternational.org

+1 415 283 4873

www.fsdinternational.org

FSD is a community of development experts, donors, and volunteers who work together to achieve locally-driven goals in Africa, Asia, and Latin America.

visit: www.gap-year.com

Friends of Waldorf Education

Germany

incoming@freunde-waldorf.de

+49 (0)721 354806 100

www.freunde-waldorf.de/en/voluntary-services

The Friends of Waldorf Education offers year-long voluntary services at Waldorf institutions in Germany for people at least 18 years of age.

Gap Africa Projects

UK

info@gapafricaprojects.com

+44 (0)207 193 7819

gapafricaprojects.com

Gap Africa Projects has a focus to provide meaningful, sustainable and memorable experiences in Africa.

Gap Medics

UK

info@gapmedics.com

+44 (0)191 230 8080

www.gapmedics.co.uk

Gap Medics organise medical and nursing placements and projects in Africa and Asia.

Gap Year South Africa

UK

info@gapyearsouthafrica.com

+27 71 383 7155

www.gapyearsouthafrica.com

Specialises in sports coaching, teaching, health awareness projects in South Africa. Our project duration is between three weeks and three months.

Give a Fig Volunteering

Sri Lanka

enquiries@giveafigvolunteering.com

+44 (0) 2032907392

www.giveafigvolunteering.com

Give A Fig Volunteering provide fantastic fully supported Sri Lanka volunteering and internship opportunities for you to make a difference.

Glencree Centre for Peace and Reconciliation

Ireland

info@glencree.ie

+353 (0) 1 282 9711

www.glencree.ie

Glencree welcomes international volunteers who provide practical help in exchange for a unique experience of working with those building peace in Ireland, Britain and beyond.

Global Media Projects

UK

info@globalmediaprojects.co.uk

+44 (0) 191 222 0404

www.globalmediaprojects.co.uk

Offers print/online and broadcast media projects in China, India, Ghana, Mexico, Romania and Tanzania.

Global Nomadic

UK

contact@globalnomadic.com

+44 (0)207 193 2652

globalnomadic.com

Global Nomadic was founded in 2009 to connect grassroots NGO's from around the world with students eager to gain hands-on experience and further their careers!

Global Volunteer Projects
UK

info@globalvolunteerprojects.org

0191 222 0404

www.globalvolunteerprojects.org

With Global Volunteer Projects you can teach conversational English in schools, help in orphanages or work with animals on conservation projects.

Global Volunteers
USA

email@globalvolunteers.org

(800) 487 1074

www.globalvolunteers.org

Join a team of short-term volunteers contributing to long-term, comprehensive community projects on a volunteer vacation abroad or a USA volunteer program.

Go Make a Difference
Tanzania

info@gomad.org.uk

+447932 052 490

Go MAD is an independent charity offering people the opportunity to serve in Tanzania, to be involved in community projects and to make a difference to people's lives.

Great Aves
UK

01832 275 038

www.greataves.org

Great Aves is a Gap Year Charity that runs volunteer projects in South America. Volunteers work on the Arajuno Road Project teaching English or working on community based conservation and development projects.

Habitat for Humanity Great Britain
UK

supporterservices@habitatforhumanity.org.uk

01295 264 240

www.habitatforhumanity.org.uk

Habitat for Humanity aims to eliminate poverty housing and homelessness. Volunteers travel to their chosen country to spend 8-16 days living and working alongside the local community.

i volunteer
India

dehli@ivolunteer.in

+91 11 65672160

www.ivolunteer.in

Volunteering opportunites are shown on their website. You could end up working in an orphanage, on a helpline, on relief effort or in a school.

ICYE UK (Inter Cultural Youth Exchange)
UK

info@icye.org.uk

+44 (0) 20 7681 0983

www.icye.org.uk

Sends people aged between 18 and 30 to work in voluntary projects overseas in including counselling centres, human rights NGOs, farms, orphanages and schools for the disabled. Registered Charity No. 1081907.

International Citizen Service (ICS)
UK

enquiries@volunteerics.org

+44 (0)20 8780 7400

www.volunteerics.org

ICS is an overseas volunteering programme for 18-25 year olds, funded by the UK Government's Department for International Development. To volunteer you don't need cash, skills or qualifications - just the ambition to make a difference.

International Service
UK

contact@internationalservice.org.uk

+44 (0)1904 64 77 99

www.internationalservice.org.uk

International Service empowers women, children and young people, and disabled people to access their rights in developing countries across the world. We offer volunteer placements overseas and work in areas such as female empowerment, disability rights and child poverty.

International Volunteer HQ (IVHQ)
New Zealand

info@volunteerhq.org

NZ: +64 6 758 7949; UK: 0808 234 1621

www.volunteerhq.org

IVHQ offers volunteer programs in more than 30 different locations worldwide including: Africa, Asia, Central & South America, The Pacific and Europe. Programs have many different start dates and a wide range of volunteer work opportunities including: Medical & Healthcare, Arts & Music, Education, Conservation and Construction.

Inxchan Volunteer Nepal
Nepal

inxchan@gmail.com

9843719599

www.inxchan.com

Inxchan means New Beginning of Life. We provide a unique philanthropically trip for participants which allows participants to support local community, children and women.

IVS (International Voluntary Service)
UK

info@ivsgb.org

+44 (0) 131 243 2745

www.ivsgb.org/info

IVS brings volunteers together from many different countries, cultures and backgrounds to live and work on projects of benefit to local communities.

Josephite Community Aid
Australia

help@jcaid.com

+61 (0) 2 9838 8802

www.jcaid.com

Australian organisation committed to helping poor and underprivileged with the aid of volunteers.

Karen Hilltribes Trust
UK

info@karenhilltribes.org.uk

+44 (0) 1904 612 829

www.karenhilltribes.org.uk

We are a community-led organisation working with the Karen people living in the poorest province of Thailand. Every year we send teams of volunteers to Karen communities to help build vital clean water systems for one month and teach English for three months or longer. Sign up today to be part of changing lives!

Kaya Responsible Travel
UK

info@kayavolunteer.com

+44 (0) 161 870 6212

www.kayavolunteer.com

Kaya offer over 200 volunteer projects worldwide working with local communities and conservation initiatives from 2 weeks to 12 months. Placements are tailored to specific needs and skills of students, career breakers', retirees, families or groups.

For further information see page 170

Khaya Volunteer
South Africa
info@khayavolunteer.com
+27 (0) 41 582 2227
www.khayavolunteer.com
Kaya Volunteer offers affordable and unique volunteering projects and programs in South Africa, Tanzania, Uganda and more.

Kidogo Adventure
UK
info@kidogoadventure.com
+44 (0)7725 996434
www.kidogoadventure.com
Kidogo Adventure is a small, personally-run organisation to enable travel through volunteering. The projects are based in Kenya and are all child-focused.
For further information see page 172

Kings World Trust for Children
UK
annemarie@kingschildren.org
+44 (0)1428 653504
www.kingschildren.org
The Kings World Trust for Children aims to provide a caring home, an education and skills training for orphaned and homeless children and young people in south India.

L'Arche UK
UK
info@larche.org.uk
+44 (0) 800 917 1337
www.larche.org.uk
L'Arche is an international movement where people with and without learning difficulties share life together. There are Communities in 34 countries. Volunteers are involved in all aspects of community life, are trained and supported, have free board and accommodation, a modest income and other benefits.

Lattitude Global Volunteering
UK
volunteer@lattitude.org.uk
+44 (0) 118 959 4914
www.lattitude.org.uk
Lattitude Global Volunteering is a youth development and volunteering charity that send young people to a huge range of challenging and rewarding placements worldwide.

Leave UR Mark
USA
info@leaveurmark.com
+1 516 998 6615
www.leaveurmark.com
Volunteer on projects that work towards development and equality in India through education, community empowerment, health, and environment.

Madventurer
UK
volunteer@madventurer.com
+44 (0)191 645 2014
www.madventurer.com
Offer group community projects in towns and villages in Ghana, Kenya, Uganda, Tanzania, South Africa, Fiji and Thailand.

Maekok River Village Resort
Thailand
rosie@maekok-river-village-resort.com
+66 (0) 53 053 628
www.maekok-river-village-resort.com
The Maekok River Village Resort offers opportunities for those on gap years or career breaks to spend time teaching and helping to improve the facilities in schools in Thailand.

Mondo Challenge Foundation

UK

info@mondofoundation.org

01604 859333

www.mondochallengefoundation.org

MondoChallenge Foundation provides sustainable support for education and livelihoods in Nepal, India and Tanzania. We believe in community-based programmes, working with local people to improve lives.

Naturally Africa Volunteers

UK

info@volunteerafrica.com

+44 (0)208 123 0301

www.volunteerafrica.com

Naturally Africa Volunteers provides opportunities for skilled and non-skilled volunteers to help make a difference in Africa.

Oggy Oggy Team

UK

support@oggyoggyteam.com

01208 220212

www.oggyoggyteam.com

We offer a range of backpacking and volunteering adventure in Asia to help local communities and to share life skills. We also offer all of our programs for free under our 'Swap it' option.

Onaris Africa

UK

info@onarisafrica.org

+44 (0)8438 866008

www.onarisafrica.org

Onaris Africa specialise in student and graduate skills-matched volunteer experiences. Our group tours are built around your skillset. Experience Africa and make an impact!

OpportUNITY

UK

office@opportunityuk.org

07767 043 837

www.opportunityuk.org

OpportUNITY is a voluntary organisation with an aim to inspire, support and empower young people.

Opportunity International UK

UK

ukinfo@opportunity.org

+44 (0)1865 725304

www.opportunity.org.uk

We provide access to financial solutions, empowering people living in poverty to transform their lives, their children's futures and their communities.

Original Volunteers Ltd.

UK

contact@originalvolunteers.co.uk

01603 280702

www.originalvolunteers.co.uk

Original Volunteers have been providing affordable and low cost volunteering placements around the world since 2006.

Regions covered: Europe, Asia, Africa, Latin America.

Otra Cosa Network

UK

info@otracosa.org

01926 730 029

www.otracosa.org

Based in Huanchaco, northern Peru, Otra Cosa Network offers a wide variety of affordable and satisfying volunteering opportunities to well-motivated volunteers from around the world.

Outreach International
UK

info@outreachinternational.co.uk

+44 (0)1903 746 900

www.outreachinternational.co.uk

Outreach International offers a personal service to committed volunteersworking in ethical projects in Cambodia, Nepal, India, Mexico, Ecuador, Galapagos, Costa Rica, and Kenya.

For further information see page 176

Oyster Worldwide Limited
UK

anne@oysterworldwide.com

+44 (0) 1892 770 771

www.oysterworldwide.com

Oyster is a specialist gap-year provider with teaching and childcare projects around the world. We offer a personal approach with experienced managers supporting you throughout your trip.

Peru's Challenge
Peru

volunteer@peruschallenge.com

+51 84 272 508

www.peruschallenge.com

Join a volunteer and travel programme and assist the work of charity organisation, Peru's Challenge, in rural communities in Peru.

Plan My Gap Year
UK

info@planmygapyear.co.uk

01892 890473

www.planmygapyear.co.uk

Award winning international volunteer placement organisation offering affordable short-term volunteer programmes from two weeks up to six months.

Pravah
India

mail@pravah.org

+91 11 2644 0619

www.pravah.org

Pravah is an organization based in New Delhi, India, working to impact issues of social justice through youth citizenship action.

Progressio
UK

enquiries@progressio.org.uk

+44 (0)20 7733 1195

www.progressio.org.uk

Progressio is an international development charity supporting poor and marginalised people, especially women, to empower themselves.

Project Trust
UK

info@projecttrust.org.uk

01879 230 444

www.projecttrust.org.uk

Project Trust (charity no. SCO25668) offers long term structured volunteering placements for school leavers (between ages of 17-19) in over twenty countries in Africa, Asia and Central and South America. Projects, lasting 8 or 12 months, include teaching, social care, journalism and outward bound.

Projects Abroad
UK

info@projects-abroad.co.uk

+44 (0) 1903 708300

www.projects-abroad.co.uk

Overseas placements. Teach English, gain invaluable experience in Medicine, Conservation, Journalism, Business, Care and Community, Sports, Law and Human Rights, Veterinary and more.

Quest Overseas

UK

info@questoverseas.com

+44 (0)1273 777 206

www.questoverseas.com

Quest Overseas specializes in gap-year adventures into the very heart and soul of South America and Africa. We offer volunteers the chance to understand life far removed from home.

Raleigh International

UK

info@raleighinternational.org

+44(0) 20 7183 1270

www.raleighinternational.org

Sustainable development charity. We are powered by young people that want to make the world a better place. We work with communities living in poverty around the world in Borneo, Costa Rica and Nicaragua and Tanzania.

For further information see page 154

Reaching Out to Cambodian Communities (ROCC)

UK

roccuk@gmail.com

www.roccuk.com

ROCC is a charitable organisation which sends volunteers out to rural Cambodia to help create sustainable communities by teaching health and English as well as implementing vital community interventions such as building water wells and health centres. They work with a local NGO called CoDeC who have worked with numerous charities such as SKIP and UNICEF

Restless Development

UK

info@restlessdevelopment.org

+44 (0)207 633 3350

www.restlessdevelopment.org

Restless Development run Health Education and Community Resource Programmes in South Asia and Africa. Volunteers are asked to fundraise a donation to the charity.

Richmond Vale Academy

Saint Vincent And The Grenadines

info@richmondvale.org

+1 784 458 2255

www.richmondvale.org

RVA runs 6 months programs with studies, courses and actions to make St. Vincent and the Grenadines ready for Climate Change meaning energy, food and disaster secure.

For further information see page 156

RIPPLE Africa

UK

+44 (0)1280 822891

www.rippleafrica.org

RIPPLE Africa is a charity which works to improve the environment and local education in Malawi, Africa. Roles are suited to your skills and interest and include work in environmental, educational and medical areas.

Sedarvp Ghana

Ghana

contact@sedarvpghana.org

+233 24 50 52 472

www.sedarvpghana.org

Volunteer & Internship in Ghana run by locals, powered by global citizens. Our volunteers and community value partnership and cross-cultural understanding, come join us!

Serenje Orphans School Home
Switzerland

contactsoa@yahoo.com

www.serenjeorphansappeal.com

Our Zambian orphanage offers a rewarding and safe experience in rural Zambia for committed volunteers.

SLV.Global
UK

info@slv.global

020 7096 1718

slv.global

SLV.Global is an international volunteering organisation running mental health placements in Sri Lanka and Indonesia, and also Educational Programs in India. All of our placements, ranging from 1 - 12 weeks long, are designed to provide maximum benefit to the communities where we work and at the same time give volunteers the opportunity to gain highly valuable experience in the mental health sector.

Smile Society
India

www.smilengo.org

SMILE Society invite international volunteers and students to join us in our welfare projects, international work camps, summer camps, internship programmes and volunteer projects in India.

Spirit of Adventure Trust
New Zealand

info@spiritofadventure.org.nz

+64 (0) 9 373 2060

www.spiritofadventure.org.nz

Become part of the volunteer crew on one of the Trust's youth development voyages around New Zealand each year.

Step Together Volunteering
UK

enquiry@step-together.org.uk

+44 (0)117 955 9042

www.step-together.org.uk

We work across England and Scotland, with a focus on helping those most in need of support, including adults and young people who face significant challenges. We provide intensive one-to-one coaching and inspire and enable volunteering placements to match the individual's needs, interests and ambitions.

Task Brasil Trust
UK

www.taskbrasil.org.uk

Task Brasil Trust is a charity helping impoverished children in Brazil. Volunteers always needed. Registered Charity No. 1030929.

Tearfund
UK

info@tearfund.org

+44 (0)208 977 9144

www.tearfund.org

We're following Jesus where need is greatest, working through local churches to unlock people's potential and helping them to discover that the answer to poverty is within themselves. When disasters strike, we respond quickly. We won't stop until poverty stops.

The Book Bus Foundation
UK

info@thebookbus.org

+44 (0) 208 0999 280

www.thebookbus.org

The Book Bus provides a mobile service and actively promotes literacy to underpriviledged communities in Zambia and Ecuador.

The Career Break Site
UK

info@thecareerbreaksite.com

www.thecareerbreaksite.com

On The Career Break Site you'll find tons of career break opportunities, like ski instructor courses, TEFL, working abroad and volunteering.

The Dragon Trip Pte Ltd
UK

info@thedragontrip.com

0203 817 5974

thedragontrip.com

The Dragon Volunteer Trips offer the chance to learn Mandarian, change children's lives and travel in breathtaking scenery.

The Humanity Exchange
USA

admin@thehumanityexchange.org

+1 778 300 2466

www.thehumanityexchange.org

The Humanity Exchange provides grassroots Volunteer Abroad programs in communities across Ghana, Cameroon, Benin and Columbia, and unique opportunities to volunteer and Learn French in Africa.

The Worldwrite Volunteer Centre
UK

world.write@btconnect.com

+44 (0) 20 8985 5435

www.worldwrite.org.uk

Join WORLDwrite's campaign for young volunteers who feel strongly about global inequality, want to make an impact and use film to do it. Registered charity No. 1060869.

The Year Out Group
UK

info@yearoutgroup.org

www.yearoutgroup.org

The Year Out Group is an association of the UK's leading Year Out organisations, promoting the concepts and benefits of well-structured year out programmes and helping young people and their advisers in selecting suitable and worthwhile projects.

Think Pacific
UK

info@thinkpacific.com

0113 335 9919

www.thinkpacific.com

Think Pacific offer you the chance to make a difference to the communities and places you visit, guiding you on a meaningful adventure through the glorious islands of Fiji.

Time for God
UK

office@timeforgod.org

+44 (0)1423 536 248

www.timeforgod.org

Time For God has 50 years experience creating full-time volunteering opportunities in the UK and abroad. Find out more about us and then get involved.

Travel Teacher
UK

info@travelteacher.co.uk

07435636460

www.travelteacher.co.uk

Travel and teach in the South Pacific. Volunteer expeditions to Fiji and The Cook Islands. Make an impact in a local community whilst stepping off the beaten track and immersing yourself deep within authentic culture.

Travellers Worldwide
UK

info@travellersworldwide.com

01903 502 595

www.travellersworldwide.com

Travellers is a leading international provider of voluntary placements and work experience internships overseas.

Uganda Lodge Volunteer Centre
Uganda

info@ugandalodge.com

Uganda: +256 774768090; UK: +44 1932 562757

www.ugandalodge.com

Rural Project offering affordable short/long volunteer placements (all ages) in school, clinic, sports coaching, community or building work etc. Safaris/Gorilla-Treks organised. British on-site coordinators.

Unipal
UK

info@unipal.org.uk

www.unipal.org.uk

Unipal (A Universities' Trust for Educational Exchange with Palestinians) seeks to facilitate a two-way process of education; providing English-language teaching in Palestinian refugee camps in the West Bank, Gaza and Lebanon and introducing British students to a knowledge and understanding of the situation and daily lives of refugees.

United Planet
USA

quest@unitedplanet.org

+1 (617) 874-8041

www.unitedplanet.org

United Planet unlocks your potential as a global citizen, empowering you to create a more peaceful, cohesive and sustainable world. With partnerships all over the world, United Planet fosters cross-cultural understanding and addresses shared challenges to unite the world in a community beyond borders.

Up with People
USA

+32 2 646 26 36

www.upwithpeople.org

A global education organization which aims to bring the world together through service and music. The unique combination of international travel, service learning, leadership development and performing arts offers students an unparalleled experience and a pathway to make a difference in the world, one community at a time.

V2 Volunteer & Vacation
UK

info@v2volunteers.com

+44 (0)203 289 4611

www.v2volunteers.com

Join us for an amazing volunteering experience on the islands of Jamaica or Trinidad and Tobago.

VAP (Volunteer Action for Peace)

UK
action@vap.org.uk
0844 209 0927
www.vap.org.uk
Organises international voluntary work projects in the UK each summer and recruits volunteers to take part in affordable placements abroad that range between two weeks and 12 months.

Volunteer for Africa
UK
info@volunteer4africa.org
www.volunteer4africa.org
Non-profit organisation that helps volunteers and responsible travellers truly make a difference. Search the site for volunteer work or organisations needing supplies in the area you plan to visit.

Volunteer Maldives PVT Ltd
Republic of Maldives
info@volunteermaldives.com
+94 77 394 1309
www.volunteermaldives.com
Volunteer Maldives is committed to making a real and tangible difference to these warm and friendly communities. When you travel with us you can rest assured that the work you do will directly benefit the islanders that have been identified by these local communities and the NGO's we work with.

Volunteer The World
USA
info@cosmicvolunteers.org
+1 215 609 4196
www.cosmicvolunteers.org
American non-profit organisation offering volunteer and internship programmes in China, Ecuador, Ghana, Guatemala, India, Kenya, Nepal, Peru, the Philippines, and Vietnam.

Volunteer Vacations
UK
info@volunteervacations.co.uk
01483 331551
www.volunteervacations.co.uk
Voluntary sports coaching, teaching and orphange work abroad helping disadvantaged children.

Volunteer Work Thailand
UK
info@volunteerworkthailand.org
www.volunteerworkthailand.org
Non-profit organisation that helps people find volunteer work in Thailand including many opportunities to volunteer for free.

Volunteer World
Germany
helpcenter@volunteerworld.com
+49 211 41 60 49 83
www.volunteerworld.com
Volunteer World helps grassroot projects and interested volunteers worldwide to get in touch. Volunteers can compare and apply for the social projects while local NGOs receive the support they need to fulfill their great cause.

Volunteering India
India
info@volunteeringindia.com
IN: +91 9716 235 166; UK: +44 (0)20 8133 9939
www.volunteeringindia.com
Volunteering India provides safe, affordable and meaningful volunteer programs in India to individuals, groups or families. A variety of programs are offered, including cultural exchange programs, internships and gap year programs. A choice of programs includes working with orphans, women empowerment programs, health/HIV programs, teaching English, summer volunteer programs, street children programs and more.

343

Volunteering Journeys
UK
hello@volunteeringjourneys.com
+44 (0)20 70971877
www.volunteeringjourneys.com
We provide quality programs in Asia and Africa at affordable prices through which one can connect with locals and contribute to local development projects.

Volunteering Solutions
India
info@volunteeringsolutions.com
+91 9871371009
www.volunteeringsolutions.com
A safe and affordable volunteer program offering the oppurtunity to volunteer in hospitals, orphanages and clinics around the world. Volunteers will be immersed into the culture and live with local families.

Volunteers for International Partnership
USA
info@partnershipvolunteers.org
+1-802-246-1154
www.partnershipvolunteers.org
VIP offers volunteer opportunities for individuals or groups to do international community service in health, social services, environment and education.

VSO (Voluntary Service Overseas)
UK
enquiry@vsoint.org
+44 (0)20 8780 7500
www.vsointernational.org
As a volunteer, you can make a unique difference to the world. With VSO, you'll get something few other volunteering organisations offer - an opportunity of using your skills and experience to have a long-lasting impact on peoples' lives.

WaterAid
UK
+44 (0) 20 7793 4594
www.wateraid.org
WaterAid is an international charity enabling the world's poorest people access to safe water and sanitation. You can volunteer to help them in the UK.

Whipalong Volunteer Program
South Africa
info@whipalong.co.za
+27 (0) 83 626 6324
www.whipalong.co.za
The Whipalong Volunteer Program invites volunteers to be a part of the on-going rehabilitation and re-schooling of abused and neglected horses in South Africa. Volunteers' responsibilities include lunging, backing of young horses, feeding, grooming, tack maintenance and general care of the horses and yard, in addition to regular riding.

Willing Workers in South Africa (WWISA)
South Africa
+27 (0)44 534 8958
www.wwisa.co.za
The core aim of WWISA is to help bring desperately needed community development services to poorly provisioned and frequently overlooked historically disadvantaged rural townships.

WLS International Ltd
UK
info@gapyearinasia.com
0203 384 7024
www.gapyearinasia.com
WLS International is one of the leading volunteer organizations with programs in Cambodia, China, Nepal, India, Indonesia, Sri Lanka, Thailand and Vietnam.

Work & Volunteer Abroad (WAVA)

UK

0800 80 483 80

www.workandvolunteer.com

Experience the world on one of WAVA's Gap Year programmes. Choose from a range of volunteer and work Gap Year travel projects around the world, and let WAVA help you See more & Do more around the world.

workaway.info

UK

www.workaway.info

Travel cheaply and stay for free, whilst making a difference to the communities you visit. Put your existing skills to good use, or try something new you'd never normally get to do and pick up new skills along the way.

WorldTeach

USA

info@worldteach.org

(857) 259-6646

www.worldteach.org

WorldTeach partners with governments and other organizations in developing countries to provide volunteer teachers to meet local needs and promote responsible global citizenship.

Y Care International

UK

enquiries@ycareinternational.org

+44 (0)20 7549 3150

www.ycareinternational.org

Y Care International creates opportunities for vulnerable young people across the globe to change their lives for the better. Inspired by and faithful to our Christian values, we work with people of all faiths and none to build a more just world, free from poverty.

Medical

A Broader View Volunteers

USA

volunteers@abroaderview.org

+1 215 780 1845

www.abroaderview.org

A Broader View Volunteers offers a variety of conservation, humanitarian and medical volunteering opportunities across Latin America, Africa and South East Asia.

For further information see page 160

Global Medical Projects

UK

info@globalmedicalprojects.co.uk

+44 (0)191 222 0404

www.globalmedicalprojects.co.uk

Global Medical Projects are specialists in arranging worthwhile medical work experience placements for Pre-university students, students on their vacation, students on their electives and qualified medical personel.

Global Nomadic

UK

contact@globalnomadic.com

+44 (0)207 193 2652

globalnomadic.com

Global Nomadic was founded in 2009 to connect grassroots NGO's from around the world with students eager to gain hands-on experience and further their careers!

International Volunteer HQ (IVHQ)

New Zealand

info@volunteerhq.org

NZ: +64 6 758 7949; UK: 0808 234 1621

www.volunteerhq.org

IVHQ offers volunteer programs in more than 30 different locations worldwide including: Africa, Asia, Central & South America, The Pacific and Europe. Programs have many different start dates and a wide range of volunteer work opportunities including: Medical & Healthcare, Arts & Music, Education, Conservation and Construction.

Kaya Responsible Travel

UK

info@kayavolunteer.com

+44 (0) 161 870 6212

www.kayavolunteer.com

Kaya offer over 200 volunteer projects worldwide working with local communities and conservation initiatives from 2 weeks to 12 months. Placements are tailored to specific needs and skills of students, career breakers', retirees, families or groups .

For further information see page 170

Médecins Sans Frontières/ Doctors Without Borders (MSF)

UK

office-ldn@london.msf.org

+44 (0)20 7404 6600

www.msf.org.uk

MSF field staff worldwide give life-saving medical and technical assistance to people who would otherwise be denied access to basics such as healthcare, clean water and shelter. Annually, around 3,000 international volunteers join local staff helping populations in danger.

Medical Projects

UK

info@medicalprojects.co.uk

www.medicalprojects.co.uk

For aspiring doctors, midwives and nurses aged 16-19 who are looking for real-life experiences to help kickstart their medical careers. Placements include working in partner hospitals in India, Ghana and Europe and are excellent for providing both UCAS points towards university applications and practical work experiences in medical care.

Outreach International

UK

info@outreachinternational.co.uk

+44 (0)1903 746 900

www.outreachinternational.co.uk

Outreach International offers a personal service to committed volunteersworking in ethical projects in Cambodia, Nepal, India, Mexico, Ecuador, Galapagos, Costa Rica, and Kenya.

For further information see page 176

Learning Abroad

Academic year abroad

African Leadership Academy
South Africa

info@africanleadershipacademy.org

www.africanleadershipacademy.org

African Leadership Academy offers high school students worldwide the opportunity for an unparalleled African experience, by studying abroad or spending a gap-year with them.

Alphappl
Portugal

apply@alphappl.com

www.alphappl.com

It doesn't matter what your background is, If you want to kick-start your life in the digital world, while experiencing things you've never imagined before - then this is the place for you.

American University
USA

+1 202 885 1000

www.american.edu/spexs/augap

Spend a semester or summer learning and participating in community service in Washington, DC and discover who you want to be. American University's International Gap Program is designed for students who are ready to build a foundation for future academic and career success and a better understanding of global issues.

Carpe Diem Education
USA

drew@carpediemeducation.org

503-446-4732

www.carpediemeducation.org

Sieze the journey. Inspiring growth and transformation through experiential education, community, and intercultural exchange.

Class Afloat
Canada

admissions@classafloat.com

+1 902 634 1895

www.classafloat.com

Sail on a tall ship to exotic ports around the world and earn university credits. Also offers Duke of Edinburgh's Award Scheme.

College for International Co-operation and Development (CICD)
UK

+44 (0)1964 631 826

www.cicd-volunteerinafrica.org

CICD offers programmes from 5 or 12 months or longer, consisting of 5 months training, studies and preparation, followed by 6 months volunteer work at a development project in Africa or India and a one month follow-up period back at the college afterwards. Ideal for those looking to do volunteer work abroad and who would prefer to have more preparation before going out there.

Connect-123
UK

info@connect-123.com

+44 (0)207 096 1201

www.connect-123.com

Connect-123 develops and administers volunteer, internship and study abroad programs in Barcelona, Buenos Aires, Cape Town, Dublin and Shanghai.

Council on International Educational Exchange (CIEE)
USA

contact@ciee.org

1-207-553-4000

www.ciee.org

CIEE offer a wide range of international study programs such as study abroad programs for US students, gap-year abroad programs and seasonal work in the USA for international students.

CRCC Asia
China

beijing@crccasia.com

+86 01 8468 3769

www.crccasia.com

All of our programs offer the unique opportunity to develop professional skills in your preferred industry, whilst also gaining exposure to China's dynamic culture and lifestyle. Since 2008 more than 6,000 participants from over 150 countries have taken part in our programs in China.

Diablo Valley College
USA

+1 925 685 1230

www.dvc.edu

Diablo Valley College offers a varity of programmes to international students, available as day, evening, summer, online or hybrid classes.

Education in Ireland
Ireland

educationinireland@enterprise-ireland.com

+353 1 7272967

www.educationinireland.com

Live and study in Ireland, earning degrees at ordinary and Honours Bachelors, Masters and Doctorate levels and undergraduate and postgraduate diplomas over a full range of disciplines.

Graduate Prospects
UK

enquiries@prospects.ac.uk

+44 (0) 161 277 5200

www.prospects.ac.uk

Prospects - the UK's official graduate careers website.

IBS Budapest
Hungary

info@ibs-b.hu

+3615888600

www.ibs-b.hu/gap-year

International Business School is a private business school offering a life-changing experience for you during a year, including learning, volunteering and travelling periods to Tanzania, Costa Rica or Cambodia.

IE University
Spain

university@ie.edu

+34 921 412 410

www.ie.edu/university

IE University is an international university which takes a humanistic approach to higher education: a university of entrepreneurs whose education and research model integrates knowledge and enables students to specialize flexibly.

Institute of International Education

USA

iiedirectories@eircom.net

www.iiepassport.org

Search for international education opportunities by country, city, subject and many other criteria.

John Cabot University

Italy

admissions@johncabot.edu

+39 06 681 9121

www.johncabot.edu

John Cabot University is an American liberal arts university in Rome, Italy, with over 350 courses taught in English and a vibrant international student body.

Leiden University

Netherlands

+31 (0) 71 527 4024

www.leiden.edu

Leiden University is one of Europe's foremost research universities. This prominent position gives our graduates a leading edge in applying for academic posts and for functions outside academia.

Maximo Nivel

USA

+1 800 866 6358

www.maximonivel.com

Maximo Nivel provides high quality, affordable study abroad programs in Latin America. Since 2003, we have offered our international programs to participants from all over the world.

Minds Abroad

China

info@mindsabroad.com

+86 (871) 532 5089

www.mindsabroad.com

Minds Abroad is a US-based organization that conducts study abroad programs in China and India for both individual students and also customized faculty-led groups from college and universities across the US and Europe.

Office of International Education, Iceland

Iceland

ask@hi.is

+354 525 4311

www.ask.hi.is

Find information on all the higher education institutions in Iceland, as well as practical things to do before arriving, visas, admissions, residence permits, etc.

Queenstown Resort College

New Zealand

+64 3 409 0500

www.queenstownresortcollege.com

Offers a diverse range of world class courses and programmes including diplomas, internships, a range of English language courses, leadership development programmes, and short courses for visitors.

Salem Kolleg GmbH

Germany

info@salemkolleg.de

+49 7553 919 615

www.salemkolleg.de/english

Salem Kolleg provides a unique gap year that offers orientation after school and aims to support those who plan to study at university or college in Germany, Switzerland or Austria. Our three terms are composed of introductory courses in many university subjects from the humanities, natural and social sciences.

Scuola Leonardo da Vinci
Italy
scuolaleonardo@scuolaleonardo.com
www.scuolaleonardo.com
One of Italy's largest provider of in-country Italian courses in Italy, for students who wish to experience living and studying in Italy.

Studies Abroad
USA
gap@studiesabroad.com
512-480-8522
studiesabroad.com/gap
ISA has a wide variety of study abroad programs for undergraduate students at accredited schools and universities throughout Africa, Asia, Europe, Latin American, The Middle East and The Pacific.

The English-Speaking Union
UK
jacqueline.finch@esu.org
+44 (0)20 7529 1561
www.esu.org
The English-Speaking Union organises educational exchanges in high schools (mostly boarding) in the US and Canada, awarding up to 30 scholarships a year to gap-year students.

The US-UK Fulbright Commission
UK
advising@fulbright.org.uk
+ 44 0207 498 4010
www.fulbright.org.uk
EAS is the UK's only official source of information on the US education system, providing objective advice through in-house advising and a variety of outreach events.

TRACC - Tropical Research and Conservation Centre
Malaysia
info@tracc-borneo.org
tracc.org/teaching/marine-science-a-level
Our Cambridge Marine Science intensive A-Level course allows you to complete an entire A-level in just 14 weeks. You could earn an extra A-level in Marine Science, valid anywhere in the world whilst working with like-minded people from diverse backgrounds, learning about the oceans and tropical ecosystems, marine biology, aquaculture, fisheries, scuba diving and conservation.

Where There Be Dragons
USA
info@wheretherebedragons.com
+1 303 413 0822
www.wheretherebedragons.com
Runs semester, gap-year and college-accredited programmes in the Andes, China, Himalayas and more.

Art

Accademia Europea di Firenze
Italy
+39 055 21 15 99
www.aefirenze.it
The Accademia Europea di Firenze is an international school located in the very heart of Florence offering studies in Italian, Music, Art, Dance and Culture.

Aegean Center for the Fine Arts

Greece

studyart@aegeancenter.org

+30 22840 23 287

www.aegeancenter.org

The Aegean Center offers small group and individualized study in the visual arts, creative writing and music. Facilities are located in two stunning locations: the Aegean islands of Greece and Italy's Tuscany.

ARTIS - Art Research Tours

USA

david@artis.info

+1 800 232 6893

www.artis-tours.org

ARTIS (Art Research Tours and International Studios) provide high quality international art and cultural study abroad programmes at affordable prices, located in beautiful art capitals throughout the world.

SACI Florence

Italy

admissions@saci-florence.edu

+1 (212) 248 7225

www.saci-florence.edu

A non-profit educational institution for students seeking fully accredited studio art, design, and liberal arts instruction.

For further information see page 192

For further information see page 192

SAI - Study Abroad Italy

USA

mail@saiprograms.com

+1 (707) 824 8965

www.studyabroadflorence.com

In conjunction with Florence University SAI offer the chance for international students to live in the heart of this bustling Renaissance city while experiencing modern Florentine life.

Studio Escalier

USA

info@studioescalier.com

+1 718 228 4109

www.studioescalier.com

Admission to their three month intensive courses in painting and drawing is by advance application only. Anyone is welcome to apply who has a dedicated interest in working from the human figure.

The British Institute of Florence

Italy

+39 (0) 55 2677 81

www.britishinstitute.it

Located in the historic centre of Florence within minutes of the main galleries, museums and churches, the British Institute offers courses in history of art, Italian language and life drawing.

The Marchutz School

France

+33 442 966 013

www.marchutz-school.org

Offers artists a unique opportunity to live, learn and grow in the incomparable Provencal setting of Aix-en-Provence, France.

Culture

Accademia Europea di Firenze

Italy

+39 055 21 15 99

www.aefirenze.it

The Accademia Europea di Firenze is an international school located in the very heart of Florence offering studies in Italian, Music, Art, Dance and Culture.

Alderleaf Wilderness College

USA

+1 360 793 8709

www.wildernesscollege.com

A centre for traditional ecological knowledge offering innovative wilderness survival, animal tracking and nature courses in the Pacific Northwest of the United States.

American Institute for Foreign Study (AIFS)

USA

info@aifs.com

(203) 399 5000

www.aifs.com

One of the oldest, largest and most respected cultural exchange organizations in the world. Their programmes include college study abroad, au pair placement, camp counselors and staff.

Art History Abroad (AHA)

UK

info@arthistoryabroad.com

+44 (0) 1379 871 800

www.arthistoryabroad.com

Travel through stylish Italy with a group of people just like you. Study beautiful art and architecture with brilliant tutors. Have fun and make friends for life.

For further information see page 188

Cultural Experiences Abroad (CEA)

USA

info@gowithcea.com

+1 800 266 4441

www.gowithcea.com

CEA sends thousands of students on study abroad programmes at multiple universities in 15 countries including Argentina, China, Costa Rica, Czech Republic, England, France, Germany, Ireland, Italy, South Africa and Spain.

Dublin Cookery School

Ireland

info@dublincookeryschool.ie

+353 1 210 0555

www.dublincookeryschool.ie

Award-winning Dublin Cookery School is a great place to start your gap year. We give you the credible skills and practical expertise needed to get a job anywhere you may travel.

For further information see page 208

Eastern Institute of Technology

New Zealand

info@eit.ac.nz

+64 6 974 8000

www.eit.ac.nz

Te Manga Mâori - EIT in Hawke's Bay offers the opportunity to study the Maori language and culture from beginners through to advanced level.

El Casal

Spain

john@elcasalbarcelona.com

+34 93 217 90 38

www.elcasalbarcelona.com

Based in Barcelona, El Casal offers the chance to soak in Catalan culture through a programme specifically for gappers who want to learn Spanish.

Istituto di Lingua e Cultura Italiana Michelangelo

Italy

+39 055 240 975

www.michelangelo-edu.it

The Michelangelo Institute offers cultural courses on art history, Italian language, literature, commerce and commercial correspondence, and 'L'Italia oggi'.

For more information please see our listing "Michelangelo Institute".

For further information see page 196

John Hall Venice

UK

info@johnhallvenice.com

+44 (0)20 8871 4747

www.johnhallvenice.com

Courses based in Venice, London, Florence and Rome with a sensational combination of lectures, visits and classes in art, music, world cinema, literature, global issues, Italian, cookery and photography.

For further information see page 190

Knowledge Exchange Institute (KEI)

USA

info@keiabroad.org

1 212 931 9953

www.keiabroad.org

Study abroad and intern abroad programmes designed to meet your academic, professional and personal interests.

Lexia Study Abroad

USA

info@lexiaintl.org

+1 800 775 3942

www.lexiaintl.org

Cultural study programmes that encourage students to connect with their community while pursuing academic research. Participate in the daily life and work of a community in countries worldwide.

Michelangelo Institute

Italy

+39 055 240975

www.michelangelo-edu.it

The Michelangelo Institute offers courses for Italian language, Art History, Art, Italian Cooking and Italian Culture, in addition to enabling an immersion in Italian culture, with visits to museums, concerts, excursions, movies, dinners in restaurants, visits to markets, and evening entertainment.

Road2Argentina

Argentina

info@road2argentina.com

+54 114 833 9653

www.road2argentina.com

Study abroad in Argentina and learn all about the country and its culture.

scenns

Thailand

scenn@scenns.com

+66 (0)806 023 184

www.scenns.com

Scenns offers accommodation and various culture related tutorials for individuals and small groups. We also offer advice for exploring the Thai-Burma border region, potential volunteer placings, and are always ready to help with any queries.

SIT Study Abroad

USA

studyabroad@sit.edu

+1 888 272 7881

www.sit.edu/studyabroad/

Offers undergraduate study abroad programmes in Africa, Asia and the Pacific, Europe, Latin America and the Middle East.

The Chalet Host Course

France

admin@chalethostcourse.co.uk

+44 (0)7761 786 756

www.chalethostcourse.co.uk

Our week long courses are ideal for gap year students and also those on a career break looking to work in the ski industry. We give you hands on, practical experience of all aspects of the role of a host so you can walk into the job you want and amaze your guests.

The Hive Cookery School Ltd
UK
chris@thehivecookeryschool.co.uk
020 3608 1213
www.thehivecookeryschool.co.uk
Based in the stunning Vanoise National Park in the French Alps, The Hive trains aspiring chalet hosts to be the best in the business. We'll teach you everything you need to know about how to run a chalet efficiently for your benefit, for the benefit of your potential employers and, most importantly, for the benefit of your future guests.

The Pimenta - Kerala Spice Garden Bungalows
India
harithafarms@gmail.com
+91 485 2260216
www.thepimenta.in
Experience of what it's like to be part of a typical Kerala homestead. Stay in a tropical spice forest garden using Indian Permaculture and bio-organic techniques. See the spices growing. Explore neighbouring villages, enjoy picnics to waterfalls, visit an elephant training centre, tea gardens, old temples, churches and temple festivals.

The Ultimate Chalet Host Cookery Course
Ireland
info@chaletcookerycourse.co.uk
+44 (0)845 222 0282; +353 1 431 1359
www.chaletcookerycourse.co.uk
The Ultimate Chalet Host Cookery Course is situated in the Alps and offers to teach you everything you need to know about running a successful chalet with style and the minimum of fuss.

Design & Fashion

Blanche Macdonald Centre
Canada
info@blanchemacdonald.com
+1 604 685 0347
www.blanchemacdonald.com
If you are looking for a career in design & fashion, the Blanche Macdonald Centre offers numerous courses in Makeup Artistry, Fashion Design, Fashion Merchandising, Hair Design, Esthetics/Spa Therapy and Nail Technology. Considered to be the premium industry leader, the college graduates over one thousand students per year and has three campuses in Vancouver, British Columbia, Canada.

Domus Academy
Italy
info@domusacademy.it
www.domusacademy.com
In 2009 Domus Academy joined the Laureate International Universities Network, an international high-level education network for art and design. The Academy offers 10 masters courses, attended by students from all over the world.

Florence Institute of Design International
Italy
registrar@florence-institute.com
+39 055 23 02 481
www.florence-institute.com
The Florence Institute is an international design school specialising in design courses for students from around the world, with all classes taught in English.

Istituto di Moda Burgo
Italy
imb@imb.it
(+39) 02783753
www.imb.it

International fashion design school Istituto di Moda Burgo offers high-quality courses in fashion design, fashion stylist and pattern making.

Metallo Nobile
Italy
school@metallo-nobile.com
+39 055 2396966
www.metallo-nobile.com

Metallo Nobile offers courses in jewellery making and jewellery design, located in the heart of Florence.

NABA - Nuova Accademia de Belle Arti
Italy
+39 02 973721
www.design-summer-courses.com

NABA summer courses are divided into three levels: introduction, workshop and advanced. They have courses in design, fashion, graphic design and visual arts.

Polimoda Institute of Fashion Design and Marketing
Italy
info@polimoda.com
+39 055 275061
www.polimoda.com

Based in Florence, Polimoda Fashion School offers a variety of summer courses for those interested in all aspects of fashion.

RMIT Training
Australia
enquiries@rmit.edu.au
+61 (0) 3 9925 8111
www.shortcourses.rmit.edu.au

Has a Career Discovery Short Course in fashion. An intensive programme which includes lectures by experienced industry professionals alongside studio workshops.

Film, Theatre & Drama

Actors College of Theatre and Television
Australia
info@actt.edu.au
+61 (0) 2 9213 4500
www.actt.edu.au

ACTT is Australia 's leading independent college for the performing arts and the only acting school in Sydney offering an extensive range of accredited acting courses and technical production courses for overseas students.

EICAR - The International Film & Television School Paris
France
inquiries@eicar.fr
(+33) 01 49 98 11 11
www.eicar-international.com

Offers short summer workships taught in English during July and September in the following areas: filmmaking, script writing, editing, HD Video and sound.

European Film College
Denmark
info@europeanfilmcollege.com
0045 86 34 00 55
www.europeanfilmcollege.com

Offering students a unique experience, an international learning environment offering young filmmakers and actors an intense eight-month course.

355

Full Sail University
USA
+1 407 679 6333
www.fullsail.edu

If you're after a career in music, film, video games, design, animation, entertainment business, or internet marketing, Full Sail is the right place for you.

Hollywood Film & Acting Academy
USA

www.hwfaa.com

The traditional film school alternative, offering shorter more intense programme in feature films, movie making and acting.

Met Film School
UK
info@metfilmschool.co.uk
+44 (0)20 8832 1933
www.metfilmschool.co.uk

Are you passionate about film and want to spend your year doing something creative and fun? Take the plunge and study filmmaking at Met Film School Berlin, where your gap year leads to a qualification and new practical skills.

NYFA (New York Film Academy)
USA
film@nyfa.edu
+1 212 674 4300
www.nyfa.com

The New York Film Academy runs programmes all year round in New York City and at Universal Studios in Hollywood.

PCFE Film School
Czech Republic
info@filmstudies.cz
+420 257 534 013
www.filmstudies.cz

Offers workshops, semester and year programmes in filmmaking including directing, screenwriting, cinematography, editing and film history and theory.

visit: www.gap-year.com

The Acting Center
USA
+1 818 386 9099
www.theactingcenterla.com

No audition is necessary but an interview is required. Classes are available in evenings during the week and on weekends.

The Los Angeles Film School
USA
323 860 0789
www.lafilm.com

Has degree programmes in filmmaking, game production and animation. International students must acquire a student visa before studying in the United States.

Tribeca Flashpoint College
USA
info@tribecaflashpoint.edu
+1 312 332 0707
www.tribecaflashpoint.edu

Tribeca Flashpoint College is a two-year, direct-to-industry college focusing exclusively on the following disciplines: film/broadcast, recording arts, visual effects and animation and game development.

TVI Actors Studio - Los Angeles
USA
+1 818 784 6500
www.tvistudios.com

TVI Actors Studio offers acting classes, workshops, and seminars for aspiring and professional actors.

Vancouver Film School
Canada
+1 604 685 5808
www.vfs.com

Centre for both training and higher learning in all areas related to media and entertainment production.

Accademia Europea di Firenze
Italy

+39 055 21 15 99

www.aefirenze.it

The Accademia Europea di Firenze is an international school located in the very heart of Florence offering studies in Italian, Music, Art, Dance and Culture.

Backbeat Tours
USA

tours@backbeattours.com

+1 901-272-BEAT (2328)

www.backbeattours.com

Backbeat Tours provide numerous tours around Mephis, from an Elvis-themed Hound Dog Tour to the Historic Memphis Walking Tour, and even a chilling Memphis Ghost Tour. All tours are available as a step-on service or as custom private tours for tour operators, conventions, corporate groups or any party of 15 or more.

Brooks Institute
USA

+1 805 585 8000

www.brooks.edu

Brooks Institute offers training in filmmaking, graphic design and photojournalism. The courses are designed for anyone who aspires to a career in photography, filmmaking, visual journalism, or graphic design.

Country Music Travel
USA

mail@countrymusictravel.com

www.countrymusictravel.com

Country music-themed vacations and escorted tours, from trips to Dollywood entertainment park, to music cities tours in Nashville and Memphis.

Jazz Summer School
UK

+44 (0) 208 989 8129

www.jazzsummerschool.com

Jazz Summer School offering places at the French jazz summer school in the South of France or The Cuban music school in Havana.

Scoil Acla - Irish Music Summer School
Ireland

info@scoilacla.com

+353 (0)85 881 9548

www.scoilacla.com

Summer school established to teach Irish Piping (Irish War Pipes), tin whistle, accordian, banjo, flute and harp.

Songwriter Girl Camps
USA

info@songwritergirl.com

+1 615 323 2915

www.songwritergirl.com

Songwriter Girl Camps offer weekend songwriting camps for girls and women of all ages and ability.

SummerKeys
USA

+1 207 733 2316

www.summerkeys.com

Music vacations for adults in Lubec, Maine. Open to all 'musical people' regardless of ability with workshops and private tuition in a variety of instruments.

7 Learning abroad

SummerSongs Inc.
USA

info@summersongs.com

+1 845 594 1867

www.summersongs.com

SummerSongs is a not-for-profit corporation dedicated to the art and craft of songwriting. It offer seasonal songwriting camps (summer and winter) on both the East and West coasts of the United States.

Taller Flamenco
Spain

info@tallerflamenco.com

(+34) 954 56 42 34

www.tallerflamenco.com

Taller Flamenco is a learning centre for Flamenco and Spanish Language in Seville. Courses include flamenco dance, flamenco guitar, singing and percussion.

United DJ Mixing School
Australia

admin@djsunited.com.au

+61 (03) 9639 9990

www.djsunited.com.au

Offer an introductory course over two weekends, which gives the basics of DJ-ing and a longer comprehensive course that runs over twelve weeks.

World Rhythms Arts Program (WRAP)
USA

www.drum2dance.com

Classes develop your working knowledge of instruments, rhythms, dances, songs, styles, methods and applications.

Photography

c4 Images & Safaris
South Africa

shem@c4images-safaris.co.za

+27 (0) 12 993 1946

www.c4images-safaris.co.za

Offers short photography workshops and wildlife safaris in South Africa with emphasis on helping you to improve your photography skills.

Europa Photogenica
USA

FraPhoto@aol.com

www.europaphotogenica.com

This company provides carefully planned, high quality, small group photo tours designed for photographers of all levels who wish to improve their photographic skills using Europe as their classroom.

Fisheye Underwater Productions
Philippines

info@fisheyeunderwater.com

+63 915 299 3964

www.fisheyeunderwater.com

Fisheye Underwater Productions specialise in underwater videography and photography. We offer services from dive centre promotional material to personalised customer video and photography for great souvenirs to take home.

Joseph Van Os Photo Safaris
USA

info@photosafaris.com

(206) 463-5383

www.photosafaris.com

Joseph Van Os Photo Safaris guide you to some of the world's finest wild and scenic locations with the main purpose of making great photographs.

Keith Moss Street Photography Courses

UK

+44 (0) 1287 679 655

www. photographycoursesandworkshops.co.uk

Specialising in black and white street photography, Keith Moss offers courses in Europe's most inspiring cities. The courses provide an insight into what it takes to capture the essence of the street.

London Photo Tours & Workshops

UK

+44 (0)7738 942 099

www.londonphototours.co.uk

London Photo Tours and Workshops specialise in short courses, tours, and small-group photography workshops, offering experienced and friendly tuition.

Nigel Turner Landscape Photography

USA

npturner@cox.net

+1 702 7695110

www.nigelturnerphotography.com

Nigel Turner Landscape Photography offers landscape photography workshops in the American West. Improve your technique with friendly and relaxed tuition and explore some of the most beautiful places in the United States.

Photo Holidays France

UK

aw@andrewwhittuck.co.uk

www.photoholidaysfrance.co.uk/index. html

A private photography school in the south of France offering one to one photography tuition specialising in landscape and portrait photography.

Photographers on Safari

UK

info@photographersonsafari.com

+44 (0(1664 474040

www.photographersonsafari.com

Photographers on Safari offer UK and International Photography Trips and Safaris. Photograph animals in their natural environment with expert Photography Tuition.

Steve Outram Crete Photo Tours & Workshops

Greece

steveoutram@gmail.com

+30 28210 32201

www.steveoutram.com

Professional photographer Steve Outram uses his local knowledge of Zanzibar, Lesvos and western Crete to show you how to make the most of photographic opportunities and develop your skill as a photographer.

Chinese

Bridging the Gap China

China

enquiries@bridgingthegapchina.co.uk

+86 777 562 8765

www.bridgingthegapchina.co.uk

Bridging the Gap offers courses which combine learning Mandarin Chinese with sightseeing and cultural activities in the Yunnan province, China.

China Study Abroad

China

info@chinastudyabroad.org

+86 10 8468 3799

www.chinastudyabroad.org

Hong Kong Institute of Languages
China
info@hklanguages.com
+852 2877 6160
www.hklanguages.com

Regardless of your goal, to become fluent in a new language for interest, to travel abroad, or to sharpen your global business acumen, the HK Institute of Languages provides the best teachers, the best experience, the most fexible hours and the best locations at your own choice!

Hong Kong Language Learning Centre
China
hkllc@netvigator.com
+852 2572 6488
www.hkllc.com

Language school in Hong Kong which specialises in Cantonese and Mandarin conversation and Chinese reading and writing for expatriates, locals and overseas Chinese.

Live the Language (LTL) Mandarin School
China
info@livethelanguage.cn
+86 10 5100 1269
www.ltl-school.com

Live the language of Mandarin by studying in China. Immerse yourself in the language and the culture as you participate in individual or group classes and explore the streets of China. Gap year programmes are also available, with opportunities for work experience and earning money teaching English.

WorldLink Education US Office
USA
www.worldlinkedu.com

WorldLink Education's Chinese language programme immerses you in Mandarin Chinese through class instruction, after-class tutoring, language exchanges with native speakers and a range of optional extra activities.

French

Accent Français
France
contact@accentfrancais.com
+33 (0) 467 58 12 68
www.accentfrancais.com

This school runs intensive French courses in Montpellier particularly for non-French speakers. They last between one week and several months.

Alliance Française de Londres
UK
info@alliancefrancaise.org.uk
+44 (0) 20 7723 6439
www.alliancefrancaise.org.uk

Alliance Française is a non-profit-making organisation whose goal is to teach French and bring cultures together (group classes and bespoke tuition available).

BWS Germanlingua
Germany
info@bws-germanlingua.de
+49 (0) 89 599 892 00
www.bws-germanlingua.de

BWS Germanlingua is based in Munich and Berlin; all staff are experienced teachers, and classes have a maximum of 12 students.

CESA Languages Abroad
UK

info@cesalanguages.com

+44 (0) 1209 211 800

www.cesalanguages.com

Perfect your language skills, experience the culture first-hand and have an amazing gap-year with CESA.

For further information see page 198

CMEF, Centre Méditerranéen d'Etudes Françaises
France

centremed@monte-carlo.mc

+33 (0)4 93 78 21 59

www.centremed.monte-carlo.mc

Located in the South of France between Nice and Monaco - Monte Carlo. An international language school with a long tradition on French language courses.

France Langue (BLS)
France

bordeaux@france-langue.fr

+33 (0)5 56 06 99 83

www.france-langue.com

Based in Bordeaux and Biarritz, BLS offer a wide range of French courses to suit your exact requirements.

Institut français du Royaume-Uni
UK

box.office@institutfrancais.org.uk

+ 44 (0)20 7871 3515

www.institut-francais.org.uk

The Institut Français is the official French Government centre of language and culture in London.

Institut Savoisien d'Etudes Françaises pour Etrangers
France

isefe@univ-savoie.fr

+33 (0) 4 79 75 84 14

www.isefe.univ-savoie.fr

An institute which specialises in teaching French as a foreign language to adults from non-Francophone countries.

Live Languages Abroad
UK

info@livelanguagesabroad.co.uk

+44 (0)1736 740000

www.livelanguagesabroad.com

At Live Languages Abroad we believe that the best way to learn a language is to live the language abroad. With our experience of providing language courses abroad, we will be able to provide you with the best course, accommodation and location.

For further information see page 200

Lyon Bleu International
France

learnfrenchinlyon@lyon-bleu.fr

+33 (0) 437 480 026

www.lyon-bleu.fr

Lyon Bleu International, in Lyon, is dedicated to teaching the French language and culture.

TASIS, The American School in Switzerland
Switzerland

admissions@tasis.ch

+41 91 960 5151

www.tasis.ch

Each year, the TASIS schools and summer programmes attracts students from around the world who share in a caring, family-style international community.

Vis-à-Vis
UK
+44 (0) 20 8786 8021
www.visavis.org

French courses offered in France. Various accommodation options are available, and there is the usual range of course length, level and intensity.

German

German Academic Exchange Service (DAAD)
UK
info@daad.org.uk
+44 (0)20 7831 9511
www.daad.org.uk

The German Academic Exchange Service is the German National Agency for the support of international academic cooperation.

Goethe Institut
UK
info@london.goethe.org
0207 596 4000
www.goethe.de/enindex.htm

The Goethe Institut is probably the best-known international German language school network.

Live Languages Abroad
UK
info@livelanguagesabroad.co.uk
+44 (0)1736 740000
www.livelanguagesabroad.com

At Live Languages Abroad we believe that the best way to learn a language is to live the language abroad. With our experience of providing language courses abroad, we will be able to provide you with the best course, accommodation and location.

For further information see page 200

Greek

College Year in Athens
Greece
programs@dikemes.edu.gr
+30 210 7560-749
www.cyathens.org

College Year in Athens offers unparalleled learning opportunities for English-speaking students seeking a programme of study in Greece.

Live Languages Abroad
UK
info@livelanguagesabroad.co.uk
+44 (0)1736 740000
www.livelanguagesabroad.com

At Live Languages Abroad we believe that the best way to learn a language is to live the language abroad. With our experience of providing language courses abroad, we will be able to provide you with the best course, accommodation and location.

For further information see page 200

Italian

Accademia del Giglio
Italy
info@adg.it
+39 055 23 02 467
www.adg.it

This quiet, small school takes about 30 students, taught in small classes. As well as Italian language courses, they offer classes in drawing and painting.

Accademia Europea di Firenze
Italy
+39 055 21 15 99
www.aefirenze.it

The Accademia Europea di Firenze is an international school located in the very heart of Florence offering studies in Italian, Music, Art, Dance and Culture.

Accademia Italiana

Italy

study@accademiaitaliana.com

+39 055 284 616

www.accademiaitaliana.com

An international design, art and language school, the Accademia Italiana puts on summer language courses as well as full-year and longer academic and Masters courses.

Centro Machiavelli

Italy

school@centromachiavelli.it

+39 0 55 2396 966

www.centromachiavelli.it

A small language school in the Santo Spirito district of Florence, Centro Machiavelli teaches Italian to those who want to use the language creatively and who are interested in the culture of Italy. Explore Florence in between lessons for a truly cultural experience.

Europass

Italy

europass@europass.it

0039 055 2345802

www.europass.it

Europass has offered individual and varied Italian language courses in the heart of Florence since 1992.

Il Sillabo

Italy

info@ilsillabo.it

+39 347 9779531

www.ilsillabo.it

Il Sillabo is a small, family-run language school in San Giovanni Valdarno, Italy.

Istituto Europeo

Italy

info@istitutoeuropeo.it

+39 05523 81071

www.istitutoeuropeo.it

The Italian Language Music Art School in Florence. Enjoy yourself learning a beautiful language: come study Italian, music, art with us.

Live Languages Abroad

UK

info@livelanguagesabroad.co.uk

+44 (0)1736 740000

www.livelanguagesabroad.com

At Live Languages Abroad we believe that the best way to learn a language is to live the language abroad. With our experience of providing language courses abroad, we will be able to provide you with the best course, accommodation and location.

For further information see page 200

Lorenzo de' Medici

Italy

info@lorenzodemedici.it

+39 055 287 203

www.ldminstitute.com

Istituto Lorenzo de' Medici is committed to delivering a high-quality international learning experience through which students advance along their formal educational paths, develop their creativity, realize their own potential, and empower themselves to impact the world around them.

Michelangelo Institute
Italy
+39 055 240975
www.michelangelo-edu.it

The Michelangelo Institute runs Italian language courses all year round, including a Specialisation course for advanced speakers and One-on-one courses for those wanting to reach a good level of Italian knowledge and fluency in a short time.

Japanese

Kichijoji Language School
Japan
+81 (0) 422 47 7390
www.klschool.com

At Kichijoji Language School you will have the opportunity not only to learn Japanese; but, also to live the culture and to explore, for yourself, Tokyo, the exciting city we call home.

The Yamasa Institute
Japan
info@yamasa.org
+81 (0) 564 55 8111
www.yamasa.org

The Yamasa Institute is an independent teaching and research centre under the governance of the Hattori Foundation. It is APJLE accredited.

Multi-languages

Ailola Cape Town English School
South Africa
service@ailolacapetown.com
+27 21 439 9834
www.ailolacapetown.com

Since 1998 Ailola Cape Town English School offers English courses to foreigners. It has 9 classrooms in Sea Point with panoramic views on Table Mountain.

Caledonia Languages Abroad
UK
info@caledoniaworldwide.com
+44 (0)1316 217721
www.caledoniaworldwide.com

Short courses in French, Italian, German, Russian, Spanish and Portuguese in Europe and Latin America, for all levels, start all year round, most for a minimum of two weeks.

CERAN Lingua International
Belgium
customer@ceran.com
+32 (0) 87 79 11 22
www.ceran.com

CERAN runs weekly intensive residential language programmes in Dutch, French, German and Spanish.

EF Education First
UK
+44 (0)207 341 8500
www.ef.edu/pg/gap-year

EF Gap Year Programs offer you the opportunity to learn a foreign language, while also experiencing a new culture and facilitating personal growth.

En Famille Overseas
UK
info@enfamilleoverseas.co.uk
+44 (0)1397 712906
www.enfamilleoverseas.co.uk

En Famille organises tailor-made homestays in France, Spain and Italy, for individuals and groups. Travellers stay in a host family and learn the language, as well as joining in the life of the family.

ESL - Language Travel

UK

info@esl.co.uk

+44 (0) 20 7451 0943

www.esl.co.uk

ESL Language Travel offers immersion language courses abroad in over 20 languages in more than 300 inspirational destinations. The start dates and durations of our courses are very flexible allowing you to easily fit language learning abroad into your Gap Year.

Eurolingua Institute

UK

www.eurolingua.com

Eurolingua is a network of institutes teaching 12 languages in 37 countries. Group programmes give 15 hours of tuition a week, according to your level.

Inlingua International

Switzerland

www.inlingua.com

Inlingua is one of the world's leading language training organizations with 309 language centers in 35 countries across Europe, Africa, Asia, North and South America.

Language Courses Abroad

UK

info@languagesabroad.co.uk

+44 (0) 1509 211612

www.languagesabroad.co.uk

Languages courses available in French, German, Greek, Italian, Portuguese, Russian, Spanish and others.

Learn Languages Abroad

Ireland

info@languages.ie

+353 (0)1451 1674

www.learn-languages-abroad.co.uk

Learn Languages Abroad will help you find the course best suited to your needs.

Live Languages Abroad

UK

info@livelanguagesabroad.co.uk

+44 (0)1736 740000

www.livelanguagesabroad.com

At Live Languages Abroad we believe that the best way to learn a language is to live the language abroad. With our experience of providing language courses abroad, we will be able to provide you with the best course, accommodation and location.

For further information see page 200

Modern Language Studies Abroad (MLSA)

USA

info@mlsa.com

(815) 464-1800

www.mlsa.com

Offers language study abroad programmes in the following countries: Spain, Italy, France and Costa Rica.

Native Monks

USA

support@nativemonks.com

nativemonks.com

Get the best value when you choose from hundreds of tutors from all over the world, send them a message, and fix a time for one-to-one lessons with your chosen tutor.

OISE Oxford

UK

oxford@oise.com

01865 247 272

www.oise.com

Have their own unique teaching philosophy which leads students to gain confidence, fluency and accuracy when speaking another language taught by a native-speaker.

7 Learning abroad

365

TalkTalkBnb
France

www.talktalkbnb.com/en

TalkTalkBnb connects travellers with hosts wanting to improve their language skills. Find free accommodation in exchange for speaking your mother tongue with your host!

The Language Gap
UK

hola@thelanguagegap.org.uk

www.thelanguagegap.org.uk

We can find language experiences that combine learning or practising a skill with language learning. You can windsurf in French, dance or paint in Spanish, help conserve wildlife, walk in the mountains, sail, scuba dive, play football, explore art, history, or politics, all in the country and language of your choice.

Portuguese

CIAL Centro de Linguas
Portugal

portuguese@cial.pt

+351 217 940 448

www.cial.pt

With schools in Lisbon and Faro, CIAL organises courses in Portuguese for foreign students.

Live Languages Abroad
UK

info@livelanguagesabroad.co.uk

+44 (0)1736 740000

www.livelanguagesabroad.com

At Live Languages Abroad we believe that the best way to learn a language is to live the language abroad. With our experience of providing language courses abroad, we will be able to provide you with the best course, accommodation and location.

For further information see page 200

Russian

Live Languages Abroad
UK

info@livelanguagesabroad.co.uk

+44 (0)1736 740000

www.livelanguagesabroad.com

At Live Languages Abroad we believe that the best way to learn a language is to live the language abroad. With our experience of providing language courses abroad, we will be able to provide you with the best course, accommodation and location.

For further information see page 200

Obninsk Humanities Centre
Russian Federation

lara.bushell@btinternet.com

+44 (0) 208 858 0614 (UK number)

www.dubravushka.ru

Learn Russian in Russia, with qualified English-speaking Russian teachers and students, at Dubravushka, Russia's leading independent boarding school.

The Russian Language Centre
UK

info@russiancentre.co.uk

+44 (0) 20 7831 5330

www.russiancentre.co.uk

The Russian Language Centre in London offers a range of courses for groups and individuals: intensive, accelerated and private.

Spanish

Academia Hispánica Córdoba
Spain

info@academiahispanica.com

+34 957 488 002

www.academiahispanica.com

Academia Hispánica Córdoba offers small-group language tuition to suit all levels. Learn Spanish in Spain, whilst immersing yourself in the wonderful culture.

AES Cabin Crew

Spain

contact@aescabincrew.com

+34 622 910856

www.aescabincrew.com

AES Cabin Crew offer 3-month courses in Spain for learners to achieve the official European cabin crew (or flight attendant) qualification, in addition to daily Spanish Classes.

An additional month of only Spanish is also available for any students who wish to improve their language skills even further, and there is plenty of opportunity to immerse yourself in Spanish culture and explore the best sights Spain has to offer.

AIL Madrid Spanish Language School

Spain

+34 91 725 6360

www.ailmadrid.com/gap-year/home

AIL Madrid offers a gap year (or bridge year) program directed to high school graduates and University undergraduates, graduates and postgraduates wanting a break from their studies or career. Use your language skills for practical work experience or for meeting new people.

Ailola Buenos Aires Spanish School

Argentina

service@ailolabuenosaires.com

+54 11 4383 7706

www.ailolabuenosaires.com

Since 2005 the Ailola Buenos Aires Spanish School offers Spanish courses to foreigners. It has 8 classrooms and is located in the famous Palacio Barolo.

Ailola Madrid Spanish School

Spain

service@ailolamadrid.com

+34 913 64 24 54

www.ailolamadrid.com

Since 2001 Ailola Madrid Spanish School offers Spanish courses to foreigners. It has 7 classrooms in Madrid's traditional Central Almond district.

Ailola Quito Spanish School

Ecuador

service@ailolaquito.com

+593 2 228 5657

www.ailolaquito.com

Since 1988 Ailola Quito Spanish School offers Spanish courses to foreigners by University-educated teachers. It has 16 classrooms in the historic city part of Quito.

Amigos Spanish School

Peru

amigos@spanishcusco.com

+51 (84) 24 22 92

www.spanishcusco.com

Non-profit Spanish school. With every hour of your Spanish classes, you pay for the basic care of a group of underprivileged children at their foundation.

Apple Languages

UK

info@applelanguages.com

+44 (0) 1509 211 612

www.applelanguages.com

The best place to learn Spanish, French, Italian or German is in a country where the language is spoken, and Apple Languages offers a variety of courses in a number of countries. They also offer courses specifically for under 18's and over 50's, so there's something for everyone.

CAPS Home to Home
Spain
caps@hometohome.es
+34 93 864 88 86
capsassistants.com
CAPS is a programme designed for young people who would like to spend a year in Spain helping in a School as Conversation Teaching Assistant.

CESA Languages Abroad
UK
info@cesalanguages.com
+44 (0) 1209 211 800
www.cesalanguages.com
Perfect your language skills, experience the culture first-hand and have an amazing gap-year with CESA.

For further information see page 198

Don Quijote
UK
+44 (0)20 8786 8081
www.donquijote.org
Don Quijote is a leading network of schools teaching Spanish in Spain and Latin America.

El Pasaje Spanish School
Argentina
info@elpasajespanish.com
+54 (11) 5032 7428
www.elpasajespanish.com
We offer a wide variety of Spanish courses in Buenos Aires at affordable rates and super-customized Stay & Learn Programs. We are located in the very heart of Buenos Aires.

Enforex
Spain
info@enforex.es
+34 91 594 3776
www.enforex.com
Learn to speak Spanish in Spain or Latin America. Over 30 centres all in Spanish speaking countries. Summer camps also available.

Expanish
Argentina
contact@expanish.com
+54 11 5252 3040
www.expanish.com
Learn Spanish in Buenos Aires located in the city centre, home to some of the oldest historical sites in the city.

International House Madrid
Spain
info@ihmadrid.com
+34 913 197 224
www.ihspanishinmadrid.com
Learning Spanish in Madrid allows you to bask in the culture of the Spanish people, converse first hand with Spanish native speakers, and enjoy the full beauty of this beautiful vibrant city.

Live Languages Abroad
UK
info@livelanguagesabroad.co.uk
+44 (0)1736 740000
www.livelanguagesabroad.com
At Live Languages Abroad we believe that the best way to learn a language is to live the language abroad. With our experience of providing language courses abroad, we will be able to provide you with the best course, accommodation and location.

For further information see page 200

Mente Argentina

Argentina
info@menteargentina.com
+44 (0)20 3286 3438
www.menteargentina.com

Mente Argentina provides two different options for learning Spanish in Buenos Aires. Learn in top Universities in Argentina or, alternatively, learn at Mente's private language institute, which allows for more flexibility.

PeachTravelingSchool

Spain
+34 952 201 742
www.peachtravelingschool.com

Learn Spanish in Spain and experience its most authentic customs, talk to its most genuine people, and discover its most incredible and hidden beauties, whilst having an expert teacher travelling with you 24/7.

Pichilemu Institute of Language Studies

Chile
info@studyspanishchile.com
+56 (72) 842488/449
www.studyspanishchile.com

The Pichilemu Language School offers accredited Spanish language courses next to the beach in central Chile. We have Spanish crash courses, intensive Spanish classes, Spanish and Surf programs, and Study Abroad for credit courses. We help arrange accommodation and activities for all our students.

Simón Bolivar Spanish School

Ecuador
info@simon-bolivar.com
+593 (2) 2234 708
www.simon-bolivar.com

One of the biggest Spanish schools in Ecuador. Spanish lessons are offered at the main building in Quito, the Pacific coast and the Amazon jungle.

Universidad de Navarra - ILCE

Spain
ilce@unav.es
+34 948 425 600
www.unav.es/ilce/english/

A wide range of programmes are offered for people who wish to travel to Spain to learn about the culture and the language.

TEFL

Cactus TEFL

UK
+44 (0)1273 830960
www.cactustefl.com

Cactus TEFL is an independent advice and admissions service working with over 125 TEFL course providers in 35 different countries.

i-to-i TEFL

UK
tefl@i-to-i.com
+44 (0)113 205 4610
www.i-to-i.com

TEFL (Teaching English as a Foreign Language) is all about exploring the world while learning new skills and getting useful experience for 'real life'. LoveTEFL offer internationally recognised TEFL training, and unique teaching/travel adventures and internship.

TEFL Toulouse

France
info@tefltoulouse.com
+33 5 61 54 76 67
www.tefltoulouse.com

Teach English in France or around the world with our 4 week externally accredited TEFL course - in the heart of sunny Toulouse!

369

TEFL Trainer

Spain

contact@teflinternshipspain.com

+34 932 082 519

www.tefltrainer.com

Our unique combination of total immersion through Teaching, Spanish lessons and subsidised accommodation across the biggest cities in Spain could turn out to be just what you have been looking for.

Sport

Air

Mokai Gravity Canyon
New Zealand
+64 6 388 9109
www.gravitycanyon.co.nz
Mokai Gravity Canyon boasts three world-class adventure activities: our extreme flying fox; our mighty 80-metre bungy; or feel the thrill of a 50-metre freefall on our bridge swing.

New Zealand Skydiving School
New Zealand
bookings@skydivingnz.com
+64 (03)3029 143
www.skydivingnz.com
New Zealand's longest established skydiving school with more programmes, facilities and experience than any other in the country.

Nimbus Paragliding
New Zealand
contact@nimbusparagliding.co.nz
64 03 326 7373
www.nimbusparagliding.co.nz
Nimbus Paragliding provides Paragliding courses and paragliding equipment in Christchurch, New Zealand.

Nzone
New Zealand
skydive@nzone.biz
+64 3 442 5867
www.nzone.biz
Experience the ultimate adrenaline rush of tandem parachuting while on vacation in New Zealand. Or train to be a Sport Skydiver yourself with an Accelerated Freefall Course, no prior training needed.

Skydive Arizona
USA
jump@skydiveaz.com
+1-520 466-3753
skydiveaz.com
Located halfway between Phoenix and Tucson is the largest skydiving resort in the world! The clear desert weather allows over 340 flying days a year.

Skydive Australia
Australia
info@australiaskydive.com
+61 (02) 6684 1323
www.australiaskydive.com.au
Skydive Australia is the largest and most professional skydiving company in Australia.
Choose to jump between our 5 unique spectacular locations at East Coast and it will become the experience of your lifetime.

Skydive Las Vegas
USA
+1 702 759-3483
www.skydivelasvegas.com
Skydive over the quiet and peaceful views of Hoover Dam, Lake Mead, the Colorado River, the Las Vegas Strip and the entire Las Vegas Valley. Tandem skydiving is the easiest, fastest, cheapest and safest way to make your first skydive.

Skydive Switzerland GmbH
Switzerland
+41 (0) 33 821 0011
www.skydiveswitzerland.com
Learn how to skydive in Switzerland. Tandem jumps, fun and glacier jumps also available.

Taupo Bungy

New Zealand

info@tka.co.nz

+64 27 480 1231

www.taupobungy.co.nz

Located in the Waikato River Valley, Taupo Bungy is considered one of the world's most spectacular bungy sites. Featuring the world's first cantilever platform and New Zealand's first 'splash cam'.

Earth

Awol Adventures

New Zealand

info@awoladventures.co.nz

+(+64 9) 834 0501

www.awoladventures.co.nz

Join us in the Waitakere Rainforest for an amazing Auckland Adventure in the rainforest and beach adventure zone of Piha. We offer canyoning and abseiling experiences, as well as boogie boarding and cater for any level of ability.

Bucks and Spurs

USA

csonny@getgoin.net

+1 417-683-2381

www.bucksandspurs.com

Horseback riding vacations in Missouri. Round up cattle, see a horse whisperer use his natural horsemanship, and enjoy the ride at this Missouri Dude Ranch.

Gravity Assisted Mountain Biking

Bolivia

gravityoffice@gravitybolivia.com; info@gravitybolivia.com

+591 767 03000; +591 2 2310218

www.gravitybolivia.com

Gravity Assisted Mountain Biking offer various downhill and cross-country mountain bike rides in Bolivia and Peru. We offer one-day to two-week long rides, as well as multi-activity trips that include biking, hiking, mountaineering and much more.

Jagged Globe

UK

+44 (0) 845 345 8848

www.jagged-globe.co.uk

Jagged Globe provides mountaineering expeditions and treks. They also offer courses which are based in Wales, Scotland and the Alps for both the beginner and those wishing to improve their skills.

Megalong Australian Heritage Centre

Australia

admin@megalongcc.com.au

+61 (02) 4787 9116

www.megalongcc.com.au

Discover the best of the Blue Mountains at this unique venue in stunning wilderness bushland. Experience horse riding, cattle, native wildlife and the rural lifestyle in our guesthouse or camping. Enjoy trail riding in the pristine wilderness of the Megalong Valley.

Mountaineering Council of Ireland

Ireland

info@mountaineering.ie

+353 1 625 1115

www.mountaineering.ie

The Mountaineering Council of Ireland has lists of mountaineering clubs in Ireland, useful information and can give advice on insurance.

Quest Japan

Japan

info@questjapan.co.jp

+81 (0)3 6902 2551

www.hikejapan.com

Guided walking holidays and tailor-made tours for individuals and small groups, from the island of Yakushima south of Kyushu, to the Kii mountain range in Central Japan, and the island of Hokkaido.

Qufu Shaolin Kung Fu School China

China

shaolinskungfu@gmail.com

+86 151 537 30991

www.shaolinskungfu.com

Qufu Shaolin Kung Fu School China is an institute for the teaching and promotion of traditional Shaolin Kung Fu and Chinese Martial Arts in China. Students of all ages and abilities can learn from Shaolin Masters in the beautiful and peaceful UNESCO World Heritage City of Qufu.

Rock'n Ropes

New Zealand

info@rocknropes.co.nz

+64 800 244 508

www.rocknropes.co.nz

A Rock'n Ropes course is 'as exciting as skydiving or bungee jumping'. Check out their website for full details.

Sporting Opportunities

UK

info@sportingopportunities.com

+44 (0)208 123 8702

www.sportingopportunities.com

Sporting Opportunities offers sports coaching projects and sports tours for gap years, career breaks and volunteer travel.

White Peak Expeditions

UK

mail@whitepeakexpeditions.co.uk

www.whitepeakexpeditions.co.uk

Specialists in trekking and climbing for small groups in Nepal, Tibet, Kazakhstan/Kyrgyzstan, Ecuador and Peru. Climbs are suitable for the less experienced climber and are generally combined with trekking expeditions.

Snow

Alltracks Limited

UK

info@alltracksacademy.com

+44 (0)1794 301777

www.alltracksacademy.com

Whether you're looking to spend a fun but challenging career break or gap year on an extended course, perfect your powder turns in a couple of weeks, learn more about backcountry riding and avalanche safety or become a qualified ski or snowboard instructor, Alltracks have a course for you.

Altitude Futures - Gap Course Verbier

Switzerland

info@altitude-futures.com

+44 7539 071166

www.altitude-futures.com

Altitude Futures run official BASI and CSIA ski and snowboard instructor courses in Verbier, Whistler and Tignes. See www.altitude-futures.com for more details.

373

Basecamp Ski and Snowboard
UK

+44 (0) 20 8789 9055

www.basecampgroup.com

Basecamp is the no. 1 choice for anyone looking to take their skiing and snowboarding to the next level as part of a gap year or career break.

BASI (British Association of Snowsport Instructors)
UK

basi.org.uk

+44 (0)1479 861717

www.basi.org.uk

Fast track your snowsport career and become a qualified ski or snowboard instructor in 10 weeks with approved BASIGap.

Cardrona Alpine Resort
New Zealand

info@cardrona.com

+64 3 443 7341

www.cardrona.com

Skiers and Snowboarders of all ages and abilities will enjoy a trip to Cardrona Alpine Resort. With wide open beginner trails, pristine groomers, fun freeride terrain and world class parks and pipes, Cardrona is a great way to enjoy the Southern Alps.

Harris Mountains Heli-Ski
New Zealand

hmh@heliski.co.nz

+64 3 442 6722

www.heliski.co.nz

If you are a strong intermediate skier or ski-boarder, then try this for that extra thrill!

ICE Snowsports Ltd
UK

info@icesi.org

+44 (0) 870 760 7360

www.icesi.org

With ICE you can attend official BASI courses in Val d'Isere, including a range of ski instructor courses and snowboard instructor courses.

iGOSKi Ltd
UK

info@igoski.co.uk

+44 (0)844 770 40 74

www.igoski.co.uk

At iGOSKI we specialise in short ski breaks with flexible travel options, fast and efficient transfers to maximise your snow-time in the finest ski resorts in the Alps. Our personal service will ensure your holiday is an unforgettable experience.

Interski
UK

enquiries@interskisnowsportschool.co.uk

01623 456 333

www.interskisnowsportschool.co.uk

Interski Gap Year Instructor Training Courses run in the resorts of Aosta/Pila and Courmayeur. The only fully-inclusive gap course on the market with guaranteed employment for all successful students.

Non-Stop Ski & Snowboard
UK

info@nonstopsnow.com

+44 (0)1225 632 165

www.nonstopsnow.com

Offering a variety of ski and snowboard instructor courses in western Canada, New Zealand and France. An ideal gap-year, career break or chance to fast track into the ski industry.

374

OnTheMountain Pro Snowsports Instructor Training in Switzerland

Switzerland

gap@onthemountainpro.co.uk

+41 27 288 3131

www.onthemountainpro.co.uk

Provides exceptional training and loads of fun, after training stay and enjoy the slopes until the end of the season at no extra cost.

Outdoor Interlaken AG

Switzerland

mail@outdoor-interlaken.ch

+41 (0) 33 826 77 19

www.outdoor-interlaken.ch

Ski/Snowboard school for complete beginners and for those who wish to brush up their skills. Have local guides who know the best trails, snow and shortest lift lines.

Oyster Worldwide Limited

UK

anne@oysterworldwide.com

+44 (0) 1892 770 771

www.oysterworldwide.com

Paid work opportunities in top Canadian ski resorts: Whistler, The Rockies and Tremblant or join an 11 week ski and snowboarder courses in Jasper, France or Romania. Intermediate skiers can become ski instructors in world-renowned Whistler with CSIA Level 1 course and qualification included.

RIDGE Mountain Academy

USA

info@ridgeacademy.com

406-730-8524

www.ridgeacademy.com

RIDGE Mountain Academy focuses on mountain sports, education, personal growth and life skills. RIDGE is designed for male and female student athletes ages 16 to 22 who are interested in expanding a passion for sports in the mountains.

Silver Ski Holidays

UK

silvers@silverski.co.uk

01622 735544

www.silverski.co.uk

Silver Ski Holidays have been operating ski chalets in the French Alps for over 32 years. Our holidays suit all age groups and all levels of skiers and snow boarders, and include flights and transfers from either Gatwick or Manchester airports.

SITCo Ski and Snowboard Training New Zealand

New Zealand

ski@sitco.co.nz

+64 21 341 214

www.sitco.co.nz

SITCo has been training keen skiers and snowboarders since 2002. Come to Queenstown NZ to start living the dream. Accommodation, lift pass, training, qualifications, and a Heli-ski, plus much more are all included.

Ski Armadillo
UK
info@skiarmadillo.com
+44 (0)1799 668726
www.skiarmadilloverbier.com

Whatever your skiing requirements, Ski Armadillo has the knowledge, professionalism and personality to ensure that you receive the skiing experience that you deserve. After all, we're skiers too, so we know how important this holiday is to you.

Ski Instructor Academy KG
Austria
info@siaaustria.com
+43 650 563 3607
www.siaaustria.com

Ski Instructor Academy offers high quality, good value ski instructor courses and private improver clinics. We have the unique ability to offer you a guaranteed job as a snow sports instructor in Austria after completing your training, giving you peace of mind that you can put your new skills straight to the test, gain valuable experience and gives you the confidence to book with Ski Instructor Academy leading to a long and successful career in the snow sports industry.

Ski le Gap
UK
info@skilegap.com
+44 (0)3309 001032 / 0800 160 1981
www.skilegap.com

Offers ski and snowboard instructor training courses based in the popular Canadian resort of Tremblant.

Ski New Generation
UK
info@skinewgen.com
+44 (0)1462 674 000
www.skinewgen.com

Here at New Generation we have a wide selection of ski and snowboard lessons and adventures for all ages and abilities. From tiny tots right through to all mountain pros. Take a closer look at our lessons then select your resort to find out more.

Ski-Exp-Air
Canada
info@ski-exp-air.com
+1 418 520 6669
www.ski-exp-air.com

Ski-exp-air is a Canadian ski and snowboard school offering quality, professional instruction in a fun atmosphere.

SnowSkool
UK
team@snowskool.co.uk
+44 (0)1962 713342
www.snowskool.co.uk

Ski and Snowboard instructor courses in Canada, New Zealand, France and the USA. SnowSkool offers four, five, nine and eleven week programmes earning internationally recognised qualifications.

The Tasty Ski Company
UK
info@thetastyskicompany.co.uk
+44 (0)7538 761 767
www.thetastyskicompany.co.uk

The Tasty Ski Company has a selection of catered ski chalets in Morzine and Le Grand Massif. Our prices include our lovely house wines, beer and soft drinks. This is an unlimited service not just confined to meal times.

The Winter Sports Company

UK

info@wintersportscompany.com

+44 (0)1736 763402

www.wintersportscompany.com

The Winter Sports Company all-inclusive ski patrol courses, ski instructor courses, snowboard instructor courses and internships, with internationally recognised qualifications, in Canada, Europe and New Zealand.

Timberline Canadian Alpine Academy

Canada

info@timberlineacademy.com

+1 403 763 3032

www.timberlineacademy.com

Timberline Canadian Alpine Academy is a locally owned Outdoor Adventure School situated in Banff, Canada. They specialize in Gap Year Ski & Snowboard Instructor Courses with paid internships.

WE ARE SNO

UK

hello@wearesno.com

wearesno.com

WE ARE SNO provide ski and snowboard instructor courses at resorts around the globe. All courses come with guaranteed paid work for winter!

Whistler Summer Snowboard Camps

Canada

info@whistlersnowboardcamps.com

+1 604 902 9227

www.whistlersnowboardcamps.com

Treeline is a residential summer ski and snowboard camp, located in beautiful Whistler, British Columbia, Canada. Improve your snowboarding skills with 1-2 week sessions for Kids (7-18), as well as an Adult's Only session for 19+.

Yamnuska Mountain Adventures

Canada

info@yamnuska.com

+1 403 678 4164

http://yamnuska.com

Located in Canmore, Alberta at the Banff National Park gates, Yamnuska are a premier provider of mountaineering, ice climbing, rock climbing, backcountry skiing, avalanche training and trekking experiences in the Canadian Rockies.

YES Tours Inc

Canada

info@yesimprovement.com

+1 604 905 2560

www.yesimprovement.com

YES is based in Whistler and has been offering Instructor training programs for over 20 years! Work as a Instructor for the season in Whistler for the time of your life!

Various

Bear Creek Outdoor Centre

Canada

info@bearcreekoutdoor.com

+1 888 453 5099

www.bearcreekoutdoor.com

Located on 500 acres, Bear Creek Outdoor Centre contains two private lakes and miles of wooded trails perfect for nature exploration, orienteering, and hiking.

Camp Challenge Pte Ltd

Singapore

enquiries@camp-challenge.com

+65 6257 4427

www.camp-challenge.com

At Camp-Challenge, we believe that every youth is a cell of this global community. We provide the platform for this growth through our programmes.

Canyon Voyages Adventure Co
USA

+1 435 259 6007

www.canyonvoyages.com

River rafting, kayaking, canoeing, hiking, horseback, mountain bike and 4x4 trips available in the canyons of Utah.

Class VI River Runners
USA

info@class-vi.com

+1 888 383 9985

www.class-vi.com

River Runners offers a variety of organised sporting trips for students, families and corporate groups.

Donegal Adventure Centre (DAC)
Ireland

info@donegaladventurecentre.net

+353 71 984 2418

www.donegaladventurecentre.net

DAC offers various camps and activities for all ages and abilities. Try your hand at surfing, high-rope climbing, archery, zip wire, abseiling, cliff jumping, body boarding and many more.

EBO Adventure
UK

info@eboadventure.com

0800 781 6861

www.eboadventure.co.uk

Get adventurous with a wide range of training activities, survival courses and outdoor instructor courses in the UK and abroad.

G2 Outdoor
UK

www.g2outdoor.co.uk

The centre, based in the Highlands of Scotland offers a full range of outdoor activities for both winter and summer.

Mendip Snow Sport
UK

info@mendip.me

01934 852335

www.mendipsnowsport.co.uk

Centre is on the edge of the Mendip hills, where you can ski, snowboard, mountain board, as well as pursue archery, rifle shooting, power kiting, 4x4 driving, quad biking, rock climbing, abseiling and more.

Peak Leaders
UK

info@peakleaders.com

01337 860 079

www.peakleaders.com

Make the most of your once in a lifetime experience in some of the world's leading resorts whilst gaining internationally recognised instructor qualifications, plus plenty of CV enhancing extras.

Raging Thunder
Australia

info@ragingthunder.com.au

+61 (0)7 4030 7990

www.ragingthunder.com.au

Selection of day tours, once in a lifetime experiences available, such as Great Barrier Reef excursions, sea kayaking, ballooning and white water rafting.

Rapid Sensations Rafting
New Zealand

info@rapids.co.nz

+64 7 374 8117; 0800 35 34 35

www.rapids.co.nz

White water rafting, kayaking and mountain biking on offer. They also have a kayaking school.

River Deep Mountain High
UK

info@riverdeepmountainhigh.co.uk

+44 (0) 15395 28666

www.riverdeepmountainhigh.co.uk

Outdoor activities and activity Holidays in the Lake District. Where you can try canoeing, kayaking, gorge walks, abseiling, climbing, sailing, walking, trail-cycling or mountain biking.

River Rats Rafting
New Zealand

+64 7 345 6543

www.riverrats.co.nz

River Rats are located in Rototua, New Zealand and are specialists in rafting. They also offer a gondola ride up Mount Ngongotaha other activities.

Rogue Wilderness Adventures
USA

webmaster@wildrogue.com

+1 (541) 479 9554

www.wildrogue.com

Hiking, fishing and rafting trips are designed to give you a thrilling, relaxing and fun experience. Based in Rogue River Canyon.

Rug&Rock Adventures Ltd
UK

info@rugandrock.com

+44 (0)8 4444 123 12

www.rugandrock.com

Sport Lived Ltd
UK

0844 858 9103

www.sportlived.co.uk

Want to discover a new country and develop your passion for sport? We make it happen. Play or coach sport during a gap year or summer break. It's the perfect way to combine sport, adventure and travel.

Wilderness Aware Rafting
USA

rapids@inaraft.com

+1 719 395 2112

www.inaraft.com

At Wilderness Aware Rafting we offer a variety of white water rafting trips suitable for all skill levels, including mild water float trips, fast-paced and splashy beginner/intermediate trips and action-packed advanced white water.

World Stage Sport
UK

lewis@worldstagesport.co.uk; sam@worldstagesport.co.uk

07939 931341

www.worldstagesport.co.uk

World Stage Sport is an exciting, fast growing company run by two driven sportsmen offering advice and consultancy to sportsmen and women looking to experience sport around the world!

Water

Adventure Bound
USA

info@adventureboundusa.com

+1 970 245 5428

www.adventureboundusa.com

Discover the relaxation of drifting down the river without a care in the world, experience the excitement of paddling an inflatable kayak through an exhilarating rapid, or feel the power of laughter and intrigue while sharing campfire stories with Adventure Bound.

All Outdoors California Whitewater Rafting
USA

rivers@aorafting.com

+1 925 932 8993

www.aorafting.com

Explore the rivers of California with All Outdoors. Choose from a choice of 10 Rivers, with mild to wild rapids and scenic canyons for beginners or advanced rafters. These professionally guided whitewater rafting trips are available in 1-day & multi-day options.

Allaboard Sailing Academy
Spain

info@sailing.gi

+350 200 50202

www.sailing.gi

Whether you are an enthusiastic novice, looking to learn the ropes and sail safely, or a seasoned mariner seeking to hone your skills and achieve the next qualification, Allabroad have the perfect course for you.

Alpin Raft
Switzerland

info@alpinraft.com

+41 (0) 33 823 41 00

www.alpinraft.com

Located in Interlaken in the Swiss Alps, Alpin Raft offers fantastic fun and adventures - join us for some thrilling and scenic rafting, canyoning or bungy-jumping!

Aquatic Explorers
Australia

+61 2 9523 1518

www.aquaticexplorers.com.au

Aquatic Explorers is an SSI (Scuba Schools International) Facility offering new divers, as well as local and international scuba divers the best scuba diving training at Cronulla Beach in Sydney, Australia.

Barque Picton Castle
Canada

info@picton-castle.com

+1 (902) 634 9984

www.picton-castle.com

Explore Europe, Africa and the Caribbean as crew on a three-masted tall ship. No experience needed. Join Barque Picton Castle. Come aboard, come alive!

Bermuda Sub-Aqua Club
Bermuda

chairman@bsac.bm

+ 1 441 291 5640

www.bsac.bm

The Bermuda Sub-Aqua Club is a branch of the British Sub-Aqua Club and offers members a varied programme of club-organised dives; a safe, structured, proven training programme.

Cairns Dive Centre
Australia

info@cairnsdive.com.au

+61 7 40 510 294

www.cairnsdive.com.au

CDC offers daily day or live aboard snorkel and dive trips to the Outer Great Barrier Reef. We also offer SSI learn-to-dive courses from beginners through to instructor level.

Catalina Tours
USA

catalinatours@gmail.com

+1 310 510 0211

www.catalinaoceanrafting.com

Catalina Tours provide a variety of ocean and land tours, day packages and overnight packages. Explore the island via electric bike or Jeep, or take to the seas for snorkelling, scuba diving, jet-skiing and paragliding. Discover the local wildlife, including dolphins and sea lions. Situated on Catalina Island itself, all of our staff live on the Island and we know the area well.

Challenge Rafting
New Zealand
challenge@raft.co.nz
+64 3 442 7318
www.raft.co.nz
Challenge Rafting offers exciting half-day whitewater rafting trips on the Shotover and Kawarau Rivers.

Coral Divers
South Africa
cdc@coraldivers.co.za
+27 63 083 7613
www.coralgopro.co.za
Join us for the experience of a lifetime and become a PADI Divemaster or Instructor. Coral Divers offers a Career Development Course aimed at giving you the best possible foundation to the dive industry.

Dart River Safaris
New Zealand
info@dartriverjetsafaris.co.nz
+64 3 442 9992
www.dartriver.co.nz
Jet boat up the Dart River and kayak back or take the bus back. In between explore the ancient forest. The Dart River Valley featured in the Lord of the Rings films.

Deep Sea Divers Den
Australia
info@diversden.com.au
+61-7-4046 7333
www.diversden.com.au
Your guide to the finest Great Barrier Reef scuba diving and snorkelling off Cairns Tropical Queensland, Australia.

Dive Kaikoura
New Zealand
divekaikoura@xtra.co.nz
+64 03 319 6622
www.divekaikoura.co.nz
Professional instructors and small groups make Dive Kaikoura the ideal place to start your diving journey or advance your diving qualification.

Dvorak Expeditions
USA
+1 719 539 6851
www.dvorakexpeditions.com
White water rafting, kayaking and fly fishing trips offered in Colorado, Utah, New Mexico, Idaho, Texas and Mexico.

Elite Sailing
UK
sue@elitesailing.co.uk
UI634 890512
www.elitesailing.co.uk
Sailing school and RYA Training Centre based at Chatham, Kent. Suitable for absolute beginner to professional skippers and crew.

Errant Surf
UK
+44 (0)208 133 6438
www.errantsurf.com
An award-winning worldwide surf company offering cost effective global surf trips to the most beautiful corners of the globe.

Gap Year Diver Ltd
UK
+44 (0)1608 738 419
www.gapyeardiver.com
Diver training and a wide range of activities and excursions included which make the entire experience more exciting and enjoyable.

Island Divers
Thailand
+66 (0)898732205
www.islanddiverspp.com

Looking for a new adventure? Then join our friendly and highly qualified staff for dive courses and dive trips for all levels, from beginner to professional.

Island Star Excursions
USA
info@islandstarexcursions.com
+1 808 661 7238
www.hawaiioceanrafting.com

Whale watching, rafting, sailing and speed boating all off the coast of Hawaii. Small groups only.

Jubilee Sailing Trust
UK
info@jst.org.uk
+44 (0) 23 8042 6868
www.jst.org.uk

Tall Ships Sailing Trust. Join their JST Youth Leadership@Sea Scheme, no sailing experience needed. Registered Charity No. 277810.

Learn In Asia (Mermaids Dive Center)
Thailand
dive@mermaidsdivecenter.com
+66 38 303 333
www.learn-in-asia.com

Mermaids offers a variety of PADI scuba diving courses, scuba diving internships, coral and wreck diving trips every day, open to complete beginners and experienced divers alike.

Mermaid Diving
Spain
melissa@mermaiddiving.co
+34 922 738 031
www.mermaiddiving.co

At Mermaid Diving we offer you a first class experience at our award winning PADI 5 Star IDC Dive Centre in Tenerife. We cater for all levels of diver - whether you want to learn to dive, continue your PADI dive education to PADI Instructor level or if you simply just enjoy diving, we are the dive team for you.

National White Water Centre
UK
info@ukrafting.co.uk
01678 521083
www.ukrafting.co.uk

Known as the home of white water rafting and kayaking, the Snowdonia-based centre boasts fantastic water conditions for paddlesports alongside beautiful scenery.

Ocean Rafting
Australia
crew@oceanrafting.com.au
+61 7 4946 6848
www.oceanrafting.com

Ocean rafting around the coast of Queensland and the Whitsunday Islands which includes exploring Whitehaven Beach.

Ocean Tribe Ltd
Kenya
+254 (0)700 934 854
www.oceantribe.co

Ocean Tribe Ltd organize professional scuba diving training packages, dive training courses and dive career internships where you can go all the way to instructor in just a few short months.

OzSail

Australia

bookings@ozsail.com.au

+61 7 4946 6877

www.ozsail.com.au

OzSail presents an extensive range of sailing and diving holidays from which to choose.

Penrith Whitewater Stadium

Australia

+61 2 4730 4333

www.penrithwhitewater.com.au

Introduction packages and courses in whitewater rafting offered and whitewater kayaking.

Plas Menai

UK

info@plasmenai.co.uk

+44 (0) 1248 670964

www.plasmenai.co.uk

Plas Menai, the National Watersports Centre in North Wales, offers RYA training courses in dinghy sailing, windsurfing, powerboating and cruising throughout the year and also run kayaking courses and sea kayak expeditions.

Pocono Whitewater

USA

info@poconowhitewater.com

+1 570 325 3655

www.poconowhitewater.com

Trail biking, paintball skirmish, kayaking and whitewater rafting available in the LeHigh River Gorge.

Reef Conservation International (ReefCI)

Belize

anthony@reefci.com

+1 513 334 9393

www.reefci.com

ReefCI offers a unique one-of-a-kind marine conservation diving experience. We offer an all-inclusive Monday-Friday diving and marine conservation trip on a small private island surrounded by turquoise coral seas situated on the Belize Barrier Reef.

River Expeditions

USA

+1 800 463 9873

www.raftinginfo.com

Rafting in West Virginia on the New and Gauley Rivers.

Sabah Divers

Malaysia

sabahdivers2u@yahoo.com

+6088256483

www.sabahdivers.com

Sabah Divers operate one of the leading scuba diving education & training centres in South East Asia, running a full-service dive shop and offer scuba diving courses as well as recreational dives.

Scuba Duba Dive

UK

dive@scubadubadive.com

+44 (0)1224 900640

www.scubadubadive.com

Scuba Duba Dive offers numerous dive holidays and training packages all over the world to suit all levels of diver, from absolute beginners to those with years of experience. Destinations include Egypt, Thailand, Malta and Honduras.

Scuba Junkie
Malaysia
info@scuba-junkie.com
+60 89 785372
www.scuba-junkie.com
Scuba Junkie is a fully licensed and insured PADI operation offering courses for beginners to advanced in the Celebes Sea.

Shotover Jet
New Zealand
info@shotoverjet.com
+64 3 442 8570
www.shotoverjet.com
World famous as the ultimate jet boat experience, Shotover Jet has thrilled over 3 million people since 1970, and now it's your turn!

South Sea Nomads
Indonesia
info@southseanomads.com
+6282145804522
www.southseanomads.com
A floating backpackers' hostel. Our aim is to provide dive and exploration safaris to locations that will appeal to anyone with a love of the sea and a sense of adventure.

Sunsail
UK
+44 (0)844 2732 454
www.sunsail.com
Sunsail offers the full range of RYA yacht courses as well as their own teaching programmes. Their instructors are RYA qualified.

Surf Camp Australia
Australia
info@surfcamp.com.au
+61 407 787 346 / 1800 888 732
www.surfcamp.com.au
Surf Camp Australia offers 2-10 day courses for both experienced and beginner surfers, complete with accommodation in beachside cabins just a short distance from the beach and a variety of meals.

Surfaris
Australia
surf@surfaris.com
1800 00SURF
www.surfaris.com
Surfaris - licensed to a greater range of surf breaks than any other operator in Australia. Located on the east coast of NSW, half-way between Sydney and Byron Bay in the coastal surfing village of Crescent Head.

Surfing Queensland
Australia
info@surfingqueensland.com
+61 07 552 011 65
www.surfingqueensland.com.au
Surfing Queensland has a surf school system with over 20 licensed surf schools operating on beaches from Coolangatta to Yeppoon.

Tall Ships Youth Trust
UK
info@tallships.org
02392 832055
tallships.org
The Tall Ships Youth Trust is dedicated to the personal development of young people through the crewing of ocean going sail training vessels. It is the UK's oldest and largest sail training charity for young people aged 12-25.

visit: www.gap-year.com

Taupo Kayaking Adventures

New Zealand

info@tka.co.nz

027 480 1231

www.tka.co.nz

Specialising in kayaking trips around the crystal clear water of Lake Taupo, under the shadow of an active volcano, and metres away from Maori rock carvings.

The Professional Association of Diving Instructors (PADI)

UK

customerservices.emea@padi.com

+44 (0)117 300 7234

www.padi.com

PADI provides a wealth of information about diving to help newcomers get started. They also provide details on a variety of scuba holidays around the world, so you can plan your perfect diving vacation.

Ticket To Ride

UK

info@ttride.co.uk

+44 (0) 20 8788 8668

www.ttride.co.uk

Ticket to Ride develop all of our worldwide surfing adventures around the combination of doing something for yourself, something for others, travelling the world and having something to show for it all at the end.

Torquay Stand Up Paddle Surfing & Kitebuggying School

UK

info@kitesurfingtorquay.co.uk

+44 (0)1803 329850

www.standuppaddletorquay.co.uk

Torquay Stand Up Paddle Surfing and Kitebuggying School offers equipment and lessons for kitesurfing, kitebuggying and stand up paddle surfing in Torquay.

Wavehunters UK

UK

mail@wavehunters.co.uk

+44 (0)1208 880617

www.wavehunters.co.uk

Wavehuntyers excel in providing people of all ages personal attention and specifically tailored surf lessons from experienced committed and professional surf coaches.

Sport Instructors

Alpine Elements Group

UK

jobs@alpineelements.co.uk

0844 770 4070

jobsite.alpineelements.co.uk

Alpine Elements is a specialist Ski and Summer Holiday Company in France, Austria and Greece offering exciting jobs varancies, both full and part time, in both the summer and winter.

Aus Diving Academy

Indonesia

info@adadivinggiliair.com

+62 878 6239 2939

adadivinggiliair.com

Aus Diving Academy offers a 4 to 6 month program for those that are looking for adventure, a unique lifestyle and a professional scuba diving certification.

Britannia Sailing East Coast

UK

enquiry@britanniasailingschool.co.uk

+44 (0) 1473 787019

www.britanniasailingschool.co.uk

Based at Shotley Marina near Ipswich, Britannia Sailing is a well-established company with first-class facilities offering all aspects of sailing instruction and yacht charter.

Coaches across Continents
USA

brian@coachesacrosscontinents.org

www.coachesacrosscontinents.org

The world's only development organization with a proven track record in using soccer as a vehicle for social change in developing communities, mobilizing volunteers, financial resources, and equipment to work with local teachers and community leaders in disadvantaged communities on three continents

Coral Divers
South Africa

cdc@coraldivers.co.za

+27 63 083 7613

www.coralgopro.co.za

Join us for the experience of a lifetime and become a PADI Divemaster or Instructor. Coral Divers offers a Career Development Course aimed at giving you the best possible foundation to the dive industry.

EA Ski & Snowboard
UK

sstraining@educatingadventures.com

+44 (0)20 7193 2647

www.easkiandsnowboard.com

EA Ski & Snowboard provides a variety of ski instructor courses at top ski resorts in Canada, New Zealand, Japan, Switzerland and the USA, which arm you with a range of internationally recognised ski instructor qualifications.

Those interested in a full season and wanting to step right into an instructor uniform with a paid Ski Instructor Job should check out the Season Internship Courses. Or, for those looking for a part season training and certification program, check out the 3 to 12 Week Ski Courses.

Elite Ski Academy
Austria

info@eliteskiaustria.com

www.eliteskiaustria.com

Elite Ski Academy offers preparation courses for becoming a ski instructor as well as a range of other camps.

Flying Fish UK Ltd
UK

mail@flyingfishonline.com

+44 (0)1983 280641

www.flyingfishonline.com

Flying Fish trains and recruits over 1000 people each year to work worldwide as yacht skippers and as sailing, diving, surfing, windsurfing, ski and snowboard instructors.

Oyster Worldwide Limited
UK

anne@oysterworldwide.com

+44 (0) 1892 770 771

www.oysterworldwide.com

Choose between an 11 week instructor programme in Jasper, Canada and our 5 month course + instructor job in Whistler. Excellent Oyster support throughout.

PJ Scuba
Thailand

pjscuba@gmail.com

+66 (0) 382 322 19

www.pjscuba.com

Offers the chance to study scuba diving to instructor level (PADI) and then teach in Thailand.

Ski Academy Switzerland

UK

info@skiacademyswitzerland.com

+44(0)113 3141510

www.skiacademyswitzerland.com

Provider of quality ski instructor programmes for gap-year students and for those on a career break or just fancy a challenge!

skivo2 Instructor Training

UK

dave.beattie@skivo2.co.uk

+44 (0)1635 278847

www.skivo2.co.uk

For those wanting to become Ski Instructors, an opportunity to train with the highest qualified coaches in the world's largest ski area! Courchevel Trois Vallées.

SkiWeekends - Snow Academy

UK

sales@skiweekends.com

023 8020 6971

www.skiweekends.com

Have you ever wanted to be a ski or snowboard instructor? How about spending a season as a chalet host, looking after guests and skiing in your free time? Sign up for one of our Snow Academy courses and you could be spending the whole winter living and working in the mountains of Canada or France.

The Instructor Training Co

New Zealand

info@sitco.co.nz

+64 (0)21 341 214

www.sitco.co.nz

The Instructor Training Co offers you the opportunity to train for your ski instructor qualification in New Zealand. Five, eight and ten week courses available.

Timberline Canadian Alpine Academy

Canada

info@timberlineacademy.com

+1 403 763 3032

www.timberlineacademy.com

Timberline Canadian Alpine Academy is a locally owned Outdoor Adventure School situated in Banff, Canada. They specialize in Gap Year Ski & Snowboard Instructor Courses with paid internships.

8 Sport

Festivals

Brighton Festival
UK
info@brightonfestival.org
+44 (0) 1273 700747
www.brightonfestival.org

A handful of volunteer posts are open during the festival in May, working in the education and press office departments.

Cheltenham Festivals
UK
01242 511211
www.cheltenhamfestivals.com

This company runs festivals throughout the year, including jazz, science, music, folk, fringe and literary events.

Edinburgh Festival Fringe
UK
admin@edfringe.com
+44 (0) 131 226 0026
www.edfringe.com

Big and long-established late summer festival that has managed to stay cutting-edge.

Harrogate International Festivals
UK
info@harrogate-festival.org.uk
+44 (0) 1423 562 303
www.harrogateinternationalfestivals.com

Harrogate International Festival hosts a number of arts festivals, and offers internships and short-term work experience placements during festivals.

Hay Festival
UK
admin@hayfestival.com
+44 (0) 1497 822 620
www.hayfestival.com/wales/jobs.aspx

One of the most famous literary festivals in the UK. Most departments take on extra workers for festival fortnight, including stewards, extra staff for the box-office and the bookshop and three interns.

Ilkley Literature Festival
UK
info@ilkleyliteraturefestival.org.uk
+44 (0) 1943 601 210
www.ilkleyliteraturefestival.org.uk

If you want to become a volunteer at the Ilkley Literature Festival fill in their online form. Jobs include stewarding and helping with mailouts.

Lichfield Festival
UK
info@lichfieldfestival.org
+44 (0) 1543 306 270
www.lichfieldfestival.org

Volunteers required backstage, to assist with stage management and to help with the education programmes. Contact Richard Bateman, volunteer coordinator, for more details.

Mananan International Festival of Music and the Arts
UK
information@erinartscentre.com
+44 (0) 1624 835 858
www.erinartscentre.com

Volunteers needed for stewarding duties, programme selling, transportation of artists, administration, catering, bar duties, technical support and manning galleries and shops.

389

Norfolk and Norwich Festival Ltd
UK

info@nnfestival.org.uk

+44 (0) 1603 877 750

www.nnfestival.org.uk

Volunteers needed from January to May to help out with administration, marketing and even event production.

Portsmouth Festivities
UK

info@portsmouthfestivities.co.uk

+44 (0)23 9268 1390

www.portsmouthfestivities.co.uk

Volunteers required to help out with the many varied festivities in Portsmouth.

Salisbury International Arts Festival
UK

info@salisburyfestival.co.uk

+44 (0) 1722 332 241

www.salisburyfestival.co.uk

Volunteering opportunities include stage manager, helping out with crowd management and leaflet distribution. Registered charity No. 276940.

Winchester Hat Fair
UK

info@hatfair.co.uk

+44 (0)1962 844600

www.hatfair.co.uk

This vibrant and entertaining festival takes over the centre of Winchester each year during the first weekend in July. Volunteers are needed to help out before and during the festival.

Youth Music Theatre
UK

+44 (0)20 8563 7725

www.youthmusictheatreuk.org

Internships are available in their London office for recent arts graduates or for professionals looking to change career direction. Also need UK-wide volunteers for one to two days per week.

Graduate opportunities & work experience

3M United Kingdom Plc
UK

+44 (0)8705 360036

www.3m.com

3M offer internships and Graduate programmes in industry and development. Gain valuable experience in an environment where you'll develop marketable skills and work on exciting projects. Whether you're heading into manufacturing, distribution, or marketing, our programs will put you in position for continued success and advancement in your career.

Absolute Radio
UK

020 7434 1215

www.absoluteradio.co.uk/about

Absolute Radio are looking for individuals with a love of music and a passion for radio broadcasting to experience working behind the scenes at some of the UK's biggest radio stations. Spend two weeks learning how radio stations work, from on-air presentation and production, through to the website, marketing and operation.

Accenture

UK

ukgraduates@accenture.com

+44 (0)808 1011169

www.accenture.com/ukschemes

Apply for graduate placements with Accenture, a global management consulting, technology services and outsourcing company.

Arcadia Group plc

UK

0844 243 0000

www.arcadiagroup.co.uk

They have placement postions in their finance and HR departments, suitable for those undertaking a year's placement as part of their degree. See their website for more details.

BBC Recruitment

UK

www.bbc.co.uk/careers

Work experience placements available across the UK in all areas. These are unpaid placements that can last up to four weeks. Competition is fierce so you need to apply at least a year in advance.

Camp Beaumont & Kingswood Camps

UK

recruitment@campbeaumont.co.uk

www.cbjobs.co.uk

Camp Beaumont offers a variety of job opportunities at its nationwide camps including team leaders, activity coordinators, child care, TEFL teaching and lifeguards. Full-time positions are available as well as work experience opportunities.

Cancer Research UK

UK

volunteering@cancer.org.uk

+44 (0)300 123 1022

www.cancerresearchuk.org

Internships of 12 week duration for people who wish to gain valuable work experience in fundraising, as well as marketing, campaigning and communications. Registered Charity No. 1089464.

Civil Service Recruitment

UK

www.civilservice.gov.uk/recruitment

There are a number of specific schemes open to new and experienced graduates looking for a career change. If you're successful, you could be posted to a number of government departments.

Engineering Development Trust (EDT)

UK

info@etrust.org.uk

01707 871520

www.etrust.org.uk

The EDT is the largest provider of STEM (science, technology, engineering and mathematics) enrichment activities for UK youth.

FCO (Foreign & Commonwealth Office)

UK

+44 (0) 20 7008 1500

www.fco.gov.uk

See the FCO website for more about careers and opportunities in the Diplomatic Service.

GlaxoSmithKline UK

UK

+44 (0) 20 8047 5000

www.gsk.com/en-gb/careers/graduates

Graduates can join us in a variety of exciting roles across several business functions. If you're enthusiastic, committed to making a difference and have a strong interest in healthcare, then we'd love to hear from you.

HSBC Holdings plc

UK

+44 (0) 20 7991 8888

www.hsbc.com/careers

HSBC has a worldwide graduate and internship programme. See their website for further details.

IBM UK Ltd

UK

ibmstudent@uk.ibm.com

023 9256 1000

www-05.ibm.com/employment/uk/

IBM run a number of Student Schemes for 'very talented individuals' in all aspects of their business.

IMI plc

UK

info@imiplc.com

+44 (0)121 717 3700

www.imiplc.com

IMI operates a global graduate development programme and offers vacation work from June to September to penultimate year engineering (mechanical, electrical or manufacturing) students leading to possible sponsorship through the final year at university.

Kraft Foods

UK

www.kraftheinzcompany.com

Each year Kraft Foods offer plenty of graduate and internship opportunities across Europe.

L'Oréal (UK) Ltd

UK

career.loreal.com/careers

L'Oréal offers internships to students in universities, business and engineering schools from diverse backgrounds and provide the opportunity to acquire substantial initial work experience in one of our areas of expertise: Operations, Finance, Marketing, Sales, Communications, Digital, and Human Resources. For three to twelve months you become a member of our teams, working on projects and achieving concrete objectives on which you are assessed.

Marks & Spencer Plc

UK

+44 (0) 20 7935 4422

careers.marksandspencer.com

The M&S Graduate scheme offers many different opportunities in Retail Management, Head Office and HR.

Penguin Group UK

UK

jobs@penguin.co.uk

www.penguinrandomhouse.co.uk

Penguin offers business internships which last for eight weeks, journalism internships at the Financial Times which last for twelve weeks, the Pearson Diversity Summer Internship Programme as well as two-week work experience placements throughout the year.

RAF

UK

+44 (0) 845 605 5555

www.raf.mod.uk/careers/

Work experience places are available in RAF bases all over the UK. As each base runs its own work experience programme you need to check the RAF website to find one near you.

visit: www.gap-year.com

Rock UK
UK

job.enquiry@rockuk.org

+44 (0)844 8000 222

www.rockuk.org

As an experienced Christian provider of Outdoor Adventure residentials and day visits for young people, Rock UK offer an exciting Gap Year Instructor Training Course. Contact us to find out more!

www.rockuk.org/work-for-us/gap-year-programme

S & N Genealogy
UK

manager@genealogysupplies.com

+44 (0) 1722 717007

www.sandn.net/vacancies.htm

Gap-year students required to do office work such as document scanning.

Santander UK
UK

www.santanderukgraduates.com

If you are a graduate interested in working with Santander UK, submit an application for consideration when a position arises.

UNHCR
UK

gbrloea@unhcr.org

+44 (0) 20 7759 8090

www.unhcr.org.uk/interns/index.html

The UNHCR have six month internships which give the participant the opportunity to gain valuable experience working with refugees.

Wesser Fundraising UK
UK

recruitment@wesser.co.uk

01462 704 865

www.wesser.co.uk

Wesser offers "live in" fundraising positions nationwide working in behalf of UK charities. All fundraisers are provided with a great pay package plus free accommodation including bills. No experience necessary.

Seasonal

Ardmore Language Schools
UK

info@theardmoregroup.com

01628 826699

www.ardmore-language-schools.com

Ardmore Language Schools run summer English courses for students from all over the world in 15 residential and two non-residential centres across the UK. Job opportunities are also available for TEFL graduates.

Brightsparks Recruitment
UK

recruitment@brightsparksUK.com

+44 (0)20 3627 9710

www.brightsparkslife.com

Brightsparks offers job opportunities to students, graduates and young professionals, providing guidance and support to help them get into their dream careers.

Camp Beaumont & Kingswood Camps

UK

recruitment@campbeaumont.co.uk

www.cbjobs.co.uk

Camp Beaumont offers a variety of job opportunities at its nationwide camps including team leaders, activity coordinators, child care, TEFL teaching and lifeguards. Full-time positions are available as well as work experience opportunities.

Crewseekers Ltd

UK

info@crewseekers.net

+44 (0)238 115 9207

www.crewseekers.net

We offer a personal service assisting people of all ages and experience levels looking for the opportunity to build up some sea miles, find professional sailing work and paid delivery jobs, gap year adventures, sailing weekends and holidays, or simply to go sailing with like minded sailors.

Facilities Management Catering

UK

resourcing.fmc@aeltc.com

+44 (0) 20 8971 2465

www.fmccatering.co.uk

If you would like to work at the most prestigious sporting event of the year then log onto our website now and click on the work opportunities page to apply online.

Fish4jobs

UK

customerservices@fish4.co.uk

0345 3000 406

www.fish4.co.uk

Search for temporary work, paid or unpaid, charity and fundraising jobs and seasonal holiday jobs abroad.

Malvern Outdoor Elements

UK

enquiries@malvernoutdoors.co.uk

01684 574546

www.malvernoutdoors.co.uk/ employment

Malvern offers job opportunities to people looking to work outdoors and help instruct visitors on a variety of exciting outdoor activities.

PGL

UK

recruitment@pgl.co.uk

0333 3212 123

www.pgl.co.uk/jobs

As the UK's market-leading provider of residential activity holidays and educational courses for children, PGL have an immense variety of Gap Year Jobs to offer for your Gap Year: and we pay you!

Robinwood Activity Centre Ltd

UK

careers@robinwood.co.uk

+44 (0)1706 811067

www.robinwoodcareers.co.uk

Robinwood is a leading provider of residential activity courses for Primary school groups, with three centres in the North of England. Job opportunities at their centres are also available.

Season to Season Employment

UK

enquiries@seasontoseasonemployment. com

0117 214 0769

www.seasontoseasonemployment.com

Season to Season Employment is a recruitment agency offering a bespoke service in both seasonal and permanent contracts within the hospitality business.

Fundraising

Home Fundraising
USA
enquiries@homefundraising.com
020 7089 4444
www.homefundraising.com
Home Fundraising offers job opportunities for fundraising in the UK, complete with training, good money and the satisfaction of working for a good cause.

Marie Curie Cancer Care (Head Office)
UK
supporter.relations@mariecurie.org.uk
0800 716 146
www.mariecurie.org.uk
Volunteer. Help in their shops, hospices and/or offices, or get involved in fundraising for Marie Curie (Registered Charity No. 207994).

Pell & Bales
UK
info@pellandbales.co.uk
+44 (0)20 7187 7187
www.pellandbales.co.uk
Pell & Bales are currently recruiting across our sites in London and Brighton and are looking for passionate, target driven people to join our team and help raise funds for some of the worlds leading charities.

Scope
UK
supportercare@scope.org.uk
+44 (0)20 7619 7100
www.scope.org.uk
Scope is a registered charity (No. 208231) for the disabled which needs your help in raising funds. Whether it's running, swimming, cycling or trekking, there is plenty you can do to help.

War on Want
UK
support@waronwant.org
+44 (0)20 7324 5040
www.waronwant.org
Run, walk, cycle, swap, bake, party - there are lots of ways to raise money for War on Want (Charity No. 208724). Whatever your fundraising challenge, your work will help in the fight against global injustice.

Volunteering

Action Centres UK
UK
enquiries@acuk.net
+44 (0)1299 272148
www.acuk.net
Action Centres UK provides international volunteers with the opportunity to gain valuable service-work experience in a safe and comfortable Christian environment.

Amnesty International
UK

sct@amnesty.org.uk

+44 (0) 20 7033 1777

www.amnesty.org.uk/volunteer

Amnesty International (registered charity No: 1051681) have a selection of volunteering vacancies throughout their UK offices. Volunteer roles are advertised on their website. Speculative applications are not accepted.

Beamish, The Living Museum of the North
UK

volunteering@beamish.org.uk

+44 (0)1913 704003

www.beamish.org.uk/volunteering

Beamish has hundreds of volunteers who make a huge contribution to all areas of the Museum in a wide range of diverse roles, and are always looking for more enthusiastic volunteers to join the team. Contribute to the running of Beamish across all areas in a wide range of roles, including engaging the visitors in the period areas, delivering family learning activities, assisting the Curatorial and Costume Teams behind the scenes and much more.

Beanstalk
UK

+44 (0)20 7729 4087

www.beanstalkcharity.org.uk

Volunteer Reading Help is a national charity, helping children who struggle with their reading to develop a love of reading and learning.

Blue Cross
UK

info@bluecross.org.uk

+44 (0) 300 777 1897

www.bluecross.org.uk

The Blue Cross is Britain's pet charity (No. 224392), providing practical support, information and advice for pet and horse owners. For information on volunteering visit their website.

Born Free Foundation
UK

info@bornfree.org.uk

+44 (0)1403 240 170

www.bornfree.org.uk

The Born Free Foundation has grown into a global force for wildlife. Volunteer with their major international projects devoted to animal welfare, conservation and education. They also list other possible overseas volunteering vacancies.

Camphill Communities in England & Wales
UK

www.camphill.org.uk

Camphill Communities in England and Wales offer opportunities for people with learning disabilities, mental health problems and other special needs to live, learn and work with others of all abilities in an atmosphere of mutual care and respect.

They welcome people from all over the world to join their work as resident Volunteers for a period of six months, a year or more.

Camphill Scotland

UK

info@camphillscotland.org.uk

+44 (0)1316 291520

www.camphillscotland.org.uk

Camphill communities in Scotland have a mixture of salaried staff, long term vocational co-workers and short term volunteers, who usually join the community for a year or two, though shorter placements may also be considered.

Cats Protection League

UK

volunteering@cats.org.uk

+44 (0)8707 708 649

www.cats.org.uk/get-involved/volunteering

Volunteering opportunities available in a wide variety of roles, please see our website for more details. Registered charity No. 203644.

Central Scotland Green Network Trust

UK

contact@csgnt.org.uk

+44 (0)1501 822015

www.csgnt.org.uk

CSGN organises volunteers to help with ecological improvements in Central Scotland. Work includes fence repairing and path building. Reg Charity SC015341

Centre for Alternative Technology

UK

fundraising@cat.org.uk

+44 (0) 1654 705 950

www.cat.org.uk

CAT has volunteer placements. Reg Charity 265239

Challenge Team UK

UK

info@challengeteamuk.org

(+44) 01323 721047

www.challengeteamuk.org

The Challenge Team UK is a group of young volunteers who educate teenagers about healthy sexuality.

Change Agents UK

UK

contact@changeagents.org.uk

01572 723419

www.changeagents.org.uk

CHANGE AGENTS UK are creating a force for a sustainable future; working with young people, graduates, businesses and communities motivated by sustainability to create change.

Children with Cancer

UK

info@childrenwithcancer.org.uk

+44 (0)20 7404 0808

www.childrenwithcancer.org.uk

Volunteer with us and help to save young lives. If you've got some spare time, and would like to help our charity, why not join our volunteer team.

Children's Country Holidays Fund

UK

volunteering@cchf-allaboutkids.org.uk

+44 (0) 1273 847 770

www.cchf-allaboutkids.org.uk

CCHF (registered charity number 206958) Volunteers required to help out on week long or weekend activity breaks for severely disadvantaged children.

Christian Aid Gap Year
UK
info@christian-aid.org
+44 (0)20 7620 4444
www.christianaid.org.uk

Have placements between mid-August and June each year for volunteers in their offices around the UK.

City Year UK
UK
info@cityyear.org.uk
020 7014 2680
www.cityyear.org.uk

City Year UK challenges young people to tackle educational inequality through a year of full-time voluntary service in schools. As well as having a huge impact on children's lives, it's a chance for you to develop leadership skills and invest in your own future.

Dementia Adventure
UK
volunteering@dementiaadventure.co.uk
01245 237548
www.dementiaadventure.co.uk/
volunteering

Dementia Adventure's mission is to enable people living with dementia to get outdoors, connect with nature, themselves and their community, and retain a sense of adventure in their lives.

Dogs Trust
UK
+44 (0)20 7837 0006
www.dogstrust.org.uk

Volunteers needed to help out in the following areas: fundraising, dog walking, dog socialising and pre-adoption home visiting. Registered Charity No. 227523.

Elizabeth Finn Homes
UK
enquiries@efhl.co.uk
+44 (0)20 8834 9200
www.efhl.co.uk

Charity (No. 207812) that aims to help those with limited resources who live in their own homes, or by providing accommodation for older people in their own care homes. Volunteers always needed.

Emmaus UK
UK
contact@emmaus.org.uk
+44 (0)300 303 7555
www.emmaus.org.uk

Emmaus Communities (Registered Charity No. 1064470) offer homeless people a home and full time work refurbishing and selling furniture and other donated goods. They list various volunteer opportunities on their website.

English Heritage
UK
volunteer.enquiries@english-heritage.org.uk
+44 (0)870 333 1181
www.english-heritage.org.uk

English Heritage are looking for people who are aged 18 and over to assist with workshops, tours and other activities associated with learning and school visits.

Friends of The Earth
UK
info@foe.co.uk
0207 490 1555
www.foe.co.uk

Friends of The Earth welcomes volunteers at their head office in London, or at any of their regional offices. Registered Charity No. 281681

Global Adventure Challenges Ltd

UK

enquiries@globaladventurechallenges.com

+44 (0) 1244 676 454

www.globaladventurechallenges.com

Raise money for your chosen charity whilst having the adventure of a lifetime. Many adventures to choose from are listed on their website.

Greenpeace

UK

recruitment.uk@greenpeace.org

+44 (0) 20 7865 8100

www.greenpeace.org.uk

Greenpeace need volunteers either as an active supporter or in their London office to help out with their administration.

Groundwork Oldham & Rochdale

UK

gor@groundwork.org.uk

+44 (0)161 624 1444

www.groundwork.org.uk

Whether you're looking to gain work experience, fulfil your passion in environmental issues or simply want to give a few hours a week to a cause that benefits your community Groundwork can help you to do something special.

Hearing Dogs for Deaf People

UK

volunteer@hearingdogs.org.uk

+44 (0)1844 348 100

www.hearingdogs.org.uk

Become a volunteer with Hearing Dogs for Deaf People (Registered charity No.293358). Contribute to the life changing work of this Charity by visiting their website and clicking on 'Get involved'.

Hebridean Whale & Dolphin Trust

UK

info@hwdt.org

+44 (0)1688 302620

www.whaledolphintrust.co.uk

Spend your break living and working aboard the Silurian, aiding in research and data collection of the Hebrides marine life. Learn about the UK's marine life with full cetacean and sea bird identification training, and gain sailing experience as you travel the British Isles.

ILA (Independent Living Alternatives)

UK

paservices@ilanet.co.uk

+44 (0)20 8369 6032

www.ilanet.co.uk

Aims to enable people who need personal assistance, to be able to live independently in the community and take full control of their lives.

Latin Link

UK

+44 (0)118 957 7100

www.latinlink.org.uk

Latin Link sends teams and individuals to work in mission with Latin American and Spanish Christians for between three weeks and four months. Registered Charity No. 1020826.

Macmillan Cancer Support

UK

cycling@macmillan.org.uk

020 7840 7875

www.macmillan.org.uk/londontoamsterdam

Share your skills to improve the lives of people affected by cancer. Assist our fundraising activities or support us in our offices and gain new experience whilst having fun. Registered Charity No. 261017.

Médecins Sans Frontières/ Doctors Without Borders (MSF)
UK

office-ldn@london.msf.org

+44 (0)20 7404 6600

www.msf.org.uk

MSF field staff worldwide give life-saving medical and technical assistance to people who would otherwise be denied access to basics such as healthcare, clean water and shelter. Annually, around 3,000 international volunteers join local staff helping populations in danger.

Mind
UK

contact@mind.org.uk

+44 (0) 20 8519 2122

www.mind.org.uk

Mind (Registered Charity No. 424348) would like to hear from you if you would like to take part in a fundraising event, or have an idea for fundraising for the charity.

Museum of London
UK

recruitment@museumoflondon.org.uk

+44 (0) 20 7814 5792

www.museumoflondon.org.uk

The Museum of London offers opportunities in a wide variety of departments across the Museum's three sites, enabling volunteers to get an insight into museum life and get involved in a number of different tasks and activities.

NSPCC
UK

recruitmentenquiry@nspcc.org.uk

+44 (0)20 7825 2500

www.nspcc.org.uk

Volunteers needed to help with fundraising, office work, manning the switchboard at Childline or even helping on a specific project. (Reg. Charity No. 216401)

OpportUNITY
UK

office@opportunityuk.org

07767 043 837

www.opportunityuk.org

OpportUNITY is a voluntary organisation with an aim to inspire, support and empower young people.

PDSA
UK

0800 854 194

www.pdsa.org.uk

A wide range of volunteering opportunities offered. Use the contact form on their website to find out about opportunities in the UK and Ireland. Registered Charity No. 208217.

Rainforest Concern
UK

info@rainforestconcern.org

+44 (0)1225 481 151

www.rainforestconcern.org

Sends volunteers to Ecuador, Costa Rica and Panama to work with important conservation programmes.

Revitalise
UK

volunteer@revitalise.org.uk

+44 (0)303 303 0148

www.revitalise.org.uk

Revitalise is a national charity providing short breaks and other services for people with physical disabilities, visually impaired people, and carers. They offer inspirational opportunities for volunteers through one of the largest, most diverse volunteer programmes in the UK.

RNLI
UK

+44 (0) 845 045 6999

jobs.rnli.org

From crewing the lifeboats and volunteer lifeguarding, to raising vital funds or awareness, or using your professional skills in our offices, there are a wide range of volunteer roles available at RNLI. You will receive first class training and equipment, guidance and support and be given the opportunity to make a difference in your local community, to save lives and be part of the larger RNLI family.

Rock UK
UK

job.enquiry@rockuk.org

+44 (0)844 8000 222

www.rockuk.org

At Frontier Centre (Northants), Rock UK operates a volunteer programme taking on overseas volunteers. Placements are for 9 months. Volunteers must be at least 18 years old and are typically up to 28 years old.

Royal Botanic Gardens
UK

kewvolunteer@kew.org

+44 (0) 20 8332 5655

www.kew.org/about/volunteer

Volunteers can help out at the Royal Botanic Gardens in four different areas: school & family, discovery, information and horticultural volunteers.

RSPB (Royal Society for the Protection of Birds)
UK

volunteers@rspb.org.uk

01767 680 551

www.rspb.org.uk/joinandhelp/volunteering

Want a career in conservation? Check out the volunteering pages on the RSPBs website for advice, volunteering opportunities and case studies (Registered Charity No. 207076)

RSPCA
UK

www.rspca.org.uk/volunteer

The RSPCA (registered charity no. 219099) are always looking for volunteers. Check out their website for vacancies in a home near you.

Samaritans
UK

volunteering@samaritans.org

+44 (0)3705 627282

www.samaritans.org

The Samaritans (Registered Charity No. 219432) depend entirely on volunteers. They are there 24/7 for anyone who needs help. Can you spare the time to help them?

Sense
UK

info@sense.org.uk

www.sense.org.uk

Volunteers always required by Sense (Registered Charity No. 289868) in a variety of areas. See their website for further details of how you can help.

Shelter

UK

info@shelter.org.uk

+44 (0) 844 515 2000

www.shelter.org.uk

Volunteers are integral to Shelter's fight against bad housing and homelessness. There are a range of different volunteering opportunities available and we support volunteers with a range of skills, experiences and backgrounds. (Charity No. 263710.)

TCV (The Conservation Volunteers)

UK

information@tcv.org.uk

+44 (0) 1302 388 883

www.tcv.org.uk

The Conservation Volunteers have been reclaiming green places since 1959.

The National Trust

UK

enquiries@nationaltrust.org.uk

0344 800 1895

www.nationaltrust.org.uk/get-involved/volunteer

Learn new skills whilst helping to conserve the UK's heritage. Volunteering opportunities can be found on their website. Registered Charity No. 205846.

The National Trust for Scotland

UK

0131 458 0354

www.nts.org.uk/Volunteering

The National Trust for Scotland is a conservation charity that protects and promotes Scotland's natural and cultural heritage. Contact them to find out about volunteering opportunities.

The Prince's Trust

UK

webinfops@princes-trust.org.uk

+44 (0)20 7543 1234

www.princes-trust.org.uk

Volunteer with the Prince's Trust (Registered Charity No. 1079675) and help young people achieve something with their lives. Opportunities in fundraising, personal mentoring, volunteer co-ordinator and training.

The Simon Community

UK

info@simoncommunity.org.uk

0207 485 6639

www.simoncommunity.org.uk

The Simon Community is a partnership of homeless people and volunteers living and working with London's homeless. They need full-time residential volunteers all year round. Registered Charity No. 283938.

The Waterway Recovery Group

UK

enquiries@wrg.org.uk

01494 783453 (Ext:604)

www.waterways.org.uk

WRG has helped restore many derelict waterways throughout Britain. Thanks to the hard work of the volunteers many canals have been reopened.

The Wildlife Trusts

UK

enquiry@wildlifetrusts.org

+44 (0) 1636 6777 11

www.wildlifetrusts.org

The Wildlife Trusts (Registered Charity No. 207238) always need volunteers. Check out their website or contact your local office for information about vacancies in your area.

Time for God
UK
office@timeforgod.org
+44 (0)1423 536 248
www.timeforgod.org

Time For God has 50 years experience creating full-time volunteering opportunities in the UK and abroad. Find out more about us and then get involved.

UNICEF UK
UK
+44 (0)300 330 5580
www.unicef.org.uk

UNICEF UK regularly recruit voluntary interns to support teams within the UK. These internships usually last between two and six months and are based at offices in London or Billericay.

vInspired
UK
info@vinspired.com
+44 (0)2079 607 000
www.vinspired.com

At vInspired we believe that your creativity, energy and optimism can change the world. We're dedicated to helping you improve your skills, confidence and employability whilst you raise vital funds to make a real difference.

Whizz-Kidz
UK
volunteers@whizz-kidz.org.uk
+44 (0)20 7233 6600
www.whizz-kidz.org.uk

Whizz-Kidz is looking for volunteers to join their national Volunteer Network, you just need to be 16 or older. If you have an open mind, tons of enthusiasm and a positive attitude there are opportunities to suit you!

Wild Futures' Monkey Sanctuary
UK
volunteer@wildfutures.org
+44 (0)1503 262 532
www.monkeysanctuary.org

Residential volunteering opportunities available, offering an ideal opportunity to learn more about primates and their conservation and welfare whilst also helping with the day-to-day running of a busy sanctuary.

World Horizons
UK
enquiries@worldhorizons.co.uk
01554 750005
www.worldhorizons.co.uk

Looking for adventure, ways to serve others and opportunities to grow in faith? Join with our teams around the world and make a difference, come on a Gap Year!

Youth Hostel Association
UK
volunteers@yha.org.uk
0800 0191 700
www.yha.org.uk/volunteering

If you've got some free time and would like to support YHA, there are many volunteering activities you can get involved with.

10

Volunteering in the UK

Archaeology

Council for British Archaeology
UK

webenquiry@archaeologyuk.org

+44 (0) 1904 671 417

new.archaeologyuk.org

CBA's magazine, British Archaeology, contains information about events and courses as well as digs. Reg Charity 287815.

School of Archaeology & Ancient History
UK

arch-anchist@le.ac.uk

+44 (0) 116 252 2611

www.le.ac.uk/archaeology/dl/dl_intro.html

Offers a series of modules in archaeology which can be studied purely for interest, or as part of a programme towards a Certificate in Archaeology.

University College London - Institute of Archaeology
UK

ioa-ugadmissions@ucl.ac.uk

+44 (0) 207 679 7495

www.ucl.ac.uk/archaeology/

UCL offers a range of short courses in archaeology many of which are open to members of the public.

University of Bristol - Department of Archaeology & Anthropology
UK

sart-ugadmin@bristol.ac.uk

+44 (0)117 954 6050

www.bristol.ac.uk/archanth

A variety of short courses offered, including: anthropology, archaeology, egyptology, history, Latin, Minoan, Roman and techniques. They also have a one week intensive 'get started in archaeology' course.

Art

Cardiff School of Art and Design
UK

csad@carditfmet.ac.uk

+44 (0) 29 2041 6154

www.cardiff-school-of-art-and-design.org

Cardiff School of Art and Design run a ten week summer school programme designed to introduce you to the variety of art and design.

London Art Portfolio
UK

julia@londonartportfolio.com

+44 (0)207 403 6881

www.londonartportfolio.com

We successfully help art, design and architecture students from all over the world to gain entry into top UK universities. We also offer art classes and summer school for enthusiasts of all abilities, and will soon be organising art-related trips to Italy.

For further information see page 248

The Heatherley School of Fine Art
UK
info@heatherleys.org
+44 (0) 20 7351 4190
www.heatherleys.org
The Heatherley School of Fine Art offers both vocational and part-time courses to students aged 18+, focusing on portraiture, figurative painting, sculpture and printmaking.

The Prince's Drawing School
UK
admin@princesdrawingschool.org
+44 (0) 20 7613 8568
www.princesdrawingschool.org
The Prince's Drawing School is an educational charity (No. 1101538) dedicated to teaching drawing from observation. Daytime, evening and summer school courses are run for artists and the general public.

University College London - Slade School of Fine Art
UK
slade.enquiries@ucl.ac.uk
+44 (0) 20 7679 2313
www.ucl.ac.uk/slade
The Slade offers various qualifications in Fine Art, in addition to evening, Saturday and Easter courses and summer school.

University of the Arts London - Camberwell College of Arts
UK
info@camberwell.arts.ac.uk
+44 (0) 20 7514 6302
www.camberwell.arts.ac.uk
The college offers undergraduate and postgraduate courses in Design and Fine Art, including Book Arts, Conservation, Designer-Maker, Fine Art Digital, Illustration and Printmaking.

University of the Arts London - Central Saint Martins
UK
info@csm.arts.ac.uk
+44 (0)20 7514 7000
www.csm.arts.ac.uk
The college offers foundation, undergraduate, postgraduate and short courses in Acting, Directing, Graphic Design, Animation, Textile Design, Fashion, Ceramic Design, Architecture, Fine Art and more.

University of the Arts London - Chelsea College of Arts
UK
info@chelsea.arts.ac.uk
+44 (0) 20 7514 7751
www.chelsea.arts.ac.uk
The college offers undergraduate and postgraduate courses in Fine Art, Graphic Design Communication, Textile Design, Interior and Spatial Design and Curating and Collections.

University of the Arts London - Wimbledon College of Arts
UK
info@wimbledon.arts.ac.uk
+44 (0) 20 7514 9641
www.wimbledon.arts.ac.uk
The college offers undergraduate and postgraduate courses in Fine Art, Theatre and Screen, Drawing, Digital Theatre, Painting and Theatre Design.

Cookery

Ashburton Cookery School
UK
info@ashburtoncookeryschool.co.uk
+44 (0) 1364 652784
www.ashburtoncookeryschool.co.uk
Cookery courses available from one to five days.

Belle Isle School of Cookery

UK

info@irishcookeryschool.com

+44 (028)66 385 228

www.irishcookeryschool.com

Essential Cooking is an intensive four week course designed for people who are interested in learning the key skills for a gap-year job in cooking

Cookery at The Grange

UK

info@cookeryatthegrange.co.uk

+44 (0)1373 836099

www.cookeryatthegrange.co.uk

Cookery at the Grange has been running the outstanding four week, residential Essential Cookery Courses since 1981. Fantastic local ingredients from the Somerset countryside near Bath, are used to learn to cook really good food, for fun, for a gap year or for a career.

Cookery School at Little Portland Street

UK

info@cookeryschool.co.uk

0207 631 4590

www.cookeryschool.co.uk/classes/cooks-certificate-in-food-wine/

Cookery School at Little Portland Street has something to offer all food lovers: check out the huge array of classes on offer on our website.

Edinburgh New Town Cookery School

UK

info@entcs.co.uk

+44 (0)131 226 4314

www.entcs.co.uk

1, 3 and 6 month courses designed for gap year students who want to work in ski chalets, luxury live aboard yachts or shooting lodges.

Edinburgh School of Food and Wine

UK

info@esfw.com

0131 333 5001

www.esfw.com

Courses of interest to gappers are the four week Intensive Certificate Course which is geared towards chalet work, and the one week Survival Course which is ideally suited to those leaving home for the first time.

Food of Course

UK

info@foodofcourse.co.uk

+44 (0) 1749 860116

www.foodofcourse.co.uk

A four-week residential course providing all essential skills to cook in a ski chalet, on a yacht or in holiday homes worldwide.

Gordon Ramsay's Tante Marie Culinary Academy

UK

info@tantemarie.co.uk

+44 (0) 1483 726957

www.tantemarie.co.uk

Tante Marie Culinary Academy is the UK's oldest independent cookery school and is now the only school in the world able to award both the internationally acclaimed Cordon Bleu Diploma and the CTH Level 4 Diploma in Professional Culinary Arts.

Le Cordon Bleu

UK

london@cordonbleu.edu

+44 (0) 20 7400 3900

www.lcblondon.com

Le Cordon Bleu has courses ranging from their famous diplomas in 'Cuisine and Pâtisserie' to shorter courses in techniques, seasonal cooking, essentials and healthy eating.

Leiths School of Food and Wine

UK

info@leiths.com

+44 (0)20 8749 6400

www.leiths.com

Learn how to cook and earn money from it on your gap year. Leiths certificate cookery courses will give you the confidence and skill to achieve this.

Swinton Park Cookery School

UK

cookeryschool@swintonpark.com

+44 (0) 1765 680900

www.swintonpark.com

Overlooking the exquisite parkland of Swinton Park, the school offers two-day, one-day and half-day classes in a range of themes from Game to Foraging courses.

The Avenue Cookery School

UK

info@theavenuecookeryschool.com

+44 (0)7958 171 787

www.theavenuecookeryschool.com

Offer one and two week courses aimed specifically at gap-year students, chalet assistants and undergraduates.

The Bertinet Kitchen

UK

info@thebertinetkitchen.com

+44 (0) 1225 445531

www.thebertinetkitchen.com

The Bertinet Kitchen offers a range of relaxed and fun courses for food lovers of all abilities and specialist baking and bread-making courses for amateurs and professionals alike.

The Cook Academy (Hampshire)

UK

kate@cookacademy.co.uk

01252 793648

www.cookacademy.co.uk

The Cook Academy offers cookery tuition and experiences for all ages, abilities and occasions.

The Orchards School of Cookery

UK

isabel@orchardscookery.co.uk

01789 490 259

www.orchardscookery.co.uk

Orchards Cookery specialises in training and recruiting Chalet Cooks and also runs Off to University courses, Designer Dinner party courses, Corporate Days and One and Two Day cookery courses.

The School of Artisan Food

UK

info@schoolofartisanfood.org

01909 532171

www.schoolofartisanfood.org

Based in the heart of Sherwood Forest, The School of Artisan Food teaches all aspects of artisan food production including baking and patisserie, butchery and charcuterie, cheese making, brewing, preserves, ice cream and chocolate making for people of all skill levels to. Offers a wide range of short courses, and a one year Advanced Diploma.

The Vegetarian Society Cookery School
UK

cookery@vegsoc.org

0161 925 2000

www.vegsoccookeryschool.org

The Vegetarian Society Cookery School is the world's premier vegetarian cookery school. We teach both the general public and professionals the many aspects of vegetarian cuisine through workshops held at our venues in Altrincham & London. Our courses are open to everyone, whether vegetarian or not.

Webbe's Cookery School
UK

+44 (0)1797 222226

www.webbesrestaurants.co.uk

Respected five-day, complete, hands-on, intensive, cutting edge foundation cooking certificate course for healthy eating and cooking for friends on a budget at university and beyond.

White Pepper Cookery School
UK

info@white-pepper.co.uk

+44 (0)1202 280050

www.white-pepper.co.uk

With informative and engaging cooking classes, White Pepper offers classes in a variety of cuisines including Japanese, Italian, Thai as well as courses in Foraging, French Patisserie and more.

Yorkshire Wolds Cookery School
UK

info@yorkshirewoldscookeryschool. co.uk

+44 (0)1377 270607

yorkshirewoldscookeryschool.co.uk

Situated in the picturesque Yorkshire countryside, the school offers Gold Residential Duke of Edinburgh courses as well as "Student Gap Year Survival Skills".

Drama

Peer Productions
UK

admin@peerproductions.co.uk

01483 476825

www.peerproductions.co.uk

This free intensive one year, full time course for 17-23-year-olds, offers practical experience, the opportunity for artistic development and support moving forward.

RADA (Royal Academy of Dramatic Art)
UK

enquiries@rada.ac.uk

+44 (0)20 7636 7076

www.rada.ac.uk

This legendary drama college runs a variety of summer school courses.

Royal Central School of Speech and Drama
UK

enquiries@cssd.ac.uk

+44 (0) 20 7722 8183

www.cssd.ac.uk/gapyear

Central offers short courses in acting, singing, stand-up comedy, puppetry, cabaret and burlesque, and directing.

For further information see page 244

Springs Dance Company
UK

info@springsdancecompany.org.uk

07775 628 442

www.springsdancecompany.org.uk/apprenticeships

Springs Dance Company offers a 3 or 9 month intensive dance course that focuses on the creation, performance and teaching of dance work inspired by and expressive of the Christian faith.

The Oxford School of Drama
UK

info@oxforddrama.ac.uk

+44 (0) 1993 812883

www.oxforddrama.ac.uk

The Oxford School of Drama runs a six-month Foundation Course, including acting, voice, movement, music and stage fighting. Registered Charity No. 1072770.

Year Out Drama
UK

yearoutdrama@stratford.ac.uk

01789 266 245

www.yearoutdrama.co.uk

Full-time practical drama course with a unique Company feel; work with theatre professionals to develop a wide range of skills; perform in a variety of productions; write and direct your own work; benefit from close contact with the RSC.

Driving

AA (Automobile Association)
UK

+44 (0) 161 495 8945

www.theaa.co.uk

The AA website has lots of useful information on driving in the UK and abroad, including stuff about breakdown, insurance and travel planning. You can find hotels, good places to stop whilst driving and you're even able to find out about up-to-date traffic news.

DVLA (Driver & Vehicle Licencing Agency)
UK

www.dvla.gov.uk

The DVLA offers information on driving licences, vehicle registration, vehicle taxation and various motoring-related matters.

DVSA (Driver & Vehicle Standards Agency)
UK

customer.services@dsa.gsi.gov.uk

0300 200 1122

www.gov.uk/dvsa

The DVSA offers information on driving instructors and schools, theory and practical driving tests and various other motoring-related matters.

RAC Motoring Services
UK

+44 (0)1922 437000

www.rac.co.uk

The RAC website has lots of useful information on driving in the UK and abroad, with breakdown, insurance and other services.

Fashion & Design

Holts Academy
UK

info@holtsacademy.com

+44 (0)20 7405 0197

www.holtsacademy.com

Holts Academy offer 1-year part-time jewellery making & design diploma courses for those passionate about jewellery. Right in London's Jewellery District, government funding available for eligible students.

Leicester College - St Margaret's

UK

info@leicestercollege.ac.uk

+44 (0) 116 224 2240

www.leicestercollege.ac.uk

Has part-time courses in footwear, fabrics and pattern cutting.

Newcastle College

UK

enquiries@ncl-coll.ac.uk

+44 (0) 191 200 4000

www.ncl-coll.ac.uk

Short courses available in fashion illustration, bridalwear design, textile dyeing and printing, pattern cutting and embroidery.

The Fashion Retail Academy

UK

info@fra.ac.uk

+44 (0)300 247 4000

www.fashionretailacademy.ac.uk

Short courses available in visual merchandising, styling, PR, buying and range planning there are also tailor-made courses for those wishing to run their own retail business.

The Session School

UK

info@thesessionschool.com

+44 (0)20 7998 7353

www.thesessionschool.com

Independent make-up school for professional make-up courses, workshops and masterclasses for all levels and abilities, with tuition by make-up experts.

University of the Arts London - London College of Fashion

UK

shortcourses@fashion.arts.ac.uk

+44 (0) 20 7514 7566

www.fashion.arts.ac.uk

Short courses available in pattern cutting, principles of styling techniques, film and TV make up, childrenswear and maternitywear, retro fashion design and how to recycle your second hand clothes.

Westminster School of Media, Arts and Design

UK

course-enquiries@westminster.ac.uk

+44 (0)20 7911 5000

www.westminster.ac.uk

Westminster School of Media, Arts and Design provides courses in Art and Design, Fashion, Television, Film and Moving Image, Journalism and Mass Communication, Music and Photography.

Land studies

Bishop Burton College

UK

+44 (0)1964 553 000

www.bishopburton.ac.uk

Short courses available in tractor driving, pest control, tree felling, sheep shearing, animal husbandry and more...

Capel Manor College

UK

enquiries@capel.ac.uk

+44 (0) 8456 122 122

www.capel.ac.uk

They have short courses in lorinery, flower arranging, CAD in garden design, practical gardening, aboriculture, botanical illustration, leathercraft and more ...

Chichester College
UK

+44 (0) 1243 786321

www.chichester.ac.uk

Short courses available In animal care, farming, bushcraft, coppicing, hedgerow planting and managment, watercourse management, moorland management and more ...

Plumpton College
UK

+44 (0) 1273 890 454

www.plumpton.ac.uk

Courses available in animal care, welding, tractor driving, machinery, wine trade, aboriculture, chainsaw, bushcraft, pond management, wildlife, woodcraft and more...

Royal Agricultural University
UK

admissions@rau.ac.uk

+44 (0)1285 652531

www.rau.ac.uk

The Royal Agricultural University offers various courses in agriculture, conservation and animal studies.

South Staffordshire College
UK

enquiries@southstaffs.ac.uk

+44 (0)300 456 2424

www.southstaffs.ac.uk

Whether you want to get into the best university or land yourself a top job, we will help you get where you want to be. At South Staffordshire College, there are lots of subjects and courses to choose from whether you're just leaving school or embarking on a course later in your career.

Sparsholt College
UK

enquiry@sparsholt.ac.uk

+44 (0) 1962 776441

www.sparsholt.ac.uk

Have part-time courses in forklift operation, tractor driving, health & safety, horticulture, floristy, landscaping and more.

The Open College of Equine Studies
UK

info@equinestudies.co.uk

+44 (0)1284 811 401

www.equinestudies.co.uk

The college offers a series of short courses available in horse and pony care, behaviour, training, physiology and breeding as well as stable and business management courses.

Warwickshire College - Moreton Morrell
UK

info@warkscol.ac.uk

0300 45 600 47

www.warkscol.ac.uk

The college spans 750 acres of countryside, offering agriculture and equine studies. Courses range from brickwork, carpentry and joinery to forestry, tree management and arboriculture, with floristry and flower arranging also available. Courses also include animal welfare and vet nursing in addition to equine and farriery.

Ardmore Language Schools
UK
info@theardmoregroup.com
01628 826699
www.ardmore-language-schools.com

Ardmore Language Schools run summer English courses for students from all over the world in 15 residential and two non-residential centres across the UK. Job opportunities are also available for TEFL graduates.

Berlitz - London
UK
+44 (0) 20 7611 9640
www.berlitz.co.uk

International language school. Intense courses in Chinese French, German, Italian, Japanese, Portuguese, Russian and Spanish available. Other schools in the UK can be found in Birmingham, Brighton, Bristol, Edinburgh, Manchester and Oxford.

Canning House
UK
enquiries@canninghouse.org
+44 (0)20 7811 5600
www.canninghouse.org

Canning House runs evening courses in Brazilian Portuguese, as well as a wide range of events on Latin America, Spain and Portugal.

International House London
UK
info@ihworld.com
+44 (0)207 394 6580
www.ihworld.com

Worldwide network of language schools offering courses in Arabic, Chinese, French, German, Italian, Japanese and Spanish.

Italian Cultural Institute in London
UK
icilondon@esteri.it
+44 (0) 20 7235 1461
www.icilondon.esteri.it/IIC_Londra

The Italian Cultural Institute has a wide programme of Italian language courses as well as a mass of information about Italy and its culture.

Native Monks
USA
support@nativemonks.com
nativemonks.com

Get the best value when you choose from hundreds of tutors from all over the world, send them a message, and fix a time for one-to-one lessons with your chosen tutor.

Oxford International Study Centre
UK
international@oxintstudycentre.com
+44 (0)1865 201009
www.oxintstudycentre.com

Spend a semester or year in the academically exciting and beautiful city of Oxford. OISC offers tailor-made programmes with a choice of over 30 subjects.

Rosetta Stone (UK) Ltd
UK
cs@rosettastone.co.uk
0800 005 1220
www.rosettastone.co.uk

Learn languages with Rosetta Stone's interactive CD-ROM software plus online features.

11

Learning in the UK

413

The Japan Foundation - London Language Centre
UK

info.language@jpf.org.uk

+44 (0)20 3102 5021

www.jpf.org.uk/language

The Japan Foundation London Language Centre provides courses in Japanese. Also has regular newsletter and resource library.

Music

BIMM 1
UK

info@bimm.co.uk

+44 1273 626 666

www.bimm.co.uk

Various part-time courses available, also summer schools, for bass, drums, guitar, vocals, songwriting and live sound/tour management.

British Kodály Academy
UK

enquiries@britishkodalyacademy.org

+44 (0) 208 651 3728

www.britishkodalyacademy.org

The Academy runs various music courses for teachers and young children, but also have courses for those wishing to improve their skills.

Dartington International Summer School
UK

summerschool@dartington.org

+44 (0) 1803 847 080

www.dartington.org/summer-school

Dartington International Summer School (Registered Charity No. 279756) is both a festival and a music school. Teaching and performing takes place all day, every day.

Drum Camp
UK

info@drumcamp.co.uk

07858 478247

www.drumcamp.co.uk

Drum Camp is an annual worldwide percussion event in Norfolk specialising in world rhythms and drum and dance programs. Offers an amazing variety of classes over four days, in music, singing and dance.

English Camerata
UK

01923 853309

www.englishcamerata.org.uk

English Camerata offer a Chamber Music Summer Course which provides extensive coaching in an exciting classical chamber music environment for ensembles and instrumentalists playing a variety of instruments.

Lake District Summer Music
UK

info@ldsm.org.uk

+44 (0)1539 742620

www.ldsm.org.uk

The Lake District Summer Music School is an ensemble-based course for string players and pianists intending to pursue careers as professional musicians. Registered Charity no 516350.

London Music School
UK

info@londonmusicschool.com

+44(0)208 986 7885

www.tlms.co.uk

The London Music School offers a Diploma in Music Technology, open to anyone with musical ability aged 17 or over. The course explores professional recording and you get to use a 24-track studio.

London School of Sound

UK

info@londonschoolofsound.co.uk

+44 (0) 20 7720 6183

www.londonschoolofsound.co.uk

Based in the recording studio previously owned by Pink Floyd, we offer part and full-time courses of between five weeks and two years in music production, sound engineering and DJ skills.

NLMS Music Summer School

UK

c.gomme@btinternet.com

www.nlmsmusic-summerschool.co.uk

Each year over 100 enthusiastic adult amateur musicians get together for a week of enjoyment.

North London Piano School

UK

+44 (0) 20 8958 5206

www.learn-music.com/nlps2

The North London Piano School runs an annual International Summer Course. Courses are intensive and tailored to each participants' skills, needs and aspirations and offer a record number of tuition hours within a week long course.

The DJ Academy Organisation

UK

andyking221@btinternet.com

07980 915424

www.djacademy.org.uk

Offer an eight-week part time DJ course (in various cities in the UK), private tuition, one day superskills course, the ultimate mobile DJ course and the superclub experience.

The Recording Workshop

UK

recordingworks@btconnect.com

+44 (0) 20 896 88 222

www.recordwk.dircon.co.uk

The Recording Workshop offer part time and full time courses on all aspects of music production, sound engineering and music technology.

Photography

Cambridge TV School

UK

bob@cambridge-tv.co.uk

01223 750890

www.cambridgetvschool.co.uk

Learn the skills required and produce broadcast-quality programmes with a full-time intensive one term course at Cambridge TV School.

DigitalMasterclass Ltd

UK

brian@digitalmasterclass.co.uk

+44 (0)1303 230958

www.digitalmasterclass.co.uk

London School of Photography

UK

lsp@lsptraining.co.uk

+44 (0)203 691 7680

londonschoolofphotography.com

Short courses available in digital photography, photojournalism, as well as travel, adventure and street photography. Small classes of up to eight people. One to one training also available.

Photo Opportunity Ltd

UK

chris@photoopportunity.co.uk

+44 (0)7850 652911

www.photoopportunity.co.uk

Courses offered lasting from one to five days in length. Tailored to suit your own particular needs and classes are small.

Photofusion

UK

info@photofusion.org

+44 (0) 20 7738 5774

www.photofusion.org

This independent photography resource centre, situated in Brixton, offers digital photography courses.

The EOS Training Academy

UK

info@eostrainingacademy.co.uk

+44 (0)1869 3317412

www.eostrainingacademy.co.uk

Experience Seminars hosts a range of workshops throughout the UK, which are designed to provide a fast track way of learning photography and digital imaging techniques.

The Photography Institute

UK

info@thephotographyinstitute.co.uk

www.thephotographyinstitute.co.uk

The Institute provides an online diploma course in photography, with contributions from leading photographers.

The Photography School

UK

info@thephotographyschool.co.uk

+44 (0)1580 201180

www.thephotographyschool.co.uk

Try your hand at photography with intensive photography courses for beginners and professionals alike at The Photography School.

The Royal Photographic Society

UK

reception@rps.org

+44 (0) 1225 325 733

www.rps.org/learning

The RPS holds various photography workshops for human, landscape and floral photography, printing and development and digital manipulation software.

The Trained Eye

UK

info@thetrainedeye.co.uk

+44 (0)1494 353637

www.thetrainedeye.co.uk

Offer creative courses in wedding and portrait photography, for amateurs or advanced photographers to improve their skills.

Sport

Ace Adventure

UK

info@aceadventures.co.uk

+44 (0)330 555 0313

www.aceadventures.co.uk

Ace Adventure offers numerous activities, situated in the beautiful Scottish highlands. Activities include exciting water and land sports such as white water rafting, canoeing, kayaking, canyoning, paintball and even bungee jumping.

Active Outdoor Pursuits

UK

info@activeoutdoorpursuits.com

+44 (0)1540 210000

www.activeoutdoorpursuits.com

Active Outdoor Pursuits provides a range of sports for all weathers. Summer activities include water sports such as white water rafting, canoeing or kayaking, whilst land sports include rock climbing & abseiling and mountain biking. Winter sports include skiing, snowboarding and mountaineering are available.

BASP UK Ltd

UK

firstaid@basp.org.uk

+44 (0) 1855 811 443

www.basp.org.uk

BASP offers First Aid and Safety Training courses designed specifically for the outdoor user, suitable for all NGB Awards.

Big Squid Scuba Diving Training and Travel

UK

info@bigsquid.co.uk

0207 627 0700

www.bigsquid.co.uk

Big Squid offers a variety of dive courses using the PADI and TDI systems of diver education.

Bowman Yacht Charters Cornwall

UK

info@bowmanyachtcharters.com

01326 210582

www.bowmanyachtcharters.com

Sailing experience day trips & yacht charters around Cornwall, including Falmouth Bay, St Mawes, Feock, River Fal, Penzance, Coverack, Helford River, Fowey and The Isles of Scilly.

British Hang Gliding & Paragliding Association Ltd

UK

office@bhpa.co.uk

+44 (0)116 289 4316

www.bhpa.co.uk

The BHPA oversees the standards of instructor training and runs coaching course for pilots. They also list all approved schools in the field of paragliding, hang gliding and parascending.

British Offshore Sailing School - BOSS

UK

+44 (0) 23 8045 7733

www.boss-sail.co.uk

BOSS offers complete RYA shore-based and practical training courses, also women only courses, from Hamble Point Marina.

British Sub Aqua Club

UK

info@bsac.com

+44 (0) 151 350 6200

www.bsac.com

With 1,000+ friendly dive clubs all around the UK (and some overseas) BSAC offers accessible, affordable scuba diving lessons. With the right training and support, you could be very soon enjoying your own scuba diving adventure.

Canyoning.co.uk

UK

info@canyoning.co.uk

+44 (0)1887 829706

canyoning.co.uk

Canyoning.co.uk offer multiple canyoning locations throughout Scotland. A combination of climbing, abseiling, swimming, jumping. Canyoning is a full on adventure activity which is sure to build confidence and adventure spirit.

417

Cornish Wave Mobile Surf School

UK

+44 (0)1637 872031

www.cornishwave.com

Cornish Wave specialise in delivering bespoke Surfing lessons, Coasteering sessions and Bushcraft Wild Camp Experiences to individuals, small groups, and families in and around Newquay, Cornwall, UK.

CricketCoachMaster Academy

UK

info@ccmacademy.co.uk

+44 (0) 7815 081744

www.ccmacademy.co.uk

The CCM Academy has a coaching programme to further develop players with the recognised potential to play at county and international level.

Curling in Kent

UK

info@curlinginkent.co.uk

+44 (0)1892 826 004

www.fentonsrink.co.uk

Come to Fenton's Rink and try your hand at this exciting Olympic sport. New season begins 1st October.

Dream Fencing Club

UK

dreamfencing@gmail.com

07581 782848

www.dreamfencing.co.uk

Dream Fencing Club aims to introduce this Olympic sport to adults and children in the London area, offering first-class and well-coached fencing opportunities for all ages. The club is for beginners and experienced fencers alike and provides high quality training which not only improves your physical condition but also your mental concentration, coordination, self-discipline and emotional control.

Fly Sussex Paragliding

UK

info@flysussex.com

+44 (0) 1273 858 170

www.flysussex.com

Learn to paraglide or hang glide over the beautiful Sussex countryside.

Glasgow Ski & Snowboard Centre

UK

info@ski-glasgow.org

+44 (0) 141 427 4991

www.ski-glasgow.org

Learn to ski, improve your existing skills or learn to snowboard. Fully qualified instructors waiting to teach you.

Green Dragons

UK

fly@greendragons.co.uk

01883 652 666

www.greendragons.co.uk

Paragliding and hang gliding centre. You do not need any experience or knowledge, just the desire to fly and follow your instructor's guidance on positions for take off, time spent in the air and landing.

Jubilee Sailing Trust

UK

info@jst.org.uk

+44 (0) 23 8042 6868

www.jst.org.uk

Tall Ships Sailing Trust. Join their JST Youth Leadership@Sea Scheme, no sailing experience needed. Registered Charity No. 277810.

London Fencing Club

UK

+44 (0)7951 414409

www.londonfencingclub.co.uk

Fencing tuition available in various centres in London - beginners to advanced training available.

London Scuba Diving School

UK

info@londonscuba.com

0845 544 1312

www.londonscuba.com

The London Scuba Diving School teaches beginners in swimming pools in Battersea and Bayswater. They also offer advanced courses for the experienced diver.

Mendip Outdoor Pursuits

UK

info@mendip.me

+44 (0)1934 834 877

www.mendipoutdoorpursuits.co.uk

Lessons in abseiling, archery, bridge building, caving, climbing, bush craft, kayaking, navigation, orienteering and more available.

Nae Limits

UK

info@naelimits.co.uk

01796 482600

www.naelimits.co.uk

Nae Limits has over 14 adrenaline-fuelled water and land adventure activities for you to experience, whether you are planning a stag do activity, family activity break, team building event or just fancy a day out to remember! Tackle some of the best White Water Rafting Scotland has to offer or kick up your canyoning a gear in one of our private exclusive venues or get dirty on our Quad Biking Trek.

New Forest Activities

UK

info@newforestactivities.co.uk

+44 (0) 1590 612 377

www.newforestactivities.co.uk

Organises group activities such as canoeing, rope work, cycling and climbing. Also offer environmental courses in the New Forest.

Newquay Activity Centre

UK

info@newquayactivitycentre.co.uk

+44 (0)1637 879571

www.newquayactivitycentre.co.uk

Newquay Activity Centre offers great opportunities for lovers of water-sports. Activities include surfing, coasteering and bodyboarding. Available to beginners or experts, with provision for Hen & Stag parties, school outings, family groups and military exercises.

North London Skydiving Centre Ltd

UK

office@ukskydiving.com

+44 (0)1354 699 088

www.ukskydiving.com

North London Skydiving Centre offers both TAFF and AFF courses to become a qualified skydiver as well as parachute jumping, wind tunnel experiences, and hovercraft piloting lessons.

Oyster Luxury Travel and Diving Ltd

UK

info@oysterdiving.com

0800 699 0243

www.oysterdiving.com

Oyster Diving is a PADI Scuba Diving and Travel Centre. Our facilities are in West London, Soho Central London, Brighton & Hove, Surrey & Berkshire and Oxford.

Plas y Brenin - The National Mountain Centre

UK

info@pyb.co.uk

+44 (0) 1690 720 214

www.pyb.co.uk

For those hoping to reach dizzy heights, Plas y Brenin offers a vast range of activities and courses.

419

Pod Zorbing
UK

info@zorbing.co.uk

+44 (0)208 935 5638

www.zorbing.co.uk

Ever fancied hurtling down a hill in a huge inflatable ball? With a choice of Harness or Hydro Zorbing, Pod Zorbing offers great, professional Zorbing experiences with a true fun factor.

Poole Harbour Watersports
UK

info@pooleharbour.co.uk

+44 (0) 1202 700503

www.pooleharbour.co.uk

Learn to windsurf and kitesurf at Poole in Dorset. Courses available for both beginners and improvers.

ProAdventure Limited
UK

sales@proadventure.co.uk

+44 (0)1978 860605

www.proadventure.co.uk

Based in Wales, ProAdventure offers different activity courses around the UK, including canoeing, kayaking, rock climbing and mountain biking.

Skydive GB
UK

info@skydivegb.com

+44 (0)1262 228033

www.skydivebrid.co.uk

Skydive GB specialises in introducing people to the exciting sport of skydiving, whether it's jumping for charity, a one-off experience or something you want to take up as a hobby or sport.

South Cambridgeshire Equestrian Centre
UK

+44 (0) 1763 263 213

www.scec.co.uk

This riding school is set in 260 acres of Cambridgeshire countryside. They offer riding tuition to the beginner and also more advanced teaching for experienced riders.

Splash White Water Rafting
UK

info@rafting.co.uk

+44 (0)1887 829706

rafting.co.uk

Splash White Water Rafting offers a host of adventure activities. Based in Aberfeldy & Glasgow. Rafting, Canyoning, Paintball, Abseiling and more. Also offering rafting in the heart of Glasgow.

Sportscotland National Centre Cumbrae
UK

cumbraecentre@sportscotland.org.uk

+44(0) 1475 530757

www.nationalcentrecumbrae.org.uk

Sportscotland national watersport centre offer a range of courses from a fully residential three weeks Powerboat Instructor or 18 weeks Professional Yachtmaster Training, to a one day introduction to Windsurfing.

Suffolk Ski Centre
UK

info@suffolkskicentre.co.uk

+44 (0) 1473 602347

www.suffolkskicentre.co.uk

Learn to ski or snowboard in Suffolk. Courses also available for those wishing to improve their existing skills.

Sussex Polo Club

UK

info@sussexpolo.co.uk

+44 (0) 1342 714 920

www.sussexpolo.co.uk

Sussex Polo is a professional and welcoming club, popular with players, sponsors and spectators. Ideal for players wanting high standards of low goal polo or to learn to play in a relaxed and friendly atmosphere all year round.

The Talland School of Equitation

UK

office@talland.net

01285 740 155

www.talland.net

World renowned BHS and ABRS approved equestrian centre offering top class training for professional qualifications. Variety of courses including competition training on quality horses.

Tollymore Mountain Centre

UK

livetheadventure@tollymore.com

+44 (0)28 4372 2158

www.tollymore.com

Tollymore have a range of courses designed to suit your own skills and experience. Their courses include rambling, mountaineering, climbing, canoeing and first aid.

UK Parachuting

UK

jump@ukparachuting.co.uk

07769 721036

www.ukparachuting.co.uk

AFF courses available. Also tandem skydiving and Accelerated Free Fall tuition slots available every day.

UKSA (United Kingdom Sailing Academy)

UK

info@uksa.org

+44 (0)1983 294941

www.uksa.org

Entry level training for work crewing on superyachts, employment in the yachting industry, or train to become a watersports instructor. Spend a few weeks at UKSA and be ready for the working season. Funding options. Travel the world!

Vertical Descents Ltd

UK

cornwall@verticaldescents.com

07891 264342

www.verticaldescents.com

Vertical Descents offer a variety of water and land sports - from surfing, body boarding and white water rafting to climbing & abseiling, go-karting and paintball - plus many more, including extreme sports. Perfect for school trips and corporate and school outings.

Wellington Riding

UK

info@wellington-riding.co.uk

+44 (0) 118 932 6308

www.wellington-riding.co.uk

A riding school and livery yard set in 300 acres of the Hampshire countryside. Wellington Riding offers junior courses for children and adult tailor-made courses to enhance riding and horse care at any level.

Golders Green Teacher Training Centre

UK

+44 (0) 208 905 5467

www.englishlanguagecollege.co.uk

Golders Green College offers high quality English language courses for overseas students, including TEFL/TESOL courses.

ITC - Intensive TEFL Courses

UK

info@tefl.co.uk

+44 (0) 8456 445464

www.tefl.co.uk

Intensive TEFL Courses (ITC) have been running weekend TEFL (Teach English as a Foreign Language) courses throughout the UK since 1993.

LTTC - London Teacher Training College

UK

lttc@teachenglish.co.uk

+44 (0)208 133 2027

www.teachenglish.co.uk

Over the years the college has trained a vast number of teachers from around the world, and prides itself on the quality of its courses and the individual attention it provides every student who enrols.

OxfordTEFL

UK

tesol@oxfordtefl.com

+34 93 458 0111

www.oxfordtefl.com

OxfordTEFL offer a four week training course, accredited by Trinity College London, at the end of which you should get a Certificate in TEFL.

TEFL course at The London School of English

UK

+44 (0)20 7605 4142

www.londonschool.com/courses/london/tefl-tesol

TEFL course in London to give you qualifications to become an English Teacher. 4 weeks, qualified team and workshop on finding a teaching job.

TESOL Direct

UK

info@tesol-direct.com

+44 (0) 121 449 2221

www.tesol-direct.com

Professionally-designed TESOL courses offered accredited by ACTDEC. Experienced tutors provide comprehensive feedback and helpful support. Free grammar guide and teaching resource book.

Appendix

Country info

Once you have chosen where you want to go, whether one country or a dozen, do some research. It would be a shame to travel to the other side of the world and then miss what it has to offer. There are loads of websites giving interesting and useful factual advice (weather, geographical, political, economic) as well as those that are more touristy.

Foreign Office warnings

It's worth bearing in mind that economic and political situations can change rapidly in countries, so check with the Foreign and Commonwealth Office that the country is still safe to travel to before you go. There's a link to their website on: **www.gap-year.com**

It's important to look at the lists of specific areas which travellers should avoid. It's also worth noting the phone numbers of all British embassies and consulates in areas where you may be travelling, in case you need to contact them for help.

Telephone, text or email home regularly to save your family a lot of worry and British embassies a lot of wasted time. The following pages contain data for countries: make sure you check with the FCO for up-to-date information.

Afghanistan, The Islamic Republic of
Capital: Kabul
Currency: Afghani (AFN)
Religion: mainly Sunni Muslim
Languages: Farsi (Dari), Pashtu (Pashto or Pukhto)
British Embassy, Kabul: +93 (0) 700 102 000

Albania, The Republic of
Capital: Tirana
Currency: (ALL)
Religion: Sunni Muslim, Albanian Orthodox, Roman Catholic
Languages: Albanian (Tosk is the official dialect), Greek, Vlach, Romani, Slavic dialects
British Embassy, Tirana: +355 4 223 4973/4/5

Algeria, The People's Democratic Republic of
Capital: Algiers
Currency: Algerian Dinar (DZD)
Religion: Sunni Muslim, Christian, Jewish
Language: Arabic (official language), French and Amazigh
British Embassy, Algiers: +213 77 00 85 000

Andorra, The Principality of
Capital: Andorra la Vella
Currency: Euro (EUR)
Religion: Roman Catholic
Language: Catalan (official), French, Spanish
British Consulate-General, Barcelona: +34 933 666 200

Angola, The Republic of
Capital: Luanda
Currency: Kwanza (AOA)
Religion: Indigenous beliefs, Roman Catholic, Christian, Muslim
Language: Portuguese (official), local African languages
British Embassy, Luanda: +244 (222) 334582

Anguilla (British Overseas Territory)
Capital: The Valley
Currency: Eastern Caribbean Dollar (XCD); US dollars accepted (USD)
Religion: Christian
Language: English
Government House, Anguilla: +1 (264) 497 2621

423

Antigua and Barbuda
Capital: Saint John's City
Currency: East Caribbean dollar (XCD)
Religion: Anglican, Moravian, Methodist and Roman Catholic
Language: English
St John's, Honorary British Consul: +1 268 561 5046

Argentina (The Argentine Republic)
Capital: Buenos Aires
Currency: Peso (ARS)
Religion: Roman Catholic, Protestant, Jewish and Muslim
Language: Spanish
British Embassy, Buenos Aires: +54 (11) 4808 2200

Armenia, The Republic of
Capital: Yerevan
Currency: Dram (AMD)
Religion: Armenian Orthodox, Christian, Yezidi
Language: Armenian, Russian, Yezidi
British Embassy, Yerevan: +374 (0) 10 264 301

Ascension Island (British Overseas Territory)
Capital: Georgetown
Currency: St Helena/Ascension Pound (SHP)
Religion: Christian
Language: English
Government House, Georgetown: +00 247 7000

Australia, The Commonwealth of
Capital: Canberra
Currency: Australian dollar (AUD)
Religion: Christian, Buddhist, Jewish, Muslim
Language: English, Aboriginal
British High Commission, Canberra: +61 (0) 2 6270 6666

Austria, The Republic of
Capital: Vienna
Currency: Euro (EUR)
Religion: Roman Catholic, Muslim and Protestant
Language: German
British Embassy, Vienna Tel: +43 (1) 716 130

Azerbaijan, The Republic of
Capital: Baku
Currency: Manat (AZN)
Religion: Muslim, Russian Orthodox, Armenian Orthodox
Language: Azeri, Russian, Armenian
British Embassy, Baku: +994 (12) 437 7878

Bahamas, The Commonwealth of The
Capital: Nassau
Currency: Bahamian Dollar (BSD)
Religion: Baptist, Anglican, Roman Catholic, Methodist, Church of God, Evangelical Protestants
Language: English, Creole (among Haitian immigrants)
refer to British High Commission, Kingston, Jamaica: +1 (876) 936 0700

Bahrain, The Kingdom of
Capital: Manama (Al Manamah)
Currency: Bahraini Dinar (BHD)
Religion: Muslim
Language: Arabic, English
British Embassy, Manama: +973 1757 4100; +973 1757 4167 (Information)

Bangladesh, The People's Republic of
Capital: Dhaka
Currency: Taka (BDT)
Religion: Muslim, Hindu, Buddhist, Christian
Language: Bangla, English, some tribal languages
British High Commission, Dhaka: +880 (2) 882 2705/6/7/8/9

Barbados
Capital: Bridgetown
Currency: Barbadian Dollar (BBD)
Religion: Protestant, Roman Catholic, Jewish, Muslim
Language: English
British High Commission, Bridgetown: +1 (246) 430 7800

Belarus, The Republic of
Capital: Minsk
Currency: Belarusian Ruble (BYR)

Religion: Eastern Orthodox Christian, Roman Catholic, Protestant, Jewish, Muslim
Language: Belarusian, Russian
British Embassy, Minsk: +375 (17) 229 8200

Belgium
Capital: Brussels
Currency: Euro (EUR)
Religion: Roman Catholic, Protestant
Language: Dutch, French, German
British Embassy, Brussels: +32 (2) 287 6211

Belize
Capital: Belmopan
Currency: Belizean Dollar (BZD)
Religion: Roman Catholic, Protestant, Muslim, Buddhist, Hindu, Bahá'í
Language: English, Creole, Spanish, indigenous languages
British High Commission, Belmopan: +501 822 2981/2717

Benin, The Republic of
Capital: Porto-Novo
Currency: CFA Franc BCEAO (XOF)
Religion: Indigenous beliefs, Christian, Muslim
Language: French, Fon, Yoruba, other African languages
Community Liaison Officer, Contonou: +229 21 30 32 65

Bermuda (British Overseas Territory)
Capital: Hamilton
Currency: Bermuda Dollar (BMD)
Religion: Christian, African Methodist Episcopalian
Language: English, Portuguese
Government House, Hamilton: +1 (441) 292 3600

Bhutan, The Kingdom of
Capital: Thimphu
Currency: Ngultrum (BTN), Indian Rupee (INR)
Religion: Buddhist, Hindu
Language: Dzongkha, various Tibetan and Nepalese dialects, English widely spoken

UK has no diplomatic representative in Bhutan. Contact British Deputy High Commission, Kolkata (Calcutta), India: +91 33 2288 5173-76

Bolivia, The Republic of
Capital: La Paz
Currency: Boliviano (BOB)
Religion: Roman Catholic, Evangelical Methodist
Language: Spanish, Quechua, Aymara and Indigenous dialects
British Embassy, La Paz: +591 (2) 243 3424

Bosnia and Herzegovina
Capital: Sarajevo
Currency: Convertible Mark (BAM)
Religion: Roman Catholic, Orthodox, Muslim
Language: Bosnian, Serbian, Croatian
British Embassy, Sarajevo: +387 33 282 200 (main); +387 33 20 4780 (Consular/Visa)

Botswana, The Republic of
Capital: Gaborone
Currency: Pula (BWP)
Religion: Christian, indigenous beliefs
Language: English, Setswana
British High Commission, Gabarone: +267 395 2841

Brazil, The Federative Republic of
Capital: Brasilia
Currency: Real (BRL)
Religion: Roman Catholic, Pentecostal, Animist
Language: Portuguese
British Embassy, Brasilia: +55 61 3329 2300

British Antarctic Territory
Currency: Sterling
Language: English
refer to Foreign & Commonwealth Office, London: +44 (0) 20 7008 1500

British Virgin Islands
Capital: Road Town, Tortola
Currency: US Dollar (USD)
Religion: Christian
Language: English
Government House, Tortola: +1 284 494 2345/2370

Brunei (Darussalam)
Capital: Bandar Seri Begawan
Currency: Brunei Dollar (BND)
Religion: Muslim
Language: Malay, English, Cantonese, Mandarin, Hokkein, Hakka
British High Commission, Bandar Seri Begawan: +673 (2) 222 231;
+673 (2) 226 001 (Consular/Visa)

Bulgaria, The Republic of
Capital: Sofia
Currency: Lev (BGN)
Religion: Bulgarian Orthodox, Muslim, Roman Catholic, Jewish
Language: Bulgarian
British Embassy, Sofia: +359 (2) 933 9222

Burkina Faso
Capital: Ouagadougou
Currency: CFA Franc BCEAO (XOF)
Religion: Animist, Muslim, Christian
Language: French, indigenous languages
British Honorary Consul, Ouagadougou: +226 (50) 30 88 60

Burma (The Union of Myanmar)
Capital: Rangoon
Currency: Kyat (MMK)
Religion: Buddhist, Christian, Muslim, Animist
Language: Burmese, ethnic minority languages
British Embassy, Rangoon: +95 (1) 380 322

Burundi, The Republic of
Capital: Bujumbura
Currency: Burundi Franc (BIF)
Religion: Muslim, Roman Catholic, Animist
Language: Kirundi, French, Swahili
British Embassy, Liaison Office, Bujumbura: +257 22 246 478

Cambodia, The Kingdom of
Capital: Phnom Penh
Currency: Riel (KHR), and US Dollar (USD)
Religion: Buddhist, Muslim, Christian
Language: Khmer, Cambodian
British Embassy, Phnom Penh: +855 23 427124/48153

Cameroon, The Republic of
Capital: Yaounde
Currency: CFA Franc BEAC (XAF)
Religion: Christian, Muslim, indigenous beliefs
Language: French, English, Pidgin, numerous African dialects
British High Commission, Yaounde: +237 2222 05 45

Canada
Capital: Ottawa
Currency: Canadian Dollar (CAD)
Religion: Roman Catholic, Protestant, Muslim
Language: English, French
British High Commission, Ottawa: +1 (613) 237 1530

Cape Verde, The Republic of
Capital: Praia
Currency: Escudo (CVE)
Religion: Roman Catholic
Language: Portuguese, Crioulo
British Honorary Consulate, Sao Vincente: +238 232 3512

Cayman Islands (British Overseas Territory)
Capital: George Town (Grand Cayman)
Currency: Caymanian Dollar (KYD)
Religion: Christian
Language: English
Government House, George Town, Grand Cayman: +1 345 949 7900

Central African Republic, The
Capital: Bangui
Currency: CFA Franc BEAC (XAF)
Religion: Christian, Muslim, indigenous beliefs
Language: French, Sangho
refer to British High Commission, Yaoundé, Cameroon: +236 2161 8513

Chad, The Republic of
Capital: N'Djamena
Currency: CFA Franc BEAC (XAF)
Religion: Muslim, Christian, indigenous beliefs
Language: French, Arabic, local languages
refer to British High Commission, Yaoundé, Cameroon: +237 2222 05 45

Chile, The Republic of
Capital: Santiago de Chile
Currency: Peso (CLP)
Religion: Roman Catholic, Evangelical, Jewish, Muslim
Language: Spanish, Mapuche, Aymara, Quechua
British Embassy, Santiago: +56 (2) 370 4100

China, The People's Republic of
Capital: Beijing
Currency: Yuan Renminbi (CNY)
Religion: Officially atheist. Daoist, Buddhist, Muslim, Roman Catholic, Protestant (the 5 state-registered religions)
Language: Putonghua (Mandarin), many local Chinese dialects
British Embassy, Beijing: +86 (10) 5192 4000

Colombia, The Republic of
Capital: Bogotá
Currency: Peso (COP)
Religion: Roman Catholic, Evangelical
Language: Spanish, indigenous languages
British Embassy, Bogotá: +57 (1) 326 8300

Comoros, The Union of The
Capital: Moroni (Ngazidja)
Currency: Comoros Franc (KMF)
Religion: Muslim, Roman Catholic
Language: Comoran, French, Arabic
refer to British High Commission, Port Louis, Mauritius: +230 202 9400

Congo, The Republic of The
Capital: Brazzaville
Currency: CFA Franc BEAC (XAF)
Religion: Roman Catholic, Christian, Muslim, traditional beliefs
Language: French (official), Lingala, Kikongo, Munukutuba
refer to British Embassy, Kinshasa, Democratic Republic of Congo:
+243 81 715 0761

Congo, The Democratic Republic of the
Capital: Kinshasa
Currency: Congolese Franc (CDF)
Religion: Roman Catholic, Protestant, Kimbanguist, Muslim, indigenous beliefs
Language: French (official), Lingala (trade language), Swahili, Kikongo, Tshiluba
British Embassy, Kinshasa: +243 81 715 0761

Costa Rica, The Republic of
Capital: San José
Currency: Colon (CRC)
Religion: Roman Catholic, Evangelical Protestant
Language: Spanish
British Embassy, San José: +506 2258 2025

Côte d'Ivoire, The Republic of (Ivory Coast)
Capital Yamoussoukro
Currency: CFA Franc BCEAO (XOF)
Religion: Muslim, Christian, indigenous beliefs
Language: French (official), Dioula, Baoule and other local native dialects
British Embassy, Côte d'Ivoire: +225 (22) 442 669

Croatia, The Republic of
Capital: Zagreb
Currency: Kuna (HRK)
Religion: Roman Catholic, Orthodox, Muslim
Language: Croatian
British Embassy, Zagreb: +385 (1) 6009 100

Cuba, The Republic of
Capital: Havana
Currency: Convertible Peso (CUC) or Peso (CUP)
Religion: Roman Catholic, Santeria, Protestant
Language: Spanish
British Embassy, Havana: +53 (7) 214 2200

Cyprus, The Republic of
Capital: Nicosia
Currency: Euro (EUR), Turkish Lira (in the north) (TRY)
Religion: Greek Orthodox, Muslim, Maronite, Armenian Apostolic
Language: Greek, Turkish, English
British High Commission, Nicosia: +357 22 861100

Czech Republic, The
Capital: Prague
Currency: Czech Koruna (Crown) (CZK)
Religion: Roman Catholic, Protestant,
Orthodox, Atheist
Language: Czech
British Embassy, Prague: +420 257 402 111

Denmark, The Kingdom of
Capital: Copenhagen
Currency: Danish Krone (DKK)
Religion: Evangelical Lutheran, Christian, Muslim
Language: Danish, Faroese, Greenlandic (an
Inuit dialect), English is the predominant
second language
British Embassy, Copenhagen: +45 35 44 52 00

Djibouti, The Republic of
Capital: Djibouti
Currency: Djiboutian Franc (DJF)
Religion: Muslim, Christian
Language: French (official), Arabic (official),
Somali, Afar
British Honorary Consul, Djibouti: +253 (3)
250915

Dominica, The Commonwealth of
Capital: Roseau
Currency: East Caribbean Dollar (XCD)
Religion: Roman Catholic, Protestant
Language: English (official), French patois (Creole)
British High Commission, Roseau: +767 275
7800

Dominican Republic, the
Capital: Santo Domingo
Currency: Dominican Peso (DOP)
Religion: Roman Catholic
Language: Spanish
British Embassy, Santo Domingo: +1 809 472
7111

East Timor - see Timor-Leste

Ecuador, The Republic of
Capital: Quito
Currency: US Dollar (USD)
Religion: Roman Catholic
Language: Spanish (official), Amerindian
languages (especially Quechua)
British Embassy, Quito: +593 (2) 2970 800/1
visit: www.gap-year.com

Egypt, The Arab Republic of
Capital: Cairo
Currency: Egyptian Pound (EGP)
Religion: Muslim (mostly Sunni), Coptic Christian
Language: Arabic (official), English and French
British Embassy, Cairo: +20 (2) 2791 6000

El Salvador, The Republic of
Capital: San Salvador
Currency: US Dollar (USD), Colon (SVC)
Religion: Roman Catholic
Language: Spanish
British Honorary Consulate, El Salvador: +503
2236 5555

Equatorial Guinea, The Republic of
Capital: Malabo
Currency: CFA Franc BEAC (XAF)
Religion: Christian (predominantly Roman
Catholic), indigenous religions
Language: Spanish (official), French (official),
Fang, Bubi, Ibo
Refer to British High Commission, Abuja,
Nigeria: +234 (9) 413 2010

Eritrea
Capital: Asmara
Currency: Nafka (ERN)
Religion: Christian, Muslim
Language: Tigrinya, Tigre, Arabic, English
British Embassy, Asmara: +291 1 12 01 45

Estonia, The Republic of
Capital: Tallinn
Currency: Kroon (EEK)
Religion: Lutheran, Orthodox Christian
Language: Estonian (official), Russian
British Embassy, Tallinn: +372 667 4700

Ethiopia, The Federal Democratic Republic of
Capital: Addis Ababa
Currency: Ethiopian Birr (ETB)
Religion: Orthodox Christian, Muslim, Animist,
Protestant
Language: Amharic, Tigrinya, Oromigna,
Guaragigna, Sidaminga, Somali, Arabic, other
local dialects, English (major foreign language
taught in schools)
British Embassy, Addis Ababa: +251 (11) 661
2354

Falkland Islands (British Overseas Territory)
Capital: Stanley
Currency: Falkland Island Pound (FKP)
Religion: Christian, Roman Catholic, United
Reformed Church, Anglican
Language: English
Government House, Stanley: +500 282 00

Fiji (The Republic of the Fiji Islands)
Capital: Suva
Currency: Fijian Dollar (FJD)
Religion: Christian, Hindu, Muslim
Language: English (official), Hindustani,
Gujarati, numerous Fijian dialects
British High Commission, Suva: +679 3229 100

Finland, The Republic of
Capital: Helsinki
Currency: Euro (EUR)
Religion: Lutheran, Orthodox
Language: Finnish (official), Swedish (official),
growing Russian speaking minority and small
Sami speaking community
British Embassy, Helsinki: +358 (0) 9 2286
5100/5210/5216

France (The French Republic)
Capital: Paris
Currency: Euro (EUR)
Religion: Roman Catholic, Protestant, Jewish,
Muslim
Language: French
British Embassy, Paris: +33 1 44 51 31 00

Gabon (The Gabonese Republic)
Capital: Libreville
Currency: CFA Franc BEAC (XAF)
Religion: Christian, Muslim, indigenous beliefs
Language: French (official), Fang, Myene,
Bateke, Bapounou/Eschira, Badjabi
British Honorary Consulate, Libreville: +241
762 200

Gambia, The Republic of
Capital: Banjul
Currency: Dalasi (GMD)
Religion: Muslim, Christian, indigenous beliefs
Language: English (official), Mandinka, Wolof,
Fula, indigenous languages
British High Commission, Banjul: +220 449 5133

Georgia
Capital: Tbilisi
Currency: Lari (GEL)
Religion: Georgian Orthodox, Muslim, Russian
Orthodox, Armenian Apostolic
Language: Georgian (official), Russian,
Armenian, Azeri, Abkhaz
British Embassy, Tbilisi: +995 32 274 747

Germany, The Federal Republic of
Capital: Berlin
Currency: Euro (EUR)
Religion: Protestant, Roman Catholic, Muslim
Language: German
British Embassy, Berlin: +49 (30) 20457-0

Ghana, The Republic of
Capital: Accra
Currency: Cedi (GHS)
Religion: Muslim, Christian, indigenous beliefs
Language: English (official), African languages
(including Akan, Mossi, Ewe, and Hausa), Fante,
Ga-Adangme, 75 spoken languages
British High Commission, Accra: +233 (0)302)
213250

Gibraltar (British Overseas Territory)
Capital: Gibraltar
Currency: Gibraltar Pound (GIP)
Religion: Roman Catholic, Protestantism,
Muslim, Hindu, Jewish
Language: English
Governor's Office, Main Street: +350 200 45
440

Greece (The Hellenic Republic)
Capital: Athens
Currency: Euro (EUR)
Religion: Greek Orthodox, Muslim
Language: Greek
British Embassy, Athens: +30 210 727 2600

Grenada
Capital: St George's
Currency: East Caribbean Dollar (XCD)
Religion: Roman Catholic, Anglican, Protestant
Language: English (official), French patois
Honorary British Consul, St George's: +473
405 8072

Guatemala
Capital: Guatemala City
Currency: Quetzal (GTQ)
Religion: Roman Catholic, Protestant, Judasim, Muslim, indigenous Mayan beliefs
Language: Spanish, there are 23 officially recognized Amerindian languages
British Embassy, Guatemala City: +502 2380 7300

Guinea, The Republic of
Capital: Conakry
Currency: Guinean Franc (GNF)
Religion: Muslim, Christian, traditional beliefs
Language: French (official), eight local languages taught in schools (Basari, Pular, Kissi, Koniagi, Kpelle, Loma, Malinke and Susu)
British Embassy, Conakry: +224 63 35 53 29

Guinea-Bissau, The Republic of
Capital: Bissau
Currency: CFA Franc BCEAO (XOF)
Religion: Muslim, Christian, indigenous beliefs
Language: Portuguese (official), Crioulo, indigenous African languages
Honorary British Consulate: +245 320 1224/1216

Guyana, The Co-operative Republic of
Capital: Georgetown
Currency: Guyanese Dollar (GYD)
Religion: Christian, Hindu, Muslim
Language: English, Amerindian dialects, Creole
British High Commission, Georgetown: +592 226 58 81

Haiti, The Republic of
Capital: Port-au-Prince
Currency: The Gourde (HTG)
Religion: Roman Catholic, Protestant, Baptist, Pentecostal, Adventist, also Voodoo
Language: French (official), Creole (official)
British Consulate, Port-au-Prince: +509 3744 6371

Holy See, Rome (Vatican City State)
Capital: Vatican City
Currency: Euro (EUR)
Religion: Roman Catholic
Language: Latin, Italian, English and French
British Embassy, Rome: +39 06 4220 4000

Honduras, The Republic of
Capital: Tegucigalpa
Currency: Lempira (HNL)
Religion: Roman Catholic, Protestant
Language: Spanish, English (business), Amerindian dialects
British Embassy, Tegucigalpa: +504 237 6577/6459

Hong Kong (The Hong Kong Special Administration of China)
Currency: Hong Kong Dollar (HKD)
Religion: Buddhist, Taoist, Christian, Muslim, Hindu, Sikhist, Jewish
Language: Chinese (Cantonese), English
British Consulate General, Hong Kong: +852 2901 3281

Hungary, The Republic of
Capital: Budapest
Currency: Forint (HUF)
Religion: Roman Catholic, Calvinist, Lutheran, Jewish, Atheist
Language: Hungarian
British Embassy, Budapest: +36 (1) 266 2888

Iceland, The Republic of
Capital: Reykjavik
Currency: Icelandic Krona (ISK)
Religion: Evangelical Lutheran, Protestant, Roman Catholic
Language: Icelandic
British Embassy, Reykjavik: +354 550 5100

India
Capital: New Delhi
Currency: Rupee (INR)
Religion: Hindu, Muslim, Christian, Sikhist
Language: Hindi (official), 18 main and regional official state languages, plus 24 further languages, 720 dialects and 23 tribal languages, English (officially an associate language, is used particularly for political, and commercial communication)
British High Commission, New Delhi: +91 (11) 2419 2100

Indonesia, The Republic of
Capital: Jakarta
Currency: Rupiah (IDR)
Religion: Muslim, Protestant, Roman Catholic, Hindu, Buddhist
Language: Bahasa Indonesia (official), over 583 languages and dialects
British Embassy, Jakarta: +62 (21) 2356 5200

Iran, The Islamic Republic of
Capital: Tehran
Currency: Rial (IRR)
Religion: Shi'a Muslim, Sunni Muslim, Zoroastrian, Jewish, Christian, Bahá'i
Language: Persian (Farsi), Azeri, Kurdish, Arabic, Luri, Baluchi

Iraq, Republic of
Capital: Baghdad
Currency: New Iraqi Dinar (IQD)
Religion: Muslim, Christian
Language: Arabic, Kurdish, Assyrian, Armenian, Turkoman
British Embassy, Baghdad: +964 7901 926 280

Ireland, Republic of
Capital: Dublin
Currency: Euro (EUR)
Religion: Roman Catholic, Church of Ireland
Language: Irish, English
British Embassy, Dublin: +353 (1) 205 3700

Israel, The State of
Capital: Tel Aviv
Currency: New Israeli Shekel (ILS)
Religion: Jewish, Muslim, Christian
Language: Hebrew, Arabic, English, Russian
British Embassy, Tel Aviv: +972 (3) 725 1222

Italy
Capital: Rome
Currency: Euro (EUR)
Religion: Roman Catholic, Jewish, Protestant, Muslim
Language: Italian (official), German, French, Slovene
British Embassy, Rome: +39 06 4220 0001

Ivory Coast - see Côte d'Ivoire

Jamaica
Capital: Kingston
Currency: Jamaican Dollar (JMD)
Religion: Anglican, Baptist and other Protestant, Roman Catholic, Rastafarian, Jewish, Seventh-Day Adventist
Language: English, Patois
British High Commission, Kingston: +1 (876) 936 0700

Japan
Capital: Tokyo
Currency: Yen (JPY)
Religion: Shinto, Buddhist, Christian
Language: Japanese
British Embassy, Tokyo: +81 (3) 5211 1100

Jordan, The Hashemite Kingdom of
Capital: Amman
Currency: Jordanian Dinar (JOD)
Religion: Sunni Muslim, Christian
Language: Arabic (official), English
British Embassy, Amman: +962 6 590 9200

Kazakhstan, The Republic of
Capital: Astana
Currency: Kazakh Tenge (KZT)
Religion: Muslim, Russian Orthodox, Protestant
Language: Kazakh, Russian
British Embassy, Astana: +7 7172 556200

Kenya, The Republic of
Capital: Nairobi
Currency: Kenyan Shilling (KES)
Religion: Protestant (including Evangelical), Roman Catholic, indigenous beliefs, Muslim
Language: English (official), Kiswahili, numerous indigenous languages
British High Commission, Nairobi: +254 (20) 284 4000

Kiribati, The Republic of
Capital: Tarawa
Currency: Australian Dollar (AUD)
Religion: Roman Catholic, Protestant (Congregational), Seventh-Day Adventist, Bahá'í, Latter-day Saints, Church of God
Language: English (official), I-Kiribati
refer to British High Commission, Suva, Fiji: +679 3229 100

Korea, The Democratic People's Republic of (North Korea)
Capital: Pyongyang
Currency: North Korean Won (KPW); foreigners are required to use Euros
Religion: Buddhist, Christian, Chondo
Language: Korean
British Embassy, Pyongyang: +850 2 381 7980 (International); 02 382 7980 (Local dialling)

Korea, The Republic of (South Korea)
Capital: Seoul
Currency: South Korean Won (KRW)
Religion: Shamanist, Buddhist, Confuciant, Chondogyo, Roman Catholic, Protestant
Language: Korean
British Embassy, Seoul: +82 (2) 3210 5500

Kosovo
Capital: Pristina
Currency: Euro (EUR)
Religion: Muslim, Serbian Orthodox, Roman Catholic
Language: Albanian, Serbian, Bosniak, Turkish
British Embassy, Pristina: +381 (38) 254 700

Kuwait, The State of
Capital: Kuwait City
Currency: Kuwaiti Dinar (KWD)
Religion: Muslim, Christian, other religions restricted
Language: Arabic (official), English (second official language)
British Embassy, Dasman: +965 2259 4320

Kyrgyzstan (The Kyrgyz Republic)
Capital: Bishkek
Currency: Som (KGS)
Religion: Muslim, Russian Orthodox, Christian minorities
Language: Kyrgyz, Russian
British Embassy, Bishkek: +996 (0) 312 69 02 32

Laos (The Lao People's Democratic Republic)
Capital: Vientiane
Currency: Kip (LAK)
Religion: Buddhist, Animist, Christian, Muslim
Language: Lao
British Embassy (resident at Bangkok): +66 (0) 2 305 8333

Latvia, The Republic of
Capital: Riga
Currency: Lat (LVL)
Religion: Lutheran, Roman Catholic, Russian Orthodox
Language: Latvian, Russian
British Embassy, Riga: +371 6777 4700

Lebanon (The Lebanese Republic)
Capital: Beirut
Currency: Lebanese Pound (LBP)
Religion: 18 registered sects including Druze, Maronite Christian, Shi'a and Sunni Muslim
Language: Arabic (official), English, French, Armenian
British Embassy, Beirut: +961 (1) 9608 00 (24 hours)

Lesotho, The Kingdom of
Capital: Maseru
Currency: Loti (LSL)
Religion: Christian, indigenous beliefs
Language: Sesotho, English
British Honorary Consulate, Maseru: +266 2231 3929

Liberia, The Republic of
Capital: Monrovia
Currency: Liberian Dollar (LRD), US Dollar (USD)
Religion: Christian, Muslim, indigenous beliefs
Language: English (official), indigenous languages
British Honorary Consulate, Monrovia: 00 231 (0) 77 530 320

Libya (The Great Socialist People's Libyan Arab Jamahiriya)
Capital: Tripoli
Currency: Dinar (LYD)
Religion: Sunni Muslim
Language: Arabic, Italian and English understood in major cities
British Embassy, Tripoli: +218 (21) 335 1084/5/6

Liechtenstein, The Principality of
Capital: Vaduz
Currency: Swiss Franc (CHF)
Religion: Roman Catholic, Protestant
Language: German (official), Alemannic dialect
refer to British Embassy, Berne, Switzerland: +41 (31) 359 7700

Lithuania, The Republic of
Capital: Vilnius
Currency: Litas (LTL)
Religion: Roman Catholic
Language: Lithuanian (official), Russian, English
British Embassy, Vilnius: +370 5 246 29 00

Luxembourg, The Grand Duchy of
Capital: Luxembourg
Currency: Euro (EUR)
Religion: Roman Catholic, Protestant, Jewish, Muslim
Language: Luxembourgish, German, French
British Embassy, Luxembourg: + 352 22 98 64

Macao (The Macao Special Administrative Region of the People's Republic of China)
Currency: Pataca (MOP)
Religion: Buddhist, Christian, Taoist
Language: Cantonese, Portuguese, English
British Honorary Consulate, Macao: +853 685 0886

Macedonia, republic of
Capital: Skopje
Currency: Macedonian Denar (MKD)
Religion: Orthodox, Muslim
Language: Macedonian, Albanian, Turkish, Serbian, Vlach, Roma
British Embassy, Skopje: +389 (2) 3299 299

Madagascar, The Republic of
Capital: Antananarivo
Currency: Ariary (MGA)
Religion: Christian, indigenous beliefs, Muslim
Language: Malagasy, French
British Consulate, Toamasina: +261 (20) 53 325 48/325 69

Malawi, The Republic of
Capital: Lilongwe
Currency: Kwacha (MWK)
Religion: Protestant, Roman Catholic, Muslim, Hindu, indigenous beliefs
Language: English (official), Chichewa (national)
British High Commission, Liongwe: +265 (1) 772 400

Malaysia, The Federation of
Capital: Kuala Lumpur
Currency: Ringgit (MYR)
Religion: Muslim, Buddhist, Taoist, Christian, Hindu, Animist
Language: Bahasa Malay (national language), Iban, English widespread, Chinese, Tamil
British High Commission, Kuala Lumpur: +60 (3) 2170 2200

Maldives, The Republic of
Capital: Malé
Currency: Rufiyaa (MVR); resort islands accept US Dollar (USD)
Religion: Sunni Muslim (other religions illegal)
Language: Dhivehi, but English widely spoken in Malé and resort islands
refer to British High Commission, Colombo, Sri Lanka: +94 (11) 539 0639

Mali, The Republic of
Capital: Bamako
Currency: CFA Franc BCEAO (XOF)
Religion: Muslim, Christian, Indigenous beliefs
Language: French (official), Bambara, and numerous other African languages
British Embassy Liaison Office, Bamako: +223 2021 3412

Malta, The Republic of
Capital: Valletta
Currency: Euro (EUR)
Religion: Roman Catholic
Language: Maltese, English
British High Commission, Valletta: +356 2323 0000

Marshall Islands, Republic of the
Capital: Majuro
Currency: US Dollar (USD)
Religion: Christian (mostly Protestant)
Language: English, two major Marshallese dialects, Japanese
refer to British Embassy, Manilia: +63 (2) 858 2200

433

Mauritania, The Islamic Repubic of
Capital: Nouakchott
Currency: Ouguiya (MRO)
Religion: Muslim
Language: Hassaniya Arabic (official), Pulaar,
Soninke, Wolof, French widely used in business
British Honorary Consul, Nouakchott: +222
525 83 31

Mauritius, The Republic of
Capital: Port Louis
Currency: Mauritian Rupee (MUR)
Religion: Hindu, Christian, Muslim
Language: English, French, Creole
British Honorary Consulate, Rodrigues: +230
832 0120

Mexico (The United Mexican State)
Capital: Mexico City
Currency: Mexican Peso (MXN)
Religion: Roman Catholic, Protestant
Language: Spanish, at least 62 other regional
languages
British Embassy, Mexico City: +52 (55) 1670
3200

Micronesia, The Federated States of
Capital: Palikir
Currency: US Dollar (USD)
Religion: Roman Catholic, Protestant
Language: English, Trukese, Pohnpeian,
Yapese, Kosrean, Ulithian, Woleaian, Nukuoro,
Kapingamarangi
refer to British Embassy, Manila: +63 (2) 858
2200

Moldova, The Republic of
Capital: Chisinau
Currency: Moldovan Leu (MDL)
Religion: Eastern Orthodox, Jewish, Baptist
Language: Moldovan, Russian (official)
British Embassy, Chisinau: +373 22 22 59 02;
out of hours +373 69 10 44 42

Monaco, The Principality of
Capital: Monaco
Currency: Euro (EUR)
Religion: Roman Catholic
Language: French (official), Italian,
Monegasque, English
British Honorary Consulate, Monaco: +377 93
50 99 54

Mongolia
Capital: Ulaanbaatar
Currency: Togrog (Tughrik) (MNT)
Religion: Tibetan Buddhist, Shamanist, Muslim
(south-west)
Language: Khalkh Mongol, Kazakh
British Embassy, Ulaanbaatar: +976 (11) 458 133

Montenegro, Republic of
Capital: Podgorica
Currency: Euro (EUR)
Religion: Christian, Muslim
Language: Montenegrin, Serbian, Bosnian,
Albanian, Croatian
British Embassy, Podgorica: +382 (20) 618 010

Montserrat (British Overseas Territory)
Capital: Plymouth (destroyed by the last
volcanic eruption)
Currency: East Caribbean Dollar (XCD)
Religion: Christian
Language: English
Governor's Office, Brades: +1 (664) 491 2688/9

Morocco, The Kingdom of
Capital: Rabat
Currency: Moroccan Dirham (MAD)
Religion: Muslim, Christian, Jewish
Language: Arabic (official), Berber dialects,
French (commerce, diplomacy and government)
British Embassy, Rabat: +212 (537) 63 33 33

Mozambique, The Republic of
Capital: Maputo
Currency: Metical (MZN)
Religion: Roman Catholic, Christian, Muslim,
indigenous beliefs
Language: Portuguese (official), over 16
African languages and dialects
British High Commission, Maputo: +258 21
356 000

Myanmar (see Burma)

Namibia, The Republic of
Capital: Windhoek
Currency: Namibian Dollar (NAD)
Religion: Christian
Language: English (official), Afrikaans,
German, and several indigenous languages
British High Commission, Windhoek: +264 (61)
274800

Nauru, The Republic of
Capital: Yaren District (unofficial)
Currency: Australian Dollar (AUD)
Religion: Protestant, Roman Catholic
Language: Nauruan (official), English
(commerce and government, widely
understood)
refer to British High Commission, Suva, Fiji:
+679 322 9100

Nepal
Capital: Kathmandu
Currency: Nepalese Rupee (NPR)
Religion: Hindu, Buddhist, Muslim
Language: Nepali (official), Newari (mainly in
Kathmandu), Tibetan languages (mainly hill
areas), Indian languages (mainly Terai areas).
Nepal has over 30 languages and many
dialects.
British Embassy, Kathmandu: +977 (1) 441
0583/1281/4588/1590

Netherlands, The Kingdom of The
Capital: Amsterdam
Currency: Euro (EUR)
Religion: Roman Catholic, Protestant, Muslim
Language: Dutch
British Embassy, The Hague: +31 (0) 70 4270
427

New Zealand
Capital: Wellington
Currency: New Zealand Dollar (NZD)
Religion: Anglican, Presbyterian, Roman
Catholic, Methodist, Baptist
Language: English, Maori
British High Commission, Wellington: +64 (4)
924 2888

Nicaragua, The Republic of
Capital: Managua
Currency: Cordoba (NIO)
Religion: Roman Catholic, Evangelical
Protestant
Language: Spanish (official), English, Miskito,
Creole, Mayanga, Garifuna, Rama
British Honorary Consul, Managua: +505 254
5454/3839

Niger, The Republic of
Capital: Niamey
Currency: CFA Franc BCEAO (XOF)
Religion: Muslim
Language: French (official), Arabic, local
languages widely spoken
British Honorary Consul, Niamey: +227 9687
8130

Nigeria, The Federal Republic of
Capital: Abuja
Currency: Naira (NGN)
Religion: Muslim, Christian, traditional beliefs
Language: English (official), Hausa, Yoruba,
Igbo
British High Commission, Abuja: +234 (9) 413
2010/2011/3885-7

Norway, The Kingdom of
Capital: Oslo
Currency: Norwegian Kroner (NOK)
Religion: Church of Norway (Evangelical
Lutheran)
Language: Norwegian (bokmål and nynorsk),
Sami
British Embassy, Oslo: +47 23 13 27 00

Oman, The Sultanate of
Capital: Muscat
Currency: Oman Rial (OMR)
Religion: Ibadhi Muslim, Sunni Muslim, Shi'a
Muslim, Hindu, Christian
Language: Arabic (official), English, Farsi,
Baluchi, Urdu
British Embassy, Muscat: +968 24 609 000;
(out of hours emergencies) +968 9920 0865

435

Pakistan, The Islamic Republic of
Capital: Islamabad
Currency: Rupee (PKR)
Religion: Muslim, Hindu, Christian
Language: Punjabi, Sindhi, Pashtun, Urdu,
Balochi, English and other local languages
British High Commission, Islamabad: +92 51
201 2000

Palau, The Republic of
Capital: Suva
Currency: United States Dollar (USD)
Religion: Christian, Hindu, Muslim
Language: English, numerous Fijian dialects,
Gujarati, Fijian Hindi
refer to British Ambassador, Manila, The
Philippines: +63 (2) 858 2200

Palestine (The Occupied Palestinian Territories)
Currency: New Israeli Shekel (ILS), Jordanian
Dinar (JOD) (West Bank Only)
Religion: Muslim, Christian
Language: Arabic, English widely spoken
British Consulate-General, Gaza: +972 (08)
283 7724

Panama, The Republic of
Capital: Panama City
Currency: US Dollar (USD) (known locally as
the Balboa (PAB))
Religion: Roman Catholic, Protestant, Jewish,
Muslim
Language: Spanish (official), English
British Embassy, Panama City: +507 269
0866

Papua New Guinea, The Independent State of
Capital: Port Moresby
Currency: Kina (PGK)
Religion: Christian according to its
constitution, Roman Catholic, Evangelical
Lutheran, Evangelical Alliance, Pentecostal,
Baptist, Anglican, Seventh Day Adventist,
United Church, Buddhist, Muslim, Hindu
Language: English, Pidgin, Hiri Motu, over 820
different languages
British High Commission, Port Moresby: +675
325 1677

Paraguay, The Republic of
Capital: Asunción
Currency: Guarani (PYG)
Religion: Roman Catholic, Mennonite,
Protestant, Latter-day Saints, Jewish, Russian
Orthodox
Language: Spanish (official), Guaraní (official)
British Honorary Consulate, Asunción: +595
(21) 210 405

Peru, The Republic of
Capital: Lima
Currency: Nuevo Sol (PEN)
Religion: Roman Catholic
Language: Spanish (official), Quechua (official),
Aymara and several minor Amazonian languages
British Embassy, Lima: +51 (1) 617 3000
(main); 3053/3054 (consular)

Philippines, The Republic of the
Capital: Metro Manila
Currency: Peso (PHP)
Religion: Roman Catholic, Protestant, Muslim
Language: Filipino (official), English (official)
British Embassy, Manila: +63 (2) 858 2200

Pitcairn, Henderson, Ducie & Oeno Islands (British Overseas Territory)
Capital: Adamstown
Currency: New Zealand Dollar (NZD)
Religion: Seventh Day Adventist
Language: English, Pitkern (a mix of English
and Tahitian)
British High Commission, Auckland, New
Zealand: +64 (9) 366 0186

Poland, The Republic of
Capital: Warsaw
Currency: Zloty (PLN)
Religion: Roman Catholic, Eastern Orthodox,
Protestant
Language: Polish
British Embassy, Warsaw: +48 (22) 311 00 00

Portugal (The Portuguese Republic)
Capital: Lisbon
Currency: Euro (EUR)
Religion: Roman Catholic, Protestant
Language: Portuguese
British Embassy, Lisbon: +351 (21) 392 4000

visit: www.gap-year.com

Qatar, The State of
Capital: Doha
Currency: Qatari Riyal (QAR)
Religion: Muslim
Language: Arabic (official), English, Urdu
British Embassy, Doha: +974 4496 2000

Romania
Capital: Bucharest
Currency: New Leu (RON)
Religion: Orthodox, Roman Catholic,
Protestant, Reformed, Greek Catholic, Unitarian
Language: Romanian (official), English, French,
German
British Embassy, Bucharest: +40 (21) 201 7200

Russia Federation, The
Capital: Moscow
Currency: Ruble (RUB)
Religion: Orthodox Christian, Muslim, Jewish,
Buddhist
Language: Russian, Tatar
British Embassy, Moscow: +7 (495) 956 7200

Rwanda, The Republic of
Capital: Kigali
Currency: Rwandan Franc (RWF)
Religion: Roman Catholic, Protestant, Muslim,
indigenous beliefs
Language: Kinyarwanda (official), French
(official), English (official), Kiswahili (used in
commercial centres and by army)
British Embassy, Kigali: +250 252 556000

Saint Helena (British Overseas Territory)
Capital: Jamestown
Currency: St Helena Pound (SHP)
Religion: Christiantiy, Bahá'í
Language: English
Governor's Office, Jamestown: +290 2555

Saint Kitts & Nevis (The Federation of St Christopher & Nevis)
Capital: Basseterre
Currency: East Caribbean Dollar (XCD)
Religion: Anglican, Roman Catholic,
Evangelical Protestant
Language: English
Honorary British Consul, Basseterre: +1 (869)
764 4677

Saint Lucia
Capital: Castries
Currency: East Caribbean Dollar (XCD)
Religion: Roman Catholic, Anglican, Methodist,
Baptist, Jewish, Hindu, Muslim
Language: English (official), French patois
(Kweyol)
British High Commission, Castries: +1 (758)
452 2484/5 (resides in Barbados)

Saint Vincent and the Grenadines
Capital: Kingstown
Currency: East Caribbean Dollar (XCD)
Religion: Anglican, Methodist, Roman Catholic,
Seventh-Day Adventist, Hindu, other Protestant
Language: English
British High Consul, Kingstown: +784 457 6860

Samoa, The Independent State of
Capital: Apia
Currency: Samoan Tala (WST)
Religion: Roman Catholic, Methodist, Latter-
day Saints
Language: Samoan, English
British Honorary Consulate, Apia: +685 27123

São Tomé & Príncipe, The Democratic State of
Capital: São Tomé
Currency: Dobra (STD)
Religion: Christian
Language: Portuguese, Lungwa Santomé, and
other creole dialects
Refer to the British Embassy in Luanda,
Angola: +244 222 334582

Saudi Arabia, The Kingdom of
Capital: Riyadh
Currency: Saudi Riyal (SAR)
Religion: Muslim (Sunni, Shia). The public
practice of any other religion is forbidden
Language: Arabic, English
British Embassy, Riyadh: +966 (0) 1 488 0077

Senegal, The Republic of
Capital: Dakar
Currency: CFA Franc BCEAO (XOF)
Religion: Muslim, Christian, indigenous beliefs
Language: French (official), Wolof, Malinke,
Serere, Soninke, Pular (all national)
British Embassy, Dakar: +221 33 823 7392/9971

Serbia, The Republic of

Capital: Belgrade
Currency: Serbian Dinar (RSD)
Religion: Serbian Orthodox, Muslim, Roman Catholic, Christian
Language: Serbian (majority), Romanian, Hungarian, Slovak, Croatian, Albanian (Kosovan), Ukranian, Bosniak, Montenegrin, Bulgarian, Ruthenian, Roma. Vlach, Macedonian
British Embassy, Belgrade: +381 (11) 2645 055

Seychelles, The Republic of

Capital: Victoria
Currency: Seychelles Rupee (SCR)
Religion: Roman Catholic, Anglican, Muslim, Hindu
Language: English, French, Creole (Seselwa)
British High Commission, Victoria: +248 4283 666

Sierra Leone, The Republic of

Capital: Freetown
Currency: Leone (SLL)
Religion: Muslim, Christian, indigenous beliefs
Language: English (official), Krio (English-based Creole), indigenous languages widely spoken
British High Commission, Freetown: +232 (0) 7689 25634

Singapore, The Republic of

Capital: Singapore
Currency: Singapore Dollar (SGD)
Religion: Taoist, Buddhist, Muslim, Christian, Hindu
Language: Mandarin, English, Malay, Tamil
British High Commission, Singapore: +65 6424 4200

Slovakia (The Slovak Republic)

Capital: Bratislava
Currency: Euro (EUR)
Religion: Roman Catholic, Atheist, Protestant, Orthodox
Language: Slovak (official), Hungarian
British Embassy, Bratislava: +421 (2) 5998 2000

Slovenia, The Republic of

Capital: Ljubljana
Currency: Euro (EUR)
Religion: Roman Catholic
Language: Slovene, Italian, Hungarian, English
British Embassy, Ljubljana: +386 (1) 200 3910

Solomon Islands

Capital: Honiara
Currency: Solomon Islands Dollar (SBD)
Religion: Christian, traditional beliefs
Language: English, Pidgin, 92 indigenous languages
British High Commission, Honiara: +677 21705/6

Somalia (The Somali Democratic Republic)

Capital: Mogadishu
Currency: Somali Shilling (SOS)
Religion: Sunni Muslim
Language: Somali (official), Arabic, Italian, English
British Office for Somalia, Nairobi, Kenya: +254 (20) 2844 000

South Africa, Republic of

Capital: Pretoria/Tshwane
Currency: Rand (ZAR)
Religion: Predominately Christian but all principal religions are represented
Language: 11 official languages: Afrikaans, English, Ndebele, Sepedi, Sesotho, Swati, Tsonga, Tswana, Venda, Xhosa, Zulu
British High Commission, Pretoria: +27 (12) 421 7500

South Georgia & South Sandwich Islands (British Overseas Territories)

Capital: King Edward Point
Currency: United Kingdom Pound Sterling (GBP)
Language: English
Governor's Office, Stanley, Falkland Islands: +500 282 00

Spain, The Kingdom of

Capital: Madrid
Currency: Euro (EUR)
Religion: Roman Catholic, Protestant
Language: Castilian Spanish (official), Catalan, Galician, Basque
British Embassy, Madrid: +34 (91) 714 6300

Sri Lanka, The Democratic Socialist Republic of
Capital: Colombo
Currency: Rupee (LKR)
Religion: Buddhist, Hindu, Muslim, Christian
Language: Sinhalese, Tamil, English
British High Commission, Colombo: +94 (11) 5390639

Sudan, The Republic of
Capital: Khartoum City
Currency: Sudanese pound (SDG)
Religion: Muslim, Christian, indigenous religions
Language: Arabic (official), Nubian, Ta Bedawie, dialects of Nilotic, Nilo- Hamitic, Sudanic languages, English
British Embassy, Khartoum: +249 (183) 777 105

Suriname, The Republic of
Capital: Paramaribo
Currency: Suriname Dollar (SRD)
Religion: Hindu, Muslim, Roman Catholic, Dutch Reformed, Moravian, Jewish, Bahá'í
Language: Dutch (official), English, Sranan Tongo (Creole), Hindustani, Javanese
British Honorary Consulate, Paramaribo: +597 402 558

Swaziland, The Kingdom of
Capital: Mbabane
Currency: Lilangeni (SZL)
Religion: Christian, indigenous beliefs
Language: English, Siswati
British Honorary Consulate, Mbabane: +268 551 6247

Sweden
Capital: Stockholm
Currency: Swedish Krona (SEK)
Religion: Lutheran, Roman Catholic, Orthodox, Baptist, Muslim, Jewish, Buddhist
Language: Swedish, English widely spoken
British Embassy, Stockholm: +46 (8) 671 3000

Switzerland
Capital: Berne
Currency: Swiss Franc (CHF)
Religion: Roman Catholic, Protestant, Muslim
Language: Swiss German (official), French, Italian, Rhaeto-Rumantsch
British Embassy, Berne: +41 (31) 359 7700

Syria (The Syrian Arab Republic)
Capital: Damascus
Currency: Syrian Pound (also called Lira) (SYP)
Religion: Sunni Muslim, Shi'a Muslim, Alawite, Druze, other Muslim sects, Christian, Jewish
Language: Arabic (official), Kurdish, Armenian, Aramaic, Circassian, some French, English
British Embassy, Damascus: +963 (11) 339 1513/1541 (consular)

Taiwan (Province of the People's Republic of China)
Capital: Taipei
Currency: New Taiwan Dollar (TWD)
Religion: Buddhist, Taoist, Christian
Language: Mandarin Chinese (official), Taiwanese, Hakka
British Trade & Cultural Office, Taipei: +886 (2) 8758 2088

Tajikistan, Republic of
Capital: Dushanbe
Currency: Somoni (TJS)
Religion: Sunni Muslim, Ismaili Shiite, Russian Orthodox Christian, Jewish
Language: Tajik, Russian
British Embassy, Dushanbe: +992 372 24 22 21

Tanzania, United Republic of
Capital: Dodoma (official)
Currency: Tanzania Shilling (TZS)
Religion: Christian, Muslim, indigenous beliefs
Language: Kiswahili, English
British High Commission, Dar es Salaam: +255 (022) 229 0000

Thailand, Kingdom of
Capital: Bangkok
Currency: Baht (THB)
Religion: Buddhist, Muslim, Christian, Hindu
Language: Thai, Yawi
British Embassy, Bangkok: +66 (0) 2 305 8333

Tibet – see China

Timor-Leste, Democratic Republic of

Capital: Dili
Currency: US Dollar (USD)
Religion: Roman Catholic (majority),
Protestant, Muslim, Hindu, Buddhist
Language: Tetum (official), Portuguese
(official), Bahasa Indonesian, English
refer to British Embassy, Jakarta: +62 (21)
2356 5200

Togo (Togolese Republic)

Capital: Lomé
Currency: CFA Franc BCEAO (XOF)
Religion: Christian, Muslim, indigenous beliefs
Language: French, Kabiye, Ewe
The British Ambassador to Togo resides in
Accra, Ghana: +223 21 221665; in a genuine
emergency contact the Honorary Consul in
Togo: +228 2222714

Tonga, Kingdom of

Capital: Nuku'alofa
Currency: Pa'anga (TOP)
Religion: Christian
Language: Tongan, English
refer to British High Commission, Suva, Fiji:
+679 322 9100

Trinidad and Tobago, Republic of

Capital: Port of Spain
Currency: Trinidad and Tobago Dollar (TTD)
Religion: Roman Catholic, Hindu, Anglican,
Muslim, Presbyterian
Language: English (official), Spanish
British High Commission, Port of Spain: +1
(868) 622 2748

Tristan da Cunha (British Overseas Territory)

Capital: Edinburgh of the Seven Seas
Currency: Sterling (GBP)
Religion: Christian
Language: English
Administrator's Office: +870 764 341 816

Tunisia (Tunisian Republic)

Capital: Tunis
Currency: Tunisian Dinar (TND)
Religion: Muslim, Christian
Language: Arabic, French
British Embassy, Tunis: +216 71 108 700

Turkey

Capital: Ankara
Currency: New Turkish Lira (TRY)
Religion: Muslim
Language: Turkish, Kurdish
British Consulae, Izmir: +90 (232) 463 5151

Turkmenistan

Capital: Ashgabat
Currency: Manat (TMM)
Religion: Sunni Muslim
Language: Russian, Turkmen
British Embassy, Ashgabat: +993 (12) 363
462/63/64

Turks and Caicos Islands

Capital: Grand Turk
Currency: US Dollar (USD)
Religion: Christian
Language: English, some Creole
Governor's Office: +1 (649) 946 2309

Tuvalu

Capital: Funafuti
Currency: Australian Dollar (AUD), Tuvaluan
Dollar (TVD) (coinage only)
Religion: Church of Tuvalu, Bahá'í
Language: Tuvaluan, English, Samoan, Kiribati
refer to British High Commission, Suva, Fiji:
+679 322 9100

Uganda Republic

Capital: Kampala
Currency: Uganda Shilling (UGX)
Religion: Christian, Muslim
Language: English (official national language),
Luganda, Swahili
British High Commission, Kampala: +256 (31)
231 2000

Ukraine

Capital: Kyiv (Kiev)
Currency: Hryvna (UAH)
Religion: Ukrainian Orthodox, Ukrainian Greek
Catholic, Jewish, Muslim
Language: Ukrainian (official), Russian,
Romanian, Polish, Hungarian
British Embassy, Kyiv: +380 44 490 3660

United Arab Emirates
Capital: Abu Dhabi
Currency: Dirham (AED)
Religion: Muslim, Hindu
Language: Arabic (official)
British Embassy, Abu Dhabi: +971 (2) 610 1100

United Kingdom
Capital: London
Currency: United Kingdom Pound Sterling (GBP)
Religion: Church of England, although all other faiths are practised
Language: English, Welsh (in Wales), Gaelic (in Scotland)
Foreign & Commonwealth Office: +44 (0) 20 7008 1500

United States of America
Capital: Washington, DC
Currency: US Dollar (USD)
Religion: Protestant, Roman Catholic, Latter-day Saints, Jewish, Muslim
Language: English, Spanish
British Embassy, Washington DC. +1 (202) 588 6500

Uruguay
Capital: Montevideo
Currency: Peso Uruguayan (UYU)
Religion: Roman Catholic, Protestant, Jewish, Atheist
Language: Spanish
British Embassy, Montevideo: +598 (2) 622 36 30/50

Uzbekistan, Republic of
Capital: Tashkent
Currency: Som (UZS)
Religion: Sunni Muslim
Language: Uzbek, Russian, Tajik
British Embassy, Tashkent: +998 71 120 1500/1516 (consular/visa)

Vanuatu, Republic of
Capital: Port Vila
Currency: Vatu (VUV)
Religion: Presbyterian, Anglican, Roman Catholic, Seventh Day Adventist
Language: Bislama (offical), English (official), French (official), plus over 130 vernacular languages
refer to British High Commission, Suva, Fiji: +679 322 9100

Venezuela, The Bolivarian Republic of
Capital: Caracas
Currency: Bolivar Fuerte (VEF)
Religion: Roman Catholic
Language: Spanish
British Embassy, Caracas: +58 (212) 263 8411

Vietnam, The Socialist Republic of
Capital: Hanoi
Currency: Vietnamese Dong (VND) (US dollar widely accepted)
Religion: Buddhist, Roman Catholic, Protestant, Cao Dai, Hoa Hao
Language: Vietnamese, minority languages also spoken
British Embassy, Hanoi: +84 (4) 3936 0500

Yemen, Republic of
Capital: Sana'a
Currency: Yemeni Rial (YER)
Religion: Muslim
Language: Arabic
British Embassy, Sana'a: +967 (1) 302480-5

Zambia, Republic of
Capital: Lusaka
Currency: Kwacha (ZMK)
Religion: Christian, Muslim, Hindu, indigenous beliefs
Language: English (official language of government), plus six further official languages
British High Commission, Lusaka: +260 (211) 423200

Zimbabwe, Republic of
Capital: Harare
Currency: Zimbabwean Dollar (ZWD)
Religion: Christian, indigenous beliefs, small
communities of Hindu, Muslim and Jewish
Language: English (official), Shona, Ndebele
British Embassy, Harare: 0772 125 160-167

visit: www.gap-year.com

Index

visit: www.gap-year.com

445

F

G

H

visit: www.gap-year.com

I

J

K

visit: www.gap-year.com

O

P

Q

R

449

T

the gap-year guidebook 2018

visit: www.gap-year.com